PENGUIN BOOKS

MINE YOUR LANGUAGE

Abhishek Borah is an associate professor at INSEAD, France. He has been an assistant professor at the Foster School of Business, University of Washington, Seattle, and a visiting assistant professor at the Wharton School, University of Pennsylvania, Philadelphia. Prior to academia, he worked for McKinsey & Company in India.

Abhishek was raised in Nagaland and studied in Dimapur, Shillong, Delhi and Los Angeles. He is the winner of the Varadarajan Award for Early Contributions to Marketing Strategy Research and is a Marketing Science Institute young scholar. He has published several articles in top-tier journals and has been cited in publications such as *Harvard Business Review*, *Fast Company*, *Nature*, *Ad Age* and *Forbes*. Abhishek lives in Paris, France. This is his first book.

T0290192

ADVANCE PRAISE FOR THE BOOK

'Fun, memorable stories and studies about how our words can make a difference . . . regardless of how large your brand is'—Seth Godin, author of *This Is Marketing*

'This book will be to marketing what *Freakonomics* was to economics—a unique, fresh and interesting way of looking at a discipline. Full of insights for anyone interested in learning about how words and language influence us'—Erin Meyer, professor, INSEAD, and author of *The Culture Map* and *No Rules Rules* (co-authored with Reed Hastings)

'*Mine Your Language* is meticulously researched and a great read. Abhishek assembles a motley set of lively, novel and rigorous information on language in business management. The book is relevant for managers looking to understand how language choices can lead to business success and also for the curious student who wants to know how text mining can be applied for generating actionable insights'—Don Tapscott, bestselling author, multiple TED Talks speaker and executive chairman, Blockchain Research Institute

'Words and phrasing matter. The use of a single word choice can dramatically affect its meaning and lead an audience to resonantly take offence, stimulate a viral response and more. This delightful book discusses real experiments and field studies on large data sets for insights that are useful to anyone wanting to get customer interactions, taglines or social media comments right'—David Aaker, Professor Emeritus, Haas School of Business, University of California, Berkeley; vice chairman, Prophet; and author of *The Future of Purpose-Driven Branding*

'Like the gold mines of data that *Mine Your Language* focuses on, this book is a gold mine for anyone who wants to understand how language is key to business and personal success. A thoroughly researched, timely and extremely useful book full of cool insights'—Vijay Govindarajan, Coxe Distinguished Professor, Tuck School of Business, Dartmouth College, and bestselling author of *The Three-Box Solution*

'*Mine Your Language* is a creative book on how language influences the world of business. Abhishek is a highly skilled management scientist whose ability to translate academic and scientific work into managerial insights is useful for business leaders. His writing is simple, sharp and stimulating. I wish I had such skills!'—Dipak Chand Jain, vice chancellor, Jio Institute;

former dean, Kellogg School of Management; former dean, INSEAD; former dean, Sasin Graduate Institute of Business Administration, Chulalongkorn University; and former co-president and global adviser, China Europe International Business School

'Reading this groundbreaking book helps us discover the profound impact of language on consumer behaviour and business strategy. Seamlessly blending academic insight with real-world examples, the book unveils the transformative power of text mining in deciphering market nuances. Essential for marketers, entrepreneurs and the innately curious, this book is a masterclass in leveraging linguistics for success in the digital and AI era'—Anindya Ghose, Heinz Riehl Chair Professor, NYU Stern, and author of *Tap: Unlocking the Mobile Economy*

'A timely and practical book in this data-driven world. Whether you are a management scholar seeking to harness cutting-edge text mining techniques to unravel exciting new research questions or a business professional aiming to leverage the treasure trove of textual data to gain a competitive edge, this book is for you. Abhishek Borah distils scientific studies, weaving them together with real-world case examples and personal stories to take us through the fascinating world of language analysis. Simply written. Deeply insightful. Immediately applicable'—Kriti Jain, associate professor, IE Business School, and Thinkers50 Radar awardee

MINE YOUR LANGUAGE

INFLUENCE, ENGAGE, PREDICT

ABHISHEK BORAH

PENGUIN BOOKS

An imprint of Penguin Random House

PENGUIN BOOKS

USA | Canada | UK | Ireland | Australia
New Zealand | India | South Africa | China | Singapore

Penguin Books is part of the Penguin Random House group of companies
whose addresses can be found at global.penguinrandomhouse.com

Published by Penguin Random House India Pvt. Ltd
4th Floor, Capital Tower 1, MG Road,
Gurugram 122 002, Haryana, India

First published in Penguin Books by Penguin Random House India 2024

ISBN 9780143461623

Typeset in Adobe Garamond Pro by Manipal Technologies Limited, Manipal
Printed at Replika Press Pvt. Ltd, India

www.penguin.co.in

For Frodo and Butter.

We don't speak the same language.
We don't need to. Some languages need no words.

Contents

Foreword

Never in the history of business has language been as crucial as it is today. The rise of large language models (LLMs) has the potential to shake up industries from music to pharmaceuticals to market research. Firms that overlook the exciting possibilities of language will find themselves facing a huge competitive disadvantage, either today or down the road. To gain a lasting advantage, businesses must understand how language is used by consumers, competitors, the media and other stakeholders.

Abhishek's book, *Mine Your Language*, delves into academic research across various domains of business. As such, it is an essential read for anyone interested in how language shapes business. The writing is straightforward and effective, and Abhishek skilfully combines stories and trivia to explain how text mining can enable businesses to extract valuable insights from data. The book is likely to benefit a broad audience, including business executives wanting to understand the influence of consumer reviews, data analysts exploring text mining possibilities, curious readers looking for an introductory understanding of language in business, and top management recognizing how attention to language can impact firm performance and stock market outcomes.

I've known Abhishek since his PhD days at the University of Southern California. He began using machine learning techniques in his research in 2009, a groundbreaking move given the current capabilities of machines to generate human-like language. Since then, his research has focused on generating insights from text, producing papers that are not only academically rigorous but also practically relevant. He is an award-winning scholar and a tenured professor at a top business school—INSEAD; he has also taught at prestigious institutions such as Wharton. Abhishek's diverse interests, including running marathons, climbing glaciers, quizzing and making rock music records, add a unique flavour to his book. His global journey from India to the US for studies, and now teaching in France and Singapore, provides a global perspective.

Abhishek's book aligns with my own books on jugaad and frugal innovation, emphasizing the role that creativity plays when businesses are faced with resource constraints. Particularly intriguing is his demonstration of how even small companies, lacking the resources of the major tech players, can use simple text mining techniques for powerful insights. Being frugal in a technical sense, as portrayed in the book, can empower managers to uncover fresh and impactful insights.

In summary, Abhishek's book covers a wide range of topics, elucidates various text mining techniques in a simple manner and employs storytelling to engage readers. I believe it is a hugely valuable resource for anyone curious about the influence of language on business.

Jaideep Prabhu

Fellow of the British Academy, Jawaharlal Nehru Professor of Business and Enterprise, and director, Centre for India and Global Business, Judge Business School, University of Cambridge

Introduction

'I hope you like scrambled eggs!'

This was the message one of the most famous twentieth-century musicians sent to a man named Richard Lester, the director of an upcoming film that featured this famous musician's band, along with a song he had composed.[1] The initial lyrics for the song went, 'Scrambled eggs, oh my baby how I love your legs, not as much as I love scrambled eggs.'[2] The musician hoped he could eventually develop more apt lyrics and fit a three-syllable word around the melody. But at the time, 'scrambled eggs' was the song's official title even as he struggled to find a three-syllable expression to replace it.

Music experts and listeners voted this song the best song of the twentieth century in a 1999 BBC Radio 2 poll.[3]

The following year, MTV and music magazine *Rolling Stone* named this song the number-one pop song of all time. There are over 2200 cover versions of this song, making it one of the most covered songs in music history.[4] Eventually, the musician found two three-syllable words to fit around the melody: 'Yesterday' and 'Suddenly'.

The song, of course, is 'Yesterday', written by Sir Paul McCartney and sung originally by The Beatles.

As geniuses go in pop music, probably few can outdo Sir Paul McCartney. For this song, while he initially struggled to find the right word, he did get the perfect combination and the words blended and flowed along with the music. Those magical lyrics about a relationship break-up instinctually wrapped around the melody like arms around a loved one.

And the song became eternal.

What would have happened if The Beatles named the song 'Scrambled Eggs' instead of 'Yesterday'? Would it be the timeless classic we know it to be? What would have been the response of music listeners? Record companies are incessantly searching for that next big hit. Would Parlophone Records, the record company that produced the album *Help!*, which contained 'Yesterday', have struck gold or, even better, platinum, as they say in music parlance? We don't know, of course, but perhaps a song called 'Scrambled Eggs' was released in a parallel universe where people appreciate music the same way we do. I bet the song would not have achieved even an iota of its monumental success.

Why? The words that we choose influence us in every way, wouldn't you agree? And 'Scrambled Eggs' as the title of a break-up song . . . does it sound like it would have struck a chord?

* * *

My interest in language developed at a very young age. I am from the state of Assam in India and Assamese is my native language. In the late 1960s, my parents moved to the neighbouring state of Nagaland, which has seventeen major ethnic groups, each with their own language, unintelligible to the others. Besides, the state also has sizeable populations of non-Naga communities, such as Assamese, Bengalis, Marwaris, Punjabis and Tibetans, among others. Growing up in a region that included people from different parts of India and where people speak different languages, I could not escape becoming a language geek. In fact, Dimapur, the district I grew up in, in the relatively untouched and remote north-east India, has the second-highest number of languages spoken in the country. Who would have thought? Can you guess how many languages are spoken in Dimapur?

103!⁵

Just four less than the megacity Bangalore, where people speak about 107 languages.⁶ As a child, I spoke five languages even without knowing I did.

Apart from Assamese, I picked up four other languages primarily because of the diversity of people living in Dimapur. I went to a Catholic school and thus learnt English as it was the primary medium of instruction. The lingua franca in Dimapur other than English, the official language of the state, is Nagamese, a creole language based on Assamese that most people living in Dimapur speak to find unity and common ground through one language. I spoke better Nagamese than Assamese at one point. I grew up in a 'para' (a Bengali word for a small neighbourhood), where our family was the only Assamese family living among Bengali people. So, I picked up Bengali and it really helped—especially when I had to cajole my friend's mother to cook a sumptuous bhetki paturi (a dish made from sea bass that is wrapped in plantain leaves and steamed). Furthermore, my father and I watched almost every Bollywood film in the late 1980s and early 1990s starring Mithun Chakraborty or Govinda, which enabled me to learn Hindi, albeit not the kind that famous Indian Hindi writer Munshi Premchand would be proud of. People from the north-east of India are known for their poor renditions of the Hindi language. However, I spoke much better Hindi than my parents.

From an early age, I used to be amazed at how I could say 'fish' in five different languages. Our family loved eating fish, as Assamese are known for their craving for fish dishes. Rarely did a week pass by in our home without a finger-licking fish curry. Sometimes, I would ask my parents to cook curry with *fish* (English), *machli* (Hindi), *maas* (Assamese), *māchh* (Bengali) and *mash* (Nagamese) without even knowing that these words were from five different languages.

Later, I moved to New Delhi for college and I just had to pull up my socks to speak good Hindi. It was when I moved to Delhi that I realized my ability to speak five different languages was a useful trait. It enabled me to start conversations with students from different parts of India. This triggered in me the desire to learn more about languages. As I was a keen quizzer, I became devoted to finding the sources of words, how words were formed and what was their lineage, and my interest in language increased.

Later on, I pursued a PhD in marketing and the first essay of my dissertation examined if tweets on X (formerly Twitter) could affect the stock returns of firms. Using methods from computer science such as support vector machines and naïve Bayes classifiers, I showed how tweets could significantly predict stock returns. My second essay examined whether brands should be worried about what users say about them online if a rival brand has a product recall. This essay helped me get a job in a research university. These forays cemented my interest in studying language and its effects on business. From then on, I have worked on uncovering meaning out of unstructured textual data and published my work in various journals. I have also keenly followed other fields apart from marketing that have studied language, such as strategy, finance, accounting and psychology. Many of these articles are deeply interesting and important, and have strong ramifications for business practice. But not too many of these insights are known to people outside academic circles. After doing some research, I realized there was no book that spoke to a wider audience about how language could affect business decisions and how one could use text mining to uncover insights. Thus, the seed for this book emerged. This book is a summation of my interest over time and contains what I believe are useful and timely insights that can help the world outside academia. Just like I found value in studying language, I hope you find value in this book about language and set out on this journey to explore the wonderful, intriguing and interesting world of how language affects business.

Why is language important?

If you have read this book up to this point, you would agree that my choice of language affects us both. My chances of holding your interest depend on it.

The language I use in this book can either make you drop the idea of reading it or pique your interest enough to continue reading. I must be attentive to how I summon the words to write—always being alert, sensitive and empathetic to my readers' temperament and tendencies. Every word matters, whether article, noun, verb, pronoun, conjunction or preposition. The style I use can make or break it for the reader.

I could convey the book's ideas and central thesis formally or casually. It is my choice whether to write in the first or third person. There are a few rhetorical modes I can choose from—

the choice matters. I can make my writing descriptive, narrative, expository or argumentative. All my choices, and the union of all these linguistic aspects, should elegantly blend and harmonize to captivate and persuade you to keep on reading.

To cut to the quick, the language you employ in your personal and professional life matters. How we express our thoughts can ease a heartbreak or shatter a heart. Our ability to speak, write and understand one another is one of the most spectacular aspects of our human experience. It is a miracle that by just assembling and arranging some letters in our brain and positioning words in a particular fashion, we can convey a thought. Scientists have likened language to a mental organ separating us from other animals on this planet. We are born with the ability to communicate. Language, as cognitive psychologist and psycholinguist Steven Pinker so convincingly argues, is an instinct.[7] Just as birds can fly, humans can communicate. The birds didn't learn how to fly from a bunch of aeronautical whizzes; their innate ability to fly is natural. Language is innate in us too. The ability to communicate develops in children automatically without conscious effort and formal teaching. Children instinctually develop complex grammar and often surprise their parents by saying something that makes their parents wonder, *where did that come from*?

Language is a remarkable and unmistakable component of how our brains are wired.

Over and above how it matters in our personal lives, language also impacts consumer and business decisions. When we hear a friend talk about their last trip to Zanzibar, we get whisked away and daydream about a vacation. We impetuously reserve seats at a restaurant that has been lauded as the best place to savour Burmese tea leaf salad by one of our office mates. We realize that a certain up-and-coming biotech firm, working on neurogenetics research, might be a good stock to hold after attending an informative and convincing presentation by its founder at a biotechnology expo in Dubai.

Firms are also attentive to how consumers react to their choice of language. Travel adventure firms in Zanzibar would be eager to know what type of content would push someone to pay $5000 for a seven-day, all-inclusive trip. Restaurants would yearn to discover what titillates someone's taste buds so that it gets simply impossible to find a spot in their restaurant if one doesn't book two months in advance. The biotech firm would try to understand how to plan a press release that persuasively showcases its vision and goals for neurogenetics research in the next decade.

Firms have a multitude of language-based decisions to make, from the brand name (supremely important) to the language and subject matter of their annual reports.

For example, you will never see a Mitsubishi Pajero in Spain or Spanish-speaking countries, though you will see the brand in the US. Mitsubishi Motors named its sport utility vehicle the Pajero after a Pampas cat (*Leopardus pajeros*), native to southern Argentina. Unfortunately, the word 'Pajero' means 'wanker' in Spanish. Mitsubishi Motors realized the potential harm of staying with the Pajero brand name and swiftly changed it to Mitsubishi Montero for Spanish-speaking countries. This example, though innocuous and amusing, undoubtedly demonstrates the effects of language. It can make or break your brand.

Firms have to be strategic in how they communicate to their customers and their counterparts. For example, how much detail about their new technology should a firm make public in the forthcoming press release? How much information is too much information? Is it possible for a greedy rival to grasp the idea behind the new technology based on the content of the press release? These questions matter.

How firms communicate with their rivals, how consumers speak to each other, how firms listen to consumers, how investors pay attention to firms and how artists write music for their fans—all these decisions have ramifications and ultimately influence a firm's performance. They have an impact on consumer attitudes, beliefs, satisfaction and loyalty, and ultimately on a firm's sales, market share, earnings and profits. Consumers reading another consumer's rant about a particular hostess can result in a loss of business for the restaurant. A firm in the habit of releasing new product announcements, which are nothing but vapourware, might make investors move away from putting their trust and money in the firm.

Bottom line: the words that consumers and firms use can be deal-breakers.

In the past, one tried to find answers to these relevant and important questions using research methods such as observational studies, interviews, surveys, focus groups and lab experiments. But, in the last few decades, there have been vast improvements and unprecedented changes in how one can unearth linguistic characteristics from firms, consumers and artists. The field of computational social science has made enormous leaps in its ability to make meaning out of the words and language we use. Using theories and methods from fields such as computer science and linguistics, social scientists have been able to answer a plethora of questions related to how consumers and firms communicate, which would have been difficult, if not impossible, in the past.

A crucial factor that has enabled social scientists to uncover insights from textual data is the availability of data from Internet and mobile platforms. Since the turn of the millennium, websites, mobile apps and web-based services have become vital to firms and consumers. Businesses can connect and correspond with clients on social media sites such as X or provide consumers with the ability to do everything from shopping on Amazon to finding vacation rentals on Airbnb to creating videos with pranks, stunts, tricks, jokes or dances on TikTok. Digital is the new normal and it is omnipresent. The average time that users spend on digital media in developed countries is about seven hours.[8] There are approximately 4.7 billion active Internet users globally, with this number rising every hour. The upswing in access to affordable and convenient mobile devices has made the Internet available to many consumers across the globe. There are about 4.3 billion mobile users in the world[9] and most of these users partake in online activities. There are about 3 billion Facebook users,[10] 1.4 billion TikTok users,[11] 465 million X users[12] and 310 million active users on Amazon at the time of writing.[13]

A crucial outcome of this phenomenon is that consumers and firms create rich, passionate, live and vast expanses of data. Consumers leave a gold mine of information, such as their likes and dislikes, perceptions and attitudes, preferences and needs, and behaviours and decisions. On the other hand, firms leave online footprints of their strategies and actions. These 'digital breadcrumbs' are a gold mine for social scientists to understand how consumers and firms use language in their various communications. Given this data availability and the digital footprints firms and consumers leave behind, social scientists have grabbed the opportunity to test various theories about how firms and consumers use language. With its flavours of velocity, volume, variety, value and veracity, Big Data has stimulated significant and steady research for answering novel, substantive, engaging and relevant problems related to language. Publicly available data on the Internet and mobile phones allow social scientists to uncover meaning out of unstructured data and quantify both the strategic and tactical actions of firms and the social and consumption activities of consumers that are otherwise exceedingly challenging to observe, record and analyse.

An array of social scientists in business management disciplines ranging from marketing, accounting and finance to strategy, information systems and psychology have used linguistic tools to answer questions relating to how consumers and firms go about their activities. Marketing scholars have looked at how marketing tactics such as advertising influence online reviews, accounting scholars have examined how X can be another information source for investors, finance scholars have explored various financial documents and their impact on investors, strategy scholars have examined the effects of how firms convey information to influence their rivals, information systems scholars have investigated the effects of information in social networks to drive sales, communication scholars have examined what forms of content lead to reader engagement, and scholars in psychology have tested various psychological theories using textual data.

This book is a collection of studies from business management scholars who use linguistic methods to test theories and examine their predictions. I shall use the term 'text mining' to discuss various linguistic methods scholars have employed. These methods range from dictionaries of words to natural language processing techniques—the chapters in this book range from studies in marketing to finance. I have explored over 400 research studies to bring you this collection, which I hope will show you how text mining can unearth novel, absorbing and valuable findings. These findings can influence firms and policymakers in their strategies and inform everyone about how language affects us.

Though a dizzying abundance of research is available, I have chosen a small set of studies. This decision is totally based on the overlap of what I find interesting and what I hope you will find interesting. My preference for these studies is entirely driven by what economists call my 'taste function'. My taste function is a combination of what I prefer—a mix of arts, creativity and sports, the intrinsic 'interestingness' of the phenomena and its overall applicability for decision-makers.

The book is written for companies, marketers, social media managers, content creators, entrepreneurs and anyone curious about how language works—whether you are a student who wants to know the utility of computational techniques in understanding consumer behaviour or someone who is inquisitive about the role of language in affecting consumer consumption and companies' behaviour.

Each chapter in the book starts with a phenomenon followed by a narrative about the phenomenon with examples and cases, academic studies and the text-mining method used in the study. The text-mining part has some knotty material that some readers might be uninterested in digesting, but I promise the exposition is suitable and friendly for everyone. I have taken care to clarify the techniques for the average reader, and many are very simple—just a dictionary of words. Consider a research team that wants to understand if the content on Wikipedia is positive or negative. They create a dictionary of positive words such as happiness, joy, etc., and a dictionary of negative words such as sad, cry, etc. They then examine the occurrence of these words in Wikipedia's content to answer their research question. You can choose to skip this portion. Finally, each chapter offers implications, which are meant for managers of firms, policymakers and any consumer.

You will look at examples ranging from Metallica to Mahatma Gandhi, Obama to Osho, Toyota to Tesla, spoilers to soccer and lenders to liars. You will get to know how one can use text to measure traits ranging from narcissism to charisma and if there are upsides to consumers making mistakes and firms being strategically vague.

You will learn how changing the use of simple pronouns like 'we', 'I' and 'you' can have massive consequences for a firm's bottom line. You will get insights on how to successfully talk to your date or effectively make a point to your colleague. You will see how four-letter words and one-letter words can influence business success. You will see how noise and profanity can be helpful. You will read about how to improvise on social media based on the Dracula-like bites of a soccer player or how you can prevent social media firestorms by paying attention to the fire-starter. You will read about how signatures portray someone's personality and how to spot a fake review online.

* * *

Every Good Boy Does Fine. Many music enthusiasts have used this mnemonic to commit the lines of the treble clef notes to memory. When I started learning how to play music, I found it hard to remember the E, G, B, D and F pattern—a fairly random sequence. Changing these letters to words and making some meaning out of them helped me in my endeavour to learn music and play the guitar. It is a wonder how, using that sentence, I suddenly understood the pattern of lines in the treble clef quickly.

The words in that sentence somehow affected my learning like magic. The way I made meaning out of the musical language, which was alien to me till then, through my knowledge of the

English language, was both simple and revelatory. I realized then that language is an instinct, and we are intrinsically and instinctively built to understand, listen, write and speak. As someone who wished his teachers 'Goooooood . . . morrrrninnngg' because of my chronic stutter (partially triggered by my ignorance of the English language), to instruct finally in English in front of a class of MBA students from across the globe, language has been a delight for me to discover, learn and research. I hope the stories in this book inspire you, make you more curious about this extraordinary gift, and provide a usable sense of how language impacts our consumption and a firm's business decisions.

I

TWISTS AND TURNS

If there is an exemplar of twists and turns in a story, perhaps it was the narrative of the final of the 2022 football World Cup. This game exemplified all the twists and turns that most audiences crave. We get entertained with such curvy narratives because such narratives break the patterns of what we are normally used to or what we forecast will happen. We get transfixed by the vistas that emerge in every curve. And we keep staying on that curvy route waiting for the final unravelling.

In this section, I will take you through stories where there are twists and turns and where our preconceptions or assumptions are turned inside out. We will discuss metal bands going pop, a soccer player with a penchant for biting others and his influence on commerce, the effects of spoilsports on movie revenues, and if there is any value in making mistakes online.

1

Improv on Social Media

What would happen if the lights go out during the Super Bowl? Or when one of the world's best soccer players bites a hard, overpowering and obstinate Italian soccer player on the shoulder during a pivotal group game of the World Cup? The Super Bowl episode mentioned above was watched by 164.1 million viewers,[1] while the soccer game mentioned above, which was just a group game, was watched by 19.2 million viewers.[2]

If we look at more recent statistics, over 113 million viewers watched the 2023 Super Bowl.[3] This number pales compared to the last soccer World Cup final between Argentina and France in Qatar in 2022, which about 1.5 billion people watched live on television. On aggregate, content related to the 2022 soccer World Cup generated around 5.95 billion interactions on social media.[4]

The first scenario above describes the power outage that shut down Super Bowl XLVII in New Orleans in 2013. In the third quarter of the game, a partial power outage in New Orleans' Mercedes-Benz Superdome suspended play for thirty-four minutes, earning the game the nickname, 'the Blackout Bowl'. In the game's aftermath, the companies that manage the Superdome, Entergy and SMG, issued a statement that blamed the cut on 'an abnormality in the system'.[5]

The other episode involved Luis Suárez, Uruguayan football superstar and a menace to defenders, biting Giorgio Chiellini, Italian defender and erstwhile captain of both the Serie A club Juventus and the Italian national team. The incident happened in the first half of Uruguay's final group game against Italy at the 2014 World Cup in Natal, Brazil, and quickly became viral news.

By then, Luis Suárez had already bitten two other soccer players in the past, Otman Bakkal and Branislav Ivanovic. The first instance was in an Eredivisie[6] match between the club he was representing, Ajax Amsterdam, and PSV Eindhoven. In November 2010, the Dutch Football Association handed Suárez a seven-match ban for biting Bakkal. His ban did not stop him from continuing his Dracula-like exploits. In a premier league match in April 2013 between Liverpool, whom Suárez was representing, and Chelsea, he sunk his teeth into defender Branislav Ivanovic's arm as the pair tussled for possession in front of the Chelsea goal. The British media quickly pounced on his serial biting behaviour and called him a 'cannibal'.

After all this, just before the 2014 World Cup tournament, Suárez was on a PR campaign to redeem himself and exhibit a more humane side. 'I want to change the bad boy image that has stuck for a bit because I don't think I am at all how I have been portrayed,' Suárez said in a *Sports Illustrated* interview.[7]

Can you imagine the disbelief and uproar when it happened yet again?

It's the seventy-ninth minute of a crucial game for Uruguay in the 2014 FIFA World Cup in Brazil. Suárez steams in on

Chiellini in front of the Italian goal and does what he said he would never do again. Continuing his bad-boy ways, Suárez bites Chiellini. The Mexican referee, Marco Rodríguez, coincidentally nicknamed *Chiquidrácula* (Little Dracula), did not think the infraction was enough for Suárez to be sent off. Nevertheless, the world saw what happened and many were eager to talk about it. From Brazil, where Brazilian television stations played Suárez's three bites on a loop, to the Boss, aka Bruce Springsteen, everyone had an opinion about it.[8]

Is there a possibility of a brand totally unconnected to such events, creatively and intelligently utilizing these incidents to generate an improvised message on social media that captures followers' attention? After all, these events are witnessed by millions, and if something interesting happens, such as a blackout in a Super Bowl, brands big or small, new or old, could leverage these events to create instant engagement.

For a while now, digital communications have emerged as one of the most important means for brands to engage with customers. Brands increasingly use social media marketing, brand communities and buzz agents to build brands.[9] Anecdotal evidence suggests, however, that a growing number of consumers have become disenchanted and have grown suspicious—if not tired—of digital communications and online advertisements.[10] Many firms utilize personal data collected from their online users to target and personalize ads.[11] This has led many consumers to find such ads intrusive, annoying, creepy and tiresome.

To help overcome this consumer annoyance, fear and fatigue, I, along with a set of friends who are also my co-conspirators in several research papers, explored the potential of 'improvised marketing interventions' (IMI) on social media.[12] By 'IMI', we meant an impromptu, humorous, timely and unanticipated social media message from a brand that capitalized on an external event not connected to it—such as the Luis Suárez incident. We examined thousands of messages on X to see if tweets with the characteristics of an IMI could excite audiences and generate virality for the brand. 'Virality' means the number of retweets or shares received by the IMI on X.

We focused on X as it allowed us to capture a rich dimension of virality via retweets. Retweeting in X is a social phenomenon where users take a message someone else has posted and rebroadcast the same message to their followers. Unlike Meta (or Facebook), X is a one-way directed social network. On X, a user A 'following' user B does not imply that B 'follows' A. This unidirectional network structure suggests that a retweet is more credible, diffuses beyond the original user's network, and is probably read more than a typical tweet because it is pre-screened and shared by a user who is followed.[13] Though there are other forms of engagement on social media, such as likes and comments, which proxy for various engagement measures, we focused on virality. Our main goal was to enable managers to improve the effectiveness of sharing a brand's digital communication on social media.

One brand that took advantage of the Super Bowl blackout was Oreo. When the entire Mercedes-Benz Superdome lost power for over thirty minutes, American football fans across the US took to social media to pass the time. Unexpectedly, Oreo, a popular cookie brand, filled the void.[14] Within moments of the power outage, Oreo tweeted, 'Power out? No problem', along with a starkly lit image of a solitary Oreo cookie.[15] The caption read, 'You can still dunk in the dark.' This now-famous tweet received 15,000 retweets in the eight hours after they posted it, creating significant publicity for Oreo at minimal expense. By contrast, a Super Bowl ad slot costs an average of $4.5 million. And this is an average. There are ads that cost much more. Amazon's ninety-second commercial, *Before Alexa,* aired during Super Bowl LIV, is the most expensive Super Bowl commercial, along with Google's commercial *Loretta,* which aired during the same Super Bowl. Both cost a whopping $16.8 million. Oreo's tweet cost the company almost nothing compared to the two above.

So, how did Oreo win the Marketing Super Bowl?[16]

One important phenomenon that Oreo used to its advantage is the modern consumer's propensity to use multiple devices, known as 'multiplexing'.[17] Sports fans now, often, use not only the TV but also their smartphones and tablets to keep abreast of what is happening. Gone are the days when the only source of entertainment was the television. Oreo's fifteen-person social media team realized they could catch the attention of these multiplexing fans when the Blackout happened. Their social media team, consisting of copywriters, artists and a strategist, was ready to react online to whatever happened in the Super Bowl within ten minutes—whether it was an amazing touchdown or, in this case, the lights going out. The team reacted quickly, and boy, did it pay dividends!

'The new world order of communications today incorporates the whole of the way people are interacting with brands right now,' said Sarah Hofstetter, former CEO of digital marketing agency 360i, which handled game-day tweeting for Oreo, in an interview with *Wired.* 'Once the blackout happened, no one was distracted—there was nothing going on. The combination of speed and cultural relevance propelled it to the forefront.'[18]

Similarly, Snickers, the chocolate bar brand, used the Suárez 'Bitegate' incident to showcase its cheeky brand of humour.[19] The Snickers social media team was one of the first to call Suárez out on X, posting an image of a half-eaten Snickers bar with the slogan: 'More satisfying than Italian'. The post generated about 17,700 likes and 1500 comments. Snickers was rewarded with 43,000 retweets in the next twenty-four hours and 38.7 million earned media impressions in two days with no paid media behind it.[20] Again, no high television advertising costs, just like the Oreo tweet.

Many other global brands chimed in to cash in on 'Bitegate', ranging from Suárez's own homeland, Uruguay, to Portugal. McDonald's Uruguay's post—*'Hola @luis16suarez, si te quedaste con hambre vení a darle un mordisco a una* BigMac*'*, which translates to 'Hello @luis16suarez, if you're hungry, come take a bite out of a BigMac' was retweeted more than 72,000 times.

Nando's (a chain of Portuguese–Mozambican restaurants based in the UK) tweeted, 'Hey @luis16suarez, if you're that hungry, why not get your teeth stuck into something really tasty?' earning them 35,138 retweets in one day.

Examples of brand posts that utilize external events, either comic or serious, to create humorous and improvised messages on social media abound. Another event that was cleverly used by Lego, the Danish toy company, to create an IMI was Tesla's Cybertruck failure. In November 2019, at the unveiling of Tesla's new and futuristic *Blade Runner*-esque Cybertruck in Los Angeles, CEO Elon Musk wanted to demonstrate how the new truck's armoured glass exemplified strength and endurance. He asked the truck's lead designer, Franz von Holzhausen, to come on stage and throw a metal ball at the armoured glass window.[21] To Elon's, Franz's, the audience's and the viewers' surprise, the ball smashed right through the vehicle's window. The failure of the glass to withstand the missile led to an avalanche of content across traditional and social media criticizing the new truck. Lego creatively jumped on the PR fiasco to create a social media message where they shared a picture of a car made from a single grey Lego brick on top of two sets of wheels with the caption, 'The evolution of the truck is here. Guaranteed shatterproof'. The post went viral on Facebook, X and Instagram, receiving about 28,000 retweets on X and generating noteworthy virality for Lego.

My co-authors and I wanted to investigate what characteristics of such tweets drive virality for a brand. Drawing on research related to quick wit,[22] we proposed that IMIs were effective because they occur in real time, offer humour and are *either* unanticipated or timely. We argued that marketers could use this combination of traits to predict message virality.[23] Humour is a universal emotion. It is a psychological response characterized by laughter, happiness or joy arising from a pun, play on words, events or images. It is often used to make people laugh and enjoy a moment of relief from our everyday burdens.[24] Timeliness is the time taken to respond to an external event and how quickly the brand leverages the event to devise an IMI. This relates to the idea of timing in slapstick comedy; a joke will only work at a certain point in time, and if the comedian is late delivering it, it will be out of place and lose its effectiveness. The other important element that could drive virality was 'unanticipation', which is defined as 'an unexpected way a communication responds to an external event'.

An array of research has found this notion of unanticipation playing an important role in the delivery of humour by creating unexpected relationships, such as unexpected events, objects or observable deviations from an implied standard.[25] Sharing amusing, unexpected or surprising content makes social media users look good to other users by demonstrating quick-wittedness.[26] Quick wit is an intelligent form of humour and requires someone to say or write things that are entertaining, unpredictable or unexpected.

Quick wit relies on situational humour that uses timeliness and unanticipation to create audience engagement.[27] While people may feel uncomfortable and therefore less willing to share an unanticipated message in certain circumstances, such as when the content of the message is sad, IMIs that contain *both* humour and unanticipation help brands to surprise and delight their followers and engage them in a light-hearted, positive way.[28] Combining humour and unanticipation in an IMI grabs the attention of social media users and encourages people to share that content with others.

There are two reasons why humour and timeliness drive virality. First, in addition to humour, the speed of the response attracts an audience's attention, which consequently triggers further conversation.[29] Take Oreo's message, for example—the Oreo team tweeted within a few minutes of the lights going out. The message was very timely. Suppose Oreo had tweeted the same message after a few days or weeks. Its witty elements would not have caught the audience's attention. Events unfold on social media in minutes, if not seconds, and consumers crave new content to hold their attention. A timely post that is entertaining can inject fuel into a message and satisfy the urge of users to share something as quickly as possible, to seem current, and to be in the know.

Our team conducted a series of five studies to evaluate IMIs' potential to attract users' attention and test whether humour, unanticipation and timeliness drive virality. First, we had to test the theory that IMI messages lead to more significant virality than non-IMI messages. We used a method known as the Synthetic Control Method to analyse Oreo's tweet and examine its effect on the company's virality, comparing it to a synthetic (made-up) Oreo post, which did not tweet the same Oreo message. In essence, the

Synthetic Control Method compares the effect of Oreo's tweet on Oreo's virality with a synthetic, hypothetical Oreo brand that did *not* post the 'You can still dunk in the dark' tweet. We needed a counterfactual (synthetic) Oreo to see what would have happened to Oreo's virality had it not made a tweet when the Blackout happened, to test the causal effect of Oreo's tweet.

The Synthetic Control Method (SCM) is a statistical approach used to evaluate the treatment effect in comparative case studies. An SCM estimates the effect of a treatment (or intervention) of interest by comparing the evolution of an outcome variable for a unit affected by the treatment to the evolution of the same outcome variable for a synthetic control group.

One important assumption in this method is that the virality of the Synthetic Control is as similar as possible to Oreo's virality before the 'Dunk in the Dark' tweet. We ensured this assumption was valid in our analysis. Based on a rigorous process to identify brands that make up the Synthetic Control, fifteen brands from the same product market of Oreo were selected using the following handles on X: @Aero, @BahlsenBiscuits, @Butterfinger, @CadburyUK, @ChipsAhoy, @KeeblerElves, @KitKat_US, @ kraftfoods, @LittleDebbie, @MarylandCookie, @McVities, @ Nestle, @NillaWafers, @PepperidgeFarm and @Twix.

We then collected all retweets for each of these fifteen brands and Oreo from X between 8 p.m. on 1 February 2013 and 11 p.m. on 5 February 2013 by writing a script that downloaded each retweet mentioning the sixteen brand names. Finally, using 10 p.m. EST on 3 February 2013 as our event hour, we analysed the data from forty-nine hours before and forty-nine hours after the event. Figure 1.1 below shows the trajectory of Oreo's virality and the Synthetic Control's virality.

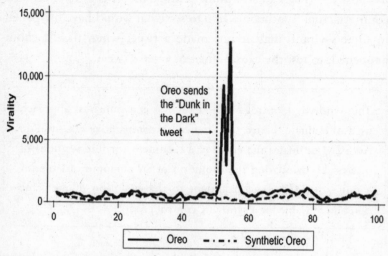

Figure 1.1: Virality of Oreo with the 'Dunk in the Dark' IMI versus synthetic Oreo without the 'Dunk in the Dark' IMI using synthetic control method.

The figure shows that after Oreo sent out its tweet, there was an increase in the real Oreo's virality compared to the counterfactual Oreo's virality. Oreo's virality peaks in the fifth hour, with a difference of 12,383 retweets between 'real' and synthetic Oreo.

We ran another experiment to examine if humour tinged with unanticipation, or timeliness, can drive virality. We wanted to examine if humour tinged with unanticipation or humour combined with timeliness causally leads to increased sharing. Experiments are more suitable than field data from X to examine causality.

Our task asked participants to watch a two-minute video,[30] which would serve as the 'event' that would inspire our fictional brand to tweet. The clip shows a unique moment where penguin chicks are rescued from a predator by an unlikely hero. Because they are cute and wobble about like drunk preschoolers, penguins are perceived unjustly to be hilarious animals. It's not a surprise the actor Danny DeVito is portrayed as the human equivalent.[31] In the clip, the wobbly penguin chicks are wending their way towards the sea. It is an adventure, but more so as this is their first time out without their parents to guard them. A giant, predatory petrel swoops in for what it thinks will be a quick kill. As they try to flee, one chick falls and the petrel tries to grab it by the neck, but doesn't quite succeed. Fortuitously, the chick returns to its group, where the chicks congregate and create a circle to protect themselves. After a taut pause, an adult Adelie (an exceptionally vigorous penguin species) arrives, seeing the petrel off. This video was a massive hit on social media and, as of December 2021, has had about 21.5 million views.

To go alongside this viral event, we created a fictitious brand called 'Wild Foods', which would appear to take advantage of the event and post an IMI. As we were interested in comparing whether the combination of high humour and high unanticipation/timeliness leads to higher tweet virality than a low humour and low unanticipation/timeliness combination, we created four different social media posts (referred to as 'conditions') each containing different text alongside the same image of the solitary adult penguin in the snow looking sideways.

The first (Condition 1, Figure 2.2A) was a tweet with a high humour and high unanticipation condition. The second (Condition 2, Figure 2.2B) was a tweet with a high humour and low unanticipation condition. The third (Condition 3, Figure 2.2C) was a tweet with a low humour and high unanticipation condition. The fourth (Condition 4, Figure 2.2D) was a tweet with both a low humour and low unanticipation condition.

Condition 1: High humour, High unanticipation (A)

Condition 2: High humour, Low unanticipation (B)

Condition 3: Low humour, High unanticipation (C)

Condition 4: Low humour, Low unanticipation (D)

Figure 1.2: Conditions for Experiment

After watching the clip, the participants in our study read a tweet that was pretested as high (or low) in humour and unanticipation. The pretest included showing these tweets to 216 participants who concurred that each of these conditions was valid. Using Figure 2.2A (condition 1), for example, the participants agreed the tweet was highly humorous and unanticipated.

Next, participants rated their willingness to retweet by answering the question 'I would like to retweet this message' using a scale from one = 'strongly disagree' to seven = 'strongly agree'. Participants then rated the IMI's humour, again by responding to three statements on a scale from one to seven. The statements to choose from were: 'The tweet content is humorous', 'The tweet content is funny', and 'The tweet content is hilarious'.

Similarly, the participants rated their unanticipation based on three statements: 'The tweet content is very unexpected', 'The tweet content is very surprising', and 'The tweet content is very unanticipated'. Note that in each case, the three statements are not truly that different. This was to ensure that the participants were not just providing scores without reading the statement and to ensure consistency in their evaluations.

Our study did not use a computerized technique because it would be difficult for a computer to classify humour, unanticipation and timeliness for a message tied to an external event. Sometimes, computerized text-mining techniques are unsuitable or challenging to execute when classifying content that requires nuance and interpretation.

As suspected, we found unanticipation tinged with humour and timely and humorous tweets drove a respondent's willingness to tweet. To strengthen our conclusion, we ran three more studies using real IMIs from X. The studies included a hand-collected dataset of 462 IMI tweets across 139 brands over a six-year period, 232 tweets by ten airlines within a two-month time frame from a third-party data provider and 477 tweets from a random sample of twenty-five firms from the Standard & Poor's (S&P) 500 company list. After following the same coding procedures for humour and unanticipation and using the number of shares of the message as a proxy for virality, we found similar results as our experiment proving humour tinged with surprise or timeliness again plays a part in driving customer engagement.

To determine if this virality results in a tangible advantage, our team evaluated the effect of these types of tweets on a firm's market capitalization following the posting of an IMI message. Utilizing the concept of the efficient market hypothesis and a method known as the event study method, we found that an IMI with high humour and high unanticipation, for example, can generate US$ 5.1 million on average in market capitalization on the event day, i.e., the day an IMI is posted by the firm that owns the brand.

An event study conducted on a specific firm examines any changes in its stock price and how it relates to a given event, which in our case is the IMI.

Social media is the preeminent source of entertainment, information and connections among users. Throughout the COVID-19 pandemic, Internet use was at an all-time high, with 90 per cent of users saying the Internet has been 'essential' or 'important to them'.[32] Social media engagement increased by 61 per cent during the first month COVID-19 hit everyone worldwide.[33] So, what do these results imply for business and social media managers?

First, many managers believe firms should plan well ahead, with the firm in complete control of the content of the message. We all know the potential advantages of such a strategy. But there is a chance that a brand can be seen as out of touch with what's happening, distant from its audience and consequently, cannot capture the trends, feelings and prevalent ideas of the time. The findings from our study should urge managers to thoroughly consider not only *what* they say but, more importantly, *how* and *when* they say it on social media. There can be a plethora of opportunities for brands to leverage an external event and craft a message that captures the audience's interest. Firms can also pre-spot events and trends and utilize these to engage more with their audiences.

Second, many times, firms do not empower their social media teams to craft messages. The results suggest firms should allow them the flexibility and capability to improvise and craft a witty message. As no one has information on events that can happen in the future, allowing social media teams to improvise can pay substantial dividends, as seen from our research.

Third, managers can utilize the findings that humour and timeliness and humour and unanticipation can generate virality. Managers can enable their social media team to craft messages that specifically have the desired characteristics (humorous, unanticipated and timely) before they send out a tweet or any social media message. The social media team could have a set of experts who can swiftly evaluate if a message has these characteristics before being sent out to the world.

Overall, social media managers must understand the nature of digital marketing and capitalize on any opportunity for advances. Our research strongly suggests IMIs using humour and timeliness or humour and unanticipation can substantially drive virality and increase market capitalization almost immediately at a fraction of traditional advertising expenses.

Marketing on social media is akin to jazz music. Its beauty is not in the expected notes but in improvising using the latest technological tools for swift, agile and exciting content. Thus, prepare, be open and adjust.

2

Should Metallica Be More Justin Bieber?

Music success is hard to predict. It is hard to know beforehand what characteristics lead a song to become a chart-topper and, say, a YouTube sensation with a million or billion views. Managers of record companies are perennially looking for that next big thing. Record companies hold the rights to the artists' catalogue, which is an asset the record company can leverage in the future.

In fact, songs that become hits are rare. In a study of about 69,000 artists, the finding was that 93 per cent never had a hit, the measure of which was an appearance in the weekly Billboard Hot 100. Three per cent had one hit, while only 2 per cent had two hits.[1] Of course, some songs are indeed truly breathtaking and thus become hits. However, most songs are neither dazzling nor dreadful. Most songs, which fall between 'getting that goosebumps feeling' and 'how bad was that', can either do very well or poorly, and it is hard to predict success for the songs that fall in this category.[2] Chance, circumstance and context play a considerable role in a song's success. Most managers work on intuition and experience to find the next Taylor Swift or Ed

Sheeran. Consequently, any hint of a formula for predicting music success is always welcome.

Have you ever wondered how listeners would react if Metallica, the heavy metal band, released a song with lyrics resembling some of Justin Bieber's greatest hits? Would their fans still remain loyal to them? Can such an atypical song become a hit? Will this atypicality be something that Metallica's record company finds useful?

When I first encountered this question, I was flabbergasted by its audacity. How could someone dare to ask such a question? Let me explain why. Cable TV entered India in 1992. Being born in the north-east of India where there is a deep fondness for Western music, I quickly became glued to watching MTV as did my friends. The music videos were what I cared about the most. These videos showed a different world, modern cultures and most importantly, I could see musicians appear in their videos. Till then, my experience of watching music videos was when Doordarshan aired five to six Grammy-nominated videos a week before the Grammys . . . once a year! I became glued to MTV and suddenly found Nirvana (excuse the pun). And Pearl Jam. And Soundgarden. And Metallica and other rock bands. I became such a grunge and metal music lover that if a pop artist such as Mariah Carey's video popped up, I would just switch channels. Even a band like Def Leppard was not spared. The music had to be raw, aggressive and not mild. So, you can understand my reaction when a research piece posed the idea of a heavy metal band writing mushy lyrics.

Metallica is probably the quintessential heavy metal band. Known for their fast tempos, machine-like, exotic and heavy riffs, and monstrous tones, Metallica basically invented the genre of thrash metal. Alongside Megadeth, Anthrax and Slayer, the other three groups that are collectively called the 'Big Four' thrash metal bands, Metallica gained popularity and critical acclaim in the 1980s with their ferocious sound, aggressive music and technical wizardry. The attitude of the band, founded by James Hetfield and Lars Ulrich in Los Angeles, is summarized by the following quote from Hetfield: 'Authority pisses me off. I think everyone should be able to drink and get loud whenever they want.'[3] Metallica's debut album released in 1983, *Kill 'Em All*, received critical acclaim and was the first thrash metal album released in the US.[4] From then on, Metallica has been one of the most well-known metal bands in music history. Their self-titled fifth album, also called the *Black Album*, endeared them to a world beyond ardent metal lovers. The album reached No. 1 on the Billboard charts, followed by a streak of number ones for their following four albums. Their awards speak for themselves—the band won eighteen Grammy nominations and eight Grammy awards starting from 1990 for best metal performance for their single 'One'.[5] After Black Sabbath and Judas Priest, MTV rated Metallica as the third-greatest metal band in history.

As you might gather, Metallica mean business and don't write lyrics about frolicking in the ocean and how beautiful the world is. The lyrics of Metallica range from suicide in 'Fade to Black' to what we all fear, the end of the world in 'For Whom The Bell Tolls'. Metallica does write ballads, too, but even they are ominous. Consider the song 'Welcome Home (Sanitarium)', which narrates the story of a man trapped inside a mental asylum while plotting a violent revolt. The US military uses Metallica's music as 'torture'—a way of tormenting prisoners by making them listen to a song on a loop at loud volumes to break them down. Their song 'Enter Sandman', a song about nightmares, was played continuously at ear-splitting levels in Guantanamo Bay and in a jail on the Iraqi-Syrian border to torture inmates.[6] They are a band that is a far cry from wholesome hunk Justin Bieber's image and musical style, which is a blend of teen pop, electronic dance music and acoustic rhythm and blues (R&B). It is safe to say that soldiers don't use Justin Bieber's music to torture prisoners.

A die-hard fan of Metallica did a keyword analysis of the most frequently occurring words in Metallica's lyrics and posted it on the band's Reddit page.[7] Their most-used word is 'never'. Other words that Metallica repeat often in their lyrics include 'one', 'take', 'death', 'hell'. One can see the themes the band generally writes about.

Another die-hard fan of heavy metal band Slipknot[8] did the same analysis of their lyrics and concluded that the most commonly used word in their lyrics was 'never,' too. As you might surmise from the words used, metal bands seem to epitomize the mindset of always seeing the glass as half empty rather than half full.

Heavy metal music originated in the 1960s and became popular in the UK in the early 1970s. The genre's name has some interesting origins,[9] which are still debated, but Steppenwolf's 'Born To Be Wild' is one of the supposed origins. Mars Bonfire, the lyricist of the song, used the term, 'heavy metal thunder' and thought about heavy metal as a combination of his idea to reflect the heaviness and noise of cars and motorcycles while driving and riding in California. Another origin story speaks of how the term comes from the Beat Generation author William Burroughs' novel, *Naked Lunch*, which supposedly used the term as a synonym for torture, when, in fact, it did not. Burroughs actually used the term in another book called *The Soft Machine*, where there is a character called 'The Heavy Metal Kid'. The actual origin, however, seems to come from music critic Lester

Bangs' review of a Canned Heat album in the 7 February 1970 issue of *Rolling Stone*, where he used the phrase to describe a cluster of bands when talking about one of Canned Heat's songs. This new form of music was then taking the UK by storm. Led Zeppelin, Black Sabbath and Deep Purple, referred to as the 'Unholy Trinity', enthralled audiences with their distorted guitar riffs, heavy chords, potent drumming, very low-range bass notes and aggressive vocals. These legendary bands, along with bands like Judas Priest and Iron Maiden, were influential for many bands in the 1980s such as Metallica, Anthrax, Slayer, Megadeth and then bands like Tool and Pantera later. Heavy metal fans could not have had a better time as many bands kept arriving with new sub-genres that fell under the umbrella of heavy metal. These fans revelled in their love for this form of music and created a subculture of their own—a 'subculture of alienation'.[10] Fans of heavy metal are known to despise commercial appeal, oppose established authority and identify themselves as separate from the rest of society. Metal fans often resist listening to other types of music, with many famous metal musicians and critics bemoaning their insularity. Metal music is against materialistic aspects and authority, and being aggressive is a part of the ethos.

On the other hand, Bieber's songs include lyrics like 'Every time I look at you, I'm lookin' at a star/ It's the way you light up every room just bein' who you are.' The contrast between someone like Justin Bieber and Metallica in their genre and lyrics could not be starker. Check the lyrics of Bieber's hit song 'Love Me', which go,

> 'Baby you can do no wrong, my money is yours,
> Give you little more because I love you, love you,
> With me, girl, is where you belong,

Just stay right here,
I promise my dear I'll put nothing above you'.

Consider the lyrics of 'Favorite Girl':

'I always knew you were the best,
The coolest girl I know,
So prettier than all the rest,
The star of my show'.

And then his superhit 'Baby' that made him a star,

'Baby baby baby oooh,
Like baby baby baby nooo,
Like baby baby baby oooh'.

In fact, there are bridal websites that have a list of Justin Bieber's songs to swoon to.[11] Justin Bieber is a global superstar and one of the bestselling artists of all time. He became the youngest male singer to debut in the US Billboard 200,[12] the first artist to occupy all top three positions in the UK singles chart,[13] and has won multiple Grammys. His remix of 'Despacito' is heralded as one of the greatest Latin songs of all time.[14] His music has been described as 'offering a gentle introduction to the mysteries and heartaches of adolescence: songs flushed with romance but notably free of sex itself'.[15] He is the king of teen and bubblegum pop. How about his fans and what are they like?

Justin Bieber's fans are called 'Beliebers'. A mix of Bieber and believer. Beliebers comprise mainly teen girls though lately, older people have become his fans too. There are also 'Boy Beliebers', who are rare and thus adored by the core 'Beliebers'. Many fans develop an addiction to him and there is a term for that—'Bieber Fever'. Bieber's fans are seen as adoring and patient.[16] He is very popular on social network sites, with about 111 million followers on X, about 248 million followers on Instagram, and is the No. 1 artist on YouTube with over 60 million subscribers. His popularity on X was so high that X changed their algorithm so that they don't have the word 'Bieber' in its trending topics consistently.[17]

So, on the one hand, there are metal heads, and on the other, there are Beliebers. In one case, the lyrics are dark and aggressive, and in the other, the songs are lovey-dovey and soft. These fan bases are opposites and they, I surmise, don't see eye to eye.

All of this leads to the question posed at the beginning of this chapter. What would happen if Metallica started writing songs that used words similar to a Justin Bieber song? Would their listeners give a thumbs up or thumbs down?

To answer this question, two researchers, Jonah Berger from the Wharton School and Grant Packard from York University (both experts in text mining), examined the relationship between lyrical differentiation, which they termed as 'atypicality', and song popularity.[18] What is lyrical differentiation, you may ask? This concept is about how the lyrics of a musician from one genre differ from those of a musician from another genre. They wanted to find out why some songs become hits while others fail. What makes certain cultural items such as songs successful? Can it be attributed to the words used in the lyrics?

Using research embedded in the psychological foundations of culture, the authors argued that people have a drive for 'stimulation',[19] and novelty can increase that stimulation. One's drive for stimulation is embedded in one's drive to feel. First espoused by psychologist Marvin Zuckerman, stimulation-seeking is an individualistic trait that explains an individual's preferences and inclination to look for new, varied and intense experiences that arouse us. Of course, sensation-seeking is a continuum; some people are high sensation seekers who get bored quickly and some are low sensation seekers who prefer calmer environments. But many of us in the current world desire experiences such as pleasure or excitement as they relieve us from the mundane things we do daily.

The world now includes a generation of obsessive email checkers and social media addicts who always look for something that catches their eye. Anything new can catch our eye. A new book, a new movie, a new shirt, a new friend. If something is new and surprising, we like such experiences. Recent research in neuroscience shows that our brain appreciably reacts when we encounter novel experiences.[20] Our brains have a 'novelty centre' called the substantia nigra/ventral tegmental area (SN/VTA). When we encounter a new thing, it activates the SN/VTA.[21] The SN/VTA is a major origin of dopamine (referred to as the 'reward chemical') in our brains. This activation increases dopamine levels, which leads us to explore and search for new information.

In essence, Berger and Packard hypothesized that cultural items such as songs, movies and books that are more atypical, or differentiated from other cultural items, may be liked more, and become more popular. Though Berger and Packard don't use neuroscience to develop their hypothesis, the idea that atypical cultural items can drive popularity is because we like novelty—it stimulates us. Liking novelty is embedded in us. Our dopamine levels increase, and most of us get motivated to search for and explore such atypical items. This leads to an atypical song becoming popular.

So how did Berger and Packard go about testing their prediction?

Using text-mining techniques, Berger and Packard measured lyrical differentiation across thousands of songs and linked their measure of lyrical differentiation with song popularity.

The authors began by collecting data on song popularity. Because their focus was on how individuals rate songs, they used Billboard's[22] digital download rankings as a baseline measurement. These rankings capture over 90 per cent of major paid song services (for example, Apple iTunes and Google Play) rather than radio play, which ensures that the measure of popularity is more likely to be driven by individual preferences than by a few institutionalized actors (e.g., radio DJs with pre-approved playlists). They also collected the genre data and obtained the popularity ranking of each song in that genre's chart (1–50). Billboard has a top 50 chart for each genre, including Christian, country, dance, pop, rap, rock, and R&B. Their sampling approach resulted in 4200 song rankings and 1879 unique songs. The authors also got the name of the artist for each song.

Next, the magic of text mining ensued. Using a website called SongLyrics.com, the authors obtained the lyrics for each of these songs. They then used topic modelling to determine these songs' main themes or topics.[23] A topic model (more about this in the chapter on movie 'spoilers') imagines that each document (in this case, a song's lyrics) contains words from many topics in different proportions. Hypothetically, let's assume that the topic model generated three topics based on all the lyrics across the 1879 songs. Say the topics are 'happy lyrics', 'sad lyrics' and 'neutral lyrics'. The names of the topics derive from the representative keywords that fall under each topic.

The topic model would then assign each song with a particular representation. Song 1 contains words that have 20 per cent of 'happy lyrics', 30 per cent of 'sad lyrics', and 50 per cent of 'neutral lyrics'. Song 2 contains words that have 90 per cent of 'happy lyrics', 5 per cent of 'sad lyrics', and 5 per cent of 'neutral lyrics'. The researchers would do this for all 1879 songs.

So, what were the topics the authors uncovered?

Common topics emerged, such as 'anger and violence', with representative keywords such as 'bad', 'dead', 'hate', 'kill' and 'slay'. See Table 2.1 below for the representative keywords for each topic. 'Body movement' was another hot topic, with keywords such as 'body', 'bounce', 'clap', 'jump' and 'shake', as were 'girls and cars' with 'car', 'drive', 'girl', 'kiss' and 'road' as representative keywords.

Topic	Example topic words
Anger and violence	bad, dead, hate, kill, slay
Body movement	body, bounce, clap, jump, shake
Dance moves	bop, dab, mash, nae, twerk
Family	American, boy, daddy, mamma, whoa
Fiery love	burn, feel, fire, heart, love
Girls and cars	car, drive, girl, kiss, road
Positivity	feel, like, mmm, oh, yeah
Spiritual	believe, grace, lord, one, soul
Street cred	ass, bitch, dope, rich, street
Uncertain love	ain't, can't, love, need, never

Table 2.1: Topics and the top 5 keywords in each topic

Berger and Packard then grouped each genre's songs to find the average topic composition. They found country songs featured a lot of lyrics about 'girls and cars' (39 per cent) and less about 'body movement' (2 per cent). Indeed, country music songwriters are fascinated by trucks. In a study, it was found that around 6.3 per cent of country songs written since 2000 talk about trucks.[24]

There is a song by country musician Corb Lund called 'The Truck Got Stuck', which mentions the word 'truck' a whopping twenty-nine times.[25] And many country songs written by male country singers talk about loving their girl or woman. Often, country lyrics say something along the lines of, 'I'm driving down the road in my pickup and heading to meet my girl'.

Songs in the Christian genre feature lyrics referring to the topic 'spirituality' and less on the topic 'street cred', while the rap genre contains several lyrics about 'street cred' and minimal use of the topic 'uncertain love'. To see how lyrically different each song is from its genre, the authors then compared the song's topic to the genre's topic by taking the absolute value difference between that song's lyrical topic composition and the genre mean for each topic and aggregated these differences across topics. So, for example, if there was a song from the rock genre like Metallica's 'Whiplash', which has words like 'bad' and 'kill' that represent the topic 'anger and violence', it would find that the lyrics of this song has low lyrical differentiation.

The results from a regression model showed that the more differentiated a song's lyrics were from its genre, the more popular that song was. In fact, a 16 per cent increase in lyrical differentiation, for example, was associated with a one-position improvement in chart ranking. So, this means that if Kendrick Lamar, a rap artist, has a song with lyrics that are 16 per cent more like country music lyrics and less of his typical rap lyrics, that will lead to an improvement in the ranking of his song by one position.

> The regression model is a statistical model that finds a relationship between an outcome (or label) and one or more predictors (or features).

In terms of which genres do well with lyrical differentiation, rock music profits the most, followed by Christian, R&B, rap and country. There was no effect on popularity if musicians in dance and pop music genres differentiated their lyrics. Perhaps, the authors speculate, it's because dance music contains few lyrics and the beat matters most. As for pop music, the genre itself focuses on being mainstream, popular culture and appealing to everyone. So, if lyrics seem different to what the mainstream audience wants, it has little effect on popularity. In fact, sometimes, when the authors ran more stringent statistical models, the finding was that differentiation, in fact, can hurt pop music.[26]

Berger and Packard also examined if songs could be successful by just including a bit of non-genre lyrics to go alongside the genre's typical lyrics. This strategy was not as successful as songs that only used fewer of the more genre-typical topics. For example, 'street cred' featured in only 2 per cent of rock lyrics and is more associated with rap music, yet rock songs containing more lyrics about street cred were more popular. Street cred contains representative keywords like: 'ass', 'bitch', 'dope', 'rich' and 'street'. Consider Good Charlotte, a rock band from Maryland, and their song 'Lifestyles of the Rich and Famous'. The song has lyrics that include the words 'rich' and 'street', and upon its release in 2002, the single reached a peak of No. 20 on the US Billboard Hot 100, which was their highest ever on the chart. According to the authors, if a musician wants to move away from her genre, the best topics helping to drive popularity are 'uncertain love' and 'body movement'. Note that their results are specific for genre-related differentiation rather than differentiation across all music.

So, what do these results imply for musicians, novelists, filmmakers and managers of such artists?

First, the study above shows that if musicians write a song that differs in its lyrical content from their genre's typical content, listeners seem to like the novelty aspect of that song. Perhaps, artists can take heart that fans like their favourite musicians experimenting with how they write lyrics. Consider Outkast, a rap and hip-hop duo from Georgia. Their biggest hit, 'Hey Ya!' did not have any of the representative words from the topic of street cred, such as 'ass', 'bitch', 'dope', 'rich' or 'street', but included words from the topic of uncertain love like 'love' and 'can't'. André 3000, the songwriter, wrote about modern relationships and how convoluted they are and even referenced his own relationship: 'We get together, oh, we get together, but separate's always better when there's feelings involved . . . know what they say, nothing lasts forever!'

'Hey Ya!' was the first song to reach 1 million downloads on Apple's iTunes[27] and was a hit across many countries. The song is one of the greatest songs of the 2000s. *Rolling Stone* placed the song in the tenth spot on their list of 'The 500 Greatest Songs of All Time'.[28] Indeed, the song's music was catchy, with elements of funk, electro, pop and hip-hop, but the lyrics were not what Outkast generally wrote about. The same goes for the song 'More Than Words' by the rock group Extreme. Extreme is a rock band mixing elements of funk and sophisticated guitar-playing. The lyrics for 'More Than Words' include words from the topic 'fiery love', such as 'love' and 'heart', a departure from how the band typically expressed themselves.

'More Than Words' reached No. 1 on the Billboard Hot 100 in the US[29] and No. 2 in the UK.[30] Indeed, even musicians want lyrical diversity, and it seems to be the case even in country music, where most lyrics are about trucks and girls. In a song called 'Songs About Trucks', country singer Wade Bowen requests his fellow country singers to refrain from writing any more 'shallow' songs about their beloved vehicles.

Second, as previously stated, the results show that if musicians want to experiment with their lyrics, the best topics to write about are uncertain love and body movement. Perhaps, someone can take a leaf out of Outkast as it seems it paid off huge for them.

Third, as Berger and Packard write, though lyrical differentiation pays off, there are also benefits to familiarity.[31] Thus, it might be fruitful for artists to get the right balance of familiarity and differentiation when they pursue their artistic endeavours. Similarity to what artists have done in the past can make fans feel at home while differentiation from their past work can stimulate, excite and arouse fans. Remixes of songs are a case in point. Many pieces get a new life after they are remixed, like the UK duo Everything But The Girl's song 'Missing'. Initially released in 1994, the song reached only the sixty-ninth position on the UK charts. After the remix by DJ Todd Terry a year later, the song became a superhit, claiming the No. 3 spot in the UK and No. 2 spot in the US. The song also made it to the Top 10 in fifteen countries.[32]

Overall, the next time you hear a Metallica song with lyrics that resemble something that Justin Bieber would write, don't be surprised if you listen to it more than their other new songs. One example where a band unknowingly tried this is the American band Pearl Jam with their song 'Wishlist', with lyrics that go, 'I wish I was a sentimental ornament you hung on, the Christmas tree I wish I was the star that went on top'. Will Metallica try this idea of lyrical differentiation? In fact, Metallica are a band quite intelligent in using data to enhance the listening experience of their fans. In my marketing class, I teach that a principal role of firms is to create value for customers. If you think of Metallica as a firm and their concerts as the product, what do you think will provide the most value to their customers? Of course, their fans having a great time. How do you deliver that? Metallica are known to have a different setlist for every city they play in. Before every show, their drummer Lars Ulrich examines Spotify data to know the most-streamed Metallica songs in the region.[33] They then create a setlist, which includes these locally liked songs. The outcome of all this—fans who sing along and love the show.

Metallica, in fact, attempted to enter country music territory with a song called 'Mama Said'. The video has about 47 million views on YouTube, and I listen to the song quite often even though I have a preference for their metal sound. Yes, 47 million views with some of the views from yours truly. We tend to like novelty and surprises!

3

Spoiler Alert: The Tale of a Nordic Thriller

You have been watching a Nordic noir on Netflix for the last two weeks. Every day, you are eager to get home, sip your favourite aperitif and immerse yourself in a world of bleak and barren landscapes where characters with complex morals intermingle. There is a murderer who is on the rampage, killing innocent children. You have finished episode nine and today is your self-selected day for the big reveal.

Who is the murderer?

Episode nine almost revealed the killer, and you waited one more day to watch the final episode. You want to prolong that ticklish nervous feeling of uncertainty and unknowing. You know that today will be the day when this thrill will be over. You intend to get home and watch the final episode along with a heady cocktail that seems to fuse well with the spartan mood of this Nordic noir fluidly. The finale is here—the finale of Nordic noir series number 17 you have been digesting every day for the last year.

As you leave the office, in the elevator going down, you hear two colleagues discussing someone. A name you seem to recall, a name that has been at the back of your mind. You also overhear them saying, 'Didn't believe Rasmussen was the one.' Slowly, as you get out of the building, as much as you try to deny the fact, you realize you now know something you should not. Your mood suddenly resembles your current favourite show's desolate and cheerless scenery.

The two colleagues have spoiled your happiness by unknowingly divulging the killer's name. You get back home. You open up Netflix and watch the final episode, knowing what you know and trying your best to unlearn what you know.

Indeed, Rasmussen, a bereavement counsellor, father and husband, is the killer. You turn the show off and order something you really don't care about from Uber Eats to go with your destructive and morose mood. All nine episodes were, for you, futile. What transpired in the elevator was that you were unintentionally offered a spoiler.

A spoiler is information about the plot of a book, movie or television show that spoils the surprise or suspense for a reader or viewer.[1] The definition is academic and flat, but the effect of a spoiler on someone keen not to know any revealing details of a whodunit is sharp, and more often than not, cruel and distressing.

If you take movies, for example, spoilers can be of different types. It can be someone telling you that the film was, in fact, a story narrated from the perspective of an untrustworthy narrator who essentially constructed the entire preceding tale or the important character in the movie who is acknowledged as dead, but is, in fact, still alive or the character in the film was someone else.

Spoilers are not just called spoilers for no reason. Movie critics ensure they don't reveal any spoilers in their reviews to ensure their readership is intact.

You would think because of the harmful effects of spoilers, websites focused on revealing a plot twist or a surprise ending would be few and far between. You're mistaken.

Despite a spoiler's mood-dampening effects, spoilers are so common that there are websites dedicated to them. For example, www.themoviespoiler.com or www.moviepooper.com for movies and www.spoilertv.com for television. The tagline for the movie spoiler website www.moviepooper.com is 'Spoiling Endings of Hundreds of Movies Since 1996'.

You would presume that moviegoers would keep away from such websites. No!

In fact, there are thousands of people who visit these sites. People seem to relish knowing key and pivotal plot elements. In fact, in November 2021, there were 332.79K visits to themoviespoiler.com and 2.11 million visits to www.spoilertv. com.[2] According to the Internet Movie Database (IMDb) data, about 93 per cent of movies released in the US got at least one spoiler review between 2013 and 2017.

Till now, I have mentioned the distressing effects spoilers can have on someone. At my end, I make sure not to meet or get into a conversation with someone about a mystery or thriller movie or television show. It's better not to take the risk as they may spill the beans without meaning to. One time, because of knowing there was a plot twist in the movie *The Sixth Sense*, I almost locked myself up and did not meet anyone for about five days before I went to the theatre. Some of my friends were infamous, veteran spoilers, and this was my strategy to stop them from spoiling the movie for me. Oh, what pains we go through to entertain ourselves!

Apart from individuals like me whose happiness is taken away because of the revelation of a plot twist, spoilers could also hurt movie revenues and television viewings. Movie and television producers and directors do their best to keep the mystery hidden and are on their toes to hide secrets pertaining to their films or TV series. In April 2019, before the release of the much-anticipated *Avengers: Endgame*, produced by Marvel Studios, the directors cautioned viewers, 'When you see *Endgame* in the coming weeks, please don't spoil it for others, the same way you wouldn't want it spoiled for you'.[3]

Should these directors and producers be worried? Do spoilers really hurt film revenues?

In an interesting study, two erstwhile co-authors of mine, Joseph Ryoo at the City University of Hong Kong and Shane Wang at the University of Virginia, along with Shijie Lu at the University of Notre Dame, examined this very question.[4] Their main task was to determine if they could use the content of online reviews about films to see if these reviews harmed a movie's box office revenues.

For their investigation, the authors first amassed a data set of 1,40,869 reviews for 993 movies released in the US between 2013 and 2017 from IMDb. IMDb is one of the primary sources of information and statistics about movies, TV shows and video games. The site also contains reviews and ratings from both users and critics. As of March 2022, the website had information on about 10 million movies and TV shows.[5] And it is a very well-visited site with 83 million registered users.

Ryoo and his colleagues used IMDb not only for its breadth of information but also because the site requires users to label their reviews with spoiler warnings. Remember, they need reviews that are categorized as spoilers to see the effects of these spoilers on box office revenues. IMDb, of course, does not want the reviews on their site to have spoilers. Like everyone else and me, IMDb is of the notion spoilers offend users and hurt movie revenues.

In fact, the website's moderators penalize users who are careless about labelling their review when it contains a spoiler. The site blacklists users who don't follow this warning.

Now let's dive into the text mining the authors utilized.

With these spoiler reviews, one can count the number of spoiler reviews for each movie and perhaps use this count or, say, a ratio of spoiler reviews to total reviews of a movie and examine the effect of either of these measures on the movie's box office performance.

However, instead of just utilizing spoiler volume, Ryoo and his co-authors ingeniously created a measure called 'spoiler intensity'. They defined spoiler intensity as the degree of information in spoiler reviews that reduces plot uncertainty. Ryoo and his colleagues wanted to use the content in the reviews to develop a measure calculating the amount of spoilage. Prior studies examining the relationship between spoilers and movie revenues did not consider the information contained in each spoiler.

Now, let's see how the authors measure spoiler intensity. They used a technique called the correlated topic model (CTM).[6] Let me quickly explain first what a topic model does. A topic model basically divides a document into several distinct topics. Imagine your task is to read the editorials in *Time* magazine for 2021 and come up with the main topics that the editorials wrote about. This would be painstaking to do manually. We may perhaps come up with topics such as 'COVID-19', 'Sustainability', 'Technology Trends', and so on. A topic model does all of this in an automated fashion. A topic model imagines that each document contains words from many topics in different proportions. For example, in my example above, a three-topic model could unearth that each editorial in *Time* magazine in 2021 has a particular representation. Say, the editorial in the first week of 2021 has 10 per cent topic A,

40 per cent topic B and 50 per cent topic C. The editorial in the second week of 2021 has 65 per cent topic A, 10 per cent topic B and 25 per cent topic C. The allocation with varying proportions depending on the content in the editorial will then be done for all the editorials that appeared each week in 2021.

Topic models are unsupervised, which means the model does not require any human supervision. You let the data speak. In a topic model, you run a particular model and the model itself uncovers the optimal number of topics based on a statistical criterion. After the model is run, the analyst must name the topics. A topic model generates the top words that belong to each topic, which helps the analyst to name them. One of the most widely used models in topic modelling is the Latent Dirichlet Allocation (LDA),[7] which has been widely used across disciplines. A correlated topic model allows correlations between topics, which standard models like the LDA don't. For example, using the example of the *Time* magazine editorial above, say the correlated topic model generates a three-topic model and you name the topics as 'Pandemic', 'Socioeconomic Trends' and 'Financial Trends'. A topic like 'Socioeconomic Trends' may have content that is also in a topic such as 'Financial Trends'.

Supervised and Unsupervised are two types of machine-learning models. In supervised learning, a model is given labelled data that it learns from and then predicts the label. In unsupervised learning, a model finds patterns in data that has no pre-specified labels.

Here is how Ryoo and his colleagues used the CTM. Their first task was to find an array of plot-related topics from the movie review texts. They used both the reviews labelled as spoilers and normal reviews for this purpose. Using the CTM, Ryoo and his co-authors identified sixty-one topics among both spoiler and non-spoiler reviews.

What were the topics the authors uncovered?

The topics spanned from 'Acting Performance', which includes representative words such as 'perform', 'actor' and 'role', to the 'Western' topic, which comprises words like 'Western', 'town' and 'magnificent'. As of now, they don't have information on what topics tend to belong to spoiler and non-spoiler reviews. Indeed, not all of the sixty-one topics can resolve plot uncertainty. Some will be more related to spoilers, and some will not. Thus, Ryoo and his colleagues used the difference between the text in spoiler and non-spoiler reviews to identify the topics that can resolve plot uncertainty.

The author team ran a binary logistic regression model to identify the topics related to spoilers.

> A binary logistic regression model is a type of regression model that estimates the likelihood of an outcome occurring versus the outcome not occurring based on one or more predictors. For example, the outcome can be 'win the lottery' or 'did not win the lottery' based on certain predictors such as age, star sign, gender, etc. An analyst tries to find which predictors are most potent in predicting an outcome.

Ryoo and his co-authors ran a logistic regression where the outcome variable was whether or not the review was a spoiler. As for the predictors, the authors used the number of words in each review that were associated with each topic. The authors identified twenty-three topics commonly related to spoilers. Guess what the top three topics related to spoilers were?

The top three spoiler-related topics were: 'Disappointment,' 'Kill' And 'Death.' Indeed, 'Kill' and 'Death' are usually involved in crucial plot points in movies. The topic of 'Disappointment' is associated with the words 'worst,' 'ruin' and 'disappoint.' The top topic related to non-spoiler reviews was 'Cinematography', which includes representative words such as 'beautiful', 'visual' and 'set'. As you probably noticed, these words are related to the aesthetics and visuals of the film and are unrelated specifically to the movie's narrative.

By counting the number of words related to each of the twenty-three topics per movie review, the authors next constructed the spoiler intensity for each film every day. Where do the authors collect the movie revenues data, and what should the timeframe be?

The authors collected the revenue and number of theatres where a movie was playing from BoxOfficeMojo.com and IMDb. Because about 97 per cent of movie revenues are generated in the first two months after a movie is released,[8] they collected figures on daily box office revenue and the daily number of theatres for the first two weeks where the movie was playing.

Okay, so the authors have the spoiler intensity metric and the movie performance data. What next? Of course, the main analysis. They estimated a regression model, which allowed them to see if spoiler intensity increases or decreases box-office performance. Note that the model controlled for many other characteristics that can influence box-office performance, such as advertising, if it was a holiday, day of the week, and many others.

What did the authors find? I will not play spoilsport and test your patience.

Voila!

Surprisingly, the study found that spoiler intensity increases rather than decreases box-office performance for a movie. Ryoo and his co-authors found, in economic vocabulary, a spoiler elasticity of .06, which means if the spoiler intensity measure changes by 1 per cent, box office revenues will increase by about 0.06 per cent.

How do they explain this? Aren't spoilers supposed to harm movie revenues?

The primary variable that the authors use, 'spoiler intensity', depends on the idea that spoilers reduce the uncertainty about a movie's quality. Especially for experiential products such as movies, it is difficult for consumers to evaluate before consumption.[9] So, the reason spoilers increase revenue is readers appreciate the quality uncertainty that is lessened.

To examine what movies benefit most from spoilers and ensure their theoretical argument that uncertainty reduction was the main driver, the authors ran a series of tests using the data they had collected.

Let's see some situations when there is more uncertainty about a movie's quality.

The first is when the user ratings for a movie are average. If I hear of a mystery movie that is doing well and has rave reviews (without spoilers of course), will I get offended if I read a spoiler? Of course, I will. I was aware that the movie *The Sixth Sense* had suspense, was rated very highly and thus almost hibernated to curb anyone from spoiling the joy of watching the suspense unravel. What about movies that are pretty bad and have a 1-star review? I will not care about these reviews anyway, spoiler or not. How about movies with mixed ratings? Films in the middle range of ratings generally signal ambiguity about a movie's quality.[10] If uncertainty reduction is a strong driver of spoilers in positively influencing movie revenues, these are the spoilers that should impact movie revenues more.

Second, another context where a movie might benefit from a spoiler is when it has less advertising. Apart from the many functions of advertising, one crucial role espoused by economics scholars is the informative aspect of advertising. Research has shown advertising reduces product uncertainty for buyers and is a credible signal about quality.[11] Thus, for films that have less advertising and more uncertainty, the effect of spoilers should be more potent.

Third, many movies have only a limited release, especially independent and arthouse films. Unlike blockbusters with a high marketing budget, these movies don't have a wide distribution and only see a limited release. This strategy is often employed by arthouse and independent filmmakers who make more artistic films. Indeed, I will have more uncertainty about the artistic quality of an independent movie than a mainstream movie.[12] Thus, movies with limited release should have more uncertainty attached to them.

Finally, spoilers should work more during the early periods of a film's release rather than later. As a movie progresses through its life cycle from its first day of screening, the uncertainty about a movie reduces because the box office revenues indicate its quality. Higher-quality movies tend to have higher box office revenues than low-quality movies.[13]

Indeed, Ryoo and his colleagues find spoilers have a more substantial effect on box office performance if a movie has average user ratings, is a limited release, has less advertising, and is in the early stages of its release.

Who would have thought that spoilers don't 'spoil' box office revenues but, in fact, have a beneficial effect on a movie's success?

So, what do these results mean for managers of works of art, such as film producers, television show makers, publishers of novels, creators of game shows and other works of art?

First, online review platforms should not prohibit reviews with spoilers. These spoilers can reduce quality uncertainty for readers of reviews and provide diagnostic information about a work of art such as movies, television shows, novels and so on.

Second, online review platforms should also maintain spoiler warning alerts if they have one. This type of mechanism first allows readers to be aware of reviews and to self-select when reading spoiler reviews if they are interested.

Third, managers of works of art with a limited release and average user ratings should be more open to online word of mouth and flexible in the types of reviews these works of art get. If word of mouth stimulates spoiler reviews, even better. Works of art with smaller marketing budgets, therefore low advertising, can monitor the online reviews of their creations and accordingly decide to keep the advertising at a minimum level if there are a lot of spoiler reviews for their products.

Fourth, managers should monitor for spoilers in reviews more in the early stages of a work of art's life cycle rather than later. Monitoring reviews for spoilers would not be worthwhile in the later stages.

Finally, apart from the volume of reviews, average ratings and the sentiment of reviews, managers can also include spoiler reviews as another component they can use for predicting a movie's success. Managers nowadays routinely collect online review data to understand the likelihood of a product's success.

As you may remember from the beginning of this chapter, even after the viewer watching the Nordic noir knew who the murderer was, he still watched the show. Perhaps the spoiler reduced his uncertainty about the show's quality.

4

Mistaking the Value of
Mistakes in Online Reviews

Consider these two reviews of a product:[1]

Review 1:

> 'When my first Sony battery expired, I bought a knock-off.
> What a mistake! It lasted about a quarter as long as the Sony.'—
> Max

Review 2:

> 'The Sony battery is essential to have. Counterfeit brands don't
> last a quarter as long as the branded Sony batteries.'—Monica

Both reviews above by Max and Monica are positive and speak
well about Sony's batteries.

But which of these two reviews should Sony feature? Which
review will better persuade consumers to consider and perhaps
purchase Sony's line of batteries?

It is well known the reviews we write online for a product or service can have strong consequences for potential buyers and affect the brand that sells the product or service. Indeed, online reviews are tremendously important for the modern-day consumer. Recent statistics show that 91 per cent of eighteen- to thirty-four-year-olds place as much trust in online reviews as personal recommendations, while 93 per cent of consumers state online reviews influence their decision to purchase.[2]

Websites also benefit from users writing a review. Having reviews on their websites increases visits and gives firms a strong handle on user satisfaction. Firms also want to know if there is anything wrong with their products to learn and improve the product and customer experience. To quote Bill Gates, 'Your most unhappy customers are your greatest source of learning.'

Let's talk about something most of us do often but don't want to admit to others, especially in a public forum—make mistakes!

To bring up a clichéd quote—'To err is human', said Alexander Pope.[3] We have all made mistakes when buying a product or using a service. For example, I remember buying fake Levi's jeans in high school. I thought I was cool, trendy and was showing off my supposedly hip Levi's jeans to my friends and family. The jeans were knee-ripped. I thought I was the next Kurt Cobain but little did I know I was making a fool of myself, as the brand name was not Levi's but Levis. Within two months, the jeans got even more ripped and, in fact, so ripped that they completely tore apart. Another example from yours truly. During my undergraduate years, I bought a Lacoste shirt, a fake one, thinking it to be an original. The shirt survived two washes. The funny thing I noticed later was the crocodile logo was facing the other side instead of looking towards the left, which the actual logo does.

Indeed, most of us realize our mistake and swear we will not fall for this trap again, and ensure we are cleverer and more competent when we buy the same product or service. However, some people go online and let their emotions out by admitting their faux pas through an online review.

Reviews often feature 'a mistake' like the one above by Max, who made a mistake in purchasing a Sony battery that turned out to be a counterfeit.

Now, my question to you was, which of the two reviews would you find more helpful?

Max's review, where he admits his mistake, or the review by Monica, who did not commit a faux pas and seems to have had a pleasant purchasing experience?

Common sense would lead most of us to believe that we do not like to read or listen to someone who has made mistakes. Many of us seek perfectionists. So, one would assume that the second review by Monica would be the preferred option.

But is there a possibility we pay attention to someone who is not perfect? Is that even possible? After all, Max seems incapable, right? One may not trust this reviewer because he was not thoughtful, intelligent and switched on enough to scrutinize the product's specifications.

Two professors in marketing, Taly Reich from the Yale School of Management and Sam Maglio from the University of Toronto in Scarborough, paired up to investigate this question.

What could be the reason a reader might be persuaded by a review featuring a mistake rather than a review that does not?

Perhaps the reader does not think the purchaser is permanently incompetent. Instead, he might have had a temporary lapse of knowledge. Max may have made an error in judgement at a particular point in time but that does not mean he is always incompetent. The reader might think he made a mistake, realized it and now has more knowledge and experience.

Research in neuroscience shows we are, in fact, very sensitive to mistakes and when we make a mistake, our brain understands what it is doing and learns. Max, for example, might have felt an array of negative emotions when he made that error of buying a knock-off Sony battery. He may have felt irritated, disappointed or annoyed. However, these emotions are a component of what the brain does to help Max do better in the future and stop making that mistake.

Our brain produces a specific type of electrical activity when we make errors, called Error-Related Negativity (ERN),[4] which allows us to know what errors we have made and correct them as we tread the various stages in our lives. This electrical activity happens at the same time we make a mistake. The brain seems to know we are making a mistake even before we are conscious of our error.

So, what is the genesis of this ERN?

From the earliest times, our ancestors had to learn from their mistakes to avoid becoming prey to predators and get more efficient and effective in their hunting adventures. So, the brain evolved for humanity's survival. What is the one thing most of us always do, even though we may read hundreds of books or listen to podcasts about being in the present? We think about our past and future. Predicting the future, among other things, also includes our ability to learn from our mistakes and change our future actions. This learning is embedded in us, and scientists have shown that ERN is a key component of how we learn.

Consider Max's situation. Max's goal is to buy batteries that are durable and last long. Max decides that instead of buying the original batteries from Sony, he will try a knock-off. He buys the knock-off and realizes it was a mistake. Although Max is disappointed and perhaps angry with his decision, the incident tells him something crucial. It tells him that his notions about how the world works and how he can influence it are not right. Now that he knows, he will buy an original Sony battery. This whole process has a neurological basis.[5]

Let's see how this happens.

Our brain cells communicate with each other using electrical 'brain waves'. When we make an error, negative electrical activity shows up at the top of our head and this activity is called the ERN. The ERN comes from a region in the brain called the cingulate cortex.[6] An ERN occurs when the cingulate cortex detects an error and sends a signal to other parts of the brain through the cingulum bundle, a nerve tract that connects several brain regions. This activation helps us focus our attention to reduce the possibility of making new mistakes.

The ERN happens so quickly we are not even aware of it. It occurs at 100 ms (1/1000th of a second) after we make a mistake. We actually come to know we have made a mistake about 200 ms later. The brain seems to know we have made a mistake, even before we do!

After we make a mistake, the cingulate cortex compares what we did to what we had planned to do. The ERN then signals to our conscious self that we did not achieve what we had intended and brings the mismatch to our attention. At the same time, we become aware that we made a mistake through a later brain signal called error positivity, which comes around 200 ms after we made an error. We tend to respond slower next time for the activity where we previously made a mistake. The brain takes some time to process it, so that we don't make the same mistake again. The stronger the ERN, the slower our response the next time we do that activity.[7]

Some people have larger ERNs than others and that seems to have positive repercussions such as good grades.[8] On the other hand, a large ERN is not always a good thing. People with large ERNs are more anxious and might react more to a mistake than is necessary. The ERN takes a long time to develop as we grow older and continues developing till our late twenties. So, if you make more errors when you are young, do not blame yourself. It just takes time. As they say, as you grow old, you get wiser. The ERN is a key component of that wisdom.

Coming back to readers' response to Max's review. A reader could consider that Max, who admitted to a mistake, which few do, now knows more about the product and has expertise in the domain of batteries.

Admitting to a mistake in a public forum signals that this person is now confident about the product's specifications. A mistaken reviewer appears more transparent and less vague than someone who does not admit a mistake. Readers know we all make mistakes and most of us try our best to rectify them. So, the reader thinks the mistaken reviewer is correcting the error. Brandon Mull has a wonderful quote in his children's fantasy book: 'Smart people learn from their mistakes. But the real sharp ones learn from the mistakes of others.'[9]

Overall, Reich and Maglio predicted:

- consumers would infer more expertise from reviewers who admit to a mistake versus reviewers who do not
- consumers are more likely to purchase a product recommended by reviewers who admit to a mistake versus those who do not as they believe that the reviewer now is an expert on the product
- these effects will only happen for the product with which the reviewer made a mistake and not for a different product.

Let's now dive into the text mining Reich and Maglio conducted with real-world data.

The authors got their textual data by scraping online reviews from the French multinational retailer Sephora. Sephora's online retail platform has plenty of reviews posted by their consumers, and review readers can indicate whether they find a particular review helpful. This was one reason the authors chose this site.

Sephora's website caters to six product categories: bath and body, fragrance, hair, make-up, skincare, and tools and brushes. Reich and Maglio randomly chose the hair product category and forty random hair care products to test their hypothesis. The authors web-scraped 5727 reviews from the site, posted between August 2017 and December 2018, and began their text-mining adventure.

The authors used a dictionary-based approach to identify reviews that admitted to mistakes.

Let me elaborate a bit on the dictionary-based approach. Dictionary-based approaches are quite effectively used in social science. There are dictionaries for a wide range of constructs or dimensions in psychology, sociology and business disciplines such as marketing. It is one of the most common text-mining methods to produce knowledge. Dictionary-based approaches have three main advantages. First, they are easy to use and understand. Second, blended with the fundamentals of linguistics, these dictionaries enable a simple and intuitive operationalization of constructs or dimensions from fields such as psychology and sociology. Third, validating these dictionaries is quite simple.[10]

For a dictionary-based approach, a social scientist first defines and calculates the measurements encapsulating the textual characteristics to characterize a construct or dimension. For example, if I am interested in the construct of negative emotion,

I will create a dictionary containing words such as 'hate', 'sad', 'angry', and so on. The most widely used measurement for the dictionary-based approach is the frequency of the words that belong to a construct or dimension in a textual corpus. The measurement is done using a computer algorithm.

We can validate these dictionary-based approaches by using human coders.

For example, say I develop dictionaries for the constructs of positive and negative emotion to measure whether a tweet is positive, negative or neutral.

One way to validate it is to ask human coders to classify 100 tweets as positive, negative or neutral. Say the coders classify sixty of these tweets as positive, thirty as negative, and ten as neutral. I can check the validity of my dictionary by running my algorithm, which counts the number of positive and negative words in each of the 100 tweets and creates the percentage of positive words and the percentage of negative words in each tweet. If the difference of the percentage of positive and negative words is positive, the algorithm classifies it as positive; if the difference is negative, the algorithm classifies it as negative; if the difference is zero, the algorithm classifies it as neutral. If the task done by the algorithm corresponds well with the human classification, the algorithm is said to be validated.

Reich and Maglio created a dictionary that included the following case-insensitive terms. In text mining, *case-insensitive* means that the words can be in upper case, lower case, proper case or any combination of cases.

- mistake: if the string 'mistake' is in the review;
- mistook: if the string 'mistook' is in the review;
- my_bad: if either the phrase 'my bad' or 'my error' is in the review;

- I_wrong: if the word 'I' is within 35 characters of a word starting with 'wrong';
- my_fault: if the word 'my' is within 35 characters of the word 'fault';
- our_fault: the word 'our' is within 35 characters of the word 'fault'.

For the latter three, note they ensured there were no punctuation marks such as a period, question mark or exclamation mark in between.

This coding procedure led to a sample of 502 reviews referencing a prior mistake. Two independent human judges verified that the coding procedure was justifiable. Because Reich and Maglio wanted to see how reviews with mistakes compare to reviews without mistakes, they randomly selected 502 reviews without a mistake. Finally, they analysed 1004 reviews to see if their effects emerged in the field.

What did the authors find?

Reich and Maglio found reviews referencing a mistake (versus those not referencing a mistake) were deemed more helpful. They also tested a stronger statistical model controlling for the length of the review, whether the review was positive or negative, the rating of the review, whether the Sephora website featured the product, whether the reviewer was a loyalty programme member and an expert in reviewing, how many images were uploaded with the review, if the review mentioned another brand and the date of the review. Their results were robust after accounting for all the above factors. The authors also found reviews with mistakes only work for the domain or product category where the reviewer made a mistake. So, if Max writes a review for Sony batteries and acknowledges his mistake, readers will only find his review helpful if they intend to buy a battery and not a smartphone, for example.

Besides the text mining, Reich and Maglio also ran a series of four experiments to find support for their arguments. In their experiments, Reich and Maglio found that participants chose the recommended products more often when they were recommended by a reviewer who admitted a mistake rather than by a reviewer who bought the product successfully.

Participants in Reich and Maglio's experiments perceived mistaken reviewers to have learnt more and gained more expertise in choosing products than successful purchasers. Figure 4.1 below shows their conceptual framework. According to the figure, readers perceive the reviewer who admits to a mistake as an expert, thus persuading them to find a review helpful and buy the product.

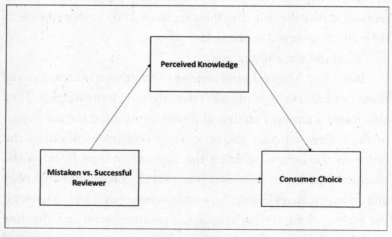

Figure 4.1: How reviews with mistakes affect purchase behaviour

Overall, Reich and Maglio found strong evidence that mistakes in a review can indeed be helpful and persuade consumers.

So, what do these results imply for practice?

And in general, how can mistakes be helpful? We tend to see mistakes in a negative light, but what are some positive consequences that can emerge from mistakes and admitting to errors?

First, Reich and Maglio suggest that revealing purchase mistakes in online consumer reviews offers firms and platforms a new way of positively influencing consumers' attitudes and purchase behaviours. Often, firms and platforms like Amazon, TripAdvisor, etc., might be cautious about featuring reviews with mistakes. However, the findings from the study above show that firms and platforms could benefit by publicizing and making these reviews more prominent. Indeed, many firms and online platforms tag reviews as 'featured' or 'highlighted,' and the study's findings indicate this strategy may be worthwhile.

Second, admitting to mistakes can build credibility for users, such as influencers on social media. We live in a world of influencers. Various influencers with millions of viewers satisfy their audience daily or weekly. But sometimes, influencers say something that leads to negative comments and backlash. Influencers could consider employing a strategy where admitting to their mistake could build their personal brands and bolster their personal equity. Consider the story of Jenna Marbles, one of the first YouTube personalities to have her wax persona in Madame Tussauds in New York. Her YouTube channel accumulated about 1.7 billion views with over 20 million subscribers by 2020. However, she was criticized on social media for racist and sexist comments. In the summer of 2020, she apologized for her mistake, mentioning her remarks were 'shameful' and 'awful,' wishing they weren't part of (her) past'.[11] She left the YouTube platform and made all her prior videos unavailable to the public. Many people responded positively to her decision.[12] Even though she is no longer on YouTube, her response was honest. The public may see her in a more positive light if she ever comes back online.

Finally, admitting to a mistake and apologizing correctly can benefit firms. We all make mistakes. Influencers make mistakes. Firms make mistakes, in fact, quite often. Nowadays, we see apologies from firms almost routinely. We see posts such as Facebook's: 'From now on, Facebook will do more to keep you safe and protect your privacy' on account of the Cambridge Analytica scandal. Then there was the instance of the Spotify CEO saying he was 'deeply sorry' for comedian Joe Rogan's racist language. But is that the right strategy? It seems like sorry is the easiest word. We are so accustomed to seeing apologies, that there is even a term for it: 'normative dilution'. Because people have become so used to seeing apologies, we have become exhausted by them, and thus, apologies have less impact and value. On the one hand, we have been taught from our youngest days we should say sorry when we do something wrong. On the other hand, there is this idea that saying sorry makes us look weak.

However, despite what one may say, owning up to a *mea culpa* and taking care of the issue seems to be the best thing to do. According to a study by the consultancy firm LRN, 'Companies whose senior managers do not properly apologize are six times more likely to have unsatisfied customers, five times more likely to see their market share stagnate, nine times more likely to struggle to adapt to change, and eight times more likely to not be recognized as a real innovator.'[13]

Thus, firms need to apologize, but there should be proper steps. First, firms may simply need better management to avoid a crisis happening. Second, firms need to be transparent. Being open and taking responsibility for a mistake shows people the firm is being honest and is trying to make a change. Third, firms should be specific about their next steps, show genuine remorse and reassure followers the mistake will not happen again. Take, for example, the admission of an error by Skittles, the makers of multicoloured, fruit-flavoured, button-shaped candies.[14] From 1979 till 2013, every Skittles candy bag consisted of strawberry, lemon, grape, orange, and lime. In 2013, they did away with this combination and removed the lime flavour from the bag. Skittles, in turn, introduced candies with a green apple flavour. More than 1,30,000 Skittles lovers got angry and posted complaints on social media. After some time, Skittles realized its mistake and reinstated the old lime flavour. The company also ran a thirty-minute press conference, where Skittles apologized to all the 1,30,880 of its angry customers for the mistake. Skittles apologized on social media, through video, and even on a Times Square billboard. This helped Skittles to demonstrate that they learnt from the mistake and improved their credibility.

Consider another example. Have any of you heard about a company called Qwikster? It is no more. Qwikster was a venture by Netflix that was shelved almost as soon as it launched. Netflix initially had a system where users would have one account with billing details for its streaming and DVD rental services. However, in September 2011, the company divided this system into two entities, Netflix with its streaming and Qwikster with its DVD service. Instead of one account, users had to take care of two. Instead of paying $10 per month, users had to dole out $8 for streaming on Netflix and $8 for renting DVDs on Qwikster. Guess what happened? Qwikster lasted twenty-one days. CEO Reed Hastings publicly apologized for his mistake saying, 'Okay, you're right. Having two billing systems was a bad idea, and we're doing away with that.' Despite the initial losses because of this event, Netflix bounced back. Admitting a mistake and taking the right steps seem to have positive repercussions on consumers and investors. One piece of research shows when top managers of firms apologize for a mistake and are perceived to be sad, stock prices rise.[15]

Overall, admitting to a mistake can have positive consequences. It can help firms rebuild their credibility and give customers real value.

It can help influencers who have had a fallout to retrieve their credibility.

It can also affect how we go about buying something online. Reading about someone's mistakes in online reviews can positively affect us. As Eleanor Roosevelt once famously said, 'Learn from the mistakes of others. You can't live long enough to make them all yourself.'

II

FIRMSPEAK

Firms communicate with a myriad of stakeholders—consumers, suppliers, investors, employees, rivals, potential consumers, governments. Moreover, there is an array of media options to communicate with these stakeholders. From traditional media such as radio and TV to newer forms including social media and online videos. As you can see, this is a complicated task. It gets even more complicated as the language utilized in each of these communications has to adhere to the needs of the targeted audience.

In this section, I will take you through stories on whether a customer service agent's usage of concrete words has any concrete benefits, why might you like Ed Sheehan's 'Shape of You' more than his other songs, how firms can reduce consumer vulnerability regarding their data, when 'I' works better than 'We' in business, and what type of environmental slogans touch the chord of their audience.

5

The Concrete Benefits of
Being Concrete in Language

Let me begin with a concrete story about abstract words. According to a recent study, how many words might it take before you encounter a word that is as abstract as 'freedom', 'idea' and 'fun'?[1] The answer is a surprisingly small number. According to a fascinating work undertaken by psychologist Gary Lupyan at the University of Wisconsin and Bodo Winter at the University of Birmingham, if there is an utterance of only five words, there is a 73 per cent likelihood of coming across a word as abstract as 'idea' and a 95 per cent chance of coming across a term as abstract as 'freedom'. Abstract words are ubiquitous.

Consider a Yelp review of a Verizon store:

'My fiancé upgraded his phone at the Apple store, but got a strange text on his new phone about his plan. We went over to the Verizon store to see what was up, and that was about as pleasant as having forks jammed in my eyes. Awful customer service. No one came up to ask us if we needed help. We had to tear a disgruntled man away from looking at his Instagram feed to help us. He didn't say there would be a wait or to sit or anything, just said "okay then" and left us. So we stood there waiting for help or even just directions for far too long, were ignored and told him we were leaving. Awful awful awful customer service.'

If you remove all the words that are relatively more abstract than concrete, the review runs like this:

'Fiancé his phone Apple store, text on his phone his plan. We (Verizon) store see up, forks jammed in my eyes. Customer. One up us we. We tear man looking his (Instagram) feed us. He said us. We stood directions long, him we leaving. Customer.'

This example shows how abstract words are essential for us to understand someone, and if we take away relatively more abstract words, 'we lose the ability to talk about, well, most of what we talk about!'[2]

Abstract words have enormous potency and when using them, we can make words take on a life of their own. Abstract words (along with abstract thinking) allow us to consider concepts, make generalizations, think philosophically, understand metaphors and use elegant, figurative language. Conceptual thinking and words can also enable solving complex problems or creating things where imagination may be required. In general, abstract words denote words referring to intangible qualities, ideas and concepts, which we can understand and know only through our intellect.

What does it mean to say 'grace' is more abstract than 'guitar'?

The inverse of abstract words is commonly defined as concrete words, which denote tangible qualities or characteristics we can understand and know through our senses—words and phrases like 'guitar', 'football' and 'nose ring'. One of the most robust and comprehensive works on concreteness comes from Marc Brysbaert at Ghent University in Belgium along with his co-authors, who asked participants to place 40,000 English words on a concreteness/abstractness scale to create a scale for concreteness.[3] Concrete words are defined as those referring 'to things or actions in reality, which you can experience directly through one of the five senses'.[4]

Concrete words and thinking have their purpose too. In the journey of our lives, we start with concrete thinking. According to Jean Piaget, the renowned developmental psychologist, babies and young children steadily progress from concrete to abstract thinking.[5] From the beginning, babies observe their surroundings and primarily learn through their five senses. In fact, their whole thinking then is based on concrete thinking. They play with objects and see predictable outcomes. Push the squeaky teddy bear and noise happens. As they grow older, they think in symbols; a thumbs-up might mean they want more milk. Gradually, between the ages of two and seven, they begin developing the ability to reason and predict. Between the ages of seven and eleven, though they still rely on concrete thinking and words, children begin to grasp why others behave the way they do and, according to psychologists, begin their adventure into the realm of abstract thought and words.

So, until around the age of about eleven, we rely on concrete thinking and use concrete words to label objects and behaviours, which are more specific, recognizable and noticeable to the eye or mind. From the age of twelve onwards, according to psychologists, we start using abstract words and thinking along with concrete terms, which we already have in our reserves. As we become older, we develop the facility and the flexibility to use either concrete or abstract words when we use our language.

Concrete and specific word choices enjoy one clear advantage, despite the romance of using abstract words, getting high marks in college writing and impressing one's peers. During my undergrad years, even though I was studying mathematics, I hung out with friends who were majoring in sociology and English. Being with them, I was riveted by the allure of abstract words and ideas. For a time, I sought to be like them and shed my unrefined hankerings. Some of my friends regularly dipped into Bob Dylan's book, *The Lyrics*, and knew some of the lyrics inside out. I, on the other hand, knew only the lyrics of the five or six unique lines of Nirvana's 'Negative Creep', which, compared to a Bob Dylan song like 'Masters of War', is far lower on the list of great lyrics. My friends read the poetry of Pablo Neruda and the prose of Salman Rushdie, while I read *The Adventures of Tintin* and *Chacha Chaudhary*. To show that I 'belonged' to their clan, I began reading books ranging from Robert Pirsig's *Zen and the Art of Motorcycle Maintenance* to Emmanuel Kant's *Critique of Pure Reason*. I did not understand anything in the latter. As for the former, I understood that I could attain Zen on a Harley-Davidson bike. Jokes aside, I remember trying to impress my friends by using abstract words like 'idiosyncrasy', 'fragility', 'hearsay' and more, which I was not even 'concretely' sure about.

Concrete words are essential for clear, memorable and effective communication. Consider the following sentences:[6]

- ABSTRACT: Americans must be willing to protect our freedoms.
- CONCRETE: Voters must be willing to give up some individual protections against wiretapping so that the

government can track down terrorists and protect the nation as a whole.

- CONCRETE: Voters must protect their Fourth Amendment right against illegal searches and seizures by calling or writing to their representatives to protest the administration's warrantless wiretapping programme.

For the purposes of this argument, let us assume that the writer of the abstract sentence likely intended the meaning of his sentence to be either of the two concrete sentences below it! But the abstract sentence, I am sure you will agree, cannot quite deliver the meaning or communicate the message clearly.

The usage of abstract words comes with an entrenched weakness—a certain loss of clarity. Using them too frequently makes the communication unappealing and not worth remembering. Concreteness, on the other hand, aids clarity.

Can this clarity be beneficial for a business situation? Duh! Of course. You always need your co-workers to be clear with you rather than meandering and rambling on using words that could fit into a philosophical treatise on existentialism (sorry, Sartre!). The ability to communicate expectations and responsibilities clearly and fluently is a prerequisite in any business environment.

But how about a customer service person on a call with a peeved customer who wants to know why the delivery of her red-striped shirt is taking so long? What should the salesperson say to the customer on such a call? Should she use abstract words like 'that' or relatively less abstract ones such as 'item', 'top' and 'clothing'? Or should she use concrete words such as 'shirt', 'red-striped', etc.? Will this seemingly inconsequential variation in language affect anything? Will the peeved customer react differently to the use of abstract and concrete words?

These fascinating questions were examined by Grant Packard at the University of York and Jonah Berger at the Wharton School of the University of Pennsylvania. They argued that this minor variation in language could have enormous consequences.

You do not need PricewaterhouseCoopers to tell you that irritation with customer service is one of life's most common complaints.[7] Customers get frustrated with customer service because of one common reason: perceived employee inattention. We often email customer support, call customer service and speak face-to-face with retail or sales representatives. Many times, as Packard and Berger mention, 'consumers often feel like service people don't care and are just "going through the motions" rather than actually listening and responding to their needs'.[8]

Excellent customer service is the most direct route to customer satisfaction.[9] It is key to a firm's growth and leads to higher loyalty, increasing the probability of customers continually using a brand's products. As a marketing professor, I can tell you there are more papers written on how to improve customer satisfaction than any other topic.

Packard and Berger argue and show that employees can improve a customer's attitude towards the employee and the company by using more concrete words, rather than abstract words, during their interactions. Using the context of the example I discussed above, instead of saying, 'I will look into that', saying 'I will look into this case of the red-striped shirt' indicates to the customer the employee is attentive to the situation at hand. Packard and Berger demonstrate that concrete words increase customer satisfaction, willingness to purchase and the number of purchases. Table 5.1 shows examples of speaking less versus more concretely in customer service.

EXAMPLES OF SPEAKING LESS VERSUS MORE CONCRETELY IN CUSTOMER SERVICE.

	Less concrete (worse)	More concrete (better)	Why?
What (adjectives, pronouns, nouns)	Those *pants* are a great choice.	Those *blue jeans* are a great choice.	Saying *blue jeans* should seem more detailed and context-specific than *pants*.
	You will receive your *refund* shortly.	You will receive your *money* back shortly.	Receiving *money* should seem more tangible and "real" than a *refund*.
	Would you like *anything* else?	Would you like *coffee* or *tea*?	*Coffee* and *tea* should seem more specific and tangible than *anything*.
How (adverbs, verbs)	Our pie is *really* good.	Our pie is *mouthwateringly* good.	*Mouthwateringly* should seem more vivid and imaginable than *really*.
	We can *get* that room for you.	We can *grab* that room for you.	*Grabbing* something should seem more tangible and "real" than *getting* it.
	I can try to *solve* that engine issue.	I can try to *fix* that engine issue.	*Fixing* something should seem more perceptible and imaginable than *solving* it.

Table 5.1: Examples of speaking less versus more concrete in customer service

Their whole thesis rides on listening. If someone uses concrete language, then an observer believes someone is attending to and understanding of their personal needs. In other words, someone is listening! These days, noise is rampant and attention is sparse and precious, the act of listening is critical. Indeed, for customer service representatives, this might enable them to convey to the customer you are being cared for.

As the employee 'listens' to the customer's message, it entails understanding the verbal messages the customer delivers and decoding the non-verbal messages transmitted.

The customer must perceive that she was being listened to. Imagine if you talk to someone, and the person provides zero response. You cannot figure out whether the person heard or understood your message. Packard and Berger argue that the manifestation of this 'listening' is the use of concrete words by the employee.

So, how did they go about testing their hypothesis? Their first study analysed customer service calls made to a major online apparel retailer to determine if customer satisfaction was higher when employees spoke more concretely. They obtained 200 audio recordings of customer service calls from the online retailer. Specifically, they collected fifty such calls for each level of customer satisfaction measure that the online retailer collected, which spanned from '1: Not at all helpful' to '4: Very helpful'. This was captured immediately after the calls were completed.

After obtaining the recordings, they converted them into text using professional transcription services. Next, instead of the concreteness dictionary developed by Marc Brysbaert and colleagues, they used a text-mining technique called Natural Language Processing (NLP) to calculate concreteness.

NLP helps machines such as computers 'read' text by mimicking the capability of humans to understand a natural language, such as English or Chinese.[10] Text mining employs a range of methodologies to process text and speech, and one of the most common and important ones is NLP. The NLP method uses the perceived concreteness scores from Paetzold and Specia,[11] who refer to the Medical Research Council (MRC) psycholinguistic database[12] as the source. It provided the concreteness score of over 85,000 modern English words on a continuous scale of 100–700.

The MRC psycholinguistic database is a dictionary comprising lexical, morphological and psycholinguistic properties for 1,50,837 words.

A lexical item is a single word, part of a word, or a chain of words forming the foundational elements of a language's vocabulary. Examples are *dog, shopping cart, by the way,* and *beat around the bush*. Morphological properties consist of the internal structure of words, how they are formed and their relationship to other words in the same language. It involves analysing the structure of words and parts of words such as stems, root words, prefixes and suffixes. For example, some simple words don't have an internal structure (i.e., they consist of only one morpheme),* such as dog, see, etc. And there are complex words with an internal structure and consist of two or more morphemes; for example, the word 'teacher' has the affix -er added to the root word to form a noun.[13] Psycholinguistics is the study of psychological processes used in determining how language is used, including the comprehension of language, production of language and acquisition of first and second language.[14]

Originally developed by Australian cognitive scientist Max Coltheart,[15] the MRC database contains four major psycholinguistic properties of words such as familiarity, age of acquisition (i.e., referring to the age at which a word is typically learnt. For example, most learn the word 'penguin' at a younger age than the word 'albatross'),[16] concreteness and imagery. Coltheart used human subjects in cognitive experiments to obtain scores for these four properties. The MRC database has the concreteness score of 8228 words that Paetzold and Specia use.

Paetzold and Specia used an NLP technique employing machine learning to provide scores for any words that have missing psychological properties for concreteness in the MRC database.

NLP is the field related to how machines such as computers understand language but for the machine to understand language, machine learning is the means. Machine learning involves developing algorithms that teach machines to automatically learn and become better from experience. Artificial intelligence (AI) is the overall term used for machines that can resemble human intelligence. Both NLP and machine learning are a part of AI.

---

* A morpheme is a unit of language that cannot be divided any further. It could be a word like 'the' or an element of a word like the 'er' sound in 'teacher'.

Paetzold and Specia used a supervised machine-learning technique to create the concreteness score for many of the words that were not initially classified in the MRC database.

Paetzold and Specia provide concreteness scores for many more words than the initial MRC database, using their NLP model to predict the concreteness scores. The authors provide perceived concreteness scores of over 85,000 modern English words on a continuous scale of 100–700.

These scores are what Packard and Berger used in their study for measuring concreteness. Instead of relying on a typology where a few words have discrete membership in a particular concreteness level, Packard and Berger used Paetzold and Specia's scores as they considered the variations in concreteness that can manifest across different parts of speech, as well as those describing objects and actions.

Berger and Packard provide an excellent elucidation of the MRC database to handle varying levels of concreteness across contexts, whereby each of these examples increases in linguistic concreteness:

Consider the kind of everyday things that different service providers might say to consumers. A waiter might ask a customer whether they would like anything, a drink or coffee. A call centre worker could respond to a caller's inquiry by saying the package will be arriving there, at their place, or at their door. An employee at a cellphone retailer could refer to a new iPhone as a product, device or phone. In each case, the options increase in specificity and imaginability. Concreteness also varies in other parts of speech. Describing a vehicle as sporty or red should make it more vivid. Rather than telling a customer, they will go to the back of the store to look for a larger size, an employee who says they will walk to the back is using more imaginable and specific language to describe this action.[17]

They finally compute a concreteness score for each turn of a conversation (averaging across all words in that turn) and for each participant in the discussion (averaging across all words over all their turns). So, each conversational turn is regarded as a separate record:

Employee: 'How may I help you?' (Turn 1)
Customer: 'I need to know about my red-striped shirt,' (Turn 2) and
Employee: 'I can help' (Turn 3).

Note the participants were the employee and the customer. Packard and Berger calculated the scores for each to account for the employee and the customer mimicking each other. Their first study found a 5.6 per cent increase in concreteness was associated with an 8.9 per cent increase in customer satisfaction. The researchers also considered about fifty other factors, including mimicry, the length of the call, the severity of the issue, the topics discussed, customer characteristics, employee tenure that could lead to higher customer satisfaction scores and how concrete the customer's language is.

Packard and Berger ran another study using 941 randomly sampled customer service interactions (i.e., customer emails and employee responses) from a large Canadian multichannel consumer durables retailer. Here, they also had access to the amount of money the customer spent three months before and after each email interaction. This enabled them to calculate the dollar impact of employees' usage of concrete language. They found that an increase in concreteness scores by one unit[18] led a customer to spend $42.80 over the ninety days following the email compared to $32.73 the customer spent over ninety days before the email interaction. Using a set of experiments, they also found that concreteness increased customer satisfaction and willingness to purchase only when customers perceived that employees were listening to them.

As Packard and Berger discuss, these results have tremendous implications. First, American firms spend more than a trillion dollars a year employing and training employees so they can provide a great experience.[19] Firms have not widely used this simple rhetorical trick, which Berger and Packard found, even though it provides a less costly, simple, elegant and powerful means to satisfy customers.

Second, training employees to use this idea may have another positive repercussion. They could become better listeners. Who knew something we innately learn as children could benefit the world of business?

Third, firms could carry out a language audit and use it to evaluate employee performance. Firms could use records of interactions between employees and customers (these records stored in databases are almost *de rigueur* in most firms) to examine if employees use concrete language.

Overall, as you can see, sometimes a simple tweak, less abstract and more concrete language, can lead to concrete benefits.

6

When 'You' Can Make the Difference

Consider the following songs:

- 'I Will Always Love You'—Whitney Houston's cover of Dolly Parton's song
- '(Everything I Do) I Do It for You'—Bryan Adams
- 'All I Want for Christmas Is You'—Mariah Carey
- 'Shape of You'—Ed Sheeran
- 'Someone Like You'—Adele
- 'Girls Like You'—Maroon 5 featuring Cardi B

The *Bodyguard* soundtrack version of Whitney Houston's 'I Will Always Love You' spent fourteen weeks at the top of the US Billboard Hot 100 in 1992.[1] The song holds the stellar distinction of being the longest-running No. 1 single from an album based on a film. The song has sold 20 million physical copies.[2]

Since its release as the lead single from *Robin Hood: Prince of Thieves*, featuring Kevin Costner in 1991, Bryan Adams' song '(Everything I Do) I Do It for You' has sold 15 million copies.[3] The song holds the distinction of having the longest unbroken

run at No. 1 in the UK Singles Chart. For four months, from
7 July 1991 to 27 October 1991, the song was a super hit that
presumably had everyone in town crooning this song to serenade
their other half. Even in India when I was growing up, many of
my die-hard metal-head friends started suddenly learning the
guitar chords of this song and for a moment moved away from
listening to bands like Guns N' Roses and Metallica. I am sure
the reason was to win over someone even though they pretended
otherwise. The song did even better across Europe, where it stayed
at the top of the charts for eighteen weeks, still an all-time record.[4]

Let's now talk about a Christmas song. 'All I Want for
Christmas Is You' by American singer Mariah Carey, recorded
in 1994 for her fourth studio album and first holiday album,
Merry Christmas, has sold 16 million physical copies to date.[5] As
of *Billboard* magazine's issue dated 8 January 2002, the song had
been on top of the Billboard Holiday 100 chart for a record fifty-
one cumulative weeks.[6] On 18 November 2021, Billboard ranked
it as the No. 1 Greatest Holiday 100 Song of All Time.[7]

That's enough nostalgia for the moment. Let's look at some
recent tunes.

'Shape of You', written by English singer-songwriter Ed
Sheeran, for his third studio album in 2017, is the second highest-
selling digital single ever, with 41.5 million copies sold. The song
is the first to hit 2 billion streams on Spotify (yes, 2 billion!).
To date, it is the second most-streamed song on Spotify, and by
December 2019, it was the most-streamed song of the decade,
with 2.4 billion plays on the same platform. In the UK, it was the
best-selling song of the decade.[8]

Since its release in 2011, Adele's second studio album, *21*, has
sold 17 million digital copies of her song 'Someone Like You'.[9]
The song became the first strictly voice-and-piano ballad to top

the Billboard Hot 100.[10] It topped year-end charts from countries like Ireland and Italy.[11]

Finally, let's look at a band instead of only solo artists. Los Angeles-based American pop/rock band Maroon 5's song, 'Girls Like You' featuring American rapper Cardi B, has sold about 12 million digital copies to date. It spent thirty-three weeks in the Top 10 and tied with Ed Sheeran's song, 'Shape of You', for the longest Top 10 run in the Billboard chart's archives.[12]

What do all these songs have in common?

First, they are super hits.

Second, they have 'you' in the title.

Like a metronome that never stops, human beings have been creating music continuously and passionately since the dawn of time. Indeed, from the Paleolithic period (roughly 2.5 million years ago), where perhaps early humans recognized that banging one rock with another created a pleasing sound, to the present, where users upload over 60,000 tracks every single day to Spotify,[13] songs are omnipresent in our lives.

Songs have various components that can lead to becoming a hit. Apart from melodies and vocals, an important ingredient that can make or break a song is the lyrics. Lyrics convey the meaning behind the song and range from romantic to political motifs. From the arguably oldest lyrics ever written, the Seikilos epitaph that was discovered in 1883 near Aydin, Turkey, during the first century CE,[14] to the lyrics of modern-day music, lyrics are a key element of songs.

Some lyrics are short, some long. Some are about God, some about the devil. Some about love, some about heartbreak. Some about togetherness, some about loneliness. Lyrics can make a song personal to us. Who has not been swayed by Leonard Cohen's poetic lyricism or gotten motivated and inspired by Kendrick

Lamar's honest, thought-provoking and socially conscious lyrics? From a linguistic perspective, lyrics include all the English language's grammatical elements. Lyrics contain nouns, articles, adverbs, adjectives and pronouns. These elements combine to form a set of lyrics, which convey meaning to us—though, I am not sure if my English grammar teacher would have approved of the way words and punctuations are swivelled around in rap, rock or hip-hop songs!

We know that song lyrics talk about love, religion, politics, technology and almost everything under the sun. But in these lyrics, we also have ordinary grammatical elements such as pronouns that identify the characters in these songs. Pronouns such as 'I', 'we' and 'you'.

Is it possible that musical success is influenced by the way songs are grammatically expressed? Can second-person pronouns, such as you, your, yours, yourself, which on the face of it appear so unremarkable, influence a song to be a hit?

For example, if there are two songs by the same musician, one with a title like 'I Need You' and the other, 'I Need It', would the former be a bigger hit if both the songs had the same melody? Also, is there any difference as to where the word 'you' ought to be placed? For example, a song can have the word 'you' in the subject case, such as 'You Can Dream', where 'you' is the protagonist. On the other hand, 'you' can be in the object case, such as 'Dreaming About You'. Here, 'you' is the target of someone's thoughts. Which of these songs will do better?

The usage of second-person pronouns is interesting and artists have the flexibility to use it in various ways. Using pronouns is important in how musicians and writers go about their art, either consciously or subconsciously. It affects the way we consume their art. The question above regarding which song would become a hit refers to using a second-person pronoun as the object of reference in a song. Musicians write about someone, which is the 'you', they are referring to. They might use a first-person perspective with lyrics like 'I need you' or a third-person perspective with lyrics like 'We will rock you'. In both cases, you is the object. There is also a second-person perspective such as 'You can dream'. There are songs with this second-person perspective. The second question above asks if 'I dream of you' is better than 'You can dream' for musical success. We shall see if this is true!

It is important to note that a second-person perspective is rarely used in another art form—novels. Have you ever read a novel where the writer uses a second-person point of view? Most writers use either a first-person or a third-person perspective. For example, J.D. Salinger's *The Catcher in the Rye* and Andy Weir's *The Martian* are in the first person. Jane Austen's *Pride and Prejudice* and Frank Herbert's *Dune* are written in the third person. Novels written in the second person are quite rare and unless you are a genius like the Italian writer Italo Calvino, who used a second-person perspective in *If on a Winter's Night a Traveler*, it is hard to pull it off. It is generally advised to use second-person perspectives in short stories rather than novels, as it becomes quite tedious for a reader. Anyway, back to the question of using second-person pronouns in songs.

I gave you some selectively chosen examples, which were super hits, but did 'any' song that contained 'you' in the object case, become a hit? This is the question Grant Packard from York University and Jonah Berger from the University of Pennsylvania examine.

Packard and Berger argue that one primary function of the narrative arts is to enable feelings of social connection. Cultural pieces that trigger those personal connections are likely to be more successful. People spend a lot of time and money consuming works of art such as music, movies or books. All of us listen, watch or read to immerse ourselves in the narratives of these works of art. We have various reasons. To get lost in the beauty of a song, wander into another universe while watching a movie, or get entranced by the stories an author weaves.

However, an important reason we listen, watch or read is to connect ourselves to others in our own social lives. Packard and Berger examine this idea and propose that narrative work predominantly including second-person pronouns (i.e., you, your, yours, yourself), can do just that. They allow us to conjure up a specific 'you' in our lives.

The authors first argue that second personal pronouns signal attentional focus—'that a speaker is directly addressing cognitively or physically present people or their things'.[15]

Consider phrases like 'you are nice' or 'your shirt is amazing'. Packard and Berger predict only second-person pronouns bring about this personal connection, and neither first-person nor third-person pronouns serve the same function.[16] If I replace the phrases above with 'I am nice' and 'My shirt is amazing' or 'They are nice' and 'Their shirt is amazing', one can see that the personal touch is lost.

However, having 'you' in a song can also mean different things to us. Let's take one song that I gave as an example in the beginning. When we listen to Bryan Adams' song, '(Everything I Do) I Do It for You', we are third-party observers. Let's consider some reactions one might have when listening to the song paying close attention to the lyrics.

- One can think Bryan Adams is directly addressing them. (Very unlikely. Prior research has shown that second-person pronouns can bolster mental stimulation and involvement.[17]

'You are going' is an example where 'you' are being directly addressed. Bryan Adams is surely not addressing a listener of the song. When I hear this song, I know that Bryan Adams is not talking to me).

- One can think Bryan Adams is conveying a norm or an imperative. (Quite unlikely. The lyrics here don't seem to convey any norm or imperative. 'You should rest more' is an example where a speaker is referring to someone and conveying a norm or imperative. Even self-talk fits in here.).

- One can put herself in Bryan Adams's shoes and feel they are Bryan Adams (very unlikely).

- One can see Bryan Adams's personal perspective, such as Bryan Adams's view about his love (unlikely).

- One can think Bryan Adams is writing about them (unless you are the protagonist Bryan Adams is writing about; statistically, there is a one/current population of the world probability that this could be true).

- One can conjure up a specific 'you' in their own life, whom the song and sentiment remind them of.

How about the last reaction?

Very possible.

The authors next argue that when we listen to a song like '(Everything I Do) I Do It for You', specifically the placement of the second person pronoun, 'you', invites us to think about a personal 'you' who is the recipient of our attention. You can imagine a 'you' whom you are currently in love with or have loved in the past. The lyrics of such a song encourage a listener to imagine their own life, which evokes personal connections. When such personal connections are activated, the song becomes more relevant, and highly likely the listener will listen repeatedly, liking the song more. Packard and Berger test this idea with a clever set of studies using text mining of the lyrics.

Overall, Packard and Berger hypothesize that songs with more second-person pronouns are liked and purchased more. And songs using second-person pronouns as the object, rather than subject, sell more because they activate thoughts of someone in our lives.

In their principal study using data from the real world, the authors collected the lyrics and chart performance for 1736 unique songs from 1187 artists to test whether songs with lyrics using second-person pronouns are more successful (i.e., purchased more) than songs that don't use second-person pronouns.

Packard and Berger first collected Billboard's digital download rankings[18] for songs from all major genres, including Christian, country, dance, rock, pop, rap and R&B, every three months for a three-year period (2014–16). They noted each song's position in the chart, which spanned from 1 to 50. To ensure they properly represented every genre, they chose 600 songs per genre.

Next, the researchers got the complete lyrics of each song from SongLyrics.com. For the text analysis part, they used a dictionary-based approach.

Specifically, the authors used the Linguistic Inquiry and Word Count (LIWC) text-analysis program[19] that has a dictionary of second-person pronouns to identify the percentage of words in each song that are second-person pronouns.

Packard and Berger then employed the simple yet powerful method of regression analysis, which analyses the relationship between an outcome variable and predictors, to examine if songs that used 'you' words more often had a higher position in the charts.

What did Packard and Berger uncover?

Per their predictions, they found that songs using 'you' words were purchased more. Their results held even after accounting for many alternative explanations. One explanation could be that more popular songwriters also use more second-person pronouns. Another could be that radio airplay might contain songs with more second-person pronouns. Perhaps the song's other topics (e.g., love, dance) drive popularity. The authors used topic modelling to arrive at a song's topics. Or the genre of the music could be a driving factor. Finally, other linguistic features such as an emotional tone in the lyrics could drive sales. The results remained strong even after accounting for all these factors in their regression model. In a regression model, a researcher can isolate the effect of a predictor (songs with 'you' in this case) on the outcome variable (song ranking on Billboard in this case), accounting for other factors. The effect lingered even for non-hit songs and even fictitious songs with titles like 'I've Known You for a While Now' and 'I've Known Her for a While Now'.

Packard and Berger also collected 1735 songs from the same artists as the analysis above, which did not make the Billboard charts, to do a real one-to-one matching. That is, comparing an artist's song that makes it to the Billboard charts and the same artist's song that does not make it to the Billboard charts. Even after using these matched pairs and re-running their analysis, the results remained robust.

Using the human coding method in text mining, Packard and Berger tested their second major question: Can 'you' songs only work when 'you' is the object of someone's thoughts or actions rather than when 'you' refers to the protagonist? Research assistants categorized if a 'you' in a song was used as the subject or object case. After obtaining the categorized data, the authors re-ran their regression analysis and found that songs containing 'you' words in the object case drive sales, in all likelihood, because of its other-activating ability. Because of their power, second-person pronouns remind someone of a personal other. In comparison, songs with 'you' in the subject case did not significantly increase in popularity.

> Human coding or manual coding in text mining is the process of labelling (e.g., positive or negative sentiment) or rating (1–low to 5–high) textual data using human assessors.

You might ponder whether songs with a first-person plural pronoun such as 'We will rock you' also drive musical success like 'I will rock you'. Packard and Berger don't find that songs with 'we' increase popularity. First, according to their data, such lyrics are quite infrequent in songs. Second, 'we' in a lyric with 'you' as the object has a lower possibility of someone conjuring up a person in the listener's life as 'we' refers to over two people and not 'you and me'.

So, what do these results imply for managers in the entertainment business, the common public and artists?

Firstly, a subtle, ignored and minor feature demonstrates that language affects us in myriad ways without us even knowing. It can drive us to consume certain works of art more than others. One of music's fundamental purposes is to inspire social connections, and it does that with the organic use of the word 'you'. We may not know why we like these songs more, but Packard and Berger now explain why we do. Songwriters might realize why some of their pieces were more popular than others. Of course, based on the study's results, one should not prescribe that songwriters intentionally write songs with a second-person pronoun and situate it in the object case. They should and need to be independent to create honest, deep and beautiful music. However, perhaps managers of such artists can understand that the possibility of some songs becoming hits is higher and thus take steps to make them more widely available.

Secondly, we pay little attention when we use or do not use words like 'you', even though it is one of the most frequent words English speakers use in their everyday life.[20] In other languages, there might be two variations of 'you'. In French, 'you' is either 'tu' or 'vous'. 'Tu' is the informal version and 'vous' is formal. In Hindi, there are three versions: 'tu' is the least formal, 'tum' less formal, and 'aap' is formal. In English, we just have this one word, but it can mean a variety of things. Sometimes, 'you' can even have a broad generic meaning.[21] It can refer to everyone and help us make meaning and derive insights beyond ourselves. Consider this sentence by Abraham Lincoln, 'You cannot escape the responsibility of tomorrow by evading it today.' Here, 'you' is meant not just for you and me, but for everyone. Indeed, how we relate to each other depends on how language, like pronouns, is used and placed. For example, pronouns can show if a marriage is rocky or sailing smoothly. Research seems to indicate that spousal conflict continues if they use more second-person pronouns and the possibility of a resolution is higher if they use more third-person pronouns.[22] Artists and writers might see the beauty of how the mere use and placement of pronouns can raise their work of art to be appreciated by millions. Everyday folks like you and me may also recognize and appreciate how pronouns can influence others.

Music is a universal language. It can pierce our heart and soul with the feelings a tune can engender. These feelings and emotions can also build bridges and brotherhood between boundaries and borders. However, sometimes when the lyrics directly speak to 'you', it becomes not only universal but also personal.

7

On the Internet,
Everybody Knows You're a Dog

Imagine you live in a suburban neighbourhood in a big city on the West Coast of the US. You are a person who focuses on the self, cherishes matters of the mind and heart, are currently practising Vinyasa yoga, taking an online mindfulness course and have a half-marathon planned in two months. You live on a street with a block of houses on both sides. You notice the person opposite your house puts some quotes up every morning through the window when you head for work. Quotes like: 'Life is beautiful. Enjoy every moment', 'The way you see things, that's what makes you special', and 'Never, never forget how amazing you are'. You value and love the ideas behind these quotes (I am being cheesy and tacky as you can see and don't even know if the quotes above make any sense, but bear with me). Every day, before you head out for work, you look forward to seeing a new quote. You appreciate this person has similar values as you and would want to know this person more. Perhaps this person could be your soulmate. You have been single for a while now. You have even told your closest friends about 'that' neighbour of yours.

One day, you decide to head to your neighbour and see who this person really is. Perhaps, ask the person out for a coffee! When you knock on the door, you observe that your neighbour is in a room with no furniture. Turns out the house is vacant. The neighbour seems a bit lost. You put on your most infectious smile, start a conversation and tell the neighbour you adore the posters. However, the neighbour looks clueless, shows no interest in you; in fact, does not stay in this house and was asked by someone in a company to do this 'job'. Because of being unemployed for a while, the 'neighbour' took up this task and was being paid for the services. You ask this person the name and address of the company and head straight to the address.

Who is sending these messages?

You enter the company's office and ask around. You run into an executive who tells you that Jim on the second floor manages your 'account'. You head to Jim, and Jim mentions all those messages were sent by Clio downstairs in the basement. You hurtle down the stairs in eagerness, keen to know if Clio is the one. The person who you think shares your values. Your potential soulmate. When you reach the basement, you don't see anyone. Where is this Clio?

Suddenly, you hear a voice saying, 'Hi, how was the run today?'

You look around again. And see no person, but a computer.

Clio is a supercomputer.

Clio knows everything about you. It knows you identify as a demisexual (which means you are attracted to someone based on a strong emotional connection), like meaningful messages, value things of the mind, body and spirit, are currently single and looking for a life partner. It knows you ran four miles today (because you tagged your running route today in your running app).

You realize this Clio probably knows everything about you because of all the data you have unintentionally shared on Facebook, Instagram, Google, Netflix, TripAdvisor, TikTok, Etsy, MapMyRun, and the other hundreds of websites you visited. Clio was sending those quotes based on your interests and preferences. And the makeshift and feigned neighbour was showing you those posters on behalf of the company, assuming you would search for them and probably buy one online. And the company, which touts itself as 'the number one destination in the West Coast for posters, wall art and fun visual products that express personal interests', ensures that when you search online for posters and wall art in your area, you will see the company's name at the top of the search results. Paid search ads and search engine optimization are both optimized for you.

I don't know about you, but I would leave the scene absolutely mindscrewed, bamboozled and enraged in this situation, thinking what has the world come to?

The story above is inspired by an episode from the TV series *Portlandia* where one of the central characters goes through a similar narrative. The story is, of course, exaggerated, totally fictional and comical. But it is also tragic and screamingly shows how our privacy online is not in our hands.

That's enough fiction for the moment. Here is a well-known and real-life horror story about how companies take our privacy for granted.[1]

All of us have our favourite stores where we buy different products. For shoes, we go to a particular store. In one store, we buy 'that' shampoo; in another, we buy the cooking oil that goes best with our chicken curry. Are there any points in one's life when one is not so fixated on using the same brand or going to the same store? Yes, there is one. When a family has had a new baby or is expecting. It is a significant life event. After a baby is born, friends of mine who are parents often say they have not slept well. At times they are overburdened, look and feel tired, and stop caring about their brand loyalties and favourite stores. What kind of company would benefit the most from knowing a family is expecting a child or had a child recently?

Big-box retailers, who sell almost everything under the sun.

The American big-box department store chain, Target, which sells everything from baby products to furniture, thought of a nefarious plan. If they could use all the data they have collected on their female customers, Target could create a 'pregnancy prediction model'. Based on the model's predictions, they could send expecting mothers advertisements or coupons to entice them, their husbands or other family members to visit Target and buy baby-related products and possibly other products. Remember, family members expecting a child would be much more flexible in their choice of stores.

Using such strategies helped Target grow its revenues from $44 billion in 2002 to $67 billion in 2010. In a meeting with investors in 2005, their president proclaimed the positive trend in the firm's performance was because of a 'heightened focus on items and categories appealing to specific guest segments such as mom and baby'.[2]

Great for the company, but this was an outright misuse of customer data. Customers did not know Target had collected such data. The prediction model could figure out the stages of a woman's pregnancy and offer products and services for each trimester. How would a woman feel when someone she doesn't know, a for-profit company, knows she is in her second trimester and is cunningly sending adverts and coupons? How would a father feel when first his family receives coupons for baby clothes and cribs, before his high-school-aged daughter reveals she is pregnant?

Another example is when a woman who miscarried twin boys kept receiving baby formula options.[3] After being casually asked if she wanted to sign up for store discounts and coupons while shopping at the Motherhood Maternity clothing store in Ontario, Canada, the woman innocently provided her name, address, email and due date. Little did she know they would sell her information to third parties. Before what would have been her due date, she received a 'Welcome to Parenthood' package from the pharmaceutical company Abbott, when she had no relationship with the company.

Firms have taken our data and entered our lives and our homes, though we did not invite them.

We share almost everything online nowadays. Our interests, likes, dislikes and preferences. We share what we do, have done or are planning to do. We share facts and opinions and things that give us joy and jubilation. We put personal stories, pictures and videos on social network sites. And all this sharing can have dire consequences for us, as epitomized by the Target case. We are an open book. Companies use various strategies, such as 'behavioural targeting' to entice us to buy something we may not want.

Using 'pixel targeting', for example, companies will show you an ad for an item on your favourite social network site after registering that you have been searching for the article on Google for a few days. For example, I get many ads to join MBA programmes. Perhaps the algorithm thinks that I am planning to do an MBA as I visit INSEAD and Wharton's websites and read the *Financial Times*. Little does the algorithm know that I am a professor, not a student, and don't intend to do an MBA.

Behavioural targeting uses people's behavioural data, such as what people are or are not doing in an app, on a website or with ad campaigns, to trigger personalized marketing, determining the advertisements that resonate most with them.

Your data is being used to manipulate you, and you seem to have no idea and control regarding 'your' data. Companies track every single thing we do online so they can feed us something we may not want. The sites most of us use, like Facebook, track our interests and likes. Instagram tracks what we share and whom we follow. Google tracks our searches.

Privacy is a word every business professional and consumer cares about nowadays. Gone are the days of the adage and memes about Internet anonymity[4] such as 'On the Internet, nobody knows you're a dog'. This is a reference to the famous cartoon with a dog sitting on the floor and another on the chair using a computer uttering this pithy observation. Created by Peter Steiner and published by the *New Yorker* on 5 July 1993, the cartoon and its catchy line symbolized the times in the pre-millennium era. Now, many firms can figure out who you are!

The digital traces of information we leave behind while browsing our favourite news outlet or reading about the exploits of *The Real Housewives of God Knows Where* can allow firms to understand not only our demographic profile such as age, location, income, etc., but also our psychographic characteristics like our values, desires, goals, interests and lifestyle choices. For example, gambling companies can identify addicts and lure them with free bets.[5] Psychographic characteristics are powerful because they can help differentiate people. Consider these two people:

Person 1: Born in 1948, raised in England, married twice, two children, successful, spends winter holidays in the Alps.

Person 2: Born in 1948, raised in England, married twice, two children, successful, spends winter holidays in the Alps.

Any guesses? Well one of them is King Charles and the other, the lead singer of the band Black Sabbath, Ozzy Osborne. These two people could not be more different if we examine their values, desires, goals and interests.

In a riposte to the original dog cartoon by Peter Steiner, Kaamran Hafeez published a cartoon in the *New Yorker* on 23 February 2015,[6] which showed a similar pair of dogs observing their owner sitting at a computer. One of the dogs asks the other, 'Remember when, on the Internet, nobody knew who you were?'

We as users are fragile in the hands of the websites we visit and because of that, consumer data privacy has become one of the most critical issues of our times. Firms are collecting, exploring and examining user data at an ever-increasing rate. This increase has been primarily due to the evidence that collecting such consumer data can generate a positive return.[7] Using digital technologies ranging from big data and artificial intelligence (AI), firms can identify what consumers prefer and need, to increase their profitability. Consumer data has value . . . a lot of it. What do you think is the value of all of Facebook's data about its users? The estimate is about $35.2 billion, which is 63 per cent of Facebook's revenues.[8]

In this whole equation, the consumer has been forgotten. Firms have been shown to disregard a consumer's privacy concerns and feelings of vulnerability. Firms are generating profits, but what about consumer welfare? Indeed, consumers are reacting strongly. Consumers who switch providers often cite privacy concerns as the reason for their switch.[9]

What can firms do to reduce such privacy concerns? Are there ways firms can alleviate some of the privacy issues we as consumers have?

To answer this question, I, along with my colleagues, Kelly Martin from Colorado State University and Robert Palmatier from the Foster School of Business at the University of Washington in Seattle, carried out a comprehensive study to see what firms could do to ease consumers' privacy concerns.[10]

We started with the idea that users nowadays feel constantly vulnerable.

Even when things are 'bright and shiny', users have every right to be vulnerable. Their data is out there. Consider this: an American company named Devumi sold followers in X and retweets to anyone who desired to become a social media influencer, arguably the hippest job in town! The company made millions of dollars and, in some cases, provided paying customers with over 200 million followers. You never know, someone might have sold a version of your profile too.

Your fake account, known as a bot, might retweet in Swedish, a language you probably don't understand. You might have your face online on X, but with a name you don't recognize. Or your name might have an extra letter added to it. And celebrities, actors, singers and politicians might have a version of you following them. X as a social network is unique. It does not need an account to be linked to a real person. No data has been stolen from X, but your data is out there, and someone can steal your social identity. While X bans buying followers, companies such as Devumi openly sold them. It was reported in early 2018 that about 48 million accounts on X were fake, simulated to look like real people. What about Facebook? In November 2017, Facebook disclosed it had about 60 million fake accounts. Imagine you are looking for a job and one of your potential employers does a social media search of your name on X like many do. There is a likelihood that someone with a similar name as you might be retweeting a pornographic picture right now.[11] Another example validating a user's right to be vulnerable is when iRobot vacuum reportedly planned to sell its consumers' floor map data to third parties.[12] Even if your data is not stolen, such as someone stealing your personal details that can be only accessed when you log in, someone can still compromise your public user profile. This can be done by outside parties or by firms themselves.

How about situations when users feel even more vulnerable? Kelly, Rob and I used a context, which is nefarious and commonplace in current times. Despite the best intentions, firms often compromise the safety, security and well-being of their users, and one of the most particularly compromising is a data breach. Data breaches are incidents in which information is stolen or taken from a system without knowledge or authorization of the system's owner.[13]

Breaches happen frequently and millions of records can be stolen. In 2020 alone, there were 3932 data breaches accounting for about 37 billion classified records.[14] All companies, big and small, have gone through such incidents. One of the most significant breaches of all time is the breach on Yahoo!, whereby hackers stole personal information from about 3 billion users. Later, it was found that although hackers stole security questions and answers, bank information had not been compromised. In September 2018, Hotel Marriott International was hacked, and thieves stole the information of about 500 million guests, such as their names, mailing addresses, phone numbers, email addresses, passport numbers, dates of birth and other personal details.[15] If I were a Yahoo! user and a guest member of Marriott, I would be seriously worried.

When we, as users, provide information to a company such as Citibank or Home Depot and they undergo a data breach, our personal information gets compromised, and our existing vulnerability multiplies as we don't know the consequences of how someone else will use our data.

Because such events make users feel helpless, they have substantial adverse consequences on a firm's financials as users feel violated and their trust in the firm reduces. There is evidence that data breaches lead to negative performance outcomes such as reduced sales and lower stock prices for the breached firm.[16]

My co-researchers and I wanted to examine if companies could suppress these negative reactions to a data breach. Was there something firms could do to mitigate the damage? To understand this, we first identified data breaches of publicly traded firms using an array of databases such as Capital IQ, Factiva, Lexis-Nexis and privacyrights.org. Using multiple sources enabled us to guarantee that the data collection was exhaustive. We then wanted to see the effect of a data breach on the breached firm's stock price. So, we collected stock price data for these firms.

We used the event study method to examine the effect of a data breach on a company's stock price. An event study is a method looking at the change in a publicly listed firm's stock price after an event, such as a new product announcement, change in CEO or a data breach in this case. The method uses the assumption of the efficient market hypothesis, which means a stock price for a publicly listed firm at a particular point in time reflects all the available information.[17] Thus, any change in the firm's stock price resulting from any new information indicates the present value of all expected current and future profits or losses from that novel information. Because data breaches are harmful, prior research suggests data breaches reduce a firm's stock price. Now, as I have been alluding, can this stock price reduction be suppressed?

We theorized that this reduction in stock price could be suppressed and so we used a concept called gossip theory to propose our hypotheses. Gossip theory is a theory in social psychology that explains how people react to the unauthorized collection, use or revelation of their private information.[18]

Using gossip theory, we first proposed that data breaches, which lead to disclosures of personal information, would have a significant and negative impact on the stock price by 'gossipers' of firms.

It is believed that about 67 per cent of our social communication pertains to gossip.[19] Gossip involves casual conversation about other people, which normally involves the sharing of details that are not confirmed as though they are true. I don't know about you but where I am from, we can gossip for hours over a cup of tea and samosas and I am sure that India must rank very high on the gossip charts. Thus, because of its frequency in our daily lives, most people are skilful in recognizing gossip, guarding against it and minimizing the threat from it.[20]

Someone who is a target of gossip reacts adversely with a range of negative emotions.[21] When a data breach happens, we predicted customers would feel emotionally violated and lessen their trust in the breached firm. This would affect customers' purchase behaviour, leading to lower sales and earnings. Investors would infer this process and reduce their trust in the stock.

Using gossip theory, we next argued that there are two ways in which firms could lessen the detrimental effects of data breaches by providing users with transparency and control. Transparency in gossip theory is related to the target's awareness of the information being shared. This lets the target know how much information is shared so that they can think of strategies to reduce the negative effects. For instance, if I am the target of gossip and know what is being shared, it reduces my distress. If it is hidden, I feel really vulnerable. Control relates to the extent of information the person targeted in the gossip can manage.[22] A target might feel more vulnerable if she has no control over the information being shared. I would feel much less anxious if I knew only my gender and city were stolen in a data breach, and I had preserved my right not to share other personal data.

Thus, if users in a data breach know what kind of information was stolen and they had control over what information was shared with the firm, we predicted the negative effects on stock price would be suppressed on such occasions. A slice of the firm's customers would still keep using the firm's products and thus the damaging effect of a breach on stock price would be lower.

Overall, we proposed a user's vulnerability can decrease if the user has knowledge about the event (which we called transparency) and the capacity to handle the diffusion and impact of the information (which we called control).[23] How do we measure transparency and control? How do we relate it to a firm's stock price after a data breach event?

Here is a trivia question. What document on the Internet has an average word count of 5372 words?[24]

Facebook's word count for this document is 4135 words, while Airbnb's word count is 8044 words.

More often than not, you might have received emails containing this document from a company you follow or subscribe to.

Any answers?

Well, it is a firm's privacy policy.

A privacy policy is a document on a firm's website describing how the firm will collect, store, protect and use personal information provided by its users.[25]

This is where we come to this book's primary focus: language and words. We intended to measure how much transparency and control a firm provided its users before its data was breached.

We used the firm's privacy policy document to measure transparency and control before a data breach. We predicted that if a data breach occurred, firms with high transparency and control would have less damage to their stock price because of a data breach.

So, say a data breach happened on 1 October 2017, for a 'Firm A'. How do we collect Firm A's privacy policy before 1 October 2017?

We resorted to using a mix of automation and human coding to create our measures of transparency and control. For each breached firm in our sample, we first gathered the privacy policy statements from the firm's website when the breach occurred using a fabulous resource for understanding how the Internet looked like in the past, the Wayback Machine Internet archive. Founded in 1996, the Wayback Machine is a digital archive of the Internet and permits users to 'go back in time' and see what websites looked like in the past using cached webpages.

To collect the privacy policies, we developed a code using the Python programming language. We scraped each iteration of all the firms in our sample over time, which allowed us to obtain the privacy policy documents that were current and active on the breach date. Thus, using Firm A above as an example, we obtained an active privacy policy from Firm A on 1 October 2017, the date of the breach.

Now, how do we measure transparency and control? We defined good transparent privacy practices as ones informing customers of what specific information firms obtain and how firms use such information. For example, this could be information like a user's search history, IP address, information being sold to third parties, etc. For control, we argued that high control is when firms allow consumers plenty of control over the usage and sharing of their data. For example, firms can allow customers to opt out of their data practices such as selling their data, sharing with partners, promotions, etc.

After obtaining the privacy policies, we looked at the language the firms used in their privacy policies. For this purpose, instead of using a computerized method, we resorted to using human assessment of the privacy policies to rate the extent to which the various privacy policies exhibit transparency and control.

How did we measure transparency and control via the privacy policy document?

For the transparency variable, we used a count of the multiple elements of a firm's privacy policy, which signals openness and readiness to offer information to customers. In particular, we coded whether the firm:

1. explains its opt-out policy,
2. explains how it captures data,
3. explains how it uses data,
4. explains its data sharing internally and with third parties, and
5. provides contact information for privacy requests.

If a firm's privacy policy did all the above, the privacy policy obtained a transparency score of 5. The lowest score a privacy policy could receive for transparency was 0. Similarly, we coded control of a firm's user data to its customers. We counted the total number of opt-out choices present in a firm's privacy policy, ranging from 0 to 5.

In particular, we coded if the consumer

1. could opt out of marketing communication,
2. could opt out of saving data usage (e.g., search history),
3. could opt out of storing personal information (e.g., credit card number),
4. could opt out of sharing data with third parties, and
5. could opt out of tracking.

If a firm's privacy policy had all the characteristics above, the policy earned a score of 5 for control.

Our sample consisted of 293 breaches across 199 unique firms. We also collected the privacy policies of these firms' competitors to examine if there were any spillover effects of a data breach on a rival. So, for example, what would happen to Walmart's stock price if the American big-box department store chain Target had a breach?

What did we find?

We found that a firm's abnormal stock market returns went down after it suffered a breach.

> Abnormal stock market returns are calculated by subtracting the expected normal stock return of a firm that would have been observed if an analysed event had not taken place from the actual stock market returns because of the analysed event.

What about the effects of transparency and control? We found that transparency by itself does not suppress the negative effect of a data breach on a firm's stock returns, but control suppresses the negative effect. And the combination of transparency and control leads to a significant reduction in the negative effect of data breaches on stock returns.

One important point to note is, we found similar results using experiments when we surveyed participants in the lab. Our experimental manipulations showed transparency and control could quell the negative effects of a user's vulnerability regarding their data. Our experiments also showed that having someone else access one's personal data can magnify feelings of violation and reduce trust.

What do you think happens to a rival of the breached firm?

Interestingly, we found that when the data breach's severity is high, in terms of the number of records stolen or hacked, the rival firm benefits. The effect was asymmetric. The more serious the data breach, the more customers move away from the weakened and breached firm to its closest rival.

So, what do these results mean for firms and investors?

First, when we look at the dollar impact of these effects, we see firms that provide both high transparency and high control to their consumers can best mitigate the damage to their market value when they undergo a breach. Let's consider the American multinational investment bank, Citigroup. When Citigroup had a data breach, which we see in our sample, using its privacy policy and the language conveyed, we found it offered both low transparency and low control. Based on our data and analysis, because of this, it exacerbated damages when the breach occurred, resulting in a loss of $836 million in market value.[26] Let's examine a counterfactual of what would have happened. That is, what would have happened to Citigroup's market value if Citigroup offered its customers both high transparency and high control?

We used a method called propensity score analysis, which allows one to create a counterfactual. In the propensity score analysis method, because Citigroup did not have high transparency and control, the counterfactual, an artificial Citigroup that has both high transparency and control, is created. This artificial Citigroup resembles the real Citigroup in terms of its characteristics such as company size, sales, market share and other metrics. This artificial Citigroup comprised a group of companies from our research study. We found that the artificial Citigroup with high transparency and control endured a loss of only about $16 million. Thus, the analysis indicates that Citigroup could have saved about $820 million from its market cap if it had endowed its customers with greater transparency and control.

> Propensity score matching is a technique used when a group of entities receives a treatment and the other group does not. This method creates a counterfactual of the control group, ensuring the predictors have the same distribution for the treated and counterfactual groups. After the matching, the treatment and control group's outcomes are compared.

In an offshoot of this study, which my co-authors and I published in *Harvard Business Review*,[27] we ranked the privacy policies of Fortune 100 companies using the language furnished in their privacy policies (see Figure 7.1). In this list, some firms provide high transparency or high control but not both. We found in our research that customers do not regard such firms well. And firms offering neither high transparency nor high control are at the highest risk of financial damage. To our dismay, we see 80 per cent of the firms listed in the Fortune 100 fall into this subset of firms. In our study, firms that failed to provide both high transparency and high control had a 1.5 times more considerable drop in stock price than firms that just provided high transparency. Firms like Citigroup, Morgan Stanley and HCA neither seem to communicate how and what information they capture from their customers nor do these firms offer their customers considerable control over the sharing and use of their information. In comparison, firms like Costco, Verizon and HP do well on transparency and control.

Second, firms can benchmark themselves using the methodology we provide. Using human coding of textual content from the privacy policies permits firms to examine how they fare versus their rivals in putting consumer welfare first. Even though the proposed measure is a proxy for transparency and control, we believe it is a strong indicator of a firm's stance on consumer privacy. Firms can use their privacy strategy as a competitive advantage against competitors. One example is the search engine called DuckDuckGo, which differentiates itself from other search engines. DuckDuckGo shows every user the same results for a given query as if it was their first visit to their search engine. The firm does not collect any user-level data and ensures user privacy.[28]

Third, firms must pay attention to how they draft their privacy policies. Privacy policies are a crucial means of communication for firms to convey the collection, use and protection of valuable customer information. Thus, it is critical evidence of a firm's strategy towards consumer privacy.

About 85 per cent of people report reading the privacy policies, which influences their trust in the firm.[29] Firms can ensure they disclose consumers' rights and information access, use and storage rules. Apart from the integrity in privacy policies, firms must ensure they draft policies that are more readable and less vague. Privacy policies over time have become longer and harder to read. Using readability scores that allow one to know the level of education one needs to comfortably read a piece of text, these policies are only understandable to someone who is a college student.[30] Regulators, too, can ensure privacy policies are visible and easy to access. For example, the California Privacy Rights Act of 2020 requires every firm to provide a privacy policy hyperlink on the firm's home page that is readily noticeable and has larger fonts with a different design.

Finally, despite the prejudice towards firms collecting consumer data as being wrong, we should note tremendous innovations have occurred due to firms understanding their customers better through data collection. For example, Netflix creates new and innovative content and delivers personalized recommendations based on data from its users. Thus, there has been the new notion of consumer's privacy calculus whereby consumers might be willing to tolerate privacy issues if the perceived value they receive in return is sufficiently high, such as financial rewards and personalization, among others.[31] Again, the central idea here is that firms are transparent in what they do with the data and allow consumers the right to control their data. If both parties agree, all is well and good.

There are a lot of steps firms can take to offer customers more trust and simultaneously gain benefits. Firms that move the needle in ensuring consumer privacy reap dividends. Consider Apple. Consumers now are even more loyal to Apple through its privacy initiatives such as App Tracking Transparency and Privacy Nutrition Labels. About 93 per cent of Apple users mention they would never consider using an Android.[32] Creating privacy policies that give customers high transparency and high control is perhaps the first step in making customers feel less vulnerable in a world where, now, on the Internet, everybody knows you're a dog.

How Good Are the Fortune 100's Privacy Policies?

A ranking of how transparent each company's policy is, and how much control it gives customers.

RANK   CONTROL (0-5)   TRANSPARENCY (0-9)

Rank	Company	Rank	Company
1	Costco Wholesale*	51	Johnson & Johnson
2	Verizon Communications*	52	Nationwide
3	Best Buy	53	Prudential Bancorp
4	HP	54	TIAA
5	American Airlines Group	55	Walt Disney Company
6	American Express	56	Chevron
7	Delta Air Lines*	57	MassMutual
8	Intel*	58	Mondelēz International
9	Target	59	PepsiCo
10	Oracle	60	State Farm Insurance
11	Deere & Company	61	AT&T
12	Microsoft	62	Cigna
13	AIG	63	Humana
14	Coca-Cola	64	ExxonMobil
15	Amazon.com	65	Fannie Mae
16	DuPont	66	Goldman Sachs Group
17	Honeywell International	67	Kroger
18	IBM	68	Marathon Petroleum
19	Merck & Co.	69	Bank of America
20	MetLife	70	Halliburton
21	Pfizer	71	Liberty Mutual Insurance
22	Valero Energy	72	Lockheed Martin
23	Walgreens Boots Alliance	73	Procter & Gamble
24	Apple	74	Wells Fargo
25	CVS Health	75	AmerisourceBergen
26	Dow Chemical	76	CHS
27	Google	77	Freddie Mac
28	Plains GP Holdings	78	INTL FCStone
29	WalMart Inc.	79	Andeavor
30	DirecTV	80	Aetna
31	Lowe's	81	Boeing
32	UPS	82	Cardinal Health
33	Anthem	83	Cisco Systems
34	Archer Daniels Midland	84	ConocoPhillips
35	Comcast	85	Enterprise Products Partners
36	FedEx	86	General Electric
37	General Motors	87	JPMorgan Chase
38	Home Depot	88	New York Life Insurance
39	Johnson Controls International	89	Tyson Foods
40	McKesson	90	United Technologies
41	UnitedHealth Group	91	Caterpillar
42	World Fuel Services	92	General Dynamics
43	3M	93	Ingram Micro
44	Allstate	94	Phillips 66
45	Express Scripts Holding	95	Berkshire Hathaway
46	Ford Motor Company	96	Citigroup
47	Safeway	97	21st Century Fox
48	Sears Holdings	98	Morgan Stanley
49	Sysco	99	Energy Transfer Equity
50	United Continental Holdings	100	HCA Holdings

0 1 2 3 4 5 6 7 8 9   0 1 2 3 4 5 6 7 8 9

*THE PRIVACY POLICIES OF THESE COMPANIES OFFER ADDITIONAL OPT-OUTS THAT DID NOT FACTOR INTO OUR RANKING.
SOURCE KELLY D. MARTIN, ROBERT W. PALMATIER, AND ABHISHEK BORAH   © HBR.ORG

Figure 7.1: Fortune 100's privacy policies scores on transparency and control

8

When 'I' Is More than 'We'

Imagine you are the customer relationship manager of a clothing store, and one of your employees is interacting with a customer. The customer, Martin, is a bit irritated, seems agitated and is not in a good mood. The customer bought a dress shirt the day before, and one of its buttons has already fallen off. Martin doubts the store's service and is almost on the verge of losing his trust in the store.

He is asking that his shirt be replaced with a new one. Sabine, one of your employees, is stellar and has done exceedingly well in her customer reviews. The month before, she was declared 'employee of the month'.

You know Sabine will address the customer's issue and ensure the matter is laid to rest impeccably and efficiently.

However, before Sabine addresses the issue, I have a question.

How do you think Sabine should engage with the peeved customer?

Should she say something like: 'We will ensure that you have your shirt replaced with a new one', or should she say, 'I will ensure that you have your shirt replaced with a new one'?

On the surface, you would think this question is trivial. But, given how important customer experience is nowadays, a simple change in pronoun use can strongly affect the bottom line. One of these sentences is likely to be much more impactful, affecting both customer satisfaction and the customer's purchasing behaviour. Customer satisfaction is the key ingredient that makes customers loyal to a company and keep purchasing. As I will explain in the chapter on 'How to Talk to Your Date', high customer loyalty means a high retention rate, which is the percentage of existing customers who remain customers after a certain period. The higher the retention rate, the higher the customer lifetime value. This helps a company generate consistent and positive cash flows, leading to high margins and market value for a publicly listed firm.

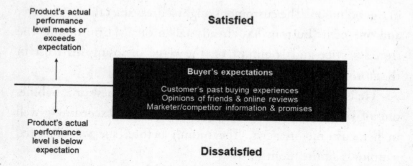

Figure 8.1: How Customers are Satisfied

Customers make loyalty decisions based on how satisfied they are. Customer satisfaction is a tricky thing. It depends on two factors: expectation and performance. Before a customer purchases, what are some things that you think shape a customer's satisfaction? Customers consider past buying experiences, friends' opinions and reviews, information about the company and its promises, and the promises of competitors. All these elements go into a customer's expectations (see the horizontal line in Figure 8.1). If a customer buys a product, and its performance is on or above the line, they are satisfied, and if it is below the line, they are dissatisfied. The figure above shows there are two ways to retain customers. One is under-promise and over-deliver. The other is making more realistic promises such as maintaining or increasing the product's performance. The former strategy of under-promising and over-delivering is misleading, untrue and not sound in the long term. Customers will know the firm's plan, and the expectation line will shift higher the next time. The latter strategy is sincere and sound. A key element that firms can focus on, to meet or exceed expectations apart from the product's performance, is customer experience. Sometimes, even if a product fails, a sincere and delightful customer experience can enable firms to meet or even exceed customer expectations. But if a product fails along with customer experience, the customer will move on and the potential to build a long-term relationship with them will be lost.

My friend once went on a date. She was trying to find someone to settle with for the long term. Sorry to bring up this analogy but if you think of the date as a 'client' and her as the 'customer', expectations were not met. In the dating profile app, the 'client' had uploaded pictures of him riding a bike, running what looked like a marathon, hiking, playing the guitar at a bonfire, and . . . he looked twenty-five! When my friend met with her date over a cup of coffee, he looked fifty-two, not twenty-five. Someone who seemed to be at home in his home. Someone who figuratively replaced the phrase 'the great outdoors' with 'the great indoors'. Someone who, in fact, used his indoor exercise bike as frequently as the rain in the Sahara Desert. Essentially, he was not the adventurous, fit and outdoorsy type that his profile claimed. So, a complete mismatch between his online profile and his real profile. My friend now hardly uses these dating apps on account of this 'bad' customer experience.

Thus, potentially bad experiences should be nipped in the bud immediately. According to a PricewaterhouseCoopers (PWC) report, even when customers love a company or product, 32 per cent of customers will stop doing business with their beloved brand after one bad experience. In Latin America, the number is just shy of 50 per cent.[1] Imagine almost half of your customers leaving your company! So, you can see the repercussions of a bad experience.

The other issue is that we live in a networked world. As Jeff Bezos says, 'If you make customers unhappy in the physical world, they might each tell six friends. If you make customers unhappy on the Internet, they can each tell 6000 friends.'[2] Customers can inform other customers about a bad experience quite easily. Peeved customers can spread negative word-of-mouth about a company with a click of a button and post an emotionally charged review disparaging the firm. These negative reviews can spread fast as bad news travels fast on online platforms and social media.[3]

The human touch is one important ingredient that ensures customers have a great experience (apart from speed, convenience and consistency). As PwC states in its report, a tangible way to provide a great customer experience is by creating genuine connections and empowering employees to create great customer experiences. Indeed, customers crave that experience. A survey found that 82 per cent of American consumers and 74 per cent of non-American consumers want more human interaction in the future.[4] In the same survey, 73 per cent of customers mentioned customer experience as a crucial element in their purchasing decisions. Customers' purchasing decisions are influenced by positive experiences in nearly every industry, particularly in healthcare (78 per cent), banking (75 per cent), restaurants (74 per cent) and hotels (74 per cent). In essence, customers bring in revenues, and employees drive the customer experience.

Often, firms spend substantial amounts of money to ensure a great customer experience. Firms spend money recruiting customer service agents, giving them adequate training, purchasing software and equipment, and renting office space. A great product, eye-catching packaging, elegant product design, coordinating with distributors and retailers, and effectively delivering a product are all things firms need to satisfy customers. So, if a firm can make its customers happier and provide them with a positive experience with just a change of pronoun use, as per my question at the beginning of the chapter, it could generate substantial rewards for the firm.

Three experts in marketing, Grant Packard from York University, Sarah Moore from the University of Alberta and Brent McFerran from Simon Fraser University, joined forces to examine which type of customer agent response might lead a customer to feel a firm has given their problem fair treatment.[5] When interacting with Martin, should Sabine say, 'We will ensure that you have your shirt replaced with a new one' or 'I will ensure that you have your shirt replaced with a new one'? Which of these strategies can increase customer satisfaction, purchase intentions and purchase behaviour?

In most cases, one of the most important ways firms manage relationships with their customers is through having conversations with them. For example, customer service agents in physical retail stores like Apple, Dell, Nordstrom, Zara, etc., deal with prospective buyers and cater to the needs and wants of customers excellently. Many case studies have been written about these firms. A customer service agent's communication style is vital in these conversations. According to Packard and his colleagues, agents' use of different pronouns when speaking with customers has substantial effects on customer attitudes and behaviour.

Packard's team first differentiates between an agent's use of 'I', which pertains to the agent, and 'we', which relates to the firm. 'I' here refers to singular self-referencing, whereas 'we' refers to plural self-referencing.

Let's see if using 'I' is a better response than 'we' in an agent and customer interaction.

Most prior research points to unwanted personality traits or states related to the 'I' pronoun. For example, first-person singular pronouns like 'I' are associated with a trait like narcissism. First-person pronouns such as 'I' and 'me' are used more with self-promoting photos on Facebook pages, for example.[6] But could 'I' have a different effect in a customer service context? A positive effect? 'I', like 'we', is a function word and function words reflect an individual's personality. These function words are powerful indicators as people are unconscious of when they use them and find it virtually impossible to control and adjust their usage of such words.[7] Perhaps during a difficult interaction, 'I' can positively affect a peeved customer if that customer infers positive aspects of an agent from her usage of 'I' words. Packard and his colleagues hypothesized that firm agents should use 'I' instead of 'we' during customer service interactions. The authors argued the usage of 'I' pronouns signals to listeners that the person talking to them is genuinely and deeply involved in an interaction.

To explore this theory, Packard and his colleagues used the concept of 'participation framework' developed by Erving Goffman, a Canadian-born sociologist and social psychologist considered by some to be 'the most influential American sociologist of the twentieth century'.[8]

Goffman theorized that using functional words, such as personal pronouns, helps to set up the roles and responsibilities of the participants in a conversation. Take the sentence, 'I understand you', as an example. This phrase creates a participation framework where the customer service agent, the grammatical subject, demonstrates understanding towards the customer, the grammatical object, by saying 'you'. Packard and his colleagues argued that a speaker's use of pronouns, implicitly or explicitly, signals their intentions, cognitions or behaviour towards the recipient.

Let's look at some examples. Take Sabine, the customer service agent dealing with Martin, who would like his defective shirt to be replaced with a new one. When Martin explains the situation to Sabine, Sabine could say, 'You're understood.' Here, Sabine is explicitly referring to Martin while keeping herself implicit. Sabine could also use the single word 'understood'. Here, Sabine is assuming Martin's implicit understanding. In other words, Martin knows what is being understood. Sabine could also say, 'We understand.' Here, Sabine is speaking on behalf of the firm. Finally, Sabine could say, 'I understand.' Here, Sabine is referring to herself while keeping Martin implicit. Packard and his colleagues propose that within a participation framework, these understated variations in how pronouns are used send signals to the listener about the speaker's involvement with the listener's needs. In this case, how Martin feels about Sabine's involvement with his need for a new shirt.

Packard and his colleagues proposed that in any customer interaction context where a customer is getting help, firm agents should use 'I' instead of any other choice like 'we'. The authors argue that it's best if Sabine uses 'I' instead of 'we' when interacting with Martin.

How can this happen?

The authors propose, in a customer-service context, that self-references like 'I' will signal the agent is customer-oriented as opposed to someone who is self-interested. Rather than 'I' words signalling narcissistic traits, we see the opposite. Using 'I' instead of other pronouns shows the speaker is truly involved and focused on the listener.[9] In fact, it signals to the listener the customer service agent is truly emotionally and behaviourally involved in the customer's needs.

Packard and his colleagues propose that a listener or a customer appreciates the use of 'I' rather than 'we' because the use of 'I' signals two things—a speaker's empathy and agency.

Empathy is the distinct ability to understand or feel what someone else is experiencing and what it is like to be in their situation. There is a beautiful Maya Angelou quote that I believe speaks a lot about what empathy can do to people. She writes, 'I've learned that people will forget what you said, people will forget what you did, but people will never forget how you made them feel.'[10] Though 'I' has narcissistic associations, its usage can also be associated with an individual's personal concern about a situation[11] and their attempt to understand the other person in an interaction.[12] The research argues that using 'I' signals a more personal customer service agent who cares and thus makes the listener think that the agent has high empathy. The use of 'I' is stronger in signalling empathy compared to a situation where no pronoun is used, such as when the speaker is left implicit. Consider Sabine just saying, 'Completely understand your issue.' The authors propose a better reaction from Sabine is, 'I completely understand your issue.'

Okay, using 'I' is good as it shows empathy. However, does using 'we' also show empathy from a firm's point of view? After all, an employee is a part of the firm and Sabine saying, 'We completely understand your issue,' also should signal the whole firm will tackle the customer's problem. Sabine here would function as the primary and direct representative of the firm, taking care of the problem.

Packard and his co-authors argue that the use of 'we' is less personal and less individualized than 'I'. It gives the listener the sense that the customer service agent is more a part of the company they represent than being a partner to the customer in finding a solution to their issue. So, Martin would want to feel that Sabine was a partner to him in finding a solution rather than being an ally of the firm.

Empathy is simple. When I go to my favourite coffee shop in the morning, the employees smile, greet me by my name and ask me about my plans for the day. It is a small thing, but it goes a long way. I go to the coffee shop because I feel they are my friends rather than being a friend of the company. There are many marketing buzzwords, such as 'customer centricity' or 'customer obsession'. Right now, in an office somewhere, a marketer is talking about how firms need to be customer-centric and that the firm should do this and do that. In the end, it is simple. Make sure employees care about their customers.

What is agency? Agency is the involvement of the customer service agent in fulfilling the customer's needs. The usage of 'I' signals a speaker's intention of responsibility and independence.[13] If Sabine says, 'I will look after the issue,' it will signal to Martin she is 'in charge' and will do the things necessary to take care of the shirt issue, giving him more confidence and ease. Using 'I' signals more agency than using no pronouns or 'we'. When no pronouns are used, such as Sabine saying, 'This will be taken care of', Martin might perceive Sabine as anonymous. There is no agency here from Sabine. She will appear to be another entity within the firm, without a face to identify her. When 'we' pronouns are used, such as Sabine using a phrase like, 'We will take care of the problem', Martin might think Sabine is distant and vague. Sabine will appear to be inaccessible and removed from the situation. While Martin might think, who is 'we'? Is it the store, Sabine, her manager, or the whole firm?

Thus, Packard and his co-authors argue that because consumers perceive agents who use 'I' as empathetic and having agency, this should lead to increased customer satisfaction, purchase intentions and purchase behaviour compared to situations when no pronouns are used, or 'we' pronouns are used.

There is ample research showing that empathy leads to higher customer satisfaction and purchase intentions and deeply involved customer service agents increase customer satisfaction and loyalty.[14]

Let's get into the text-mining method Packard and his colleagues used to test their hypotheses.

Packard and his co-authors ran both experimental studies using participants in a lab and a field study to test their predictions. I will focus on the field study as it is the study where they collected real data from a company and ran text-mining algorithms. For the field study, Packard and his colleagues collected and analysed over 1200 email interactions between the customers and staff of a large multi-category and multinational online retailer of entertainment and information products. The online retailer had a 'contact us' link on its website, which allowed Packard and his colleagues to link 1277 of these interactions (from an initial sample of 2098 interactions) back to a specific user account. This linkage enabled the authors to get the date of the interaction and the number of goods purchased before and after the interaction. The authors used this interaction as the medium to collect textual data on how customer service agents responded to their customers.

After obtaining the email correspondences between customers and customer service agents, Packard and his co-authors removed the generic headers and footers present in these interactions as these headers and footers did not include any content related to the actual interaction between the customer agent and the customer. Then the authors used a dictionary-based text-mining method on the email correspondences. For this, the authors used the dictionary of pronouns from the Linguistic Inquiry and Word Count (LIWC) software to evaluate the effect of different types of pronoun use on customer behaviour. Using LIWC, the authors calculated the percentage of 'I', 'we', and 'you' words from the content of the correspondence between the firm's agent and the customer. For their percentage of pronoun use score, the authors only took the initial email from the customer and the first response from the agent. Note that, most of the time, the third interaction was a simple 'thank you' from the customer.

The authors then ran three separate regression analyses[15] to test their predictions. The outcome variable was the customer's purchase volume in dollars up to ninety days after the interaction. So the authors looked at how much the customers purchased after the email correspondence. The predictor for the first regression analysis included the percentage of 'I' pronouns used by the customer service agent and the customer. The second regression replaced the percentage of 'I' pronouns with 'we' pronouns, and the third regression replaced the percentage of 'I' pronouns with 'you' pronouns.

What did the authors uncover?

Packard and his colleagues found that an agent's use of 'I' pronouns significantly increased customer purchase volume, and even the interaction between the agent and the customer using 'I' pronouns significantly increased purchase volume. That is, when both the agent and customer used 'I' words, it increased the customer's purchase volume after the email correspondence. However, neither the agent's use of 'we' pronouns nor the interaction between the agent's use of 'we' pronouns and the customer's use of 'we' pronouns increased purchase volume.

As for the regression analysis where purchase volume was the outcome variable, and the predictor was the percentage of 'you' words, Packard and his colleagues found that the 'you' pronoun used by the agent did not increase customer purchase volume. In fact, the interaction between the agent's use of 'you' pronouns and the customer's use of 'you' pronouns decreased purchase volume. So, when an agent used 'you' and a customer also used 'you', that led to a decrease in the customer's purchase volume after the email correspondence. In essence, their field data showed that customer agents using 'I' worked best to increase a customer's volume of purchases after an agent-customer interaction.

Packard and his colleagues ran a series of further experiments and showed that the positive impact of agents using 'I' on customer satisfaction and purchase intentions was due to customers' perceptions of the agent's empathy and agency.

So, what do these results mean for managers?

First, firms need to train their employees to use more 'I' pronouns in customer interactions rather than 'we' pronouns. It seems that employees of firms currently do not use 'I' pronouns. Using 'we' pronouns seems to be the norm. When Packard and his co-authors explored how customer service agents generally speak to their customers by running a pilot study in which they analysed the text in email agent-customer interactions, they found the service agents preferred using 'we' over 'I'. In another pilot study, the authors sent bogus customer emails to a random selection of 40 of the top 100 online retailers (per *Internet Retailer* magazine) and examined personal pronoun use in their responses. Here again, they saw a higher prevalence of responses using 'we' and 'you' pronouns than 'I'.

So, the usage of 'we' seemed to be rampant. What is the benefit of replacing 'we' words with 'I' words in a firm agent and customer interaction context? The authors found that when customer service representatives increased their use of 'I' by 10 per cent, it led to a 0.8 per cent increase in customer purchase volume. If agents could shift their use to 'I' instead of 'we' (which Packard and his colleagues state could be achieved in about 90 per cent of 'we' cases in their data), this would lead to an increase of about 7 per cent in revenue. Even though it seems trivial and superficial, just by a subtle change in pronoun use and change in the way language is spoken, we see that firms can garner an increase in customer satisfaction, purchase intentions and purchase behaviour.

Second, who would have thought that 'I' statements could have positive effects when these pronouns are criticized as a pronoun with negative connotations and associated with traits like narcissism?[16]

First-person singular pronouns also seem to have positive effects in other domains. The use of first-person singular pronouns appears to be positively associated with marital satisfaction.[17] The overall takeaway is that different pronouns can have different effects depending on the context. Managers need to know that if they use a pronoun as a proxy for understanding employee or customer behaviour and text mine a relevant corpus of documents, they should always consider the business context. In a context where there is participation by a firm agent with a customer, the use of 'I' trumps the use of 'we'.

Sabine stands to win more brownie points using the phrase, 'I will ensure that you have your shirt replaced with a new one' rather than 'We will ensure that you have your shirt replaced with a new one'.

Martin's expectations will be met or exceeded, and he will surely be satisfied.

9

Do Not Read This Book in Print: Save the Trees

Discount the name of this chapter–I am trying to be smart and witty. You can do as you please, depending on your stance towards environmentalism. Okay, let me get to the point.

Imagine you are a copywriter at an advertising agency. You've been asked to write an advertisement for a non-profit company that focuses on environmental and social issues. The non-profit focuses on reducing the number of forest fires in the western United States. Your main goal is to write a slogan that moves people to action, persuades them to act socially responsibly and makes them understand that most of the time, people are responsible for forest fires.

You have two interns eager to learn all the tricks and gimmicks you have employed over the years to win the best advertisement awards at Cannes and get many an advertisement into the One Show book. Interns who will do everything you tell them to. I was an intern once in a very famous ad agency. Yearning to be a copywriter and thinking I was on my way to becoming the next David Ogilvy, regarded as the 'father of advertising' and founder of the advertising agency Ogilvy & Mather, I obeyed everything the senior creative director and other copywriters told me to do. Though I learnt some tricks of the trade, I remember I did more copying on the photostat machine than copywriting. It used to be part and parcel of ad agencies in the past where interns would do a lot of the drudge work, but I am sure things have changed a lot now.

Okay, back to the interns. The interns, Maggie and Sheila, are polar opposites.

Maggie graduated with a communications degree from the Annenberg School of Communication at the University of Southern California (USC) in Los Angeles. She is nice to everyone, a bit reserved, measured and unassuming.

Sheila has a communication degree, too. She's from the university that USC *loves to love*, the University of California, Los Angeles (people who went to these schools would notice the sarcasm). Sheila is confident, generally speaks her mind, cares little about what others think and is always firm.

Because you have been busy with another project, you ask both of your interns to come up with slogans.

Maggie comes up with: 'Please be considerate and try to stop forest fires.'

Sheila's slogan goes like this: 'YOU need to act. YOU can stop forest fires.'

Which of the two slogans do you think is better?

In your opinion, which is more likely to influence how the target audience behaves? Remember, the final goal is to make consumers take action and ensure they don't inadvertently start a fire.

Before we go ahead, let's do a historical overview of the word 'slogan'. You may not believe it, but the word 'slogan' has a belligerent past. The word has a history strongly tied to battle. Around the early 1700s, the term meant 'the distinctive note, phrase or cry of any person or body of persons'.[1] The word 'slogan', in fact, comes from the word 'slogorn', which means 'battle cry'. Slogorn was used by Scottish highland or Irish clans. Something that Mel Gibson, who portrayed Sir William Wallace in the movie *Braveheart*, might have used in the First War of Scottish Independence against King Edward I of England. The word 'slogorn' is an Anglicization of the Scottish Gaelic and Irish word 'sluagh-ghairm'. Sluagh means 'army' or 'host', and ghairm means 'cry'.[2]

Slogans were used frequently in the Middle Ages as passwords to identify individuals at night or during battle.[3] Indeed, the association with battle has continued with the use of slogans in protest movements often operating as social symbols such as 'Black Lives Matter' or 'We shall overcome'.

What are the characteristics of slogans? Slogans are never neutral and can be used for various purposes. Researchers have proposed that slogans help simplify complicated ideas, emphasize a point, create attention, convert people, make people join a movement or group, build solidarity and even polarization, among others. A slogan can also be cathartic, as it allows one to release repressed frustrations, especially for social movements and protests.

Even in the past, we see the use of slogans in protest. For example, in the Nika revolt, where rebels used the cry 'Nika!' (victory in Greek), which almost brought down the Byzantine Empire. Besides social movements and political campaigns, firms use slogans to create their identity. We know right away 'Just Do It' means Nike (yes, the same word 'Nika' is how the brand name Nike came into being). Every brand has a slogan (known as

122 Mine Your Language

taglines in the US, straplines in the UK, or baselines in Europe).[4]
Slogans help firms differentiate themselves from others and help
create a distinctive brand identity. Brands, in fact, convey their
identity through their name, symbol and slogan.[5] So, using the
right language, making it consistent with what the brand stands
for and making it likeable are extremely important in creating an
effective slogan. Slogans play a very important part in influencing
us, be it purchasing a brand, rallying behind a political candidate
or supporting a movement. Indeed, from Barack Obama's 'Yes,
We Can' to Ho Chi Minh's 'Even the dead still keep the character',
slogans have influenced many and driven people to act.

Having got a sense of what slogans are, let's answer my
question regarding which slogan you should choose—Maggie's
or Sheila's?

Regarding the effectiveness of the two environmental
slogans or any environmental slogan, it is important to note
that changing people's stances towards environmentalism can
be quite challenging, particularly for those who have never really
considered their impact on the environment.

Indeed, environmentalism and social responsibility have
become increasingly important. However, not all of us are Greta
Thunberg. Many of us don't care about these issues because we
think we do not directly benefit from issues like preventing forest
fires. Still, the benefits are large and more macro, involving society,
the planet or consumers. The world is heading towards a gamut of
social and environmental problems and if we as consumers don't
take steps at our end to change, Planet Earth will see cataclysmic
changes, which may be hard to reverse.

Among many issues, let's consider plastic pollution. Can you
imagine 55 million jumbo jets? That is the equivalent of how
much plastic was out there in 2017.[6] Despite these statistics,

some consumers are not motivated enough to recycle better. And even if we recycle, the issue is compounded because even though plastics are recyclable, it is costly for firms to make products from recyclable plastic. Only about 8.7 per cent of all plastic waste was recycled in 2018 in the US.[7] Non-recycled plastic ends up in landfills or incinerators, leading to the emission of undesirable gases, which can harm us. This means that consumers need to examine their behaviour and reduce unnecessary consumption. However, consumers don't seem to be mindful of their harmful consumption habits. For example, the most common reason people use plastic such as in water bottles and bags is that they forget the reusable version at home.[8] Again, it is a simple change, but many people don't seem to realize the consequences of plastic harm and don't see how these changes can have harmful effects on the planet at a global level. The ability to see the larger picture falls into the background. Consumers changing their behaviour is a tall order, and many feel they can do anything they want.

Individually, the incentive to change for a person neutral in her stance towards environmental issues is weak. So, changing people's stance towards the environment is not an easy task. It is cunningly complex and behaviourally challenging to pull off.

Now let's get back to the options of the two interns. The two messages from the interns differ in one important aspect. One is assertive and the other is not. Could this difference in the language play a role in how users react to the messages?

Maggie's slogan: 'Please be considerate and try to stop forest fires', is an example of a non-assertive message.

Sheila's slogan, 'YOU need to act. YOU can stop forest fires!' is an example of an assertive message.

Research in communications and psycholinguistics tells us Maggie's message should work because this non-assertive message aligns with consumers' drive for freedom. In contrast, the more powerful statement written by Sheila goes against an individual's need for freedom.[9] Indeed, most of us don't like being told to do something. In fact, across different contexts such as anti-smoking, safe sex and exercising, it has been proven that assertive messages are less effective than non-assertive messages.[10] Moreover, asking consumers to go green or pro-environment using a softer appeal may be better than assertive messages in reducing the conflict between their personal goals and demands for responsible behaviour. A non-assertive message sounds more humane and takes the addressee's side, such as acknowledging possible obstacles to compliance (e.g., inconvenience, lack of time), which has worked to increase the user's compliance with a particular request.[11]

So, based on the arguments above, what do you think? Which one should you choose? The winner seems to be Maggie. Great! But now, let me give you the actual slogan by the Ad Council for forest fires:

'Only YOU can stop forest fires.'

And here are some other slogans by various environmental or social entities:

- 'Stop the catastrophe' by Greenpeace
- 'Stop talking. Start planting' by Plant for the Planet
- 'Take the Fossil Out of Fuel . . .' by European Environment Agency
- 'Stop hiding problems. Let's start by participating on the 25, 26 and 27 of September in Puliamo il Mondo. Live sustainably.' by Legambiente
- Save and protect our endangered animals . . . Do it now!' by www.saveourplanet.com
- 'Use only what you need' by Denver Water

This contradicts what we just argued when comparing Maggie and Sheila's options. Maggie seemed to be the winner. But what we see in reality is the other way around.

All the examples above use imperative words: 'do', 'go', 'stop', and so on. The imperative form is a grammatical mood that requires or demands an action be performed. The slogan is authoritative and is asking you to act. Not just sit. They are all assertive, not soft, and there is little option for denying the command.

Why are these environmental and social entities using an imperative or assertive form when prior research has suggested otherwise?

Marketing professors Ann Kronrod at the American University, Amir Grinstein at Northeastern University, and Luc Wathieu at Georgetown University explored these very questions.[12]

Should environmental slogans be assertive and when do these assertive slogans work?

The authors first examined the prevalence of such assertive slogans. I gave you a self-selected sample of powerful examples of environmental slogans, but are most of them assertive? First, the authors used www.ThinkSlogans.com to compare seventy-eight actual environmental slogans (e.g., EarthDay, GoGreen) to 187 randomly selected samples of slogans for consumer goods like cereal, computers and coffee. To identify assertive vs non-assertive slogans, the authors employed a human coding method to analyse the grammatical phrasing of slogans.

What did the authors find?

Astoundingly, they found that while only about 19 per cent of the slogans in consumer goods were assertive, more than half of the environmental slogans (about 57 per cent) were assertive. This went against the notion of what we discussed before, which was assertively phrased requests decrease compliance compared with more gentle requests (e.g., 'Please save the trees'; 'Please recycle.').

Why is assertive phrasing more prevalent in environmental slogans?

According to Kronrod, Grinstein and Wathieu, the role of one key variable is missing in the argument for why assertive slogans can be more powerful than non-assertive slogans in engaging consumers. The key variable is how important the issue is perceived by the target audience. Assertive slogans will be seen as encouragement rather than pressure if the target audience perceives the issue as important. Non-assertive slogans might be seen as meek, which will fail to recognize their commitment to the cause.

Indeed, for some time now, researchers from fields such as interpersonal and social communication have demonstrated that the more people believe a cause to be important, the more they comply with a slogan promoting the cause.[13] And this compliance is greater if the person can choose to comply based on her own volition.[14]

Kronrod and her colleagues further argued that the issue's importance also influences the expectations of the language served to them. They argue that the assertive slogans can encourage urgency and show that there is a strong mission behind the issue. Indeed, when you see a message such as 'Stop talking. Start planting', you believe climate change is important and needs action now. The authors suggest assertive slogans will be more persuasive when the audience also perceives the issue to be important, since the language matches the way users expect the slogans to sound. On the other hand, they hypothesized that people who do not believe an issue is important may respond to non-assertive slogans because they acknowledge their lack of interest in the cause. So, how did the authors go about testing their theory?

The team ran three lab studies to test their hypothesis and one field experiment using Google AdWords. My focus will be on the Google AdWords field experiment, where they creatively tested their idea in a real-world setting for this study.

The environmental cause for the field experiment study was to protect the Mediterranean Sea from pollution. In the call to action, users were asked to sign a petition on the website of an organization called Zalul, whose mission is to protect and maintain clean water along Israel's rivers and shorelines. Kronrod and her colleagues created a sponsored link using Google AdWords.

The authors first created a dictionary of words users might use relating to the sea, and then the authors bid for those words in Google AdWords. If anyone typed in these keywords related to the sea in Google Search, they would see the ad for the Zalul petition. In addition, if they clicked on the ad, they would arrive at Zalul's main landing page. It was assumed that these users were concerned about saving the Mediterranean. The authors then created another dictionary, which included general keywords such as 'news', 'knitting machines', etc., and bid for these keywords on Google. Similar to the process above, if users used these 'non-sea-related' keywords in their online searches, they would see the ad for the Zalul petition. If these users clicked on the ad, they would arrive at Zalul's main landing page too. This set of users was assumed to not be concerned about saving the Mediterranean, as they weren't searching for information about sea-related topics.

The authors then showed two ads with different messages to both groups. Let's call one group 'sea-related searchers' and the other group 'generic searchers'.

The assertive message read: 'You must save the Mediterranean. You must sign a petition to reduce water pollution in the Sea. To sign the petition, you have to click http://www.zalul.org.il.'

The non-assertive message was: 'You could save the Mediterranean. You may sign a petition to reduce water pollution in the Sea. To sign the petition, it is possible to click http://www. zalul.org.il.' (The original messages were in Hebrew.)

The researchers ensured any Google search related to the keywords showed these two advertisements in random order. Members in the 'sea-related searchers' group could see either the assertive or non-assertive message. Similarly, members in the 'generic searchers' group could see either the assertive or non-assertive message. The authors ran these ads, collected and analysed 309 clicks during seven weeks in January and February 2010. So, what did the authors' analysis reveal?

Users who thought that saving the Mediterranean was important (e.g., sea-related searchers) were more likely to click on an assertive message than those who clicked on a non-assertive message according to the analysis. In contrast, the non-assertive message (see Figure 9.1) had the opposite effect. The likelihood of a user clicking on a non-assertive message, when the user thought the issue of saving the Mediterranean was not important (i.e., 'generic searchers'), was higher than the likelihood of a user clicking on an assertive message.

Now, which slogan would you choose? Maggie with her non-assertive slogan or Sheila with her powerful slogan? As with everything in social science, it depends. Sheila's slogan makes sense if your audience believes forest fires are an issue. Maggie's slogan works if you think your target audience is neutral or couldn't care less about forest fires.

So, what do these results imply for managers of firms and policymakers?

First, creating messages persuading consumers to commit to a cause depends on the objective of the communication campaign.

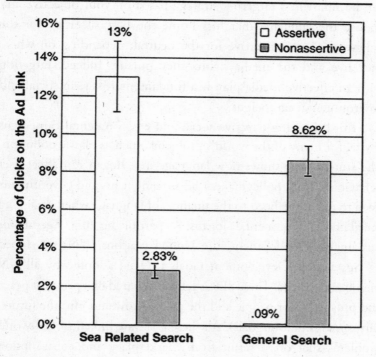

Figure 9.1: Percentage of Clicks on Advertising on Google

There have been examples of successful behaviour change in the past. If you've ever driven through the US, you must have seen the 'Click it or Ticket' slogan. This campaign was launched in the 1990s to encourage people to use seat belts. The tagline, as you can see, is assertive. You can't have a neutral opinion about wearing seat belts. It is for your and everyone's safety, and most people seem to understand the repercussions of not wearing seat belts.

Second, once the communication objective is clear, the trick, as everything is nowadays, is figuring out where your target audience will be. Where do they live? What media do they consume? You can be smart in a targeting strategy based on your objective and choose the language that hits home the best: assertive for the believer and non-assertive for the neutral, depending on where they live and the media habits they pursue. Indeed, targeting with an effective media plan is a fundamental issue in social and environmental campaigns.

Third, creating effective social and environmental campaigns is vital for many of the world's problems, such as plastic pollution. The study above shows how language in a slogan can affect user behaviour. Thus, policymakers, advertising firms and governments need to pay more heed to the nuances of language when designing social and environmental slogans. As part of the 2030 Agenda for Sustainable Development, the United Nations (UN) developed 17 Sustainable Development Goals (SDGs) adopted by all UN member countries. These SDGs reflect 'a shared blueprint for peace and prosperity for people and the planet, now and into the future' (https://sdgs.un.org/goals). All these goals are linked to real-world problems that often result from marketplace and consumption practices. If consumers can be motivated by intelligent slogans that use language effectively, marketers can pat themselves on the back. Marketing personnel need to understand how to create slogans that are beyond WEIRD samples[15] (i.e., Western, Educated, Industrialized, Rich, Democratic) to address the needs of consumers and households that are underrepresented, underserved or vulnerable. For example, consumer decisions about healthy foods are different for middle-class Western consumers. Some consumers are living in food deserts with access to an abundance of unhealthy foods, while some consumers live in famine with little or no access to food. It is important to consider both the target market and the type of language, which can be most effective.

Overall, we see in the study by Kronrod, Grinstein and Wathieu how language in slogans can persuade people. If slogans ably use the right rhetorical device, they can drive the intended point home. Consider the slogan, 'Make Love, Not War', the anti-war slogan associated with the American counterculture of the 1960s. If we look at the language used, the slogan could be characterized as sarcastic, and a mockery of America's stance on Vietnam and traditional capitalist cultural institutions like marriage. The slogan remains one of the most important slogans of the twentieth century.[16] Sarcasm worked in this case, but in another context, another rhetorical device like irony might work too.

The UN estimates that the world population will increase to 11 billion by the end of the century.[17] This will lead to higher demand for water, land, trees and fossil fuels, which will have disastrous effects on flora and fauna. Creating effective social and environmental slogans is needed now more than ever. And most importantly, using the right language will be essential.

III

CONSUMERSPEAK

What do you think is the median number of likes or retweets for any post on X?

It is 0.

Yes, 0.

Most tweets hardly see any engagement. Yet, people write because they want to build connections, do good to others, enhance their status or social capital, among various other reasons. People trust other users as they see them as peers and trust the authenticity of their opinions.

In this set of chapters, you will read about how consumerspeak, via the language and words consumers utilize, can have significant repercussions on business outcomes. We will discuss if profane words like 'fuck' have a place in business, or if using a word like 'God' can identify someone who is likely to default on a loan, how one can don the hat of Sherlock Holmes to detect fake reviews, and what content and who can create chaos for a firm on social media.

10

The Force of Four-Letter Words in Online Reviews

This chapter is about words like fuck, shit, piss, bollocks and bugger!

I am sorry to be offensive. You might think, why even discuss words like this, and how can such terms have a place in business? After all, we are supposed to dislike people who use such words.

However, as Timothy Jay, a psychology professor, states in a *Time* magazine article, 'If you don't study this kind of language, you're missing an important part of being a human.'[1]

Most of us swear or curse sometimes and 0.5 per cent to 0.7 per cent of all the words we speak in our day-to-day lives are swear words.[2] From a survey conducted in 2006, a robust 64 per cent of Americans said they use the F-word. Some use it several times a day (8 per cent), and some a few times a year (15 per cent).[3] Sure, most of these words aren't exactly polite, but they are part and parcel of everyday life for many. Younger people use cuss words more than folks from other ages—about 62 per cent of eighteen- to thirty-four-year-olds versus 39 per cent of those thirty-five and older. The use of swear words is rife. The average American now

uses about eighty to ninety swear words daily.[4] Yes, that is about
five cuss words every hour one is awake.

If we look at modern-day music and lyrics in the West, the
use of four-letter words is quite commonplace. We see swear
words used by artists ranging from Ellie Goulding to Beyoncé.
Gone are the days when the Federal Bureau of Investigation
(FBI) would get involved to investigate a song's lyrics. In 1963,
the FBI investigated the song 'Louie Louie' by The Kingsmen
for profanity. The lyrics were so muddled and confusing that the
FBI was asked to examine the lyrics for expletives. Since then, the
use of swear words in music has come a long way.[5] Consider the
song 'WAP' by Cardi B, for example. The Netflix documentary, *A
History of Swear Words*, features the song as an exemplar. Swearing
is so ubiquitous now that a quarter of the top 40 singles in 2016
are categorized as explicit on Apple iTunes, with music albums
even higher at 35 per cent.[6] One in every 234 words in lyrics is a
swear word.[7] Swearing is also common online. For example, 7.7
per cent of posts in tweets[8] include at least one cuss word.

Swear words are omnipresent, all over the world. All languages
have their share. I live in France, so I know what 'con' means.[*] I
know what 'mahikney' means[†] as I studied in a boarding school
with a lot of Nepalis. They are in every culture. Some use swear
words referring to body parts, and some refer to sex. In my younger
years and even now, if I want to show eagerness in learning a new
language, the first words I learn apart from 'Hello' and 'Thank
you' are cuss words. Somehow, swear words stick in my brain

---

[*] It is a word meaning 'asshole' or a part of the female anatomy, but it can also mean 'jerk'
or 'idiot'.
[†] Nepali slang that is used for insulting and showing anger to someone. It typically means
'motherfucker'.

better than normal words when trying to learn a new language. Don't ask me why!

What makes a swear word, well . . . a *swear word*?

For every 'shit' or 'pissed', there's another word that is blander and more usable, such as poop or angry. So, swear words become swear words because we consider 'shit' more offensive and vulgar than 'poop'. 'Pissed' is considered more derogatory and uncouth than angry.

So, the question really is: why do we swear?

Of course, we swear when we feel like swearing. Humour aside, using a cuss word allows us to convey our mental state and the intensity of that state, be it angry, excited, upset or aroused. As we age and are conditioned over time, we understand cuss words are related to strong feelings. Our body gets conditioned to physically relate to swearing. Our heart rates rise, pupils dilate, pores open, and we start sweating.[9]

Cuss words have both constructive and destructive purposes. Swearing involves taboos and clusters around topics such as lavatorial matters ('shit'), sex ('fuck'), religion ('hell') and words describing other groups of people. The words in the last category are mostly destructive.

In essence, swear words can be both constructive and destructive, and their functions can be wide-ranging.

Consider the F-word. In his wonderful book, *The Stuff of Thought: Language as a Window into Human Nature*,[10] Steven Pinker wrote there are five different ways we can swear using the F-Word such as 'descriptively (Let's fuck), idiomatically (It's fucked up), abusively (Fuck you!), emphatically (This is fucking amazing), and cathartically (Fuck!!!)'. Osho or Bhagwan Rajneesh, the Indian godman, once said: 'One of the most interesting words in the English language today is the word "fuck". It is one magical word: just by its sound, it can describe pain, pleasure, hate and love. In language, it falls into many grammatical categories. It can be used as a verb, both transitive (John fucked Mary) and intransitive (Mary was fucked by John), and as a noun (Mary is a fine fuck). It can be used as an adjective (Mary is fucking beautiful). As you can see, there are few words with the versatility of "fuck".'[11]

Thus, a swear word like 'fuck' has a lot of versatility.

Cuss words have a range of positive facets too. Philosopher Rebecca Roche mentions swearing can be relieving, 'If you're angry or particularly happy, swearing is a catharsis.'[12] Sometimes, swearing can even have benefits when we are going through pain. Apparently, it is more comfortable to keep one's arm in a bucket of ice-cold water if you are swearing at the same time. I have resorted to swearing when I am doing something difficult, like the last stretch of a marathon or near the approach of a mountain peak when my body just gives up.

Cursing could also help you on your journey to get fitter and calmer. Using swear words helps bikers pedal faster, and it can also lessen stress and anxiety.[13] Next time you are in the gym, perhaps you could try this silently to yourself, or it may be the last time you enter your gym.

Do you practice 'lalochezia'? I can see a lot of benefits of it in the streets of Istanbul. In 2021, Istanbul took the number one position as the world's most congested city, followed by Moscow, Kyiv, Bogota and Mumbai.[14] On average, a person loses 142 hours yearly in Istanbul due to traffic congestion. Lalochezia is the emotional relief that comes into play when drivers spew out expletives when pedestrians unlawfully cross a street.

Foul language can also help people bond. I became friends with many people from foreign lands by learning how to curse in their language. I am sure they were amused and must have wished I didn't greet people with these newly learnt words when I visited their country.

In these instances, we see swearing has some benefits despite its potential to violate norms and offend people. But what about the world of business? Can swear words be helpful in the context of business when swear words violate norms and offend people?

Let's consider two reviews of a product.

Review 1 reads: 'This product is super, and I will wholeheartedly recommend it.'

(Parental guidance advised) Review 2 goes like this: 'This product is fucking good, and I will wholeheartedly recommend it.'

Which review will a reader and potential buyer find more helpful?

Most of us don't like someone who curses, and we view them as crude and morally tainted. Could being potty-mouthed like the second reviewer be helpful in an online review context?

Okay, before I go ahead, let me address the larger issue of why reviews are helpful and important for businesses. Do reviews matter? Of course they do and are helpful for websites like amazon.com.

Websites like Amazon incentivize reviewers to provide helpful content for consumers. Helpfulness is defined by how well a review assists the consumer during a purchase. For instance, researchers have stated that a helpful review 'facilitates the consumer's purchase decision process'[15] and 'enables consumers to better assess a product'.[16] Many firms, such as Amazon and Apple's App Store, ask their visitors to rate the helpfulness of reviews. For example, for every review, Amazon asks the reader to answer, 'Yes' or 'No' to the question: 'Was this review helpful to you?'

In 2009, it was estimated that Amazon's helpfulness feature was responsible for more than $2.7 billion of new revenue every year.[17] Besides increasing sales, helpful online reviews can have other positive downstream effects, such as increasing conversion rates[18] and a consumer's tendency to shop at a website.[19] Likewise, we as reviewers are incentivized to write helpful reviews for both egoistic reasons (e.g., to impress others with our superior shopping skills) and altruistic reasons (e.g., to help others make good decisions). Thus, understanding how websites can assist reviewers in providing helpful reviews is of strong managerial importance and examining if swear words can affect a review is an important question.

In a very interesting study, marketing professors Katherine C. Lafreniere from the University of Lethbridge, Sarah Moore, and Robert Fisher from the University of Alberta argued and demonstrated that swear words indeed have power and the use of profanity can have beneficial outcomes even in a business context.[20]

Lafreniere and her colleagues argued that swear words can be impactful and helpful for readers in online reviews because they convey meaning about 1) the reviewer and 2) the topic/product under discussion.

Let's get into the psychological process behind both of these reasons.

When a reviewer uses the proverbial four-letter word in a product review, its usage conveys the strength of the speaker's feelings about the product. This, in turn, increases the emotional power of the review. Most readers are well aware of the taboo status of using swear words, so when we read a review containing them, we infer the reviewer has strong feelings about this product. They risked using a word considered offensive. Thus, when a reviewer writes a review such as 'this movie is fucking funny', readers will infer the reviewer has stronger feelings about the movie's funniness than an instance where the reviewer did not use the swear word.

As for the topic or product, when a reviewer uses a swear word for a product ('this book is fucking amazing'), the swear word here will convey to the reader that the book is actually good. So, the cuss word will work as a mixed-meaning expression, such that the word conveys meaning not only about the reviewer's feelings but also about the topic or product under discussion. In other words, like a content word, an expletive will provide information about the product, which could be good or bad.

Having established that cuss words can affect us when we read reviews, is it also possible that a swear word can be less effective or less impactful in an online review? Lafreniere and her colleagues argue that overusing swear words will not improve the usefulness of reviews. What could cause cuss words to lose their effectiveness in online reviews? Imagine a review written by someone who has sprinkled the page with different expletives—words she's been meaning to spew out to her boss, who fired her for no reason. She sees an online review as an outlet to let it out and goes haywire. Here, the authors argue, the review becomes unclear for a reader to determine whether the reviewer is swearing to convey the product's attributes or is prone to be reactive with a tendency to exaggerate.

There are three types of cuss words. Some expletives are uncensored such as 'fuck', some are euphemistic such as 'frick' and then there are the censored such as 'f***'. Do you think each type has the same effect on people who are reading reviews?

Euphemistic cuss words have the same effect as uncensored swear words. This is because 'frick' still retains an association with the word 'fuck'. Using 'frick' does not dilute the meaning behind the intent. Another thing to note is that a euphemistic word is pronounced quite similarly to the actual word. This allows the word to preserve the negative undertone.

So, the uncensored 'fuck' and the euphemistic 'frick' have similar effects on a reader of a review but what about the censored, such as 'f***'? Lafrenière and her colleagues propose that censored words such as 'f***' don't have the same effect on readers as 'fuck' and 'frick' because a word such as 'f***' is a symbolic stand-in or an acronym, does not sound the same as 'fuck' or 'frick', and using such a word indicates that the reviewer does not strongly approve or refute her opinion about a product.

Now, how did they go about testing these ideas?

The authors got two field data sets and ran four experiments to ensure their results were robust.

They first collected Yelp reviews to test their theory. They collected the reviews from the 2017 Yelp Dataset Challenge. This is a great dataset to play with if you ever want to examine something interesting regarding reviews and want to test your programming and text-mining chops. I have also used it for my projects.

The original dataset contains around 4.7 million reviews of 1,56,000 businesses in twelve metropolitan areas from four countries.[21] Lafrenière and her colleagues selected a random sample of 1,00,000 reviews, which involved 76,544 unique reviewers for 42,883 different businesses. The data included the content of the review, the star rating (varying from 1 to 5, with 5 as the best), the date when the review was posted and whether the readers found the review useful.

The authors also obtained reviews from amazon.com. Ruining He, from Google Research, and Julian McAuley, from the University of California in San Diego, collected and shared about 82.8 million product reviews on Amazon from May 1996 to July 2014. I have used this dataset too. It is an excellent piece of charitable work that He and McAuley have done for many researchers and practitioners to understand the intricacies and impact of Amazon reviews.

Lafreniere and her colleagues randomly selected 2,00,000 of these reviews, which spanned twenty-four product categories (e.g., books, baby, electronics), where 1,90,240 reviewers posted a review for 1,61,092 different products. Similar to Yelp, the data includes the content of the review, the star rating (varying from 1 to 5 with 5 as the best), the date when the review was posted and whether or not the readers found the review helpful.

Let's get into the text-mining method that Lafreniere and her co-authors used to figure out the effectiveness of cuss words in these online reviews. They used a dictionary-based approach, specifically the ubiquitous Linguistic Inquiry and Word Count (LIWC) software, to identify reviews containing at least one swear word.[22] As I have mentioned before, LIWC has a dictionary of constructs. LIWC categorizes words into substantiated, pre-existing dictionaries[23] and then provides the percentage of words in a textual document in each of these dictionaries. LIWC has a pre-existing dictionary of fifty-three word stems that fall under the swear word construct.

Lafreniere and her co-authors updated this list with new words such as 'frick' and 'f*ck' and also excluded words such as 'bloody' (the word 'bloody' could be used in a non-swear word context). They finally used 145 word stems.[24] If a review included a swear word, they coded it as censored, uncensored or euphemistic.

Let's look at the frequency of swear words on Yelp and Amazon. They found that 8947 Yelp reviews, about 8.9 per cent of the overall Yelp reviews, and 6965 Amazon reviews, about 3.5

per cent of the overall Amazon reviews in their sample, contained a swear word. Who would have f**king thought!

Their Yelp analysis found that reviews with swear words received significantly more useful votes than reviews without swear words. Similarly, on Amazon, they found that reviews with swear words received more helpful votes than reviews without.

The authors found that the effect of swear words becomes insignificant in influencing useful votes and the proportion of helpful votes after four swear words and two swear words on Yelp and Amazon, respectively. So, if you want to help someone or be considered a top-notch reviewer, don't use more than four cuss words on Yelp and two expletives on Amazon.

Let's examine whether censored ('f***') cuss words are indeed weaker than uncensored ('fuck') and euphemistic ('frick') swear words in influencing review helpfulness. Lafreniere and her colleagues found no difference in the effects of uncensored, euphemistic and censored swear words in affecting useful votes on Yelp. However, they found that uncensored and euphemistic swear words had a positive and similar influence in increasing the proportion of helpful votes on Amazon and that censored swear words had no effect on increasing the proportion of helpful votes on Amazon. So, if you are writing a review on Amazon, stay away from using words such as f***. Instead, go for either the uncensored or euphemistic version.

All I have discussed now is agnostic to the sentiment in an online review. For example, a review can be damning or laudatory. All the analysis and results above regarding the effects of cuss words being helpful are indifferent to the sentiment. Thus, Lafreniere and her colleagues also tested whether swear words influence usefulness or helpfulness, depending on the sentiment of the review. One would surmise that swear words will generally be more potent in negative reviews than in positive reviews. Swear words can jack up a negative review and make it more appealing to a reader. Cuss words in a negative review (e.g., 'This washing machine is fucking loud!') can increase review helpfulness as it can aggravate a reader's dislike for a product. The authors used the 5-star rating to categorize a review. They used the categorization of negative for a 1- or 2-star rating, neutral for a 3-star rating, and positive for a 4- or 5-star rating.

What did the authors find? Using their field data, they discovered that swear words were valuable to readers for both negative and positive reviews. Swear words in a positive review not only increased review helpfulness but also increased a reader's liking for a product. So, a review like 'I fucking like this book' increases helpfulness.

Thus, swear words work for both positive and negative reviews. One thing that might occur to you is how cuss words compare to words like 'super' or 'insanely', which could have similar effects. In linguistic terms, words like 'super' are referred to as mixed-meaning words and, like swear words, can convey feelings about the reviewer and strong attributes of a product. Words like 'insanely' are called negative-degree adverbs and can again qualify attributes about a product strongly. They found swear words were more potent in influencing reviewer helpfulness even when compared to such mixed-meaning words as 'super' or 'insanely'.

In essence, Lafreniere and her co-authors show that being potty-mouthed in online reviews can have positive effects on a firm's business.

So, how does this affect platforms and businesses with forums where reviewers can post their opinions about their products?

First, it shows it would be unwise for firms such as amazon. com to prohibit the use of swear words. As the study above shows, swear words in an online review can not only increase the value of an online review but also positively influence a reader's attitude towards a product.

Second, though the use of cuss words should be allowed, it would be prudent for firms to ensure excessive use of swear words is not encouraged.

Third, allowing a censored cuss word like f*** but eliminating the uncensored or euphemistic version may not be the ideal strategy for firms, as censored swear words don't convey the same meaning to the reader and are thus less impactful compared to the uncensored and euphemistic versions.

Finally, I want to point out that these results may not be generalizable across different ages, cultures and geographies. Some generations curse more, and some cultures refrain from using swear words in their daily lives or use them subtly. So, an adequate sense of how swear words are used in particular age groups, cultures or geographies may help a platform get a strong sense of the power of swear words.

Overall, though we may detest someone who is potty-mouthed, we tend to find moderately potty-mouthed reviewers on online platforms helpful.

The study above represents another example of an effective use of a swear word like 'fuck'. But this time in a context where one would think expletives have no place. The world of online commerce.

Perhaps Osho, if he were alive, would agree.

11

Words That Are Gonna Make
You Sweat (Virtually)

'A man who pays his bills on time is soon forgotten.'[1]

Who better to quote than Oscar Fingal O'Flahertie Wills Wilde, the great Irish poet and playwright, regarding one's relationship with money? Oscar Wilde, thank heavens we don't have to spell out his full name, had a tumultuous association with money. Though he was born to a financially well-off family and had a successful writing career, he ultimately died impoverished and destitute. The quote above resonates well with the credit scores that financial institutions bestow on us.

Wilde makes the point that it is better to be forgotten than remembered by your creditors. Indeed, it is much better to be a less prominent borrower who pays bills consistently and on time than someone who conspicuously 'forgets' to pay. As we all know, being a lousy debtor can significantly damage one's credit scores. A credit score has tremendous ramifications for someone who wants to live, especially 'the American way of life'. Getting good credit substantially impacts social inequality as many necessary amenities can be out of reach for someone with bad credit scores.

A credit score predicts how likely one is to repay a loan on time. Most credit scores in the US range from 300 to 850. A low score can make it impossible, if not difficult, to qualify for a loan and most often results in very high interest rates. These credit scores are based on a mathematical model. FICO, developed by Fair Isaac Corporation, is one of the most widely used credit scoring models in the US, used by 90 per cent of all financial institutions in their decision-making process.[2]

How are these credit scores calculated?

As it is difficult to predict whether someone will repay a loan over a long period, lenders collect and analyse as much information as possible to avoid making Type I (false positive) or Type II (false negative) errors. A Type I error occurs when a borrower who will eventually default is incorrectly given a loan, while a Type II error occurs when a creditor rejects a loan application from a creditworthy borrower. In general, for creating an individual credit score, these models use the individual's payment history, the amount owed, the length of the credit history, any new credit, and a mix of different credit that the individual currently has, which could range from mortgages to instalment loans.

Apart from such financial data showing a borrower's financial strength, lenders use demographic variables such as age, location, race, income, education and employment, among other characteristics. Apart from these two categories, lenders also use the specifics of the requested loan (e.g., asked amount, interest rate) and any insights they can gain through the transactions, which could be through email, phone calls or in-person interactions between the lender and borrower.

The last piece of information is vital as it is difficult to know a borrower's true intentions, personality, circumstances and ability to pay a loan back. This issue is compounded by the direction our world is trending. As a result of the COVID-19 pandemic, almost all of our transactions have become virtual. Even before the pandemic, virtual banking was on the up. I remember the days when I would dress up in a suit or formal wear, shave, go to the nearest bank and be on my best behaviour to open a bank account or apply for a loan. Virtual interactions have replaced human interactions between borrowers and lenders. Banks, other lending institutions and crowdfunding platforms use virtual platforms to interact with lenders.

Because of the difficulty in gauging someone's personality via in-person meetings, financial institutions nowadays use various pieces of information that we provide online. You may not believe it, but your information on social network profiles affects your credit scores. Companies calculate credit scores based on information on social network sites such as Facebook, LinkedIn or X.[3] Companies use information about our social connections, such as the number of followers we have, who our friends are, and information about our friends. On LinkedIn, for example, companies may check the seniority of your professional connections.[4]

Clearly, such information is valuable and predictive.[5] You would think this is a total invasion of our privacy, and it is unethical for firms to connect our social life with our financial life. However, this practice is prevalent, with an array of companies using such data. Facebook has a patent that uses its users' connections to create a score for loan approval. The patent goes by the name 'Authorization and Authentication', based on an individual's social network.[6] The information we share online, both personal and professional, affects our credit scores. Basically, institutions seek any information they can use to assess a borrower's creditworthiness.

Wait till you hear this! China now has a new social credit system where individuals are ranked on creditworthiness based on every interaction and transaction made. So, your quotidian affairs like how quickly you eat or how often you walk your dog also go into this ranking system.[7] If you display bad judgement, good luck with your loan application! In light of the volatile gas prices and how much Americans rely on cars, where do you think firms could find other useful information? Gas stations! If you pay at the gas pump itself, you are deemed more credit-worthy than paying inside the store.[8]

In the US, even though there is a lot of debate regarding the rights and wrongs of using such data, regulators are moving towards taking a more optimistic stance in letting firms use online data to generate credit scores. As the official statement from the Federal Deposit Insurance Corporation (FDIC) explains, alternative sources of data 'may help firms evaluate the creditworthiness of consumers who currently may not obtain credit in the mainstream credit system'.[9] The regulation means well. About 45 million consumers in the US don't seem to have adequate credit history to generate a reliable credit score.[10] This is a good thing as more people can now come under the purview of the credit system, especially people who are out of the mainstream financial system. For example, immigrants like me and students who don't have a long credit history. However, many argue that such data will make consumer targeting even more sinister, as lenders can discriminate against people based on such information.

Overall, our online profiles and what we say or do online matters. Even for getting loans!

If what we say online matters, then what about the words borrowers use when applying for loans on lending platforms? Could the words consumers use on their applications help lenders predict their ability to pay back a loan? The information on an online loan application is just as valuable as the behaviour people used to exhibit in front of a loan officer. In those days, we walked into our neighbourhood bank wearing our best attire. This is the behaviour (information) a lender uses to make a decision. Today, this can be detected in the way we use language when applying online for loans.

A group of marketing professors, Oded Netzer, professor at Columbia Business School, Alain Lemaire, professor at the University of Texas at Austin, and Michal Herzenstein, professor at the University of Delaware, got together to answer this very question.[11]

Their principal piece of inquiry: What is the power of words in predicting loan default?

To answer their research question, Netzer and his co-authors used text-mining tools on over 1,20,000 loan requests, which contained textual data that borrowers write while submitting their loan applications from the online peer-to-peer lending marketplace, Prosper.

What is Prosper? Founded in 2005, Prosper.com is the first online crowdfunding platform in the United States and has facilitated over $20 billion in loans to more than 11,80,000 people.[12] When potential borrowers put up a request on Prosper. com, they need to specify the general loan information such as the amount they wish to borrow, the maximum interest rate they can pay, their debt-to-income ratio and if they own homes. Like all creditors, Prosper.com checks all this information and gets the borrower's credit score from Experian, the American-Irish consumer credit reporting agency, which has information for about 1 billion people.[13] After which, Prosper.com assigns credit grades ranging from AA (lowest risk for lenders) to HR (highest risk for lenders). Now, here comes the interesting part. Apart from the financial information, borrowers also can upload pictures and write any information they wish to convey in an open text box. The potential borrowers have no restriction on the amount of content they wish to convey to lenders. For example, I could write, 'Hi I am a small business professional and need a loan of $1 million to start my business. I have run successful businesses in the past,' and upload my best professional picture to appear trustworthy and reliable.

The words that the borrowers in Prosper write are what Netzer and his colleagues used to examine if words can predict loan default.

The authors examined loan requests posted between April 2007 and October 2008 for 1,22,479 listings for their text-mining research. They used both natural language processing and the dictionary-based method for answering their research questions.

Their first question was if textual information was useful in predicting defaults.

Because the authors had the information on whether a borrower paid a loan or did not, they used loan repayment as the outcome variable. They coded a loan repayment as one and a default as zero and checked what words could predict if someone paid or did not.

To ensure they did not miss any pertinent textual information, Netzer and his co-authors looked at the following linguistic information on the 3.5 million words (with 30,920 unique words that were at least three letters long) they assembled from the content in the loan requests:

- The number of characters in the title and the text box in the loan request. Why?

- - Apparently, liars write much more text when communicating than non-liars.[14]
- Percentage of words with six letters or more. Why?
  - - On the one hand, this indicates higher income and higher financial literacy, reducing loan default likelihood.[15] On the other hand, using complex words can signal deception.[16]
- How unclear is the text measured by the 'Simple Measure of Gobbledygook' (SMOG) index?[17]
  - - This index measures writing clarity. As with a similar index called the FOG index, explored in another chapter, this index can indicate the level of formal education.
- A count of spelling mistakes. Why?
  - - Past research indicates that spelling mistakes are associated with a lower probability of being granted a loan in traditional loan channels.[18]
- Two-word combinations from the corpus of 3.5 million words. Two-word combinations are called bigrams, such as 'thank you'. Netzer and his colleagues use 1052 bigrams.

The authors then used 80 per cent of the textual data for training the model. Their main goal was to build a better predictive model than models using only financial and demographic data. They trained several predictive models and created an ensemble of models.

Ensemble models allow researchers to have a deeper understanding of the data because they use many models to get a sense of the patterns in the data. Suppose you are trying to predict if Argentina will win the FIFA World Cup in 2026 by analysing the team's past performances against other nations. You run one model and find that having Lionel Messi on the team is an important predictor and a significant reason for them winning. Another model might say having a coach who is strict and friendly is a significant predictor. Running different models allows you to see data patterns you may miss by running just one model. Because you combine many patterns using different models, which lowers variance[19] and bias, ensemble models have been shown to have better predictive performance than individual models.[20]

Netzer and his co-authors' modelling approach involved two steps.

In the first step, they trained each model on 80 per cent of the data. This means they use 80 per cent of the listings (1,22,479 listings), i.e., about 98,000 listings to build a model. Note that they know the identity of the person who posted these listings. They know if someone paid off a loan or defaulted because they have the information on whether someone did or did not. The authors used the textual characteristics listed above, such as the percentage of words with six or more letters and spelling mistakes, to predict if the person who posted the listing defaulted or not. After running this set of models, the ensemble, the authors stored these different models. In the second phase, Netzer and his colleagues built a weighted model that optimally combines the models calibrated in the first step on 20 per cent of the remaining data. So, say Model 1 finds spelling mistakes as the best predictor. Model 2 finds usage of the percentage of words with six letters or more as the best predictor. Imagine there are just four applicants. You build an ensemble model using the first two applicants. You know that applicant 1 defaulted and applicant 2 did not. If Model 1 accurately predicts that applicant 1 is a defaulter and Model 2 accurately predicts that applicant 2 is not a defaulter, the weighted model in the second step gives higher weight to Model 1 for applicant 3 as this applicant has similar characteristics to applicant 1 and lesser weight to Model 2 for applicant 3 who has characteristics that are similar to applicant 1 but dissimilar to applicant 2. In the same manner, the weighted model will give higher weight to Model 2 for applicant 4 as applicant 4 has characteristics that are like applicant 2 and lesser weight to Model 1 as applicant 4 has characteristics that are similar to applicant 2 and dissimilar to applicant 1.

The authors estimated five models in the first step, which included two logistic regressions and three different types of decision trees.

> A decision tree is a supervised machine-learning approach that is used for both classifying labels and for regression tasks. Each tree starts with a root node, which has outgoing branches that feed into internal nodes. In each node, based on a test for a feature or predictor, the data is divided into two or more nodes so that the subsequent nodes have data that are homogenous in the feature or predictor utilized for the test. Each branch is the outcome of the test. The terminal node contains the class label.

Netzer and his colleagues next estimated this calibrated and weighted model using the tenfold cross-validation technique, obtaining the prediction accuracy. The tenfold cross-validation technique is used when a researcher only has a training set and test set. It is generally used when there is insufficient data for a validation set.* Say you have 100 data points where you know

---

* Generally, in machine learning, one uses a training set to train the model that includes all possible variations of the data so that the model can predict any unseen data, a validation set to fine-tune the model and validate the model's performance, and a test set to gauge the model's accuracy. The training set has to be much larger in volume compared to the validation and test data.

whether a borrower defaulted or not. The researcher randomly picks ninety borrowers, fits a model and then checks the accuracy on the remaining ten borrowers. This process is done ten times and the researcher uses the accuracy across these ten predictions for a different set of ten borrowers to determine the model's accuracy.

Enough of all this Greek. What did the authors find after their meticulous efforts?

First, Netzer and his co-authors found the model including the textual, financial and demographic data outperformed the model with only the financial and demographic information. The model with only textual data was nearly as predictive as the financial and demographic information model. As Netzer and his colleagues mention, textual data can be helpful in 'thin file' situations when the financial information for the potential borrower is sparse. Indeed, this syncs with the idea of why social network data can be beneficial. Such information can be useful for lending credit to people with little or no credit history.

The authors' next task was determining what words, topics and writing styles are related to a borrower not paying back a loan. Here their methods spanned from Naïve Bayes classifier* to logistic regression to topic modelling (we talked about this in the chapter on Spoilers) and Linguistic Inquiry and Word Count aka LIWC (we talked about this dictionary in other chapters). What did the authors uncover?

First, words related to hardships, both financial, such as 'payday loan', 'child support', and 'refinance', and general hardships such as 'stress', 'divorce', and 'very hard' were more likely to be used by defaulters.

---

* Another machine-learning method that takes advantage of probability theory and Bayes' Theorem and is mostly utilized for classification tasks; for example, determining if an email is spam or not.

Second, words that elucidate their current situation, such as 'loan explain', 'explain why', and their state of work, such as 'hard work', and 'worker', were more likely to be from defaulters.

Third, polite and well-mannered words such as 'God bless', 'hello', and imploring lenders for help such as 'need help', and 'please help' were more likely to be written by defaulters.

Fourth, words suggesting others such as 'God', 'son', and 'someone' were more likely to be written by defaulters.

Finally, time-related words like 'total monthly', 'day', and words denoting future tense such as 'would use', and 'will be able' had a higher probability of being written by defaulters.

Next, Netzer and his colleagues used the LIWC dictionary to find other word usage patterns among defaulters and non-defaulters. The LIWC dictionary, which you may see is dispersed across this book, signifying its heavy utilization by social science scholars, contains 4500 words and categorizes words into sixty-four linguistic and psychologically meaningful dictionaries. Some dictionaries include tenses, pronouns and social, positive and negative emotions, which were used to uncover the circumstances and personalities of the defaulters.

Note that these results are correlational and not causal. Borrowers using an online lending platform might be more tech-savvy, educated and different from traditional borrowers.

Let's see what the authors found.

- Defaulters used more present- and future-tense words. Prior research indicates that liars are more likely to use such terms as they characterize unconcluded situations.[21]
- Defaulters used more motion-related terms such as 'drive', 'run', etc., and fewer relative words such as 'closer', 'higher', etc. Relative word use likely indicates more complexity in

thinking and suggests higher academic education vis-à-vis motion words that suggest the reverse.

- Defaulters also use more social words (e.g., 'mother', 'father', 'he', 'she', 'we', 'they') while repayers use more 'I' words.
- Finally, defaulters used more time-based words (e.g., 'January', 'Sunday', 'morning', 'never') and space words (e.g., 'above', 'inch', 'north'). Deceptive statements written by prisoners use these words as they draw attention from the self.[22]

A very interesting inference the authors finally made out of their analysis with the LIWC dictionary is that the writing style defaulters use mirrors the way extroverts write. Extroverts use words such as 'adults' and 'boy', which are social and human words,[23] and more motion words such as 'go' and 'drive'.[24] Extroverts have a tendency to take more risks, have little restraint in buying lottery tickets and don't save as much. This also shows that perhaps what Netzer and his colleagues are measuring is extroversion as their text-mining model cannot infer causality and is only a predictive model. For example, I can build a prediction model to predict someone's GMAT score. Say, I find that prior work experience is a significant predictor of knowing someone's GMAT score. But perhaps, the underlying variable I have not measured is a person's ambition, which is the real cause.

Overall, in this excellent research, Netzer and his colleagues find that defaulters use simple and wordier language, write about hardship, explain why they need the loan and refer to family, God and chance. Then using the LIWC dictionary, their results show that defaulting borrowers write similarly to extroverts, who tend to be liars.[25]

These results again show the power of words in providing managers with a novel and powerful tool for understanding how consumers behave and will behave in the future. Words could indeed suggest people's psychological states, traits and opinions. Indeed, when loan applications are written, as Netzer and his colleagues cleverly state, they sweat, albeit virtually.

So, what do these results imply for managers and policymakers?

First, according to the above study, how one writes a loan application predicts how one will behave financially in the future. As lenders have to work with a lot of uncertainty in being able to detect if someone is going to pay back or not, it would be a helpful venture for lenders to collect textual information from prospective borrowers, text-mine such content and use various textual predictors in their credit scoring models. Also, understanding the textual behaviour of the partner(s) of the person seeking the loan could be useful. The members of the household make decisions together rather than independently.[26]

Second, lenders have little facility to meet potential borrowers in person nowadays. Text mining the borrower's content in online settings can allow lenders to understand the behavioural signals one might have employed in in-person settings. Meeting in person may lead a prospective borrower to be on her best behaviour and 'talk the talk'. It would be difficult, if not impossible, to record such in-person conversations. However, online settings allow lenders to get some naturalistic data, such as using function words like pronouns. These function words are not premeditatively used, and writers usually don't even know they used such words.[27] These words can enable lenders to get an idea about the psychological traits of potential borrowers in their natural state.

Third, lenders can use text mining in 'thin file' situations with little financial history of potential borrowers. If the eventual goal is to enable people who have difficulty getting credit because of their short credit history to obtain credit, this seems like a wonderful endeavour.

Fourth, the textual and social network data that I discussed earlier are known as alternative data. Alternative data is any consumer information not traditionally used by the three leading credit rating agencies when calculating a credit score.[28] Though the idea of using such data seems noteworthy, there are substantial ramifications on social inequality, unfair targeting and discrimination that can emerge from using such personal information. This data can be used as a tool for lenders to discriminate among borrowers. It would be worthwhile for policymakers to ensure lenders do not use such data in a fashion that harms consumer welfare.

12

How to Become Sherlock Holmes Online

What do you think of the review below, in which a customer left her opinion of a hotel in Chicago on Yelp? Do you think it's helpful? Will it change your attitude about this particular hotel? Will it persuade you to stay in this hotel?

> *What an awesome place to stay. The staff is amazing and so friendly. The perks, such as free bike rental, are nice. The history (and restoration) of the building is really cool. Thanks for making my stay so memorable.*

Will you be persuaded to like this hotel? The reviewer has given a few details here about how the staff is so amazing, how one can get nice perks such as free bike rentals, and also added some perspective about the building and its history.

Well, I will not keep you waiting any more. The review above is fake.[1]

Yes, FAKE. And as you can see, it is pretty hard to know if this review is fake.

Fake reviews have infested the online world. From March to September 2020, online fake reviewers detection firm Fakespot assessed 720 million Amazon reviews and found about 42 per cent to be unreliable.[2] Yes, over 302 million reviews in seven months! If we focus on Amazon alone, 61 per cent of electronics reviews posted there are fake, as are 64 per cent of the reviews for supplements.[3]

How would consumers react if they knew some online reviews, that matter so much to consumers and influence their attitudes and behaviours, are fake? According to recent statistics, 82 per cent of adults in America check reviews.[4] It is estimated that online reviews increase conversion rates (i.e., for consumers who purchase an item) by as much as 270 per cent. For lower-priced products, conversion rates increase by 190 per cent, while for higher-priced products, conversion rates increase by 380 per cent.

No wonder there is an incentive for many sellers to increase their conversion rates by posting fake reviews. Firms intending to increase their conversion rates often pay some consumers to write positive reviews for their brand while writing depressing and negative reviews for their rivals.

There are nefarious companies that make money by posting fake reviews, and then there are monitoring companies that try to detect the possibility of fake reviews. On Google itself, if I type 'fake reviews', I get a mind-boggling 3,850,000,000 results with an array of websites spanning from articles about this issue to websites dedicated to finding fake reviews such as fakespot.com and reviewmeta.com. There are numerous articles such as '7 Easy Steps to Spot Fake Reviews', 'How to Spot a Fake Review on Amazon', and on and on. As you can see, this is a big issue.

How do you identify fake reviews? It is not an easy question. As you saw from the review at the beginning of the chapter about the hotel in Chicago, the review looks legit. The review was judged as fake as per Yelp's fake review detection algorithm developed by Yelp's engineers.[5]

What would Sherlock Holmes do? All of us know about this master of detecting deception. We all have read Sir Arthur Conan Doyle's masterful works or seen him on television enacted by various actors such as Benedict Cumberbatch, Jeremy Brett and Jonny Lee Miller. His obsessive, analytical and observant traits enable him to find a needle in a haystack or decipher an unsolvable murder. Perhaps Sherlock Holmes would start by looking at the characteristics of these reviews. Can linguistic nuances and traits enable him to figure out fake reviews? How could he use text mining to detect fake reviews?

All right, put on your Sherlock Holmes hat and let's begin a journey to understand the linguistic characteristics of fake reviews online.

Let's first play a game where I ask you to figure out whether the statements below are true or false. Each correct answer will get you ten points. After you've read this chapter, you can tally up your score. The maximum score is eighty points.

- Fake reviews contain less future-oriented language.
- Fake reviews contain references to third person like she, he, they, etc.
- Fake reviews do not contain too many quotes and quotations.
- Fake reviews contain words that denote power.
- Fake reviews contain emotionally exaggerated language.
- Fake reviews contain no exclamation marks.
- Fake reviews contain work-related content.
- Fake reviews contain exact details about the location of the experience.

I hope you can figure out some of the above. Detecting deception has been long studied in academia.[6] Most of this research has examined verbal and non-verbal cues such as speech patterns, posture, body language, eye contact, facial expressions, gestures, etc., to identify deception.

How many times do you think people lie every day? On average, we tell a big lie once or twice every day.[7] What do we lie about?[8] We lie most frequently about our feelings, preferences, achievements or failures, and opinions. We lie less about our plans, actions and whereabouts.

We all want to know if someone is telling the truth. It affects our relationships and trustworthiness and saves us from falling prey to deceivers. Does anyone remember the Tinder Swindler? People have been researching how to detect lies or deception for centuries.[9]

Let's first define lying or deception. It is an intentional attempt to deceive others. Note, children may behave differently from adults when lying; everything I am talking about here pertains to adults.

Researchers have categorized four factors that can be used as signals to detect deception during in-person settings.[10] Note that the signals within these factors are indicative. It is hard to be fully sure if someone is lying even after a lot of research on detecting lies.

One factor is arousal. Some ways we can figure out if someone is lying rather than speaking the truth are increased dilation of the pupils, more blinking, more disturbed speaking patterns and a higher pitch.

The second factor is feelings. Liars say more negative things, appear tense, don't maintain eye contact, provide fewer details, fidget more than usual, rub or scratch more and sound more unpleasant because of guilt and fear.

The third factor is cognitive. As it is cognitively more challenging to tell a lie, liars respond slower, pause more, hesitate, say more generic and irrelevant things, and use their hands less to illustrate what they are saying.

Finally, the fourth factor relates to the control of verbal and non-verbal behaviours. Liars are less spontaneous than truth-tellers, perhaps because they make up stories. Also, because they attempt to control their behaviours, their responses are short. They hesitate, sound high-pitched, look tense and overall seem inhibited.

Though we all need to know if someone is faking, lie detection is an important part of the work of police officers and crime investigators. We all know about the polygraph and how it detects lies by examining if there are any changes in someone's physiological characteristics, like a person's pulse and breathing rates. But police officers and crime investigators also get trained to spot verbal and non-verbal signals encompassing the four factors above. Their training helps them to put a murderer where he belongs or not misidentify an innocent person as a culprit. How do you think these investigators fare in detecting lies? Well, not great. Even with all the training, knowledge and experience, lie detection is still hard for police officers and crime investigators.[11] Research shows that experts such as polygraphers, police officers, psychiatrists and lawyers don't have superior skills in detecting lies and are more or less the same as normal folks like businesspeople and students. It seems only the United States Secret Service is well-equipped to detect lies. Well, the Secret Service does not interview suspects who are being questioned for stealing someone's wallet.

You would think if you knew someone long enough, you could detect a lie. In fact, being in a long-term relationship does not guarantee one's ability to detect lies. No wonder infidelity is the most important reason for divorce across the world.[12] Also, culture can affect how we can detect lies. People find it hard to detect lies if someone is from a different culture than their own.[13]

It is now clear that during in-person settings, even with verbal and non-verbal cues, it is hard to pinpoint a lie. In fact, it has been consistently shown that one's ability to detect lies is no more accurate than flipping a coin.[14]

How about online settings? There are no non-verbal cues in online settings, and you don't hear how someone speaks. Humans are likely to be less accurate in identifying deception with visible cues than audible ones.[15] Thus, detecting deception in an online context is even more challenging and cumbersome. However, even with various constraints, there has been a spate of scholarship to figure out deception in online settings.

In an interesting study, Eric Anderson from the Kellogg School of Management and Duncan Simester at Massachusetts Institute of Technology came across product reviews at a prominent private label apparel company, whereby they struck upon a puzzling conundrum.[16] The authors found that customers who had no record of ever purchasing the item from the company wrote about 5 per cent of the product reviews. Who were these folks? Why were these customers writing reviews when they did not even buy the product?

The products the company sells are essentially all private-label products, which are not sold by other retailers. Moreover, the products are only sold through the company's retail channels, which include a few stores, catalogues and Internet channels. One important aspect of the company, which helped the authors' analyses, is that the company could match customers in its retail stores with customers from its catalogue and Internet channels using sophisticated matching algorithms. This allowed the company to have identifying information about its customers across different channels. The authors analysed the data at the household level so that even if a husband and wife bought different items, the purchase was recorded at the household level. Note that all of their findings, which I explain below, cannot be attributed to purchases by other customers in the household as their analyses took this issue into account.

On the company's website, users submitted product reviews that included a product rating scale from 1 to 5 (highest rating) and almost all reviews included textual comments. Something that helped the authors in their attempt to characterize the reviews is that registered users can only submit online reviews on the website. These registered users can post a review for any item, whether or not they have purchased it. As I have mentioned, fake online reviews are common, and firms often manipulate innocent readers and harm competitors. For example, a restaurant can easily benefit by deceptively posting positive online reviews for itself and negative reviews for a competitor.

Anderson and Simester began their study by examining 3,25,869 reviews on the website. They first examined 5 per cent of these reviews where there was no record of the customer having purchased the item. These reviews were clearly fake.

What were the characteristics of these fake reviews? Anderson and Simester turned to data analysis and text mining of the reviews to find out.

First, looking at the star ratings, Anderson and Simester found that reviews without a confirmed transaction had twice as many reviews with a 1-star rating (10.7 per cent) compared to reviews with a genuine transaction (5.3 per cent). So, using the star ratings as a measure, fake reviews tend to be negative.

Let's get into the text mining part.

Because apparel purchasers talk about the fit and feel of their item, Anderson and Simester chose to compare the usage of *fit* and *feel* words in the reviews without a confirmed transaction against the rest of the reviews. To do this, they used a dictionary-based approach and created a dictionary of words related to 'fit and feel' to do this. See Table 12.1 below for the list of 'fit' and 'feel' words.

The 'fit' words	The 'feel' words
tight	soft
loose	cosy
small	snug
big	heavy
long	light
narrow	weight
fit	smooth
fitting	stiff
blister	warm
	coarse
	felt
	feels
	comfort
	comfy
	flimsy
	they feel
	it feels
	the feel
	sturdy

Table 12.1: Dictionary of Feel and Fit Words

What did the authors find?

Anderson and Simester found that reviews with no confirmed transactions had fewer words related to the *fit* or *feel* of the products compared to reviews with confirmed transactions. It's probably because these reviewers never wore the garment!

Next, Anderson and Simester examined the linguistic cues among the reviews.

The authors again created a dictionary of words to identify reviews in their whole dataset where the reviewers who claimed to have purchased the product, in fact, did not. Their dictionary included the following words: 'bought', 'buy', 'purchase', 'order', 'gave', 'I got myself', 'I have been looking', 'searching', 'I waited', 'I read', 'we got' and 'sold'. With these reviews indicating that the poster made a purchase, Anderson and Simester investigated whether these reviews had some known and proven linguistic indicators of online deception.

What are they?

One of the strongest indicators of deception in online settings is using a greater number of words than one would use in a non-deceptive context.[17] A potential explanation for this is the reviewer's need to give more detailed explanations so that the deceptive review seems more convincing.

The second indicator of linguistic deception is the length of the words. Deception is generally hard, complex and cumbersome for the deceiver, and this leads deceivers to use less complex language.[18]

Another feature of deceptive language is when a reviewer does not provide concrete details in a message. In fact, researchers in a study of online reviews for hotels found deceptive reviews talked more about the reviewer's family than the actual hotel.[19] It is possible, of course, that there were some family issues during a hotel stay. We have all been there! But jokes aside, deceptive reviews contained more references to family than the hotel, which should always set alarm bells ringing. Deceptive reviews also have many more exclamation marks (!) than necessary.

When Anderson and Simester analysed their data, they found that compared to reviews with a purchase, reviews without a purchase showed the following three markers:

- higher word count
- more use of words associated with the reviewer's family and personal life
- many more exclamation points than usual.

Let's see a review that the authors flagged as deceptive:

> I have been shopping at here since I was very young. My dad used to take me when we were young to the original store down the hill. I also remember when everything was made in America. I recently bought gloves for my wife that she loves. More recently I bought the same gloves for myself and I can honestly say, 'I am totally disappointed'! I will be returning the gloves. My gloves ARE NOT WATER PROOF!!!! They are not the same the same gloves!!! Too bad.

Indeed, the review above shows the three markers listed as deceptive traits.

Anderson and Simester go on and test a theory in their paper, which I will come to later, but finding deception in reviews is a task that is being continuously investigated.

In a study by Sangkil Moon at the University of North Carolina in Charlotte, Moon-Yong Kim at the Hankuk University of Foreign Studies, and Dawn Iacobucci at Vanderbilt University, the authors laid down several markers helping managers discern fake reviews online.[20]

One big issue in using text mining to unearth fake reviews online is that one cannot truly discern with absolute certainty if a review is bogus. Same as in a face-to-face situation! However, Anderson and Simester got lucky with the data as they could check the registered users and see if they bought anything, but this is not something that is known on online review sites and social media platforms. We do not know if the reviewer actually wrote a real review, even if we might think she might have written a fake review, according to fake-review-detecting algorithms.

Instead of making assumptions about the authenticity of online reviews, Moon and his colleagues first ran a survey using Amazon's Mechanical Turk crowdsourcing platform, asking participants who stayed in hotels in the past to write a real and a fake review under identical conditions. Their main survey to obtain fake and genuine reviews asked survey participants to provide four types of reviews:

1. a real positive review,
2. a real negative review,
3. a fake positive review, and
4. a fake negative review.

The authors ensured that the survey participants provided a real review based on actual experience. Of course, the participants had to conjure up a fake review.

Because Moon and his colleagues knew whether a review was fake or not, they used various dictionaries from LIWC and used a dictionary-based approach to assess the pattern of fakery in reviews. Moon and his colleagues then classified these dictionaries into four categories: emotions, pronouns, cognitive heuristics and time orientation. The authors then used these categories to identify the linguistic characteristics of fake reviews. Probably what Sherlock Holmes would have done!

Let's start with emotions. The analysis showed that fake reviews:

- were emotionally exaggerated
- contained more negative emotion words
- used more exclamation marks. A likely reason for this is that deceivers use exclamation marks to emphasize their yearning to be believed. This syncs with the findings by Anderson and Simester.
- contained words that denote power. One reason for this finding could be that deceivers use words that connote power and superiority to affirm their credibility and authority.

How about pronoun use?

- Fake reviews used more first-person pronouns (e.g., I, me, myself). A reason for this could be the deceiver tries to persuade and show that she has actually experienced the purchase she is describing.
- Fake reviews used fewer third-person pronouns (e.g., he, she, it, they). One possible reason for this is that using third-person pronouns needs greater imagination and is thus cognitively demanding.

How about cognitive heuristics?

- Fake reviews had a lot of quotation marks. A reason for the use of quotation marks is that it eases a deceiver's cognitive effort while also trying to persuade the reader.

- Fake reviews had few spatial details. Spatial details refer to details about the location of the experience. This result could be because deceptive reviewers find it challenging and cognitively demanding to come up with a narrative about the actual location.

- Fake reviews had more details of work-related content. Consider this fake review: 'Our company had a conference, and we were able to have our meetings, and the hotel was conveniently located for several team members who came in from different locations.' A review like this is broad, easy to process cognitively and write, and displays shared interests. However, it's also a review with few details, is imprecise and requires little mental work.

Finally, time orientation. What is time orientation? Time orientation is related to the way the reviewer writes about time and the kinds of tenses they use.

Moon and his colleagues found fake reviews contained more use of present and future tense. One would think if someone had an experience in a hotel, they would use the past tense to describe the experience. But, because writing fake reviews requires a completely made-up narrative, the authors of fake reviews often forget they need to write in the past tense. Because the intention of fake reviews is generally to make a reader purchase a product or use a service in the future, fake reviewers write about the future. For example, a review like, 'I think this restaurant will get a Michelin star soon.'

Voila! You now have quite a few markers to detect fake reviews and are on your way to becoming the Sherlock Holmes of online reviews. It may also be helpful to know who these fake reviewers are.

Indeed, both Anderson and Simester and Moon and his colleagues examined the traits of these fake reviewers. Both these sets of authors had information on individual characteristics. Anderson and Simester found that reviewers without a purchase are:

- younger
- have more children in their homes
- less likely to be married
- less likely to have a graduate degree
- live in less expensive homes
- come from lower household income brackets
- tend to buy items at discounted prices
- write more than twice as many reviews as other users

What about Moon and his colleagues? Moon and his colleagues found that fake reviewers:

- had high trust in social media such as Facebook and X. This is probably because deceivers who trust social media a lot may believe whatever fakery they write in reviews will be believed by consumers as well. Thus, they are taking advantage of the trust consumers have in social media.
- cared less about the quality of a product. This could be because consumers who put quality as an important attribute in their purchases may not want to influence others in their purchasing decisions falsely.
- were users who didn't look for deals. This result could happen as consumers who look for deals don't want to influence others who are looking for a good price and may feel guilty about doing so.

- were users who were not prosocial. This is completely understandable, as users who want to help others would be less inclined to deceive people looking for input on their purchases.
- were generally from individualist cultures rather than collectivist cultures. Individualist cultures focus more on oneself than others, and a sense of competition often motivates people from such cultures.
- were younger. As younger users use and enjoy social media much more than older users, they may have much fewer qualms about posting deceptive reviews.

As you can see, there are many linguistic markers and individual characteristics that can help firms understand the big bad world of fake reviews better. This field is an ongoing study where researchers from various domains are trying to understand fake reviews.

So, what do these results imply for managers?

First, it is essential that firms have text-mining algorithms that can detect fake reviews and differentiate them from real ones. I have provided two studies identifying the textual characteristics of fake reviews. It is a hard task but needs work, and machine learning researchers, computational linguists and psychologists are still figuring out ways to detect lies. For example, how do you find a difference between a 'white lie' and the truth? What are the differences between a high stakes lie and a white lie?

Second, given the current privacy concerns, it may be difficult to use the finer details of a user's personal information to detect if a review is fake or not. Many truthful individuals may have the same traits that Anderson and Simester and Moon and his colleagues mention as associated with fake reviewers. Thus, the best strategy may be to combine different markers of fakery, such as user information and textual characteristics, to detect if a review is fake.

Third, as you might expect, there are many other markers of a review being fake apart from textual markers or knowing individual characteristics. For example, instead of individuals posting such reviews, one can also look at firms that pay individuals to write fake reviews or write fake reviews themselves. In an interesting study,[21] the authors used the difference in the openness of online travel platforms to examine the characteristics of fake reviews. Anyone can write a review on TripAdvisor, but only a consumer who has booked a stay in a hotel using Expedia can post a review of the hotel on Expedia. To find fake reviews, the authors compared reviews that appeared at the same location, hotel and time of a review on both TripAdvisor and Expedia. The reviews on TripAdvisor, which were fake, tend to come from independent hotels with a single unit owner rather than chain hotels, which have multi-unit owners. Moon and his colleagues, in an additional analysis using TripAdvisor data, find that hotels with low star ratings have more fake reviews and hotels with more rooms have more fake reviews, possibly because the monetary gains of fake reviews are higher. One can also use the time dimension as an indicator to find fake reviews. Moon and his colleagues found reviews that come in early are more likely to be fake than later reviews. This is a result that has been found in earlier work on fake reviews as well.[22] Managers can use such firm and time characteristics to identify if a review is fake.

Finally, if we think fake reviews have evil intent, can they also have good intentions? This is Sherlock Holmes at his best and what he would have probably been proud of! After identifying the linguistic traits of fake reviews and the characteristics of the reviewers, Anderson and Simester posed an interesting theory. On the apparel platform that Anderson and Simester studied, there were thousands of apparel firms listed, and there was a much weaker reason to write a review about a competitor's product. Because each of the firms on this platform sells thousands of products and sales are so dispersed across these firms, the likelihood that a negative review for one firm will hurt another is quite low. So, why should anyone write a review for a product they have not purchased?

Would customers who are deeply loyal to the brand, who want to improve the brand, possibly write fake reviews about inferior products that may be detrimental to the brand? Could these be reviewers who are loyal to the brand and acting as 'self-appointed brand managers'? For example, say there is a customer who purchases men's shirts from a brand and suddenly notices the firm is selling clothing for pets. This may prompt a customer who thinks of himself as a self-appointed brand manager to provide a review of the brand. Anderson and Simester found people provided fake reviews mostly for products with relatively smaller sales volumes, newer items, niche and very niche items, younger products and products in newer categories. Indeed, this is consistent with what self-appointed brand managers might do. These consumers are more likely to provide reviews for products and give feedback to the brand when they see new and unexpected products. But what about the possibility that these reviewers may also just want to enhance their social status rather than act as brand managers? There is a subtle difference between the two. Reviewers who want to promote their social status are more likely to advise other customers, whereas reviewers who see themselves as brand managers are more likely to provide feedback to the seller.

Anderson and Simester again turned to text mining to disentangle the two effects and distinguish between reviews that are directed at customers and those directed at the brand. They used a dictionary-based approach and created a dictionary for identifying reviews directed at the brand, which included words like 'please', 'bring back', 'offer more', 'carry more' and 'go back to'. The authors then created another dictionary for identifying reviews directed to other customers including words like 'if you are looking', 'if you need', 'if you want', 'if you like', 'if you order', 'if you own', 'if you buy', 'if you purchase', 'if you wear' and 'if you prefer'. When the authors examined the deceptive reviews, the authors found reviews without a purchase are three times more likely to include content directed at a brand than content directed at the customers. Indeed, even though these reviews were fake, they seemed to have come from a good place. So, sometimes as in this unique case, fake reviews mean good rather than evil. In essence, this study shows the deep and unique insights that text mining can uncover. Firms that sink their teeth into data using text mining can find interesting and important insights that are maybe hard to discern using non-textual data analysis.

I am guessing you have got a gist of what text mining can do to understand fake reviews—both in terms of identification as well as intent.

Now you can claim to your friends that you are a Sherlock Holmes of online deception.

The game is afoot!

By the way, how many points did you get in the task of figuring out the general characteristics of fake reviews?

80, 70, 60?

If you scored less, hope you got some idea of how to spot a fake review online.

If you scored any of the points above, great and congrats, but I hope you are not faking it!

13

#Boycott[Insertyourfirmname]: Shunning Shitstorms on Social Media

#Boycott[Insertyourfirmname]!

If you don't want the firm you manage or work for to have this hashtag attached to it, read on!

No one wants to be embarrassed or disparaged. Especially on social media, where news travels fast and we have little control. We might have some friends and friends of friends who might inadvertently or intentionally see our embarrassment, but for firms that have thousands to millions of followers, not only do such embarrassments hurt their reputation, but also their sales and market share. Thus, such humiliations can have harmful effects on firms.

Typically, firms create social media messages that are of an everyday nature. We see them and we move on. Sometimes, firms come up with interesting, novel and provocative messages that help them attract audience attention. Some of these messages work. They drive virality, buzz, engagement, love, likes, sharing and a million other words marketers have created to describe the much-desired, sought-after and cagey phenomenon known as

179

'social media ROI'. However, sometimes, some of these messages don't work. And by don't work, I mean they really don't. They create what you could call the inverse of all the million words above, which marketers crave.

They create a mess.

Consider the #DeleteUber campaign, for instance. The campaign created a firestorm in January 2017 when Donald Trump, the then US President announced what came to be known as the 'Muslim Travel Ban'. This referred to a series of executive orders from the Trump administration, which prohibited travel and refugee resettlement from predominantly Muslim countries. After the ban was announced, it was met with protests, including one from taxi drivers at the John F. Kennedy (JFK) International Airport in New York City. However, good old Uber continued to operate its services at the JFK airport and put out the following tweet on X: 'Surge pricing has been turned off at #JFK Airport'.[1]

Immediately, users hammered Uber. The hashtag #DeleteUber gained exponential momentum on X and lasted for several days, accompanied by raging emotional tweets. In fact, the campaign hurt Uber's bottom line and reputation. In the paperwork needed to be submitted for filing an IPO, Uber said that 'hundreds of thousands' deleted the Uber app and deactivated the account after the fiasco. The company included the viral movement as a risk factor in its S-1 filing. This crisis is considered one of the factors that led to Uber co-founder Travis Kalanick's resignation as its CEO.[2]

Uber and many other firms routinely go through these 'firestorms'. You might think they are rare and only happen with big firms. No. These kinds of firestorms, in fact, occur on an almost daily basis and even small firms face such crises.[3]

What are 'firestorms', you may ask?

Academically, firestorms are 'the sudden discharge of large quantities of messages containing negative WOM (word of mouth) and complaint behaviour against a person, company, or group in social media networks'.[4]

Let's consider some other firestorms.

On 24 November 2017, McDonald's Corporation accidentally tweeted a message, from its verified handle on X, that read, 'Black Friday ****Need copy and link****'. This unfinished tweet, which was undeniably due to the social media team's gaffe whereby the team perhaps forgot to have their coffee and updated their scheduled tweet into the 'need copy and link' space, attracted a barrage of negative sentiment from social media users. Users on X had a field day with this particular social media fail, with comments such as offering to work for McDonald's social media team, write copy for them and feeling pity for the social media staffer who probably lost their job. The impact of this message lingered as the flow of negative attention kept on arriving till about one week from the day they posted the tweet.[5]

In other words, McDonald's was entrapped in a firestorm. What about its arch-rival? On 8 March 2021, International Women's Day, Burger King posted a tweet that read, 'Women belong in the kitchen'. This tweet triggered a profound negative response on social media. Chelsea Peretti, an actress from *Brooklyn Nine-Nine*, who has about 1.5 million X followers, in response to the Burger King tweet tweeted, 'Burger King belongs in a trashcan'.[6] To mitigate the damage caused by the tweet, Burger King apologized and deleted the original tweet within hours of posting it.

As you can imagine, for a firm that yearns for one of those million words that stand for social media ROI, this is hara-kiri. Though the intent of the tweet may have been well-meaning or triggered by an employee who made a mistake, as all humans do, such tweets have enormous consequences.

Essentially, these actions led the audience to ridicule these firms, and the criticism lasted for days. The difference between firestorms today and similar instances in the past is that, in times past, you would read about misdemeanours in newspapers and magazines, a day or a few days later. Firms could keep such issues at bay since they had the luxury of time. However, today, firestorms are visible to thousands in minutes, spread fast and can be fanned in various ways. A peeved customer can write a song ridiculing a firm, put it up online, have it liked by millions and generate a negative reputation for a firm.

You have probably heard the story when Dave Carroll, a musician, wrote a song called 'United Breaks Guitars' about how United Airlines mishandled his guitar and his situation. The video, at last count, had about 21.5 million views[7] and generated strong negative sentiment towards United Airlines. Here is a funny aside on the 'United Breaks Guitars' case. Once, I was showing the video to my marketing class to explain the speed with which negative news spreads on social media. The class was made up of eighteen- to-twenty-one-year-old undergraduates. After I showed the video, I asked the class, why they thought this video had so many million views. One of the students responded, 'Because every professor shows this video to their class.' The whole class erupted in laughter, including me. Indeed, this video is popular with professors because it clearly demonstrates the power of negative sentiment in social media. The rise of social media has shifted power from firms to consumers.

What characteristics of such firestorms lead users to get angry and perhaps drive them to stop using these firms' products and services?

With the help of three different studies, I will provide a glimpse of why such crises occur and the characteristics of such turmoil. One study will only discuss the content, another the triggers and firestorm attributes, and another will look at the relationship between senders and receivers of such firestorms.

Let's begin with the first study. My co-authors, Sourindra Banerjee at the University of Leeds, Yuting Lin at the University of Sydney and Andreas Eisingerich at Imperial College, wanted to investigate the following question: Can we identify or characterize the ingredients of firestorms? What is in the content of these messages that drives negative sentiment on social media?[8]

We began with a theory of why these messages fail. We proposed that these statements drove negative sentiments on social media on account of the age-old notion of insensitivity. Insensitivity, in general, refers to the sender's attitude towards a receiver without considerable thoughtfulness and not paying adequate attention to understanding the receiver's emotions and feelings.[9]

The opposite of insensitivity—being sensitive—means being wary about the consequences of one's actions on others, caring about the well-being of others and avoiding behaviour that could offend or hurt others. Insensitivity, in contrast, lacks such a caring disposition.[10] Specifically, insensitivity signals that the sender of the message lacks perceptiveness of the feelings of others and attentiveness to caring about the effects a certain message may have and whether it harms or hurts others.

In these current times, firms have almost an obligation and need to respect the sensitivities of their social media users.[11] Brands need to tune and craft their social media messages ensuring they avoid hurting or offending the sensitivities of any group of customers or stakeholders. We argued statements that hurt or offend customers' sensitivities would likely become an Achilles' heel for the culprit.

Using this concept of insensitivity, we then got into the various characteristics of messages that lead to a firestorm. We proposed three elements driving negative sentiment: sloppiness, incongruence and dissonance.

We started with the most basic characteristic that might push users to talk negatively about a brand: sloppiness. I am sure you have seen messages from firms with typos or grammatical errors. And you wonder, *are these folks for real? Such a big and reputed firm and they can't get their spellings right?*

Sloppy messages signal to consumers a firm's lack of care and lack of attentiveness. Such insensitivity and sloppiness might manifest through typos, grammatical errors, wrong web links in messages, etc. When a consumer's expectation of a firm as a professional entity is violated, customers begin to question its capability to deliver on other promises it makes to customers.[12] Sloppy messages may be insulting to consumers, who perceive the firm as lacking sensitivity and perceptiveness of how such unprofessional behaviour may affect people.

Consider the tweet by McDonald's, which I discussed before, 'Black Friday ****Need copy and link****'. It signified complete carelessness on the part of the social media team. In fact, according to our calculations, the market value of McDonald's went down by US$209 million on the day they posted the sloppy tweet.

Besides sloppiness, we argued that incongruent messages could lead users to talk negatively about a firm that made a faux pas. Incongruent messages contradict the positioning of the focal firm in the marketplace and are, in fact, antithetical to the extant tenets of good marketing, namely to post messages that resonate with customers. Incongruent messages confuse consumers and can signal a firm's insensitivity and lack of care for how such confusing and contradictory statements make its audience feel. These days, social media users expect a firm's messages to be congruent with what they perceive the firm to stand for. If a firm is positioning itself as embracing diversity, and then tweets a message that conflicts with this positioning, the message would be an example of an incongruent message.

Finally, we looked at a characteristic that is more macro—being dissonant with the norms, values and mood of the times.

Firms need to word messages carefully to capture their audience's current zeitgeist and mood, addressing their potential audience's sensitivities. An apposite article by Manuel Castells[13] argues that social media has paved the way for individualism to emerge as the dominant culture of many societies on the one hand, and the formation of social groups through communication technologies on the other. Neil Alperstein, in his wonderful book, *Celebrity and Mediated Social Connections*, points out that social media has not only become a place for information exchange but also social movements and competing forms of culture, ideology and knowledge.[14] For example, movements like #MeToo and its ideas were generated and communicated via sites like X. Consequently, firms are now strictly held against social media users' current social acceptability standards. In her *Harvard Business Review* article entitled 'The Era of Antisocial Social Media', Sara Wilson proposes that any firm that transgresses the zeitgeist of the audience is in danger of hurting or upsetting the sensitivities of the audience and antagonizing them.

So, how do we measure these characteristics? Instead of using text-mining methods such as natural language processing (NLP) or a dictionary-based approach, we relied on human coding. Human coders classified the extent to which the content of the message exhibited specific characteristics that our hypotheses focused on (i.e., sloppiness, incongruence and dissonance) because automated coding systems were not available for these variables.

We measured a message's level of sloppiness, incongruence and dissonance using a seven-point scale, ranging from 1 to 7 (low to high). We focused on X as our source to analyse firestorm messages. Thus, tweets with content that were extremely sloppy in their exposition, exceedingly dissonant and completely incongruent with the brand's image got scores in the higher ranges of the scale.

In our first study, our goal was to examine if these tweets indeed generated negative sentiment on social media. Specifically, we used the tweet by McDonald's, 'Black Friday ****Need copy and link****'. Within a few hours, this tweet attracted a barrage of replies with negative sentiment on X, such as:

- 'I saw this and thought of you. #caring—Not so fast! Here are 6 things to check before you push Tweet'
- 'As a PR minor, this made me cringe'
- 'What do you think guys, abuse or neglect of the template . . .? LOL'
- 'Now that's an informative tweet!'
- 'Bernie #Sanders is Delusional. What will a $15 Minimum Wage Do for America? More Job Losses! McDonalds is installing Kiosks to replace workers due to the high cost of labour. Bernie's Policies Don't Work in America.'

Our goal was to calculate the negative sentiments generated by this tweet, from any user mentioning McDonald's in their content before and after McDonald's posted the tweet. To calculate the dependent variable, the negative sentiment of users, we used an array of machine-learning techniques and estimated eleven different machine-learning models (such as random forest, gradient boosting, etc.) following the formal and time-tested procedures for training, validation and prediction. Because we used eleven models and these models may have predicted differently, we used a voting scheme among the estimated machine-learning algorithms to determine if the tweet was negative. For example, say we have three models instead of eleven. Model A might predict a user tweet as positive, Model B might predict the same user tweet as negative, and Model C might predict the same user tweet as positive. We would categorize the tweet as positive as two out of three models assessed the tweet in the same manner. A substantial benefit of using a voting scheme is that it effectively reduces false positives. The final classification was based on achieving a simple majority vote among the eleven classifiers.

A random forest model is a machine-learning model that divides a dataset into decision trees and takes the majority voting across the decision trees for the final classification. The idea is that although a single tree may provide an inaccurate prediction, taking the collective decision will likely lead to a more correct prediction. Gradient boosting takes a dataset and creates a decision tree one at a time. It takes wrongly classified samples from a prior decision tree and corrects errors from the previous one in the next decision tree. In essence, each subsequent tree improves upon the earlier ones and learns from the previous tree's mistakes. The final classification is based on weighting each decision tree's performance in the classification. In essence, it aggregates weak models to create an overall strong model.

The dependent variable we finally used was the ratio of negative sentiment to the sum of all tweets. We called it a Negative Sentiment Ratio or NSR.

Because comparing the NSR for McDonald's before and after the tweet may not be enough to infer causality (e.g., followers may have got angry at McDonald's at the same time for some other reason apart from the tweet), we compared the NSR of McDonald's' with a group of brands that are like McDonald's, during the same timeframe. The other firms served as the control group, with McDonald's as the treatment firm. In economics, this method is known as a Differences-in-Difference specification.[15] We analysed the data around the ninety-seven-hour window of the McDonald's tweet at the one-hour level to determine if it led to a more significant increase in NSR for McDonald's compared to its closest rivals. What did we find?

We found that after McDonald's posted the tweet, there was a significant rise in the NSR of McDonald's compared to the other brands. We also found the firestorm tweet increased the NSR of McDonald's immediately, and the effect died down finally around the thirty-sixth hour. One and a half days of social media mayhem for McDonald's.

We next compiled a dataset of tweets that were exemplars of the phenomena of firestorms. We identified these tweets by manually sourcing a range of well-known and established marketing agency websites, which consisted of keywords such as 'social media fails', 'mishandled responses', 'misguided campaigns' and 'offensive campaign', resulting in forty-eight tweets by firms from several industries over the nine years between 2010 and 2019.

As in our first study using just McDonald's, we figured out the closest rival for each of these firms and examined if such tweets generated negative sentiment by collecting user tweets on

X that mentioned the posting firm and its corresponding rival for a window of fifteen days around the day the firm sent the tweet (i.e., seven days before, event day and seven days after each specific tweet).

As explained earlier, we content-coded the three characteristics—sloppiness, incongruence and dissonance for each of the forty-eight tweets. What did we find?

When we examined the effect of the three content characteristics, we found incongruent tweets significantly increased the NSR of the firm that posted a firestorm of messages. Similarly, dissonant tweets significantly increased a post's NSR. Dissonant messages had the most damaging effect on a firm's sentiment on social media, with the impact of dissonant messages proving 1.5 times more than the effect of incongruent messages on a firm's NSR. Sloppy messages did not increase NSR.

Overall, we found that incongruent and dissonant tweets have tremendous repercussions for firms. A firm's carelessness in creating a message that is incongruent with the brand's image and its inability to sync with society's current norms and values (i.e., dissonance) all drive negative sentiment.

Okay, so, we know the content characteristics of firestorms that can drive negative sentiment for firms on social media. What about triggers and characteristics? What aspects of firestorms can hurt firms? In a wonderful study on seventy-eight firestorms in Germany, Nele Hansen and her colleagues at the University of Muenster investigated this question.[16]

Hansen and her colleagues theorized that firestorms create havoc for firms using the Elaboration Likelihood Model (ELM) lens. This model is one of the most well-known models in psychology developed by professors Richard E. Petty and John Cacioppo.[17] The ELM model seeks to explain how we process stimuli and how the attitudes we develop from this process influence our behaviour. When we encounter a persuasive message, we process the message with either a low or high degree of elaboration. That is, we either overlook the message without too much deep thought, or we deeply think about it. In order to process the information, this level of elaboration depends on our motivation, ability and opportunity (MOA). If the MOA is high, we engage in central route processing, which is high elaboration, and if the MOA is low, we engage in peripheral route processing, which is low elaboration.

Hansen and her colleagues argued a firestorm motivates us to develop a negative attitude towards the firm because the issues pertaining to the firestorm hit close to home and have high personal relevance to the audience. Using the ELM, the authors looked at firestorm characteristics that have a short-term impact (through the peripheral route) and a long-term impact (through the central route). Then the authors derived factors influencing how consumers process and remember firestorm information based on a consumer's MOA.

So, what characteristics did Hansen and her colleagues examine?

They examined characteristics observed at the beginning of such a crisis, which they termed 'trigger characteristics' and characteristics that evolve during such a crisis.

First, let's see what the trigger characteristics are:

They began by looking at performance versus value-related firestorms. For example, in 2009 and 2010, Toyota drivers weren't able to stop their vehicles. This was a Toyota acceleration issue and it was performance-related. On the other hand, the Uber example I provided above is a value-related issue. They further broke down value-related firestorms on social issues such as poor working conditions for a firm and communication problems due to offensive communications from a company.

Next, they looked at the vividness of these firestorms. For example, someone can just post a tweet, a photo or a video. Indeed, we find videos to be the most vivid as they are dynamic, engaging and have life in them.

Hansen and her co-authors argued that performance and social failures would have a stronger effect on consumer perceptions of the brand and a consumer's ability to recall the memory of it. This is because performance issues might affect a user directly while a social issue might affect others the user cares less about. Communication failures don't have a strong reaction from users because they are the least harmful to users. For vividness, the authors postulated that the more vivid a firestorm was, the stronger its effect on consumer's perceptions and memory. So, videos will have the most impact.

Let's next see what the firestorm characteristics are:

Hansen and her colleagues looked at the strength of the firestorm, which is determined by the number of times people mentioned it on social media. If a firestorm has a lot of mentions, there must be something seriously wrong. Next, the authors looked at the length of the firestorm, which is the number of days the firestorm lasted. Some firestorms were short and disappeared within hours, while others lasted for some days. Finally, the authors looked at the breadth of the firestorm, which is the amount of coverage the firestorm received from media outlets apart from social media.

So, how did they collect the data? The authors wanted to look at the short-term and long-term impacts of these firestorms. So, they used a widely used brand perception dataset from YouGov, which provided information on each of these brands for the following perception dimensions: brand quality, brand value, brand satisfaction, brand recommendation, brand identification and overall impression. For the long-term impact, they ran a survey on 997 consumers after two years for each of the firestorms in their data. The authors asked survey participants if they remembered the firestorm and if they could correctly identify it.

Let's look at the text mining used in the study.

They used human coding or assessment to identify if a firestorm was a product, social or communication failure.

To create the strength measure, the authors used the 'Top Tweets' on the first day of the firestorm. This step allowed the authors to generate words related to the firestorm topic.

Some of these words related to the firestorm-related hashtags and other terms described the critical incident that started the firestorm. Then the authors created a dictionary of words related to 'shitstorm' in Germany, which is how they were referred to there, and then whenever someone mentioned a brand name, they accumulated these tweets to develop the strength measure. Hansen and her colleagues ensured they counted all these tweets from the first time they appeared to their last occurrence.

So, what did the authors find?

Product or service failures, compared to communication failures, harmed short-term brand perceptions and people remembered these firestorms. On the other hand, social failures compared to communication failures did not hurt brand perceptions and people forgot about those social issues. Vividness negatively impacted brand perceptions but not long-term memory. A firestorm's strength negatively impacted brand perceptions and increased recall of the event two years later. The authors found no significant impact of length or breadth on the two outcome measures.

Then they created an illustrative ranking of what characteristics of firestorms lead to damage towards short-term brand perceptions and an increase in long-term memory (see Table 13.1 below). You can see from the table that if a firestorm is because of a product or service failure, then someone posted the issue with a video, and if it had a high volume of tweets related to the incident, it would have the most damaging effects on firms.

Until now, I have only talked about the content and characteristics of these firestorms. However, we are missing something. We haven't considered the people who post these tweets and the people who respond to these tweets. What about these interpersonal characteristics that can drive support for firestorms? They surely deserve to be examined, and this is what Dennis Herhausen of KEDGE Business School in France, along with his co-authors, examined.[18]

Herhausen and his co-authors examined every occurrence of these firestorms on Facebook. The authors downloaded every message from the official Facebook brand communities of each US firm listed on the S&P 500 between 1 October 2011 and 31 January 2016. Next, they looked at each of these communities and saw what made a firestorm go viral in them. In essence, they examined how relationships between community members influence a member's support for a firestorm.

Imagine you are a community member of a brand called 'Inspire Brands' that sells coffee makers. Someone in your community named Jenny posts a message about how the new coffee maker she bought is not working properly. The issue is that the flow of water into the coffee maker is too slow. What would you do? Would you like or comment on her post? What could be the reason for you to like or comment and show support?

	Short-term brand perceptions			Long-term brand perceptions	
	Strength	Vividness	Reason	Strength	Reason
1.	High	Video	Product or service failure	High	Product or service failure
2.	High	Picture	Product or service failure	High	Social failure
3.	Medium	Video	Product or service failure	High	Communication failure
4.	High	Video	Social failure	Medium	Product or service failure
5.	High	Only text	Product or service failure	Medium	Social failure

Table 13. 1: Ranking of Most Harmful Firestorms

Herhausen and his colleagues argued that you would respond and show support for a message like this for the following reasons. First, the message contains high-arousal emotions rather than low-arousal emotions. Jenny, in fact, might be angry or sad, but your support differs depending on the level of arousal in her message. She might write, 'I am so angry at this', or 'I am so very disappointed with this'. Most users are not in a deep and thoughtful mood in these online communities. We don't get into the details and mostly use heuristic processing. So, if someone uses high-arousal words, users tend to support these messages because they become aroused. People who are more expressive tend to transmit their emotions more powerfully.[19]

Second, if Jenny has a strong tie with you and the other members of the community, you will support her. If Jenny strongly connects with many members, she could be an influencer or opinion leader. We tend to listen to someone who is well-connected. They measured this variable by the frequency of communication between the poster (in our case, Jenny) and the other members of the community.

Third, if Jenny writes a message in sync with the way the community communicates, the users will side with her. This is because linguistic similarity creates a psychological bond between people, which induces us to perceive we are similar. This leads to more trust and approval.[20]

Herhausen and his colleagues examined 4,72,995 negative customer posts across eighty-nine online brand communities on Facebook to see if these characteristics drove more support for these posts.

Let's get into the text mining the authors pursued.

The first question is: How do you identify a firestorm? The authors collected every message from the communities. These were positive, negative and neutral. The authors only looked at negative messages in these communities to identify firestorms. How did they determine whether a message was negative?

In the first step, the authors used the Linguistic Inquiry and Word Count (LIWC) software to calculate the positive and negative emotion words in the messages. However, just using LIWC can be problematic and despite its widespread use, it has some issues. What if a sentence read: 'This is not good!'? The LIWC would provide just the count of emotions; so, this message would be categorized as positive. The LIWC does not consider the negation 'not' before it. Thus, the authors used the Stanford Sentence and Grammatical Dependency Parser[21] to divide a message into sentences and find which emotion words were associated with negations. To do this, the authors looked at sets of two words called bigrams. The parser they used finds an emotion word first and then reverses the emotion if there is a negative word next to it. So, negated negative words translated to positive emotions and negated positive words translated to negative emotions. Overall, if a message had more negative feeling than positive emotions, they classified the message as negative.

The authors used the negative emotion words in LIWC software to measure high and low arousal words. The LIWC has dictionaries for three negative emotion words. Two are high-arousal: anger and anxiety, and one is low-arousal, sadness. Because the authors saw a lot of the posts also had 'disgust', they created a dictionary for the emotion of disgust, which is also a high-arousal emotion. Next, they created the percentage of high-arousal and low-arousal words in each message.

To measure linguistic similarity, the researchers used function words. They saw how much correspondence existed between the linguistic style of the person posting the message and the linguistic style of the community. I shall explain the measure of linguistic similarity in detail in the chapter called 'How to Talk to Your Date'. In effect, the authors used dictionary-based approaches for their analysis.

So, they have the measure of the outcome variable, which is the sum of likes and comments, and the predictors, which are high-arousal words, connectedness and linguistic similarity. What did their analysis show?

The authors found that both high- and low-arousal messages drive community support, but the influence of high-arousal messages is a tad higher. They also found that connectedness and linguistic similarity drove support for a firestorm. The influence of connectedness was, however, the strongest.

In essence, the authors showed that the relationship between senders and receivers matters too for causing firestorms.

What do these findings imply for managers?

First, firms should ensure they shun messages that are incongruent with the firm's stance. Consider the Delta Airlines tweet sent on 14 June 2014, 'Congrats team #USA! Nice goal @ clint_dempsey @soundersfc! #USAvGHA #USMNT #DeltaSEA pic.twitter.com/7C8iRzPzoa'. The picture with this tweet showed the Statue of Liberty, representing the US, and a giraffe representing Ghana. Social media users interpreted this tweet as arrogant and racist and went against what the brand means to its social media users. Delta positions itself as a mission-driven brand and an airline carrier whereby it commits to be a force for positive local and global change. After they posted the tweet, there was an increase in negative sentiment about Delta on social media, and the tweet harmed Delta as it lost about US$120 million, which was about 0.4 per cent of its stock market value on that day.

Second, messages that are dissonant with society's contemporary values and norms should be avoided. Firms that send out discordant messages are seen as out of touch with their audience. The findings in the first study here encourage firms to better understand the underlying spirit of a time (what consumers are worried about, what they desire, fear, aspire for, hope, etc.). With the help of social media trends, data and consumption habits and patterns, firms can gauge the zeitgeist of the times they are operating in.

Third, product or service issues seem to have the most damaging impact on consumer perceptions and long-term memory. Firms should classify the various firestorm triggers, prioritize product or service issues compared to social and communication failures, and come up with remedial actions.

Fourth, if there are a lot of tweets related to a firestorm, firms should not just lie in wait but should take the developing firestorm seriously. As I have mentioned, news in social media travels fast and the faster and more strategic a response, the better the consequences for the firm facing the crisis.

Fifth, messages from more connected individuals in a community can strongly influence the spread of a firestorm. Thus, firms need to measure the connectedness of individuals in their communities and take proper and robust steps to curb the spread if well-connected individuals post related messages.

Sixth, firms can use text-mining tools to check firestorm messages that are linguistically in sync with a community's linguistic style. Such firestorms can spread faster.

Finally, high-arousal messages spread more than low-arousal messages. Again, text mining can come to the rescue. Firms can divide messages by their arousal levels and be able to gauge which messages can go viral. After identification, firms can focus more on high-arousal messages than on low-arousal ones.

Call it whatever, firestorms or shitstorms are the new omnipresent danger firms face nowadays. It would be neglectful for managers to disregard the characteristics of these storms.

It is wiser to be aware and prepared before the shit hits the fan.

IV

MONEY AND MARKETS

What do the following have in common?

Plutus, Juno Moneta, Kubera.

They are gods or goddesses of wealth of myth. Plutus, the ancient Greek god of wealth, Juno Moneta, the ancient Roman goddess of wealth, and Kubera, the Hindu god of wealth.

In fact, the word 'money' comes from Juno Moneta's name. Since ancient times, wealth has been desired, and humans have prayed to supreme beings to bestow them with wealth in its various flavours. These gods were supreme beings who deemed wealth not only as material wealth but also wealth as a spiritually good life. One arena where wealth in its monetary form is the singular concern is the stock market where firms raise money by selling their shares to investors.

In this section, I will take you through how language, the size of it, and the distortion of it can influence stock markets. We will discuss how a few characters on social media influence stock prices, Donald Trump's tweets and their link with the US stock market, the sizeable benefits of a computer file in the financial world, and if noise has financial information.

14

When Bytes Matter More than Words

Let's start with a test. Don't become apoplectic. Bear with me, please.

What do these words mean?

Ectomorphic, funambulism, nudiustertian, honorificabilitud initatibus, floccinaucinihilipilification?

Any guesses?

How many did you get right?

3/5 or 4/5 or 0/5?

3/5?

Okay.

4/5?

Good.

0/5?

Even better!

Well, unless you're trying to win the Scripps National Spelling Bee or time travel to the 1700s when a group of wealthy British elites wasted time creating long words in the English language, you have no reason to know these words. All the above, including the word 'apoplectic', are complex words with a simple meaning.[1]

Let's see what they mean.

A confession. When I first read these words, I only knew the meaning of one of them. Yes, all my GRE verbal power has vanished. It has been years since I took the test. However, I wonder if the Educational Testing Service (ETS) too knows that these words are quite meaningless. Let's start with 'ectomorphic'. It means skinny. 'Funambulism' means a show of mental quickness. Literally, it means the art of tightrope walking. By the way, *funis* means 'rope' and *ambulare* means 'to walk' in Latin. 'Nudiustertian' means relating to two days ago or the day before yesterday. 'Honorificabilitudinitatibus' means being able to receive awards. It is the longest word in the English language, comprising alternating consonants and vowels. Two of the greatest writers have used this word—William Shakespeare in *Love's Labour's Lost* and James Joyce in *Ulysses*. Unless you believe you are an incarnation of one of these two, I would be quite wary of using them in a sentence. What about floccinaucinihilipilification? Created by British elites in jest, this word means an abstract sense of uselessness. It is, in fact, pretty useless to know this word. The word itself conveys what it is. The magic of language! How about apoplectic? The word I used before this list. It means angry.

Someone using such words is actually making things complex and impairing our understanding. Unless we have a dictionary with us (maybe there are people reading this whose vocabulary is much richer than mine), we will spend time and resources to find out what these words imply. In this world, which is already quite complex, simplicity is a virtue. I don't have to quote Albert Einstein or Richard Feynman to drill this down for you. We appreciate simplicity. We admire those teachers, professors and speakers who have the finesse to convey something complex in the most straightforward manner.

Using complex words in a sentence makes things foggy for us to understand.

If you want someone to understand you, you wouldn't use a word like 'tenebrous' in a sentence; you would use 'dark'. What about firms? Firms are answerable to their employees, customers, shareholders and the government.

Would they try to make things unclear? And do they derive any benefit from making things complex?

Before we get into these questions, let's first see how content can become unclear and if there is a way to measure unclearness!

Consider using a word for experiencing a feeling of positivity, satisfaction or enjoyment. I can think of the word 'happy'. If I want to show how smart I am (or think I am) and that my GRE or GMAT verbal score is above par, I could use the word 'jocund'. Happy and jocund are synonyms.

In the same manner, I could write the following sentence, 'Leo Messi is a great footballer and probably the best ever in the game's history,' or I could write it as 'Leo Messi is a splendorous soccerist and mayhap the epitome of excellence in the history of the game'.

Which of the two sentences above is clearer? It is obvious to us, but can we measure it?

There are measures. One popular and widely used measure is the Gunning Fog Index. The Gunning Fog Index score for my former sentence is 13.86, while it is 16.4^2 for the latter. The Gunning Fog Index is a test for readability in the English language, developed in 1952 by Robert Gunning, an American textbook publisher. As Gunning was keen on understanding what makes a book become a bestseller, he observed that most high-school graduates did not have competent reading skills. He was even cleverer to observe that much of this reading problem was, in fact, a writing problem.

His opinion was that newspapers and business documents were filled with 'fog' and pointless complexity. Wonder what he would have thought of those English elites!

Gunning took this issue to heart and became an ardent advocate of readability research. In 1944, he founded the first consulting firm specializing in readability. He later worked with over sixty prominent daily newspapers and popular magazines, helping writers improve their writing. In 1952, to make his point and spread it far and wide, he published a book, *The Technique of Clear Writing*, which included the widely used Gunning Fog Index. The main idea of the Gunning Fog Index formula is that short sentences written in plain English are more readable than long sentences written in complicated language. The Gunning Fog Index formula goes like this:

$$0.4 \left[\left(\frac{\text{words}}{\text{sentences}} \right) + 100 \left(\frac{\text{complex words}}{\text{words}} \right) \right]$$

The Gunning Fog Index gives a lower score or index for short sentences written in plain English (therefore more readable) than longer sentences written in complex language (less readable).

Let's go back to my two sentences above about Lionel Messi. A Gunning Fog Index score of 13.86 is appropriate for an audience between a college sophomore and a freshman. In contrast, the score of 16.4 is intended for audiences between college graduates and college seniors. In other words, the first sentence can be most likely understood by a student entering college, while the second sentence can be understood by someone on their way out into the world, outside university. So, if I want this book to be read by a broad audience, I will need a fog index of less than 12.

If I want this book to be the game-changer in moving middle schoolers away from TikTok and whatnot, I will need an index of less than 8.

Back to my question on whether firms try to make their content unclear.

Indeed, they do and strategically.

Let me give you some examples from business—accounting and finance, in particular.

Firms can try to make their content hard to read to hide the fact they are doing badly. In a seminal study that triggered a wave of research on the readability of financial documents, Feng Li from the University of Michigan found that the annual reports of firms with lower earnings have a higher Fog index (i.e., are harder to read) while firms with annual reports that are easier to read have more persistent positive earnings.[3]

Firms intentionally try to make things unclear so stakeholders such as investors can't decipher their problems.[4] Why would managers do this? Well, firms always want investors to see them positively, making investors optimistic about a firm's prospects. If a firm is not doing so well, managers of such firms intentionally use complex language to distract and confuse investors. Firms use these vile strategies in financial distress and when they want to transmit a garbled message.

In other studies, readability measures have revealed that firms using accounting techniques to enhance financial reports, present less readable annual reports.[5] Firms using more complex language in their annual reports are less efficient in their investments.[6] Complicated firm reports are less readable because they lower trading activity, primarily due to the reduced trading activity of small investors.[7] Perhaps, the intention of these firms is to reduce small investor activity and increase large investor activity. Small investors are like normal people. Indeed, they will find complex documents hard to read.

The readability of a financial document is a strategic instrument that firms can use.

Can you think of any other example where you might see firms strategically making things harder to read?

What about warranties?

In the US, despite the Magnuson-Moss Warranty Act,[8] a federal law enacted in July 1975, which aims to improve the clarity and accuracy of information in consumer warranties, warranties on many products and services are still virtually unreadable.[9] In a study, albeit one which is old, the authors state, 'All warranties (sic) examined in this study clearly would not be easy to read or understand by 50 per cent of the American adult population unable to read at an eighth-grade level.' Perhaps some firms don't want to be bothered by their customers. Perhaps their philosophy might be, 'buy, goodbye'. This is suicide in modern-day business.

As you can see, firms are strategic in providing information. They use various strategies to hide information in certain documents for their benefit. The Fog Index is one of the most used methods to measure such fogginess in business documents.

Is the Fog Index perfect? No. I will address its problems later in this chapter. However, the Fog Index is straightforward. But is there an alternative to measure fogginess? An even simpler measure? Less complex, unlike the complex words one might use to make things unclear.

Let's start with this simple idea of how letters aggregate to form a document or an online file.

Letters make up words. Words make up sentences. Sentences make up paragraphs. Paragraphs make up a chapter. Chapters make up a book. As we progress in creating a document with all the necessary figures, tables, references, footnotes and whatnot, in the online realm, an online file also increases in size, measured by the byte.

The size of a file can also correspond to a document that uses more complex words and sentences and, therefore, paragraphs, and so on that are difficult for a reader to understand.[10]

Two finance professors who are experts in linguistics, Tim Loughran and Bill McDonald at the University of Notre Dame, argued that the size of an online file is a better proxy for readability than the Fog Index. Since the authors are deeply interested in how computational linguistics affects financial outcomes, they hoped to show that the 10-K document file size provided by firms offers a simple readability proxy that outperforms the Fog Index. The file size can better gauge how effectively managers can transfer valuation-relevant information of a company to investors and analysts.

How did Loughran and McDonald go about their venture? They started by collecting many 10-K reports from various firms over the years. The US Securities and Exchange Commission (SEC) requires public companies in the US to provide comprehensive financial statements that seek to inform investors of a company's financial condition. The 10-K is an all-inclusive report filed annually by a publicly traded company about its financial performance. The SEC requires every company in the US to submit it. Compared to a company's annual report, a 10-K contains much more detail, including its history, organizational structure, financial statements, earnings per share, subsidiaries, executive compensation and any other relevant data.[11]

Using a series of tests, Loughran and McDonald first wanted to provide evidence that the Fog Index is not a proper measure of readability in financial documents.

The Fog Index has two components. Loughran and McDonald argued that measuring the first component, 'average words per sentence', is a reasonable measure of readability. However, they argued that the second component, 'complex words', is inadequate for measuring readability in business documents such as the 10-K. As we know, an increase in the number of complex words (e.g., more than two syllables) decreases readability using the Fog Index calculation. In fact, this component accounts for half of the Fog Index's inputs.

Loughran and McDonald claimed that business content frequently comprises multisyllabic words used to refer to a firm's operations. For example, consider words like *corporation*, *company*, *agreement*, *management*, *operations* and *telecommunications*. You will see such words frequently in documents submitted by an array of firms. These words will be the leading complex (as per the Fog Index) words in 10-Ks. Consider an investor, Jackie. Will she get deterred from reading a document packed with these words? No. These words will not deter Jackie from continuing to read the 10-K, nor will they make her consult a dictionary to understand what these words mean. In fact, Loughran and McDonald found that 52 complex words out of over 45,000 complex words that appear in their 10-K sample account for over 25 per cent of the complex word count. Notably, almost all of these words were simple business terms.

Overall, the authors argued that complex words add measurement error. Furthermore, they found that the Fog Index had little predictive power when it came to explaining both unexpected earnings for a company and analyst dispersion, which measures uncertainties about a company.

After identifying the Fog Index as an inappropriate measure for readability, Loughran and McDonald developed an ingenious, effortless, and yet potent measure for readability: using the file size of the 10-K complete submission text file as a readability measure. The authors found file size aligned well with their measures of the information environment. The file size was also strongly correlated with other measures of readability.

What advantages does the file size of the 10-K have over a measure like the Fog Index?

First, a 10-K file size is as easy as ABC to determine. Second, the measure is not prone to measurement errors, such as the Fog Index. Third, one does not have to collect the text and run text-mining algorithms, which other measures like the Fog Index require. Fourth, it promotes replication.

Loughran and McDonald argued that if firms were trying to obscure information relevant to investors, they were more likely to bury the results in longer documents than use polysyllabic words or complex writing. Moreover, the legal risks of failing to provide complete information would encourage managers to provide it, whether or not it was useful. They, however, contended that a large file size could be an artefact of a firm's structural complexity, and though they ran some tests to unknot the two, firm complexity and file size may be related.

An average 10-K contained over 38,000 words.[12] That was a lot of words, along with hundreds of pages that investors and analysts need to read through. This information-gathering was necessary for investors to find out whether a firm was a good bet. The longer and more tedious a 10-K, the higher the file size. From 1994 to 2011, Loughran and McDonald conducted a string of tests using all 10-K documents available on the SEC's website for an eighteen-year period. After controlling for other factors such as firm size, book-to-market, past volatility, industry effects and prior stock performance, they found that larger 10-Ks were significantly associated with high return volatility, earnings forecast errors and earnings forecast dispersion. In effect, we see that a simple measure is more powerful than a somewhat complex measure.

So, what do these results imply for managers and investors?

First, investors need to be aware of the various strategies firms might resort to when providing public information. In important and consequential documents such as the 10-K and 10-Q, which are read by eager and uncertain investors, there is evidence that firms can be manipulative. Here is a quote by the guru of investing himself, Warren Edward Buffett, in his preface to the SEC's 'Plain English Handbook':[13]

> For more than forty years, I've studied the documents that public companies file. Too often, I've been unable to decipher just what is being said or, worse yet, had to conclude that nothing was being said.

Maybe we simply don't have the technical knowledge to grasp what the writer wishes to convey. Or perhaps the writer doesn't understand what he or she is talking about. It may even be that a less-than-scrupulous issuer doesn't want us to understand a topic it feels legally obligated to address. If the guru himself found it difficult to understand what firms mean, God help us!

Second, investors and analysts should be wary of using an index like the Fog Index, which does not consider the context. The SEC has even deliberated on using such indices for measuring readability in financial documents. However, as you saw in the study I explained, the Fog Index has problems such as context independence.

Third, investors and analysts can use the file size as a proxy for the complexity and perhaps unreadability of a document instead of readability indices. Loughran and McDonald recommend using the 'complete submission text file' available on the Securities and Exchange Commission's Electronic Data Gathering, Analysis, and Retrieval (EDGAR) website. Investors and analysts can readily see the file sizes and interpret them accordingly.

Fourth, and more general, is that simple measures are powerful and perhaps sufficient to capture a phenomenon. Managers need to be conscious of this. I will spend some time on this idea in the chapter below.

There are many simple measures or constructs that can answer a business problem firms are facing. Complexity is exciting but requires time, skill, money and adequate motivation. I can give you some other examples when a simple measure, even though not that sophisticated, is used more than a complex measure and may be enough for your goal.

One example is a measure that calculates customer satisfaction. Though there are many critics of the Net Promoter Score (NPS) for measuring customer satisfaction, including me, it is the most widely used metric. Why, you may ask.

Before that, a quick definition of the NPS. The NPS is a survey tool measuring customer satisfaction and assesses if customers like your firm enough to tell their friends about it. It comprises a straightforward question: 'How likely are you to recommend (Firm X) to a friend or colleague?'

Customers are asked to provide a rating from 0 to 10 on a 10-point scale. Customers who give a score from 0 to 6 are called detractors, 7 and 8 are called passives, and 9 and 10 are called promoters. The higher the difference between promoters and detractors, the better it is.

Why is it so popular? The first and perhaps most important reason is that it is simple. You don't require machine-learning experts to analyse this data. Second, you can send it via an online poll or post it on your website. Customers can finish answering the question in a jiffy. Third, because of its simplicity, which led to its wide use, you can benchmark your company against your rivals and your industry, as other firms use it too. Finally, NPS has been proven to affect firm performance.[14]

Here is another example of a simple measure. How do you estimate poverty?

In many policy situations, policymakers need to understand poverty levels in order to implement effective measures such as aid and programmes to alleviate it. However, getting poverty statistics is hard and takes an enormous amount of time. How do you estimate poverty in a country? You run a census, which is very cumbersome and expensive. No wonder that in India, the census is a once-in-a-decade affair! In the case of Angola, forty-four years passed between two of their censuses.[15] But despite the enormous preparation time, there are many instances where data from surveys, which ask for income levels are unreliable or missing. Is there a simpler way to measure poverty?

Researchers came up with a clever and simple way to measure poverty by analysing phone call details. These call details included records of calls, text messages, purchases, usage of mobile money and other user data.[16] The researchers estimated the poverty levels of people in Rwanda and Afghanistan using only two months of call detail records. Their measure realized the similar accuracy of a census at much lower costs. When I was a student and had little money to buy a full phone plan, I would make missed calls to my parents and friends so that they would call me back. Missed phone calls can indicate low income.

Another example.

How do you measure customer preferences and their valuation for product features of cameras, laptops, computers and cars? For example, the features of cars include reliability, design, eco-friendliness, fuel economy and many others. One widely used method to figure this out is called conjoint analysis. Conjoint analysis is a survey that allows firms to understand how customers value a product's or service's various features or attributes. Despite the advantages of this technique, it is complex to design, the analysis is intricate and requires complicated statistics, and it needs ample resources to acquire customers for the survey. A straightforward way to measure people's preferences is by looking at what people search for. We all use web searches, be it Google or Bing or Opera. Why not just look at what people are searching for and get a handle on their preferences?[17]

Where can you get such search data? Google Trends. Google Trends analyses the popularity of search queries across time in Google Search across various regions and languages. If I want to understand consumers' valuation of certain car features from 2004 till now, I can use Google Trends. Below is a graph from Google Trends (see Figure 14.1), which shows the search in the US for three attributes of cars. The diagram clearly indicates that 'fuel economy' became very important for users during 2008 when the recession happened in the US. And by the way, Google Trends is free. I am not saying you should not do a conjoint analysis, but if you are low on resources and time, this measure is a useful alternative. Perhaps you can also complement your sophisticated analysis with this measure.

Another use of Google Trends has been to measure investor attention. How do you do this?

Instead of running costly and time-consuming surveys, which may get biased and unclear responses from investors, why not use searches for tickers?[18] Tickers are the symbols that firms use when they are listed on a stock exchange. For example, AAPL is the

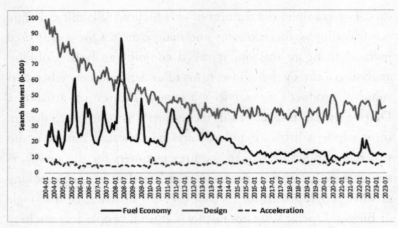

Figure 14.1: Interest for Car Attributes in Google (2014 to July 2023)

ticker for Apple. Unless you are a terrible speller, you will never search for a term like AAPL. But if you are an investor, you surely will. This simple investor attention measure has been shown to affect many stock market metrics.

Overall, simple measures, though not sexy and sophisticated, can sometimes be a wiser and nifty choice.

As they say, KISS (keep it simple, stupid).

15

Can Noise Be Information?
A 'Sound Story' about Financial Markets

Words convey meaning to a listener. One person talking to another most often does.

However, when many people talk, this meaning is turned inside out and becomes gibberish. A confused noise made by several voices. This noise is incomprehensible to anyone trying to understand what is being said.

Taking a very scientific perspective, noise is unwanted sound. Sound is a mechanical, longitudinal wave, which requires a medium. Noise, too, is a longitudinal mechanical wave that requires a medium. But it is something much more specific. Just like something obstructing a clear image, noise is anything that interferes with the intended sound.[1] Scientifically, there is no difference between noise and sound. Both are vibrations travelling through air or water.[2] The difference arises when we bring in what the brain wants when the brain receives and perceives the sound.[3]

Most of us don't want unwanted sounds. Sounds that are noise. A car honking or someone working on a construction site or the mixture of a lot of voices. These sounds are made up of irregular waveforms, which constitute a random distribution of the two fundamental constituents of sound—the frequency (how fast the waveform is vibrating per second) and amplitude (the size of the waveform).

This is noise—that we dislike.

Are there times when we enjoy noise? In Latin, noise means nausea. It's hard to think of noise as something we would enjoy, but are there times when we do enjoy noise?

Indeed, sometimes we crave noise.

White noise, anyone? The constant hum! In many cases, white noise can help people who get distracted easily to focus or sleep better. In contrast to the randomness of a shouting voice or inconsistent guitar playing, white noise is a consistent and reliable form of noise.[4]

In audio engineering, there is a range of these coloured noises, each with its own properties. These different noises have different colourful names. Sound and colour have a relation here. Noise, whatever its hue, refers to the sound of various random frequencies.

Many of us are familiar with white noise. White noise is recommended in many settings. You can buy white noise machines to fall asleep. Have you ever woken up because your dog suddenly barks in the middle of the night, or because your partner snores away to glory? We wake up at night not because of the noise itself but because of the change in noise. White noise blocks this noise and allows our brains to benefit from a more consistent sound environment. White noise is spread broadly from low to high frequency across the sound spectrum. It resembles the sound of TV static or a rushing waterfall.[5]

We then have pink noise, which is noise but with reduced frequencies. Pink noise is louder at the low frequency and softer at the high end. And it is flatter, as it does not have many low and high frequencies. It resembles the sound of light to medium rainfall. It is often considered more soothing than white noise, which some folks find displeasing. Pink noise has benefits too. It helps in deep sleep and can be beneficial for the consolidation of our memories.[6]

Finally, we have brown noise. It lowers the frequency even more. This type of noise is stronger and deeper at the low end of the frequency but without the high-frequency sounds that one hears in white and pink noise. The bass is boosted in brown noise. An example of brown noise is hard surf that comes with a storm or thunder. Brown noise has many benefits. In fact, there is a tag in TikTok called #brownnoise, which as of today has 147.7 million views.[7] The hashtag represents how brown noise has been helpful for people in managing stress, anxiety and attention-deficit/hyperactivity disorder (ADHD). One TikTok user named @natalyabubb shared a post that got about 9 million views, 1.1 million likes and 26,000 comments, which said, 'It makes my brain feel soft in the best way possible', and 'It's like driving with the window down'.[8]

All these colourful noises are useful for sleeping and managing stress. They are consistent and constant.

We see cases here when noise can be helpful.

But what about loud noises?

If you are about 82 feet away from a jet's takeoff, the noise level would be 150 decibels in terms of its amplitude, or sound intensity.[9]

If we don't wear outdoor noise barriers in this situation, our eardrums will rupture. Well, no one in their right mind would like such a loud noise. Other unpleasant, noisy apparatuses such as riveting machines, which join materials together, make a noise that reaches 110 decibels.

However, there is a group of people who don't mind these loud noises and, in fact, like them.

These people attend events, which make sounds of around 108 to 114 decibels.* Any guesses who these people are?

Metalheads.

Metalheads are fans of musical genres such as noise metal or other genres of metal such as thrash metal or industrial metal. Some metal bands intentionally make their songs noisy, loud and chaotic. And then there is the genre of noise metal bands or noise-influenced metal bands that use noise in making music.

Indeed, as metalheads intend to listen to such loud music, perhaps these folks don't see it as noise.

However, music in these genres is noise to people who don't subscribe to it. In my younger years, I listened to many bands, from Anthrax to Megadeth to Nine Inch Nails. My parents hated me for it. They must have thought, *what is wrong with our son?* Moreover, the way the folks in these bands looked, they must have sincerely prayed that I didn't become one of them. Their dreams of their son becoming the proverbial doctor or an engineer would vanish.

Why do metalheads like such loud music? And can it have any benefits whatsoever?

Music genres affect us in various ways. Some listen to pop music because it is catchy, makes our blood pump and emotions race. It relaxes listeners and even affects our brains. For example, our beta brainwaves are emphasized when we listen to pop music. It makes listeners feel like dancing and singing, and we pay attention. Our brains are connected via millions of neurons that communicate

---

* The highest recorded decibel level in a metal concert is 139 decibels by the American heavy metal band Manowar back in 1984 in Hanover, Germany.

through signals. This communication occurs through fibres called axons; where these axons connect, we call them synaptic joints. These signals are called brainwaves.[10] If we categorize the brainwaves in humans depending on their frequencies, there are five types: Delta brainwaves (below 4 Hz), Theta brainwaves (4–7 Hz), Alpha brainwaves (8–13 Hz), Beta brainwaves (13–38 Hz), and Gamma brainwaves (above 38 Hz).[11] Alpha brainwaves are related to meditation and beta brainwaves to attention. While pop music activates the beta brainwaves, listening to classical music, on the other hand, activates our alpha brainwaves. We feel calm and meditative.[12] Music thus affects our brains and our moods.

Does metal music help metalheads with their mood?

Indeed, two studies show that listening to metal helps control one's anger. Fans who were made to feel angry and then listened to heavy metal music did not become angrier. In fact, the music increased their positive emotions and these fans even felt inspired.[13] This is probably because of their capacity to better handle their emotions due to the music they listen to. The music perhaps helped them to explore the full range of emotions they felt, which made them feel more active and inspired.

Another study found that after cheesy hits from the 1980s, heavy metal was another genre that lowered blood pressure and heart rate.[14] The study's leader speculated that perhaps listening to heavy metal made these listeners process their feelings better. On the other hand, cheesy pop music from the 1980s might have induced feelings of nostalgia and warmth. I will try listening to Bette Midler's 'Wind Beneath My Wings' or Culture Club's 'Karma Chameleon' the next time I feel a bit stressed.

Is metal music good for computer coding?

A study by a motley group comprising a writer, data scientist and programmer found that 3.2 per cent of software developers of an estimated 26 million worldwide[15] listed some type of metal music as their main music choice when coding. The coders knew more genres of metal than even the study's authors, who themselves were metal listeners. Coders preferred metal music because when they heard clean singing, their attention would move towards the lyrics. On the other hand, with 'vokills' (vocalization in black or death metal where the voice is virtually unrecognizable and unintelligible), it is just background noise.

In effect, we see that heavy metal music, which is loud and noisy, can be helpful too.

Okay, we see that noise benefits sleep, controlling anger and even coding.

However, can displeasing noise be helpful in a business context? Can noise provide information for traders in a stock market, for example? Traders who seek to pinpoint accurate information, playing with precision using numbers and graphs, don't want ambivalence, as they live most of the time with uncertainty.

Could noise be informative for traders?

Finance professors Joshua Coval from Harvard Business School and Tyler Shumway from Brigham Young University marvellously examined this question in their article in a premier academic journal.[16]

First, when is there noise in a stock market context?

Not in a mosh pit, of course, which is a playground for metalheads. But in a trading pit, the playground for traders. A trading pit is an area in a stock exchange that is earmarked for trading securities. In the trading pit, brokers buy and sell various securities using a system called open outcry, which I shall explain later in this chapter. Traders match the customers' orders by shouting and through hand signals.[17]

As you might sense, the phrase 'open outcry' does not bring to mind a beautiful visualization of blue waves hitting the shores by a serene mountain. In fact, it literally means yelling, screaming and shouting at the top of one's voice along with gesticulations and whatnot, to convey information about buy and sell orders pertaining to security (e.g., equity stocks, bonds).

The noise emerging from the open outcry in a trading pit, a financial Tower of Babel, is what Coval and Shumway claim has information and can, in fact, be useful. Coval and Shumway argue that the ambient noise level in a trading pit conveys economically meaningful information and can even forecast important financial metrics.

Let us take a backseat and look at why Coval and Shumway are looking for information that can be useful for them to forecast financial metrics.

For ease of exposition, I will use securities for a firm in the stock market as the financial instrument and use equity stocks, which most people have heard about, including hopefully even the less financially inclined.

Say you are an investor interested in Apple, which goes by the ticker AAPL on the NASDAQ, the stock exchange where one can buy and sell Apple stocks. Investors interested in Apple will constantly look for information from Apple, the press, social media and any other sources that give them an upper hand.

Investors are perennially looking for new and valuable information. For example, information on X could be one source, such as the volume of tweets and consumer sentiment about Apple. Bloomberg continuously monitors tweets and alerts its customers if many people are suddenly sending tweets about a company such as Apple. Could the noise on a trading floor be information that investors could use?

To examine this, Coval and Shumway focused on two goals.

The first goal was to predict financial metrics such as price volatility, market liquidity decline and increased information asymmetry using the information content of the ambient noise level in the Chicago Board of Trade's thirty-year Treasury Bond futures trading pit. Second, they wanted to show that face-to-face interaction still matters in a world where everything is measured in bits and bytes.

In recent times, only a few exchanges persist with face-to-face trading, that is, floor trading using open outcry. Exchanges from the Bombay Stock Exchange to the Johannesburg Stock Exchange have switched to electronic trading.[18] Coval and Shumway argue that the exchange sound level, also known in trader jargon as the 'buzz' of the exchange, has valuable information that electronic exchanges cannot capture.

Let's see how this 'buzz' could be informative and go beyond the information in electronic exchanges. Indeed, there could be information that is often transmitted across an open outcry pit but cannot be easily communicated over electronic exchanges. Signals conveying information regarding the participants' emotions on the trading floor, such as fear, excitement, uncertainty, eagerness, etc., are difficult to communicate via a computer.

Frequently, traders resort to yelling, shouting, waving, jumping up and down, and so forth. In electronic markets, if two traders submit market orders of the same price, the trader who submits first is given priority. On the other hand, in open outcry settings, priority is not always perfectly observed, and traders go by the order they first notice based on how loudly a trader yells among other actions to fill an order. Note that this jumping up and down requires energy, both physical and mental, by the trader. Thus, there is a likelihood that such frenetic activity will only occur when a trader is eager to execute a trade.

Indeed, traders monitor what is happening on the trading floor. In a study published in the premier journal *Nature*, when the authors interviewed professional traders, a former trader quipped, 'On a trade floor, you live in a carefully calibrated sound field. Overall, there was a buzz from each area on the floor. If you heard some noise from FX, you quickly checked that sector.' Another floor broker in New York said, 'There are lots of times when you can kind of feel the buzz on market moves (. . .) Most of the time, floor is slow so you definitely focus more when you feel it hopping.'[19] Coval and Shumway argue that the 'buzz' proxies the degree of trader anxiety on the exchange floor. The frenetic activity surely means something.

Increased sound levels can foreshadow an array of market condition changes, making traders fearful and weak at their knees. Traders might be anxious for various reasons, making them more vocal and frantic. For example, the costs of trading could rise, or the costs of holding on to their current positions are high or higher or when they have too much inventory and want to flatten it by reducing the price.

Coval and Shumway hypothesize that increased sound level increases future price volatility (traders expect price changes and thus more noise to move their orders), reduces future market depth (traders anticipate the market to be less liquid and thus more noise to move their orders), and high information asymmetry (traders anticipate they will have less information about the market and thus more noise to move their orders).

So, how did Coval and Shumway collect the data?

They wanted to capture the noise.

The authors first collected second-by-second sound-level readings from the Chicago Board of Trade's bond pit for two months during the summer of 1998. To obtain the sound level readings, the authors pointed a microphone directly into the pit. This microphone stood on top of the 20-foot price recorders' tower, which was at the edge of the pit. They then sampled the sound level across 128 different frequencies and collected the timestamp when the sound was recorded.

In conjunction, Coval and Shumway also collected the Treasury bond futures contract's price and trading volume data of the Treasury bond futures contract. The price data was gathered from a dataset called 'time and sales', which has prices that are documented by observers who stand in a price-recorder tower called 'Radio'. These observers continuously monitor and look for signals of executed trades and instantly document whenever a trade occurs at a new price. After ensuring many checks that the data was valid and as precise as possible (remember the trades happen within seconds), they ran their analysis on 10,75,447 seconds of data.

To measure the level of sound, Coval and Shumway then took the sum of the log (base 10) of each frequency's level. By the way, this is the standard metric of sound level in the sound engineering field.

Let's venture into what ambient sound looks like on a trading pit. In this case, the Chicago Board of Trade's trading pit. See the figure below.

The figure above gives us some interesting information.

First, if you observe deeply, there is high intra-day or within-day seasonality. That is, the sound level experiences regular and predictable changes that recur every day. Second, the average sound level reveals a U-shaped intraday shape. The sound level

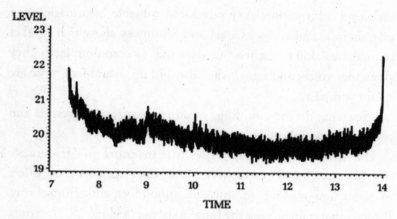

Figure 15.1 Daily noise patterns on a trading day[20]

seems to rise at the open and close of the trading day compared to the middle of the day.

After the initial rise, the sound level recedes over the next hour and steadies after 8 a.m.

Then, just before the close, when the warning bell is rung, signalling the last minute for trading, the sound level spikes and remains there until the close at 2 p.m. You also observe spurts of jumps at 7.30 a.m., 9 a.m., and 10 a.m. These are the times when Treasury news is generally announced. Overall, just by looking at how sound behaves on an average day, we can observe that there seems to be a correspondence between noise and the financial market.

So, there is correspondence, but can such noise be predictive?

Using different regression methods for various outcome variables and the deseasonalized (removing the effect of days and hours) sound measure as their predictor, Coval and Shumway found that sound levels forecast price volatility, depth of market and customer orders.

Ambient noise of the gibberish sort can indeed be useful. As I mentioned and wrote before, investors are like hunters searching for novel information. Any novel and valuable information can give them a slight edge. Coval and Shumway show that market participants don't just rely on data that is commonplace. They show that voices and signals that also add up to ambient noise are useful compasses.

So, what do these findings mean for managers, investors and even common folks?

First, the study clearly shows that investors and traders are not just looking at easily observable data such as past prices of securities, trading volumes or announcements from firms. Professional traders 'seek the buzz' to better 'feel risk'.[21] The study shows that subtle and intricate communication, such as sounds and gestures, can also be predictive of financial data.

In fact, noise combined with our visual perceptions can also help traders get a better sense of the risk of an asset. Recent research on multisensory perception has found that what we hear can influence our perception of financial risk.[22]

The presence of ambient sound makes our visual perception of extreme risk sharper. Risk assessment is crucial in financial decision-making, as traders must constantly decide under uncertainty.

How can such a sense of danger help? On trading floors, when times are turbulent and there is high volatility in asset prices, ambient noise and graphs are shown on screens. On the other hand, when there is low volatility, there is less noise, and the frenetic activity on the floor ebbs. This provides traders with an opportunity to make use of the ambient noise in their trading strategies. Noise can be your enemy or friend depending on the type of trader you are, as the *Nature* article authors argue.

Consider a trader, Susan, who uses a market timing or momentum strategy for trading. She must know any changes in the market, so her auditory radar must be fully operational in order to detect any shift to a high volatility period. However, she can be out of her zone when the extreme volatility goes away. In her case, it is optimal for her to be exposed to any noise. Consider Jack, a trader who invests using a value-based strategy. Value-based strategies generate profits by trading against investor sentiment. He does not want to be distracted by noise and requires silence to detect when volatility shifts away from high or low volatility periods. This is when he can enter trades that take advantage of the mispricing caused by the change in volatility. Being exposed to noise does not help him in this case.

Second, the study shows that machines cannot replace everything that the human voice and body can convey, which is complex and multidimensional yet subtle and singular. Electronic trading cannot replace the human side of the stock market. Traders must 'feel risk' through sound. Despite advances in electronic trading, many decisions made by human traders are still based on gut instinct. These decisions, which are based on how the trader 'feels risk,' are what ultimately influence trading. Noise matters in determining risk on the trading floor.

Third, frequent noise might be a good thing on many occasions and could be used as a measure or statistic in business contexts. What about noise in concerts, theatres and stadiums? Maybe just measuring the sound levels might be more than capturing very detailed data, which might put off consumers who are keener now than ever to protect their privacy.

Fourth, as we have seen, noise can have benefits for us. Not only us, but it also helps animals stay safe. The presence of noise induces an elevated level of arousal in animals.[23] Noise can be unpleasant and unwanted, but we need to be more aware that it can have some benefits in finance or heavy metal music. Here is one last example of the benefits of noise that may bewilder you.

Here's an example from the aviation industry.[24] You would presume any distraction due to noise might be hazardous for pilots on planes. But noise, in fact, may not be that bad a thing to have in the cockpit. When pilots are in the cockpit, they overhear various exchanges happening between air traffic controllers and other pilots. These exchanges are called party-line information or PLI. This immaterial noise could interfere with the pilot's tasks, such as flying the aircraft soundly. However, many pilots have claimed that this immaterial noise is useful, as it helps them form a mental representation and enables them to maintain an awareness of their surroundings. A state of 'situation awareness'.[25] The irrelevant information helps pilots get a sense of where they are and what their tasks involve.

Noise is noise or information, depending on how we see it.

Keep your eyes and ears open to know when noise can be information that could be valuable.

In some cases, noise can even be economically significant.

16

Is All That Twitters Gold?

Can a few characters influence stock markets?

To be precise, 280 characters.

It may seem that these 280 characters are a small number, trivial almost, and many may think that being on a social network site is wasteful, but could there be information in these seemingly insignificant characters that could move stock markets? My dissertation was focused on using tweets from X and when I told my parents I was working on something called tweets, they were completely clueless.

My parents would have loved for me to be a doctor or engineer or a high-ranking bureaucrat. But here I was, doing a PhD in business administration using machine-learning techniques to understand a newly minted word called 'tweet' and convert that understanding to meaningful information. They didn't at all understand what a PhD in quantitative marketing meant. I can say with absolute certainty my father would have never said something like, 'Our son works on Twitter data' when a band of parents would meet up. These meet-ups were in reality a boasting contest, where parents would extol their children's virtues and

brandish their professional exploits over some duty-free Chivas
Regal whisky, most likely purchased from where else but Dubai.
By the time I joined the PhD programme in 2007, MBA was the
rage in India. The only way I regained their belief in me was by
telling them that I was doing a 'PhD in MBA'. They appeared
somewhat pleased with my answer.

Let's start with what we know about X. X is one of the most
popular social networking sites in the world today and it provides
a cornucopia of digital chatter about almost everything, such as
entertainment, sports, politics, science and brands, among others.
Launched on 15 July 2006, the site has over 396.5 million users[1]
and hosts around half a billion tweets per day.[2] Eighty per cent of
usage on X happens on mobile devices.[3] The mobile nature of X,
along with its short character limit, captures instantaneous feelings
and sentiments. These reactions contain helpful information,
which on occasion, is even better than information from more
traditional sources.

Let's consider something which we generally and naturally
react to.

#Earthquake.

Yes, when the earth shakes and rumbles, we instantaneously
react.

Consider this: the fastest earthquake alerts now come
from X rather than from scientific agencies. Immediately after
an earthquake strikes, users on X flood the site with brief and
spontaneous tweets. For example, the United States Geological
Survey (USGS) uses tweets about earthquakes to identify the
epicentre of an earthquake in less than sixty seconds. Without
these tweets, the USGS would take about two to twenty
minutes to locate an earthquake. The USGS tracks the word
'earthquake' in various languages that enable the scientific team

to accurately locate the source of an earthquake and then judge its characteristics, such as the quake's size. For example, users tweeted at about 10,000 tweets per minute as soon as the massive 2011 Tohoku earthquake in Japan began. Tweets are more helpful in the detection of an earthquake rather than its magnitude. But sometimes, tweets also provide an idea about the magnitude. In April 2014, when an 8.2 magnitude earthquake struck Chile, Chilean tweeters used the word 'teramoto' instead of 'temblor'. Teramoto is used for big quakes and temblor for average quakes.[4]

Indeed, X is now one of the fastest sources of information across any media. Across any domain, X is the first to report the news. For example, the news of Seal Team Six killing Osama bin Laden first broke on X. The Arab Spring uprising was first covered via X. The death of former British Prime Minister Margaret Thatcher was first reported on X. More and more, the first word one gets about a major event comes from X.[5] X has now even become a powerful tool for journalists. It is the go-to social media site for journalists in the US.[6] About 94 per cent of American journalists use a social media site for their jobs and X dominates, with about seven out of ten journalists using it. For example, journalists use X to locate experts as sources, to find eyewitness accounts, and to find tweets, pictures and videos from eyewitnesses using geocoding.

In this 'attention economy'[7] where human attention is a scarce commodity, digital chatter on X now provides a new and rich forum for understanding the mood and behaviour of users. Certainly, such chatter can allow firms to gauge consumer attitude, attachment and advocacy for their products and brands. Moreover, such consumer feedback could be an important source of information on firm performance as it reflects the truth about the firm and involves real chatter laden with emotion. Such consumer feedback could be leading indicators for the firm's future sales, revenue and earnings.

Besides the consumer feedback, could such chatter also be useful for investors looking to make money in the stock market? Could these short tweets that seem trivial because of their pithiness and ephemerality influence something as big and imposing as the stock market?

Among the many researchers who have tried to answer this substantive and important question, one of the first and seminal studies to examine it was a team composed of Johan Bollen at Indiana University, Huina Mao at wissee.com and Xiao-Jun Zeng at the University of Manchester.[8] The authors analysed the text content of daily tweets to examine if tweets could, in fact, influence stock returns.

Why should tweets have an impact on stock returns? X has now become a powerful tool for traders, investors and journalists. Even the Securities and Exchange Commission (SEC) has recognized the value of the information on X. Anecdotal evidence suggests that X is investor relations (IR) professionals' new technology of choice for breaking firm news.[9]

Let's first see why investors should care about those seemingly trivial tweets.

Investors in a company typically seek additional information from sources other than the company. They react to information from journalists,[10] experts[11] and consumers[12]. A primary reason for this information search lies in the information asymmetry that exists between the firm and investors.[13] Though firms attempt to reduce the asymmetry by providing reports, these are sporadic (e.g., press releases) or infrequent (e.g., sales reports). Thus, investors continuously look for any novel information about the firm. Investors could consult media stories, analyst reports or expert reviews. However, the low frequency of such reports (at the most monthly) only whets the appetite of investors. Tweets are available at a high frequency compared to traditional sources. For example, an interested investor can look at the total number of tweets for their brand even at a second or minute level.

Can tweets contain useful information for investors?

Indeed, tweets may possess valuable information for investors for several reasons.

First, on aggregate, tweets are written at a much higher frequency than consumer reviews or forum discussions. Every second, 6000 tweets pass through X's servers.[14] We can attribute this high rate to the number of active users on X. Users' sheer volume of tweets, each with a unique perspective, can provide new information about themselves, firms and the economy.

Second, the simplicity of the user interface, short word limit and the option of tweeting from mobile devices enable users to react and tweet instantaneously. Such conversations may not be available in other online media.

Third, X facilitates the phenomenon of users sharing links to varied content on the Internet (e.g., videos, blog posts, news articles, music streams). These links increase the likelihood that tweets contain useful information.

For these reasons, investors may conclude that information on tweets represents a good source of the 'wisdom of crowds' about the latent quality of the brand or the mood of the economy.[15] Thus, investors may process the number of tweets, retweets and sentiments to infer the brand's quality or status of the economy and use this information for their trading decisions.

Bollen and his colleagues intended to examine if tweets could indeed affect investor decisions. Their main research question was whether the public mood on X could predict how the stock market behaves.

Let's start with their theoretical reasoning. The authors began with the well-known idea that the way we as human beings process our emotions has substantial repercussions on our behaviour and decisions. They went a step ahead and asked if this applies to societies at large and if one can calibrate how a society's mood is at one point in time. If one could measure public mood, could they use this mood to assess if that led to changes in the public's behaviour, such as stock market decisions?

Note that predicting the stock market is challenging.

One of the most important tenets of how stock markets work and prices get set is called the Efficient Market Hypothesis (EMH).[16] It is closely associated with Eugene Fama, Nobel Prize winner and the Robert R. McCormick Distinguished Service Professor of Finance at the University of Chicago Booth School of Business. He is generally regarded as the 'father of modern finance' because of his theoretical and empirical work. According to the EMH, and there are three versions of this hypothesis (strong, semi-strong and weak), stock market prices are principally driven by new information rather than past and present information, such as past and present stock prices. New information could be news about a firm, such as a firm merging with another, appointing a new CEO or a product recall. One new means of information affecting stock prices is the volume of positive or negative sentiment about brands on social media sites. Burgeoning research shows that early indicators of how a firm is perceived, such as if there is more positive sentiment about the firm at one point in time, which we can extract from social media and online sites, can predict changes in several economic and commercial outcomes.[17] Tweets have been used to predict wins and score differences of sports matches, such as soccer matches in the English Premier League.[18] Investors might use dashboards of sentiment information about brands on social media sites to make their decisions. These decisions will manifest in stock prices, and thus sentiment information about brands can predict stock returns for a brand.

Bollen and his colleagues argued that public mood measured on a social media site could also play a role in influencing stock markets. As discussed, humans react based on their moods or emotions. Research in behavioural finance has demonstrated that one's mood and emotions considerably drive many financial decisions. Thus, Bollen and his co-authors put forward the idea that mood states can also be predictive of the stock market apart from information such as news or sentiment in social media.* One may speculate that this public mood captures both the general public's attitude and the mood of traders, and thus, the mood affects stock returns through two processes. The first process is where investors, through their social networks and perhaps dashboards of social media information, infer that the general public may make financial decisions, such as purchasing more goods and services if they say they are in a 'happy' mood. The second process is that traders may be 'happy', which affects their trading behaviour. Note that the first process is still information if we consider the EMH theory. The second process is based on mood rather than information. Bollen and his co-authors are silent on delineating the process by which public mood affects stock markets.

---

* Bollen and his co-authors separate news, sentiment in online media and public mood into three distinct categories. I have combined sentiment in online media with news and called it information, meaning that information is one category and public mood is the other.

So, how did Bollen and his colleagues go about testing their idea?

The authors first needed to measure mood and since X was their focus, they obtained a dataset of about 10 million tweets posted by about 2.7 million users from 28 February to 19 December 2008. Note that this was when X had a limit of 140 characters. X did away with the 140-character limit as this short character limit led many users to spend a lot of time cramming a tweet into 140 characters. X now has 280 characters to make it even easier for us and indeed many things have happened since someone called Elon Musk became the boss of X. But people tweeting in Chinese, Japanese and Korean still use 140 characters,[19] as these languages can convey much more with fewer characters owing to the nature of their script. For example, 'Good morning' is only three characters in Chinese, while in English, it is twelve characters with a space in the middle.

For each tweet in the dataset, Bollen and his colleagues recorded the identifier for the tweet, the time when the tweet was posted, the type of submission and the number of characters in each tweet.

Next, the authors used text-mining techniques to uncover the public's mood.

Let's get into the brass tacks of the data-processing steps that Bollen and his colleagues used.

If one is focused on measuring mood or sentiment in tweets, an analyst removes words that are the most common in any language and add little information. These types of words are called stop-words in text-mining parlance. Examples of stop words include articles, prepositions, conjunctions, etc.

After removing the stop-words, Bollen and his colleagues removed all punctuations in these tweets. They did this to focus on the words and infer the emotions from the tweets. To ensure they took out irrelevant information and spam, they eliminated tweets that had links by matching 'http:' or 'www.' in the tweets. Next, the authors grouped all tweets posted on the same date, allowing them to create a daily measure of the public mood.

Now, let us examine the text-mining method the authors used to measure mood. All the techniques the authors used are dictionary-based approaches.

As the authors were focused on capturing individual emotions, they only took tweets that categorically had a user's mood states. Thus, their analysis only used tweets that had characters like 'i feel', 'i am feeling', 'i'm feeling', 'i don't feel', 'I'm', 'Im', 'I am' and 'makes me'. This is an example of a dictionary-based approach, as the authors used a dictionary of such phrases to cull out emotional tweets.

Then they dived into the two text-mining tools to capture mood. They analysed the text content of daily tweets specifically using two mood tracking tools, namely OpinionFinder (OF) and Google-Profile of Mood States (GPOMS).

OF is a dictionary of positive and negative words.[20] The original Profile of Mood States (POMS) is a psychological rating scale used to assess transitory, distinctive mood states.[21] The GPOMS is an algorithm developed by Google that measures mood. The GPOMS measures mood in six dimensions (Calm, Alert, Sure, Vital, Kind and Happy).

For the OF, Bollen and his colleagues only selected positive and negative words, marking them as either 'weak' or 'strong'. This resulted in 2718 positive and 4912 negative words. After that, for each tweet, they used the OF algorithm to determine whether a tweet contained any positive or negative words and for each match, they increased the score of positive or negative tweets by one. They finally calculated their mood measure by taking the ratio of positive vs negative tweets posted on a given day.

Because the OF only provides mood scores on the positive and negative continuum, Bollen and his colleagues used the GPOMS text-mining tool as it provides scores for six different moods. Indeed, mood may not be just one way or the other but can be multidimensional. The GPOMS tool, as I mentioned above, uses the original POMS mood dimensions and the words that fall under each of the six different moods. The original POMS dictionary has been vetted by a wide range of scholars and is used often. Because X has its own set of norms and usage, Bollen and his colleagues used the GPOMS lexicon. Google expanded the original POMS lexicon to a glossary of 964 associated terms. Bollen and his colleagues then matched the text in a tweet with this enlarged lexicon of 964 terms and mapped them to their respective POMS mood dimensions. This enabled the authors to calculate the six mood states per day.

Now, let's get to the outcome variable. Remember, stock returns!

To analyse the effect of the mood states on stock returns, Bollen and his co-authors extracted the closing prices of the Dow Jones Industrial Average (DJIA) from Yahoo! Finance. The DJIA, Dow Jones or the Dow, is a price-weighted stock market index of the thirty prominent blue-chip companies listed on the New York Stock Exchange (NYSE) and the NASDAQ and is one of the most widely used indices to measure the American economy.

Voila! We have both the measures of public mood and stock returns. Let's see what they found based on their analysis.

The authors first carried out an exploratory analysis in order to examine the validity of their mood indicators. Were these text-mining tools adequately capturing mood? To do this, they examined how their mood indicators matched with events that affect public mood. The two events chosen were the United States presidential election (4 November 2008) and Thanksgiving (27 November 2008).

The authors found that positive sentiment went up after Barack Obama's election on 4 November and Thanksgiving on 27 November. Indeed, the public in the US were in a joyous and happy mood during these days and the mood indicators reflect that. Using the GPOMS mood indicator, one can also see that there is more variance and richness in the mood indicators, which the sentiment measure of OF missed. For example, the authors found that there was pre-election anxiety and energy before 4 November and there was general happiness on election day and Thanksgiving Day. Thus, their measure seemed to correlate well with events that made people happy or anxious.

They next analysed the relationship between GPOMS and OF with the DJIA.

For this analysis, they used a method called Granger Causality.[22] We all know that correlation does not prove causation, but Granger causality analysis tests for temporal causality, i.e., can one variable measured at a prior time be useful in predicting the outcome variable at a later time?

Correlation is not causation. One can find that there is a high positive correlation between ice-cream sales and drownings. But this does not mean that enjoying an ice cream will lead to death. The variable, which is leading to this strong correlation, is the summer season. Causation is when a variable or an event causes another variable or event to occur. Establishing causation is hard and can only be determined from an appropriately designed test. Granger causality or temporal causality uses the assumption that if a variable X causes Y then changes in X will systematically happen before any changes happen in Y. Thus, in a statistical sense, lagged values of X will show a statistically significant correlation with Y.

Based on their analysis, they found that the only metric across both OF and GPOMS that is statistically significant in predicting DJIA is the calm dimension, where changes in the public mood in calmness match shifts in the DJIA values that occur three to four days later. Just using the sentiment of positive and negative words in tweets using the OF was not informative in predicting the DJIA. Frequently, an overall sentiment of positive or negative may not capture relationships between variables, and finer and richer measures may be needed. Indeed, the six mood dimensions enabled the authors to see that public mood can be predictive of stock market returns.

This study shows the incredible power of words in being able to predict an outcome that is very hard to predict—stock price!

The effort by Bollen and his colleagues, in fact, led Capital Markets, a London-based hedge fund to launch a US$40-million hedge fund. The fund used Bollen and his colleagues' ideas to help guide its trading strategy for the FTSE 100, FTSE 250, DJIA indices and oil, gold, other precious metals and currencies.[23]

Following the work of Bollen and his colleagues, there has been a stream of research examining whether information in online reviews (e.g., Amazon), blogs, user forums, user tags (e.g., 'delicious') and a variety of other online content can predict stock returns of firms, and the answer is yes.

Bollen and his colleagues analysed the effect of tweets on the DJIA index, which is a composite index of firms' stock prices. Recent work has also demonstrated the impact of user tweets about firms or a firm's tweets on a firm's stock price. For example, I along with my co-authors have shown that tweets about firms from consumers can affect the firm's stock price at a daily level.[24] New research has investigated that tweets can influence the variance of a firm's stock price even at the sub-second level. Yes, within seconds! About 92 per cent of firms send out messages in the form of tweets multiple times a day. These messages from firms can serve as a valuable source of information for investors.[25] Every tweet with a timestamp can be precisely recorded at the second level and then linked with corresponding trading activity in the stock market. Lacka[26] and her co-authors used about 8 billion trading activities for S&P 500 information technology firms and found that the informative effect of a firm's tweets has an impact that is about 147 times larger than the average trade's impact on a firm's stock price. Yes, 147 times larger! Moreover, the authors found that tweets about rivals, which are negative in nature, have the highest impact on a firm's stock price.

So, tweets from both the public, consumers and firms do impact stock price and those 280 characters do indeed matter!

Tweets from celebrities or politicians are one effect that I have remained silent about until now. Do these well-known people's tweets impact stock prices?

What do you think?

I am sure you have read one of Donald Trump's tweets!

His posting behaviour on X is now, I guess, legendary. From the time he was elected as President of the US in November 2016, he tweeted more than any other high-ranking political official.

Between May 2009 and October 2019, Donald Trump tweeted 40,376 tweets and more than 10,000 of them were during his presidential reign.[27]

Donald Trump used X not only to rally his supporters but also as a forum to extol, condemn and criticize an array of companies. If you are interested in what the erstwhile POTUS had to say on X, you can collect all his tweets from the 'Trump Twitter Archive'. All his tweets have been collated and stored.

Could Trump's tweets have affected the stock markets?

To investigate this, Peder Gjerstad from the Norwegian University of Science and Technology and his co-authors[28] examined all the 8686 tweets sent out by Trump during his presidency, beginning on 22 September 2019 and used minute-by-minute stock price data from the S&P 500 to examine if his tweets influenced the stock market.

Let's look at some characteristics of Donald Trump's tweets.

He generally tweeted during lunchtime and in the evening. Of course, he was the POTUS, and he reserved the morning for presidential matters, I suppose.

Let's see what his tweets talked about in terms of the content. Figure 16.1 provides a list of the top words that Trump used in his tweets. The figure shows that Trump used the word 'great' in over 2000 tweets, followed by 'people' and 'us'. The high frequency of these words perhaps indicates his propensity for being boisterous, narcissistic and grandiose, and his rhetoric to rally his supporters. He also talked about issues related to the trade war with China and used words such as 'products' and 'tariff'. We often saw these words in tweets where he commented on the trade war and wrote about imposing tariffs on certain products.

First, the authors found that irrespective of their content, Trump's tweets had a significant effect on the US stock market.

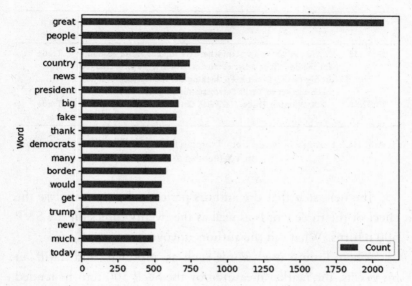

Figure 16.1: Most common words used in Donald Trump's tweets

In the first thirty minutes after his tweet, the market tended to decline. Then, the authors carried out text mining on his tweets to see what kind of content led to negative returns in the stock market.

Gjerstad and his colleagues did two kinds of analysis. The first analysis only used words from the tweets and focused on the word 'great', as it was the most frequently used, and other words such as 'products' and 'tariff' because they relate to the economy. The second analysis involved running a topic model, which enabled the authors to arrive at twenty topics that Trump tweeted about the most. Some topics were: 'Bragging', 'Border Security', 'Illegal Immigrants', 'Trade War', and also a topic called 'TV Shows'. Yes, the POTUS talked about TV shows too.

Some of Trump's tweets on the subject of 'Trade War' are listed below.

Time	Tweet	Main topic
13:44:02	....We can't have a system where we run our entire economy for the benefit of other countries, which have long charged us big tariffs. Don't keep ducking the reality. The U.S. has been subject to Tariff Terrorism for 50 years. (...)	Trade war
13:52:58	"U.S. Winning Trade War With China In Dollars." CNBC	Trade war

Figure 16.2: Example of tweets from Trump referring to the topic of 'Trade War' on 4 September 2019

The next step that the authors performed was to analyse the effect of the three words as well as the twenty topics on the S&P 500 returns. What did the authors uncover?

When Trump used words such as 'products' and 'tariff' in his tweets, the market measured by the S&P 500 returns tended to decline. Indeed, tweets that imply possible restrictions in international trade are often negative news.

On examining the topics, the authors found that the topic 'Trade War' had a large and significant effect on the S&P 500 index. Investors perhaps considered the trade war to be bad news for the economy and became insecure and uncertain. The authors also found that the topic 'Border Security' had a negative and significant impact on the S&P index. Perhaps 'Border Security' was related to cross-border trade issues, and this may have led investors to react negatively. Overall, Donald Trump's tweets increased investor uncertainty and trading volume, and led to a decline in the US stock market. President Trump not only stirred up the public but also the investing community.

What do all of these X-stock price correlation findings mean for businesses and capital market participants?

First, firms should monitor online chatter on X, Facebook and other websites, and include it as part of their marketing research. Indeed, conversations on such sites contain information about a firm's future performance, such as sales and market share. This information is beyond other sources of information and can be a leading indicator of a firm's future performance.

Second, businesses must ensure that they have the adequate text-mining skills to measure different emotions and moods that content on sites such as X can contain.

Third, investors can use the information on social media sites for their trading strategies. As Bollen, his colleagues and several other researchers have found, information on social media, online reviews, blogs, forums, etc. affects stock returns. Using the findings of the Donald Trump study, the authors claim that implementing an 'S&P 500 portfolio with hedging' strategy, that is, holding the S&P 500 index except for the first seventy-five minutes after Donald Trump tweets 'Trade War,' would lead to an annualized return of 21 per cent. In other words, a trader who held the S&P 500 index, sold it immediately after Trump's tweet on the topic of 'Trade War,' and then bought it back seventy-five minutes later would have made a significant and positive return.

Finally, recent work in connecting the information content of intra-day tweets and intra-day returns shows that firms should craft their messages on X or other social media sites more strategically. For example, using the high-frequency trading data from the study by Lacka and her co-authors, tweets that express positive or negative sentiments regarding their rivals or customers can have a permanent price impact on stock prices.

In essence, X and other social media sites are one of the primary ways the public, consumers, firms, celebrities, journalists and politicians interact. In this increasingly open and complex market environment, content on these websites can enable investors to find new information.

All that Twitters is gold because information is the new gold.

V

BOSSES

If you were a student graduating from Stanford University on 12 June 2005, you would have your ears and eyes wide open to see and listen to a man who singlehandedly changed how consumers think about product, design, innovation, technology and branding in the twenty-first century.

Steve Jobs was the commencement speaker on that day. He spoke about life, striving to fulfil our ambitions, and how death can also have a purpose. His words 'Stay Hungry. Stay Foolish' resonated with the audience that day and still speak to many. You can watch the video on the Internet. It has been viewed more than 10 million times on TED.com. However, visionaries like Steve Jobs are rare. Most bosses are mediocre and there are some infamous ones who left their companies, countries and clubs in ruins.

In this set of chapters, we will discuss how one could learn to become a charismatic leader by understanding how Obama and Gandhi made use of language, how bosses can signal a firm's future innovation focus with a few choice words, and answer the question: Is having a narcissistic boss good for business?

17

A Crash Course on Charisma from Barack Obama and Mahatma Gandhi

We often see or meet someone whom we are captivated by, can't resist and who goes into our good books. If you grew up in India like I did, you'd probably understand when I say I was blown away by an actor called Shah Rukh Khan in the 1990s. Even though he wasn't the typical movie star who was tall and muscular, he became the darling of the nation and the new superstar.

When a friend asks us why we find a certain person so appealing, among other superlative adjectives, an adjective we often use is that the person is charismatic. What is it about charisma and why do we get swayed by it?

Shah Rukh Khan exuded charisma. And the whole nation fell for it.

Many of us think that rock stars and actors have charisma. Sure, who can say Elvis Presley, Ranveer Singh, Freddie Mercury, Audrey Hepburn or James Dean didn't have charisma? But there are some politicians and heads of corporations whom we find charismatic too. If you pick up a magazine or go to a website on politics or business, you often read that someone is a charismatic leader, and you would most likely concur. Think Winston Churchill, Martin Luther King, Nelson Mandela, Hillary Clinton and others for politics. For business, think Indra Nooyi, former chairperson and CEO of PepsiCo, Satya Nadella, CEO of Microsoft, Elon Musk, CEO of Tesla Motors and SpaceX or Lido Anthony 'Lee' Iacocca, erstwhile president of Ford and CEO of Chrysler. Lee Iacocca's charisma was legendary. He was apparently so charismatic, he made other CEOs look drab and there was even talk of him running for President of the US.

Charismatic leadership is a quality that is in high demand nowadays. Firms and political parties are always on the lookout for a leader who has charisma. There are hundreds of articles that extol charisma, and how it is vital to leadership. There is ample research linking charismatic leadership to an increase in the effectiveness of organizations and effective leadership. Moreover, charismatic leaders increase follower effort, satisfaction and performance.[1] There is even evidence that the selection of celebrity CEOs, who seem to exude charisma, drives up the market value of a company's stock.[2] Hiring such CEOs positively influences the company's perception of outsiders and enhances the morale of employees and other stakeholders. What could be some reasons for the pull of charismatic leadership?

Some argue that there are just three ways to influence others: force, reason and charm. Force and reason are rational. However, charm is not. Some argue that charismatic leaders influence others with charm rather than reason, and when they run out of charm, they use force.[3] Max Weber, one of the most influential theorists and sociologists in the nineteenth and twentieth centuries, said that rationality and charisma couldn't coexist.

Is charismatic leadership just charm? Or are there other attributes or characteristics that define a charismatic leader? Can we pigeonhole charismatic leadership to be this sole quality?

Before we dive into these questions, let's first look at the history of the word 'charisma'.

The word 'charisma' has an interesting etymology. The English word 'charisma' comes from the Greek word χάρισμα (khárisma). 'Khárisma' in Greek means a 'favour freely given' or 'gift of grace'.[4] The word derives from the Greek χάρις (charis), which means 'grace' or 'charm'. In antiquity, Greeks used charisma as a term for their gods, attributing notions of charm, beauty, nature, human creativity or fertility to goddesses they called Charites (Χάριτες).[5]

The word is now rarely used in both the divine sense and the personality sense. However, the term retains a certain sense of aura and myth. In his wonderful and engrossing book, *A History of Charisma*, John Potts sums up what charisma currently means:

> Contemporary charisma maintains, however, the irreducible character ascribed to it by Weber: it retains a mysterious, elusive quality. Media commentators regularly describe charisma as the 'X-factor'. . . . The enigmatic character of charisma also suggests a connection—at least to some degree—to the earliest manifestations of charisma as a spiritual gift.

In essence, it is thought to be an individual's gift to attract and influence other people, a mysterious quality that someone either has or doesn't have.

One person who comes to mind when we talk about charismatic leadership is Barack Obama. In fact, there is even a *Harvard Business Review* article on his charisma.[6] Barbara Kellerman wrote in that article that what was genuinely striking about the inauguration of the forty-fourth President of the US was that the day mirrored the months preceding it. An astonishing number, two million, yes, two million people attended his inauguration. Barack Obama's silver tongue moved many to the point of tears who themselves moved mountains to make him President.

Is Obama indeed a charismatic leader? Was he born with this gift? Or, as some have argued, can the abilities of charismatic people be learnt and cultivated? And if it can be learnt and developed, is it just the quality of charm that one needs to pay heed to?

There has been a spate of research across sociology, political science, psychology and management trying to delineate and understand this mysterious quality and perhaps measure it, by which individuals can learn how to be charismatic. In fact, even though the mysticism of charisma continues, the construct of charisma has been steadily and increasingly demystified by scholars.

How does one measure charismatic leadership? Can we just focus on the quality of charm, measure it and be done with it? Or is it much more multidimensional? Could the language used by a leader indicate charismatic leadership? Could we scientifically investigate whether Barack Obama is actually charismatic by using the language he speaks, his silver tongue, as they say?

Past research in leadership and organizational behaviour has convincingly argued that rhetoric is a vital method for demonstrating leadership in some contexts.[7] We all can agree that someone who is eloquent and mixes analogies, metaphors and stories in their communications elegantly, has the ability to sway us. Rhetoric, conceptualized by Aristotle (believe it or not, sometimes called the 'Father of Marketing' by none other than marketing legend Philip Kotler from the Kellogg School of Management)[8] is the art of persuasion, which along with grammar and logic, is one of the three ancient arts of discourse. Leadership has been described as a 'language game,' and the language that leaders use is a crucial method for charismatic leaders to influence followers to adopt their vision.[9] Of course, the style of delivery matters too. Though it is up for debate whether style or issues of content matter more, researchers have cautioned that though the delivery style is helpful, it is not sufficient to generate charismatic attributions and that what matters is the vision of the leader and the meaning behind the message.[10]

Many researchers have tried[11] to measure charismatic leadership by using the rhetoric that political leaders use in their communication with their audience.

Now you might think, how does knowing the ingredients or attributes of charismatic leadership, that too of political leaders, help firms and organizations? How can we know if Satya Nadella or Elon Musk or even Mark Zuckerberg is charismatic, using the language used by political leaders? Prior research[12] in management has argued that the two archetypal skills both political and organizational leaders need are charisma and verbal skills. Indeed, both types of leaders require language to explain their vision to followers and to persuade them to abandon their personal ambitions in order to adopt the organization's vision. If leaders have the charisma and thus the power to persuade, followers self-sacrifice and take on the leaders' vision as their own.

Based on earlier conceptual and seminal work by Boas Shamir from Hebrew University and his colleagues, a set of researchers at Claremont Graduate University came up with eight dimensions and their respective words to define charismatic leadership.[13] Yes, eight different dimensions—not just charm. These dimensions emerge from the self-concept-based motivational theory of charismatic leadership,[14] which states that 'charismatic leaders, by their verbal and symbolic behaviour, raise the salience of certain values and collective identities in followers' self-concepts and articulate the goals and required efforts in terms of those values and identities'. Charismatic leadership seems to depend on the eye of the beholder. The rhetoric and language used by a leader in linking collective goals and followers' self-concepts enable a leader to be impactful.

In a recent study, J.E. Baur of the University of Nevada and his colleagues examined how each of these eight dimensions independently described different types of charismatic leaders.[15] They even ventured further to understand the effects of these eight dimensions on election outcomes. Let's examine what Baur and colleagues did.

Baur and his colleagues measured charismatic rhetoric in the transcripts of a leader's debate using a software called DICTION. DICTION is a text-mining software program that has been developed and validated in political science literature.[16] This software has been used across a variety of contexts, such as politics, communication and business. The text mining here is a dictionary-based approach. DICTION is a dictionary of dimensions or constructs with a set of words that make up each dimension or construct.

The DICTION software program uses thirty-three different dictionaries, which contain over 10,000 search words, to analyse a passage. The dictionaries only have individual words, and homographs* are taken into account by a weighting scheme that considers the context of the comment. Baur and his colleagues,

---

* Two or more words that are spelt the same but not necessarily pronounced the same and having different meanings and origins.

in their study, generated eight compositive dimensions from the various dictionaries in DICTION. So, for example, 'Present Concern' and 'Past Concern' were two dictionaries used for the Temporal Orientation dimension. See Table 17.1 for the list of the eight dimensions and the example words used to calculate if the leader reflects a particular dimension of charismatic leadership in their debates.

Construct	Sample Words
1. Collective Focus	
- *Collectives*	Crowd, choir, assembly, team, humanity, army, congress
- *People References*	Classes, residents, constituencies, majority, citizenry, population
- *Self-reference (-)*	I, I'd, I'll, I'm, I've, me, mine, my, myself
2. Temporal Orientation	
- *Present Concern*	Sing, govern, care, taste, desire, make, need, request, take
- *Past Concern*	Sang, governed, cared, tasted, desired, made, needed, requested, took
3. Followers' Worth	
- *Praise*	Dear, kind, lovely, intelligent, witty, mighty
- *Inspiration*	Honesty, virtue, self-sacrifice, courage, dedication, devotion, merit
- *Satisfy*	Cheerful, passionate, happiness, smile, welcome
4. Similarity to Followers	
- *Levelling*	Anybody, everybody, fully, obvious, permanent, totally, each, always
- *Familiarity*	Over, across, through, this, that, for, who
- *Human Interest*	He, his, ourselves, them, cousin, wife, grandchild

Construct	Sample Words
5. Values and Moral Justifications	
- *Spirituality*	Charity, church, blessing, eternal, faith, hope, mercy, conscience
- *Patriotic Terms*	Equality, emancipation, freedom, justice, inalienable, liberty, homeland
6. Tangibility	
- *Concreteness*	Animal, ship, eyes, lips, factory, silk
- *Insistence*	Score calculated based on repetition of key terms
- *Variety (-)*	Score calculated by dividing the number of different words in a passage by the number of total words
7. Action	
- *Aggression*	Blast, crash, explode, collide, conquest
- *Accomplishment*	Establish, finish, achieve, proceed, motivated, influence, succeed
- *Passivity (-)*	Allow, tame, submit, accept, acquiesce, appeasement
- *Ambivalence (-)*	Allegedly, perhaps, might, almost, confound, hesitate, vacillate
8. Adversity	
- *Blame*	Mean, guilty, naïve, sloppy, stupid, incompetent, mediocre
- *Hardship*	Earthquake, starvation, bankruptcy, conflict, loss
- *Denial*	Aren't, Shouldn't, don't, nor, not, nay, nothing, didn't

Table 17.1: List of the eight dimensions or constructs with sample words to measure charismatic leadership[17]

Let's quickly walk through each of these eight dimensions, which, according to organizational behaviourists and leadership scholars, exemplify charisma in leaders. Note that the negative sign in parenthesis next to a concept under each dimension indicates that the concept is reverse-coded. So, for the concept of self-reference, lesser self-reference means higher collective focus.

- Collective focus refers to the usage of collective-oriented content that communicates the importance of a group or organization's mission over individual self-interest. A leader who has this dimension uses more words like 'humanity', 'team', 'residents', and fewer words like 'I', 'me', and 'myself'.

- Temporal orientation denotes charismatic content that will make repeated references to the continuity between past and present and clearly link the past to present and future goals. A leader here would use a word both in the present and past tense, like 'govern' and 'governed' or 'take' and 'took'.

- Followers' worth includes rhetoric that shows confidence in their followers and strengthens followers' collective sense of faith in themselves. Example words used by someone with this dimension would be 'mighty', 'self-sacrifice', 'courage' and 'passionate'.

- Similarity to followers comprises rhetoric that recognizes similarities between leaders and their followers, highlighting similar values, backgrounds and experiences. A leader with this dimension would use words like 'everybody', 'through' and 'ourselves'.

- Charismatic content has more references to values and moral justifications than non-charismatic content. Examples of words here include 'conscience', 'blessing', 'emancipation' and 'homeland'.

- Charismatic leaders reference tangible and long-term goals and a leader with this dimension would use concrete words like 'ship', 'eyes', 'lips', etc., repeat key terms, and have lesser variety in their word use.

- Messages with action mobilize followers to act and provide them with a sense of adventure and excitement. Someone with this dimension would use more words that denote aggression and accomplishment like 'conquest', 'establish', 'proceed', etc. and use less words that signify passivity and ambivalence like 'tame', 'allow', 'perhaps', 'might', etc.

- Adversity is the final, key element of charismatic rhetoric, which is the ability of leaders to convey the unbearable nature of the current situation to motivate followers to attain a better future. A leader who tends to have this dimension uses words like 'guilty', 'bankruptcy', 'aren't', 'not', etc.

To examine how leaders used these words and thus the dimensions across their speeches, Baur and his colleagues collected a census of American presidential debates from 1960 to 2012, representing all the general presidential debates in US history. There were eleven elections in which general election debates were held during the period namely in 1960 and then from 1976 to 2012. They collected these debates from the United States Commission on Presidential Debates and the American Presidency Project at the University of California in Santa Barbara.

After running the DICTION software that measured how these various candidates used the words within these eight dimensions, they first divided the candidates into four clusters by a technique called cluster analysis that organized the candidates in such a way that leaders in the same group are more similar to each other than to those in other groups.

> Cluster analysis is a method that groups similar observations into a number of clusters or segments.

What did the authors find?

They found that there were four unique profiles of charismatic rhetoric based on a leader's use of it in speeches. This result indicated that leaders use multiple and distinct configurations to articulate their mission and vision. Each of the four clusters used the words belonging to the eight dimensions in varying degrees. See Figure 17.1 for how the four clusters used each of the eight dimensions. For example, Cluster 1 uses the dimension of tangibility the most compared to other clusters.

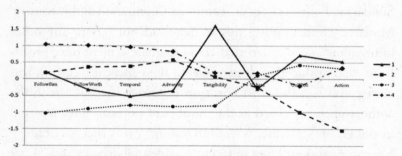

Figure 17.1: Chart showing clusters and their utilization of the eight dimensions

Let's now see how these clusters with different strategies mapped to a leader's rhetoric.

When leaders used the strategy identified in Cluster 1, they focused on words that belonged to the tangible, collective focus and action dimensions. Incumbent Presidents mostly used this strategy. Indeed, incumbent Presidents would need to become more tangible and action-oriented if they plan to continue and realize some of the promises made when they first won. Challengers used Cluster 2's strategy towards an incumbent President. Their speeches were distinguished by personal rather than collective focus, a low rather than high level of action and a lack of specificity in any of the other dimensions. The strategy in Cluster 3 was the most used (37 per cent). When leaders followed this strategy, they used the least amount of charismatic rhetoric (i.e., they were below the mean and displayed the lowest usage for five of the eight dimensions). These leaders also downplayed the dimensions of follower worth and similarity, temporal orientation and adversity. Unsurprisingly, candidates employing this strategy rarely won the election. When leaders used the strategy in Cluster 4, whose representation was the second highest, they used the following dimensions more than any other cluster: Follower Similarity, Follower Worth, Temporal Orientation and Adversity. Moreover, leaders using this strategy did not ignore any other dimensions and ensured that they adequately mentioned words from each of the eight dimensions in their speeches. In fact, this cluster also had the most effect on influence success, which the authors operationalized as the number of popular votes received in the general election. More interestingly, this rhetoric strategy has appeared most often in recent presidential debates and 74 per cent of the debates in the 2000 election or later used this rhetoric.

Whose speeches do you think exemplified Cluster 4?

Indeed, Barack Obama consistently used this strategy in his 2008 campaign.

Barack Obama used references to shared adversity to connect with his followers and express their worth concerning how they handled this adversity. For example, in one of these speeches, Obama says, 'You know, a lot of you remember the tragedy of 9/11 and where you were on that day and, you know how all of the country was ready to come together and make enormous changes to make us not only safer, but to make us a better country and a more unified country.'[18] Candidates who won or were elected as President while using this strategy include Bill Clinton (1992, 1996), George W. Bush (2000, 2004), and Barack Obama (2008, 2012). Note that all these candidates were also incumbents on their way to re-election.

Overall, there are distinct profiles of charismatic rhetoric and these profiles have varying levels of efficacy in influencing success. Leaders who use the strategy in Cluster 4 appear to be more successful in persuading their followers to support their vision than leaders who use the strategy from other clusters.

Let's get deeper into the language that leaders in Cluster 4 utilize. What were the ingredients in Obama's speeches?

The strategy in Cluster 4, in essence, involves a relatively balanced use of each of the eight dimensions. These speeches avoid using too many (or too few) words from each of the eight individual rhetorical dimensions, and balanced usage of words from each of the eight dimensions is entertained. It makes sense that using all eight dimensions may be necessary if one wants to influence large masses of followers with different lives, motivations and needs.

In his speeches, Barack Obama tried to speak to all, and carefully and eloquently expressed his vision using the words from each of the eight dimensions of what a charismatic leader epitomizes.

He engaged with his followers, and followers engaged with him. As one of his followers said, 'He does a great job of coming down to our level and not talking above our heads. He makes himself seem as common as you are.' Obama used words like 'everybody', 'each', and 'ourselves' to make his audience feel he

was on the same level playing field as them, was familiar with their
lives and backgrounds, and showed a keen human interest in their
lives. Indeed, his listeners felt that Obama was like them. A ten
out of ten on the dimension of follower similarity here.

Overall, it was not just his charm. He used a combination
of dimensions that mesmerized, motivated and rejuvenated not
only those 2 million people who attended his inauguration but
millions of others who watched on TV.

They cried in joy and saw hope for a new America.

This excerpt is a perfect example of Obama's usage of the
eight dimensions during his presidential debate:[19]

> I think we all know America is going through tough times right
> now. The policies of the last eight years—and Washington's
> unwillingness to tackle the tough problems for decades—has left
> us in the worst economic crisis since the Great Depression. And
> that's why the biggest risk we could take right now is to adopt
> the same failed policies and the same failed politics that we've
> seen over the last eight years and somehow expect a different
> result. We need fundamental change in this country, and that's
> what I'd like to bring. You know, over the last twenty months,
> you've invited me into your homes. You've shared your stories
> with me. And you've confirmed once again the fundamental
> decency and generosity of the American people. And that's why
> I'm sure that our brighter days are still ahead . . . But it's not
> going to be easy. It's not going to be quick. It is going to be
> requiring all of us—Democrats, Republicans, independents—
> to come together and to renew a spirit of sacrifice and service
> and responsibility. I'm absolutely convinced we can do it. I
> would ask for your vote, and I promise you that if you give
> me the extraordinary honor of serving as your president, I will

work every single day, tirelessly, on your behalf and on the behalf of the future of our children.

So, what does uncovering the mysteriousness of charismatic leadership mean for organizations and even normal folks?

First, firms looking for a charismatic leader can examine the language use of potential candidates vying for a leadership position. Many top management officials provide interviews, presentations, writings and speeches. If firms are really looking for a charismatic leader, one of the best places to start could be an analysis of the potential candidates' language use.

Second, stakeholders of a firm who want to evaluate if their current CEO or president has the traits of a charismatic leader could use text-mining approaches as the study above.

These results also have implications for the ordinary person. Many of us are in positions wherein we want to move on to leadership positions. Consider a mid-level executive seeking to rise through the ranks in her firm. Such a person could do a personal audit of their use of language in their professional or perhaps even private sphere. Such an analysis could allow the individual to understand where she falls in the continuum of charismatic leadership.

Third, we observe that charisma can be demystified, and a sense of charismatic leadership can be gauged from the language leaders use. Barack Obama exemplified what charismatic leadership means, and his silver tongue seems to have hit the right notes. But does this conception of charismatic leadership hold for other parts of the world? What about leaders in other parts of the world? Cultural norms and expectations for how leaders should conduct themselves indeed differ between the US and other countries.

Geert Hofstede, a well-known Dutch cultural psychologist, conducted one of the most complete examinations of how nations and their citizens are influenced by culture.[20] He proposed six dimensions by which nations differentiated from one another. He argued and showed that nations differ in how societies deal with inequalities among people: power distance (the strength of a society's social hierarchy), individualism vs collectivism, masculinity vs femininity, how people avoid uncertainty, long vs short-term orientation, and indulging in fun vs restraint.

Because of these cultural differences, is there a likelihood that charismatic leadership might mean something different in non-Western countries?

Who else to test this than India's 'Father of the Nation', Mohandas Karamchand Gandhi, Mahatma Gandhi? If I type quotes in Google Search, www. goodreads.com provides a list of 976 quotes attributed to the Mahatma.[21] His sayings such as 'Be the change that you wish to see in the world' and 'The best way to find yourself is to lose yourself in the service of others' have moved, resonated with and deeply affected millions. With India under the colonial regime, Mahatma Gandhi asked his followers to risk all they had for a better future, influencing not only millions of Indians but also leaders such as Nelson Mandela and Martin Luther King, Jr, to name a few. Gandhi, despite being a shy person, successfully reached an audience that was mostly illiterate and did not have the modern means of communication that we all now take for granted and most likely cannot live without.

Max Weber's definition of charisma was that it is 'an extraordinary quality of a person' that evokes a devout following due to 'supernatural, superhuman, or at least specifically exceptional powers or qualities'.[22] If you ask a follower of Gandhi in India, you will get a definite yes if someone wants to know if Gandhi had charisma.

However, would Gandhi's rhetoric be considered 'charismatic' according to what charisma means in the Western world?

To answer this very question, Michelle C. Bligh at Claremont Graduate University, along with Jill L. Robinson at the University of Redlands, examined sixteen of his speeches dating from 1914 through 1948.[23] They used the same eight dimensions as above. They compared his speeches to both i) social movement leaders such as Malcolm X, Andrea Dworkin, Ralph Nader and Paul Ehrlich who spoke on a variety of topics, including feminism, environmentalism, civil rights, labour grievances and nuclear disarmament and ii) former US Presidents such as Franklin Roosevelt and John F. Kennedy using a sample of their inaugural and pivotal speeches.

What did the authors find?

When compared against social movement leaders, Gandhi's speeches were mostly similar on the eight dimensions. On the other hand, when comparing against speeches by Presidents, as in the main study of this chapter, the content of Gandhi's speeches was not similar on the eight dimensions.

Compared to social movement leaders, Gandhi's speeches incorporated significantly less collective and active speech. Gandhi frequently used more self-referential terms (I, myself) than collective terms (us, we), and more passive than active terms. He also used more temporally oriented references to past and present, and less tangible language. When compared to the sample of US Presidents, his speeches contained less support for followers' worth and less similarity to followers.

When compared to both groups, Gandhi used more passive and fewer aggressive terms than either. This finding is consistent with his ideal of 'ahimsa,' or non-violence as exemplified by his quote,[24] 'If India can discover a way of sublimating the force of violence . . . and turning it into constructive, peaceful ways whereby differences of interests can be liquidated, it will be a great day indeed.'

Thus, was Gandhi charismatic?

Using the lens of charisma that is more amenable for western leaders, he is more like charismatic social movement leaders but unlike charismatic former US Presidents. It seems the language theorists in the Western world use to describe charismatic leadership for political leaders may not truly correspond directly to other parts of the world. Norms, values, ideas and cultures differ across nations. For example, Indians compared to Americans care more about power and are long-term oriented.[25] On the other hand, compared to Americans, Indians are more collectivist, more feminine, more open to uncertainty and less indulgent (see Figure 17.2 below). Perhaps to understand true charismatic leadership in other parts of the world other than the US, one would need to understand what drives and motivates the people in those regions and then come up with a newer text-mining method to characterize charismatic leadership.

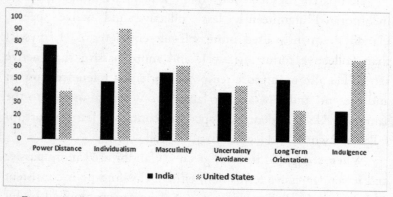

Figure 17.2: Hofstede's scores on cultural dimensions for India and the US

Overall, charismatic leadership is not just charm and it is not immeasurable.

It is multidimensional. It is measurable. And one can perhaps learn how to be charismatic.

18

Letter-Writing Skills for Leaders

CEOs are movers and shakers. They move engines to space and move heads with their social media messages. They shake beliefs by pursuing the impossible and shake financial markets with their words, gestures and actions.

In general, though, only some CEOs are the Elon Musk type. In 2019, he was christened the most inspiring leader in the tech industry.[1] He has been characterized as a CEO who is constantly pushing the boundaries, ten steps ahead of his team in terms of ideas and actions. As an employer, he has been declared lord of a workplace that relentlessly fosters innovation with one report stating, 'Tesla is an engineer's paradise where the pencil is literally never down.'[2] Other examples of CEOs with passion and commitment for innovation include Steve Jobs at Apple and Andy Grove at Intel. They were revered for their avowed success in advancing innovation in their firms.

Obviously, for a firm to do well, the people who head and lead firms have a pivotal role in creating innovative products and services for their firms. Indeed, innovations are critical for survival, growth and success in today's globally competitive markets.

However, not all CEOs are known for such an ardent and unflagging attitude towards innovation. CEOs are so often occupied with their day-to-day activities or preoccupied with their past that, more often than not, they do not recognize that the social, technological and cultural environment has turned on them.

CEOs, in many instances, are so fond of and attached to the prevalent technologies that they resist new ones. Many CEOs get attached to what they currently sell, do not focus on the future and resist new trends. In fact, researchers have found that the proportion of time they spend on the future is less than 3 per cent. Famous examples of CEOs who infamously failed to anticipate the future and think about what technologies would be in demand in the future include An Wang, then CEO of the word-processor maker Wang Labs, who mentioned, 'The PC is the stupidest thing I ever heard of.'[3] Wang Labs was a US computer company founded in 1951 by An Wang and G.Y. Chu. At its peak, the company generated about US$3 billion in the 1980s. However, An Wang was unwilling to shift the company's focus from selling minicomputers to personal electronic computers. Minicomputers is almost a misnomer. These devices sold to offices and businesses were still quite big but smaller in size than the mainframes of that era. Wang Labs filed for bankruptcy in August 1992.[4] In another instance, Ken Olsen, the then CEO of minicomputer maker Digital Equipment Corporation (DEC), prohibited his employees from using the phrase 'personal computer' while employed at his firm.[5] Ken Olsen was proclaimed as 'America's most successful entrepreneur' by *Fortune* magazine in 1986. At its peak in the late 1980s, DEC generated about US$14 billion in revenues. Ken Olsen resisted the idea of personal computers and similar to An Wang, focused on selling minicomputers. Mr

Olsen was resistant to change and thought of personal computers as 'toys' used for playing video games. Instead, DEC focused on its minicomputers that targeted research labs, engineering firms and other types of professions that required heavy computer use instead of the emerging trend of desktop machines.[6] In both these cases, these CEOs didn't think about future customer needs and thus drive innovation.

Given that some CEOs drive innovation and some do not, is there a way to understand their commitment to advancing knowledge and driving innovation for a firm?

A firm's stance towards innovation matters not only for the firm itself but also for its stakeholders. Stakeholders such as investors are always keen to acquire information from the firm about where it is headed innovation-wise. There is an inherent information symmetry between the firm and such stakeholders. Firms have inside information whereas investors, who are interested in seeing if a firm can be innovative in the future and perhaps reap profits, only have public information. Is there a way for such stakeholders to know if the CEO at the helm will drive innovation from the information publicly available?

Before I go ahead, let's talk about something that we used to do a lot earlier, but do less and less of now: writing letters.

Letters have been written since antiquity. They have served various purposes, from sending information to exchanging ideas. Letter-writing was even considered an art form and still is to many who care.[7] In the ancient world, letters were written on metal, lead, wood, animal skin, and papyrus. Sometimes, the medium was unusual. Acontius, a beautiful youth on the island of Ceos, wrote a letter in an apple to Cydippe, a well-born Athenian maiden, as recounted by the Roman poet Ovid in his collection of epistolary poems, *Heroides*.[8] But gone are the days when we would write letters with our fountain pen, read them, re-read them, find a stamp, head to the post office and send that letter to someone you were corresponding with. I was in a boarding school and still remember the eagerness and excitement every day when our housemaster would call out our names to hand us our letters. The staple form of communication in India was the blue-coloured letter with three flaps—the inland letter—before everything went tech. It meant everything to me when I received a letter from home. Opening those flaps, sometimes almost tearing the letter in my youthful enthusiasm, reading about how my parents were doing, what sumptuous meals they were cooking, what cricket matches my father was watching and his cheeky predictions, the situation in my terrorist-ridden hometown and, of course, the gossip on Indian movie stars, which was my father's speciality. I sometimes still write letters to my most loved ones and send them by mail. It's a thing that I cherish. These letters are, of course, private. And unquestionably meant for that other person whom you want to share your thoughts and feelings with.

However, there is a letter that is public. A letter that is typed. A letter sought by not just one or two people but by thousands, sometimes millions.

The letter from the leader. The CEO. A shareholder letter.

Letters from CEOs are narratives about a firm that have strong repercussions in moving both product and financial markets. For example, these letters are influential in investors' investment decisions, both institutional and retail.[9] These letters appear in a firm's annual report, which is a coveted piece of public information from a firm. Firms put loads of effort into the creation of these annual reports and spend a great deal on producing them.[10] And investors dig into these reports for any usable data that can reduce the information asymmetry that I was talking about earlier.

Besides the matter-of-fact reporting that goes into these annual reports, which contain all sorts of numeric information that you may have learnt in your accounting class (think balance sheets, income statements, cash flow statements), the CEO's letter to shareholders is one piece of content that can provide clues to where the business is headed. And this letter is from the horse's mouth. Letters to shareholders provide a rare glance at how CEOs think, which is difficult, if not impossible, to discern. CEOs play a keen role in drafting these letters. Letters by some CEOs, such as Warren Buffett of Berkshire Hathaway, have an enthusiastic audience of thousands eager to hear from him. Investors and the wider investment community scrutinize the letter to gain an insight into Buffet's decision-making while the press absorbs, garnishes and amplifies it for maximum reach.

The financial statements in the annual report enable investors to make swift decisions about buying and selling stocks. Indeed, the quantitative numbers matter and the extensive analysis that these statements undergo can be predictive of firm performance in the future. However, these financial statements often may not be enough for you to outsmart the other smarts. There could be cues hidden inside some other content within an annual report, such as the letter to shareholders, which can enable an investor to gain a surplus from their trades. In fact, relying on financial statements may be quite fruitless for some types of investing, such as value investing.

The philosophy of value investing is to buy stocks at low prices but aim to book large profits. However, if you consider how firms such as MAMAA (yes, one more new acronym: Meta, Apple, Microsoft, Amazon, Alphabet) go about their innovation strategies, value investing would perhaps not pay too many dividends. Firms in the modern world spend considerable money on innovation, hiring talented engineers, developing new products and commercializing their innovations. However, the current rules in accounting do not see these forms of spending as assets but as costs that go into the calculation of profits. So, the more a firm invests in the future, the lower its profits are. If you are a value investor, such a stock would appear as a costly stock instead of a stock full of promise.[11]

One more reason for investors to look for other sources from a firm, such as the CEO letter. Maybe it might matter even more for investors who are value-investing.

Why are CEO letters important?

First, these letters go beyond the boundary of traditional financial reporting. Second, they provide a means for the CEO to communicate her vision, spell out strategies and explain business models. Third, out of all the content in an annual report, the CEO letter contains the highest diversity in vocabulary and a variety of lexical tools.[12] These linguistic assortments strengthen its potential to direct a reader's attention and perhaps influence them. Fourth, CEO letters can provide a personal touch with an affective and interpersonal appeal from the boss, showing commitment and inspiring confidence among the firm's stakeholders. CEOs can use these letters to more proactively signal a firm's private information and perhaps convey some implicit beliefs about the firm and its relationship with the outside world.[13] Fifth, these letters are also largely unregulated, allowing for differences in individual CEO and firm narratives and enabling one to get hard-to-find information that a more structured template cannot provide. Sixth, many people might think that a CEO letter is artificial and created by public relations experts. However, CEOs spend a substantial amount of time on the content of the letter, changing and proofreading it to make sure it is per their taste.[14]

An interesting study found that cognitions expressed in letters to shareholders and internal planning documents of a firm had high correspondence.[15] Moreover, CEOs have principal fiduciary responsibility for the content of the letters. Finally, even though the income statement in the annual report is perhaps the most crucial information for decision-making, it is believed that the CEO letter is the most widely read section.[16] Because of their utility, these letters have been put to excellent use by business scholars, particularly in determining whether these letters have value beyond typical financial data. For example, past research has shown that the tone of these letters contains informational value to predict the future performance of a firm beyond quantitative financial data.[17] However, can one use this letter to understand if a CEO can drive innovation for a firm?

Three marketing professors, Manjit Yadav from Texas A&M University, Jaideep Prabhu from the University of Cambridge, and Rajesh Chandy from the London Business School, took it upon themselves to answer this question.

Their key study question was, 'Do CEOs influence business innovation results, and if yes, how?'[18]

Let's understand the theory that the authors espoused. Their approach relied on an attentional perspective on how CEOs can impact innovation. As noted above, CEOs are busy—very busy folks. In general, most of us have limited attention and CEOs, I am sure, have much more limited time than you or I do (unless you are a CEO or someone who must take care of dozens, if not thousands of folks under them). Attention is scarce and more so for managers at the helm with competing matters to pay attention to. Thus, if a CEO pays attention to something, it is consequential for the firm. Yadav and his co-authors proposed that some top managers have a greater impact on innovation because such CEOs do better in 'noticing, interpreting, and focusing of time and effort'. Within any firm, 'levers of power are uniquely concentrated in the hands of the CEO'.[19] CEOs have the wherewithal to move the firm in a particular direction. They enable firms to achieve their goals partly by their symbolic actions and partly by their communications. Both these sets of activities reflect a CEO's attentional focus and drive activities in a firm, which involve steering employees towards specific goals.

Yadav and his co-authors proposed that successful innovation requires a series of tasks and each of these tasks requires attention. The authors put forward three critical tasks: detection, development and deployment. Detection is identifying a new technology, recognizing its potential application and creating an initial product based on the latest technology. Development is the realization of the initial product into a developed product. Deployment is the improvements and additions to the developed product after launch. All these three tasks need two components. One is being able to detect opportunities outside the firm. The second is being able to anticipate events in the future. Thus, a CEO needs to exercise attention both on a spatial component (external opportunities) and a temporal component (future events). When CEOs can attend to these two components, their communications and actions drive employees towards being on the lookout for external opportunities and anticipating events in the future. This, in turn, leads to swifter detection of novel technologies and new opportunities and a greater readiness for the future. While greater attention to internal issues in a firm leads to slower detection, slower development and weaker deployment of such technologies.

Enough of all this theory.

Is there a way to capture such attention from a CEO's perspective towards a firm's innovative needs?

You know where I am going.

Yadav and his co-authors demonstrate that, yes, it is possible. The shareholder letter can be an instrument that enables one to figure out a CEO's attention to a firm's innovation needs.

They came up with a novel and creative approach to measure a CEO's focus on innovation involving a linguistic analysis of CEOs' communications, which they argued provides a reasonably unique aperture into their cognitive thinking.

As their focus was on CEOs' attention patterns and innovation outcomes, they needed a setting whereby they could analyse the content in the CEO letter and see the consequent innovation outcomes. Innovation outcome data is generally hard to obtain.

The US retail banking industry served as a nice setting. This choice was driven by data availability that is mandated by a number of regulatory agencies and also because, at the time of the study, the retail banking industry was going through significant changes, such as the introduction of Internet banking. From Citibank being the first bank to register a domain name in February 1991, the number of banks with Internet-based transactional banking services grew rapidly between 1995 and 2000, peaking in 2000. Their data spanned from 1990 to 2004.

To measure innovation outcomes, the authors chose three outcome variables that were strongly tied to their theory of three innovation tasks: detection, development and deployment. All related to Internet banking. Internet banking was the innovation that the CEO needed to pay attention to.

Speed of detection, they measured as the date when a bank registered its primary domain name. They obtained this information from InterNIC's Whois registry. Speed of development, they measured as the month when a bank went online with transactional capabilities. They obtained this information from the Internet Archive's Wayback Machine, press releases, the Thomson Directory of Internet Banks, the Online Banking Report, and even by making phone calls to banking managers. Breadth of deployment was the number of features that these banks offered online, such as Internet business banking, mobile banking, Internet tax filing, etc. The sum of all these features made up the measure of the breadth of deployment. They obtained this information too from the Internet Archive's Wayback Machine. Next, Yadav and his co-authors used the CEO letters from the retail banks to identify three factors related to the CEO's attention: future focus, external focus and internal focus. They used 867 letters to shareholders from the 176 banks in their sample.

Now let's get into the text-mining bit.

Like the outcome variables, Yadav and his co-authors wanted to use textual variables that matched their theory. Remember the spatial component, i.e., being able to detect external opportunities and the temporal component, i.e., anticipating changes in the future. They utilized a metric called future focus to capture a CEO's temporal component. They used measures that captured both a firm's external and internal focus to quantify a firm's spatial component. For all three criteria, the authors used a dictionary-based approach.

For determining a firm's future focus, the authors wanted to use words that portray that the CEO is attending to events that have yet to occur. Past research in psycholinguistics directed them to the following words, which suggest attention addressed to events yet to occur: will, may, might, shall, be, and tomorrow (and their related contractions such as we'll, I'll, they'll, you'll, etc.).[20] After examining words used in the CEO letters, the authors concluded that sentences containing the word 'will' were most apt to measure future focus. They also ensured that sentences containing the word 'will' but with a different meaning were dropped from their analysis. This is the simplest example of a dictionary-based approach but very powerful, as you will see. The authors ensured that the coding was accurate. Two independent coders manually checked a sample of sentences containing the word 'will' and ensured that this simple rule of using just the word 'will' to measure future focus was quite accurate.

External focus is the attention directed at entities outside the firm, while internal focus is the attention directed at entities inside the firm. Thus, external focus was measured with the number of words that characterized attention to customers and competitors. To measure internal focus, the authors used the number of words that represented attention to inward and organization-specific issues. See Table 18.1 for the dictionaries for external and internal focus. The authors used an iterative approach to finalize their dictionary by either adding or deleting words at each step of the process until the authors judged that the impact of any deletion or addition would be minimal.

External Focus		Internal Focus	
Customers	Competitors	Organizational	
Customer	Competitive	Organization	CEO
Customers	Competitiveness	Organizational	President
Consumer	Competitor	Reorganization	Vice-president
Consumers	Competitors	Management	Vice-presidents
Buyer	Compete	Retire	Director
Buyers	Competition	Retired	Directors
Market	Peer	Retirement	Officer
Markets	Peers	Employee	Officers
Market-place	Companies	Employees	Subsidiary
Marketplace	Banks	Staff	Subsidiaries
Communities	Firms	Stakeholder	Diversification
	Position	Stakeholders	Diversify
	Positioning	Board	Diversified
	Positioned	Manager	
		Managers	

Table 18.1: Dictionaries for measuring external and internal focus

So, how did they go about the analysis? They used a hazard model to measure the effect of the textual variables on the speed of development and deployment. This is an oft-used model in social science whereby the investigator studies the relationship between the time to an event (the outcome variable) and predictors. To measure the effect of the textual variables on the breadth of deployment, they used a regression model that examines the relationship between the outcome variable and predictors.

So, what did the authors find?

The authors found that a greater future focus enables banks to detect new technological opportunities, develop initial products based on new technologies and enhance their ability to implement initial products based on the new technologies.

External focus enables faster detection of new technological opportunities and facilitates speedier development of initial products based on these technologies. As for internal focus, while it slows the detection of new technological opportunities, it promotes faster development of initial products based on these technologies. The authors find no link between internal and external focus on deploying novel technologies.

Through this innovative and creative approach, Yadav et al. show that we can quantify the attentional patterns of CEOs. The power of this approach is that it is simple, easy to quantify and takes care of many issues that befall research when they intend to measure CEO behaviour. CEOs are difficult to reach directly, surveys are too long for them (imagine Elon Musk finishing a ten-minute survey), and it is hard to make causal inferences from surveys. Though it is very tricky and hard to model causality from archival data like the research setting attempted here, Yadav and his colleagues ensured that their outcome metric is a time period ahead when they evaluate the relationship between their text-based factors and innovation outcomes.

In essence, Yadav and his colleagues argue and show that CEOs lead and think for the firm. How CEOs attend to a firm's needs and exercise their power to steer it towards those needs can have a direct and long-term effect on a firm's innovation performance. The ones that attend to a firm's need for innovation, prosper. Think Elon Musk. Tesla surpassed a market value of US$1 trillion on 25 October 2021, making it the fifth firm to reach the milestone.[21] You must have guessed that the other four firms are Apple, Microsoft, Amazon and Alphabet. Four firms were led by CEOs who embodied attention to innovation. These past CEOs have now stepped down: Steve Jobs, Bill Gates, Jeff Bezos, Sergey Brin and Larry Page.

The next time you see Elon Musk on social media, don't just assume it is for fun and triviality. He is also attentive to what customers say. In fact, Elon Musk refocuses a team's priorities if a customer's social media post catches his eye. As a former Tesla employee states, 'What ultimately triggers him to act and make a decision is what he reads on social media. When you're in a business meeting with him, he will pivot the direction of the organization literally overnight. So manufacturing could be a problem today, and as soon as it stops being reported on social media, as soon as it stops being reported in the news, then he'll move on to whatever the news is claiming the new problem is.'[22]

Not all CEOs are as active, reactive and proactive as Elon Musk on social media. For most other CEOs, it is hard, if not impossible, to gauge if they mean business.

Yadav, Prabhu and Chandy, via text-mining methods, show that letters to shareholders provide a lens to capture a CEO's attention to innovation.

So, what do these results imply for managers?

First, the research shows that it would be judicious for firms to have CEOs at the helm who are more focused on the future than those who scan the external and internal environments. The results from the study discussed above imply that CEOs who don't focus on the future, are doomed to fail. In their dataset, out of the 867 letters to shareholders from 176 public firms, only about 9 per cent of all the CEOs' thoughts, i.e., sentences, were categorized as future-focused. This shows that CEOs have ample opportunity to influence how innovation is carried out within a firm by paying more attention to the future.

Second, CEO letters can be useful information to not only the external world but also internal stakeholders, such as a firm's employees. These letters can enable employees to get a sense of the CEO's vision and more vigorously instil in them the drive to reach that vision.

Third, innovation is a process rather than a one-shot event. It involves steps such as detecting, developing and deploying innovations. Firms that understand this can succeed.

Finally, the study discussed above shows the usability of CEO letters as another means of understanding the thinking of CEOs. A document that is publicly available and easy to retrieve, comes at a regular periodicity and at no cost.

CEO letters, in essence, can shed light on what they will shake or where they will move next.

We would be remiss not to read these missives carefully.

19

Me, Myself and I: Can Narcissism Be a Good Thing?

Here is a question. Imagine you are the owner of an apartment building that has fifteen floors. You have a set of tenants who have been quite happy with the amenities in the building and are generally satisfied. However, one day, one tenant on the fourteenth floor comes to you and informs you that the main elevator is way too slow and takes aeons for her family to get home or come down. As it happens, there is just one elevator. The other tenants start complaining too. You don't want your tenants to feel unsatisfied and want to solve this issue quickly. However, you also don't want to spend too much money. Repairing the elevator to make it go faster will likely be quite costly, and you want to minimize your expenditure as much as possible. What do you think is the best and one of the least expensive ways to find a solution to the issue? Think about it for a minute or two.

Well, one cost-effective way is to place 'something' in the elevator that will keep the tenants entertained, stay preoccupied, and the time then wouldn't seem too long.

What might that 'something' be?

Maybe a TV?

Any other guesses?

One other solution, perhaps a cheaper one than a TV, is to put a mirror in the elevator.[1]

It is more than likely that when there is a mirror, it will occupy the tenants with their own reflection and voila, the elevator will not seem so slow any more. What better way to entertain the tenants with what they most care about? Themselves!

All of us care about ourselves, but some people care a bit too much. And this caring too much about oneself is a personality characteristic.

Personality makes a huge difference in both our personal and professional lives.

Apart from skills and experience, personality ranks as one of the most important attributes in terms of what people are looking for in a job applicant. In fact, about 77 per cent of employers state that personality matters when an employer hires a potential candidate.[2]

One character trait many of us dislike is someone with a grandiose sense of self-importance. Someone who thinks very highly of themselves, needs constant admiration, believes others are below them and lacks any kind of empathy for others. You guessed it; in other words, narcissistic.

Today, this trait is prevalent like never before. Social media sites such as Instagram, TikTok, Facebook, Snapchat and LinkedIn are playgrounds for someone with narcissistic traits. Have you ever seen anyone post something on LinkedIn that says, 'Today was a normal day at work'? Usually, the posts you see on LinkedIn are of the following flavours: mentioning their recent talk to an audience of thousands, receiving the 'best whatever' award, showing off their new job, finishing some degree or course, and so on. Many of these posts have a bit of humility inserted in them (think humble brag). But in the end, it is still bragging. LinkedIn is the platform of choice to boast and brag about one's professional conquests. And the majority of these posts have dollops of narcissism in them.

Most of us believe narcissism is bad, that it is not a noble trait, and something that we should ensure we don't develop in our personalities.

The word 'narcissism' has a rich etymology and a narrative that has led to its common and frequently misplaced use in our everyday use of language. It comes from a story from the Roman poet Ovid in his *Metamorphoses Book III*.[3] It narrates the tragic tale of a handsome young man named Narcissus, who rejects the nymph Echo, and the gods then punish him by making him fall in love with his own reflection. Narcissus yearns for love and slowly succumbs to his death as he discovers that the object of his interest cannot love him back.

The idea of falling in love with one's reflection or oneself has persisted since then. And mostly, the term 'narcissism' is seen in a negative light. The negative characterization of narcissism has been exacerbated over the years as psychologists, including the great Sigmund Freud, have generally taken a negative view of it. The notion of narcissism had a significant influence on Freud, and he identified various indicators of narcissism such as self-admiration, self-aggrandizement and a disposition to view others as an extension of oneself.[4] In fact, by the 1980s, over a thousand books and articles had been written about narcissism, and most, if not all, took the perspective that narcissism was a clinical disorder.[5]

But the question is, is narcissism a clinical disorder or a personality trait? Is it a distinguishing quality that makes you 'you'?

Though clinicians still see it as a disorder, there has been an array of research that now looks at narcissism from a more neutral perspective and sees it as a personality dimension.[6] These researchers view narcissism as a personality construct that can veer from low to high. It has been defined as 'the degree to which an individual has an inflated sense of self and is preoccupied with having that self-view continually reinforced'.[7]

The idea here is that narcissism occurs in degrees. As a result, we can all range from someone who continually and regularly wants to acquire 'likes' on our Facebook or Instagram profiles to someone who is unconcerned about the previous photo a buddy shared, making it tough to tell the difference between Yoda and you. FYI, Yoda is one of my favourite fictional characters, along with Gollum. So, you know my preferences pretty well.

In essence, narcissism is not necessarily a good or bad trait. It depends on the situation and the outcome of narcissism for the concerned person on herself or others. For example, one positive repercussion of narcissism includes self-esteem[8] and feeling good about oneself. One of the negative consequences includes rating oneself very highly rather than objectively, warranted on abilities such as intelligence and creativity.

This craving for constant admiration, applause and affirmation has both its pros and cons.

However, how does it pan out for firms that are dependent on someone at the helm of the company who is narcissistic? Companies at the behest of thousands of stakeholders, such as consumers, employees and investors? What are the upsides and downsides?

This someone, known by various names as CEO, president or founder, can strongly influence a company's fortunes. More often than not, many of them show narcissistic tendencies and appear as such to the curious and observant among us.

Consider one commonly agreed archetype of such personalities: Elon Musk, the CEO of Tesla, SpaceX and the Boring Company. Musk has never been shy about saying what he thinks. His grandiose narcissistic tweets have disrupted crypto markets and misled investors, among many other consequences. Indeed, many scholars might contend that given his behaviour on X, he can be described as someone who constantly craves attention. Even on the dark side of the Internet, Anonymous, the worldwide hacking collective, describes him as 'another narcissistic rich dude who is desperate for attention'.[9]

But Elon Musk is also a risk-taker and willing to take on enormous challenges, which have transformed the auto industry, and is on his way, perhaps, to change space travel and underground transportation. Currently, Tesla's market capitalization is around $1 trillion.[10] Many of the modern business world's most successful CEOs—Jeff Bezos, Bill Gates and Steve Jobs—who might fall high on the narcissism continuum, became phenomenally successful by blending confidence (or overconfidence) and risk-taking along with excellent execution of their strategies.

So, in this case, using the examples above, narcissism could be a valuable trait for stakeholders interested and invested in a firm.

The narcissism of a company's head could thus be a double-edged sword. Sometimes, it might lead to foolhardy mistakes and sometimes it can lead to striking bonanzas.

What happens when a narcissistic CEO is at the helm? What strategies are pursued? When can it be ruinous? When can it be beneficial?

To answer these questions, let's start with an excellent piece of research by Arijit Chatterjee, professor at ESSEC Business School, and Donald C. Hambrick, chaired professor of management at the Pennsylvania State University, who examined how CEOs influence a company's strategy and performance.[11]

Let's consider some of their arguments about what happens when a narcissistic CEO is the ship's captain.

First, Chatterjee and Hambrick considered some organizational strategies. For example, industries like Blockchain, streaming services, mobile gaming, renewable energy and e-commerce are some of the most dynamic nowadays. The Blockchain market is estimated to be worth about $39.7 billion by 2025,[12] with various applications of blockchain technology emerging in logistics, supply chain, finance and many others. In an industry like Blockchain, perhaps a narcissistic and dynamic CEO might be valuable as she will make swift, brave and impactful decisions to publicize herself. Second, as acquisitions are one of the most visible, bold and daring organizational decisions, narcissistic CEOs will pursue more and grander acquisitions. We saw this in 2022 with Elon Musk buying X. Who knew?

Next, the authors consider performance outcomes. Rightly, they argue that because narcissistic CEOs engage in adventuresome and flamboyant moves, the performance outcomes of their firms will be extreme, i.e., either huge benefits or major losses and the performances will fluctuate wildly. Because narcissistic CEOs focus more on themselves and perhaps disregard the objectivity of their decisions, their tendency to go for the jugular will manifest in either making a massive killing or leading to dire straits.

So, how did the authors go about testing their hypothesis? And how do you capture CEO narcissism? CEOs generally have heavy demands on their time and perhaps will never answer a questionnaire that asks them to rate their behaviour. And good luck moving a narcissistic CEO away from themselves and their lofty vision of themselves.

To measure narcissism, Chatterjee and Hambrick used a motley set of indicators. They based their selection of indicators on two main criteria. One was an indicator that demonstrated a CEO's voluntary choice. Second, each indicator reflected one or more facets of the personality of a narcissist. These indicators were guided by the four facets of narcissism first identified by Emmons.[13] These four facets are:

- superiority/arrogance
- exploitativeness/entitlement
- self-absorption/self-admiration
- leadership/authority

Chatterjee and Hambrick used a measure of narcissism including textual and non-textual indicators. As this book is about language, I will first lay down the non-textual indicators. The first indicator is the prominence of the CEO's photograph in a company's annual report. Yes, that critical document again. As you can see, this document has many markers for the curious to understand the behaviour of a firm's personnel and the firm itself. Based on interviews with communication specialists, the authors verified that CEOs are quite focused on how annual reports look. Past research in leadership demonstrates evidence that large and successful employers tend to recruit CEOs whose faces are perceived to be more competent.[14] And that the faces of CEOs influence firm performance. For example, a study finds that a CEO's facial width-to-height ratio (WHR) predicts firm performance. The WHR of a face, which is the 'ratio of the distance between the two cheekbones to the distance between the brow and top of the lip, is a sexually dimorphic trait and related to aggressive behaviour in men'.[15] Thus, CEOs would be keen to show off their best selves as it can affect how investors perceive them. And if it's a narcissistic CEO, they will ensure that they are conspicuous, and everyone knows they are the boss. Based on these findings, Chatterjee and Hambrick used photograph size on a page in the annual report to come up with ratings of CEO prominence. For the next two narcissistic indicators, which are more compensation-focused, the authors measured i) the relative cash of the CEO's compensation (salary and bonus) and divided it by that of the firm's second-highest-paid executive and ii) the CEO's similar non-cash pay (i.e., deferred income, stock grants and stock options) divided by that of the second-highest-paid executive. These two indicators are more related to a CEO's focus on benefiting most from a firm's performance, which indicates that they think they should be the prime beneficiary of a firm's profits and windfalls.

The next two indicators relate to textual characteristics. Let's get into the text-mining method that Chatterjee and Hambrick used. They used two methods.

The first textual indicator reflected the CEO's prominence in a company's press releases. This text-mining method is an example of a keyword-matching approach. In this approach, a social scientist counts the number of matches for a particular keyword in a document. The keyword in this instance is the CEO's name. Based on interviews with communication specialists, the authors found CEOs have strict rules for any announcements that go to the outside world. CEOs themselves read and review almost all press releases except very routine ones. Thus, a very narcissistic CEO will demand that she be mentioned in press releases as often as possible. The authors operationalized this measure by calculating the number of times a CEO was mentioned by name in a company's press releases, which they further divided by the total number of words in all its press releases.

The second textual indicator relates to pronouns, specifically first-person singular pronouns. This indicator is an example of a dictionary-based approach that I have discussed previously in other chapters. The idea for using this textual indicator is that using first-person singular pronouns such as 'I', 'me', 'mine', 'my', and 'myself' reflects a person's self-absorption, which is an indicator of narcissism. To measure this indicator, the authors collected digital transcripts of CEO interviews conducted by journalists or financial analysts. The authors finally calculated the number of first-person pronoun words divided by all first-person plural pronouns ('we', 'us', 'our', 'ours', 'ourselves') and first-person singular pronouns to create their indicator. Usage of first-person plural pronouns indicates someone who thinks more collectively than individually.

Finally, the authors created a narcissism index for each CEO by taking the simple mean of the five indicators, after standardizing (i.e., subtracting the mean and dividing by the standard deviation) each of the indicators.

They tested their ideas on CEOs in the computer software and hardware industries between 1992 and 2004.

What did their analysis reveal?

Chatterjee and Hambrick found CEO narcissism was positively associated with strategic dynamism (measured by changes in advertising, innovation, marketing and financial leverage) and a greater number of acquisitions and grander acquisitions. These findings hold well and have good external validity. Jack Welch, the former CEO of General Electric (GE), who some commentators have regarded as narcissistic, made many

innovative changes to GE, including about 1000 acquisitions and
hankering after big firms such as Honeywell International.[16] On
the performance front, the authors found CEO narcissism was
related to extreme performance (measured by return on assets
and shareholder returns), and higher performance fluctuation
for a metric like return on investments. One recent example of
a considerable acquisition bid that seems to have had an adverse
and extreme reaction from the investor community is Tesla's
acquisition of X.

Tesla's stock plummeted about 20 per cent after Elon Musk
disclosed his plan to buy the social media communications
giant.[17]

Now you're thinking, how do you know that the narcissistic
index is valid? The authors verified this by running surveys with
security analysts. They also found that CEOs were narcissistic
across different firms, and it was not due to an ingrained practice
of a firm only appointing narcissistic CEOs. Their analytic
models also ensured that the narcissism index was measured
before the outcome variables, such as dynamism, acquisitions and
performance measures, which to an extent shows that the effects
are not merely correlational.

So, in effect, we see narcissistic CEOs are bolder and more
grandiose in their strategies and this, in turn, leads to radical
changes and wild swings in performance.

This excellent study was the forerunner of several other studies
that examined various consequential outcomes with narcissistic
CEOs as the main protagonists. Other studies asked different
questions. For example, is it a good idea for an innovative and
entrepreneurial firm to be led by someone narcissistic?

German scholars Andres Engelen, Christoph Neumann, and
Susanne Schmidt asked whether narcissistic CEOs should head

entrepreneurially oriented firms for forty-one S&P 500 firms from 2005 to 2007.[18]

What is 'entrepreneurial orientation', you may ask.

Entrepreneurial orientation (EO), which is regarded as a key ingredient nowadays to succeed in the business world, is the idea of an entrepreneur being quick to adapt to customer needs, always keeping an eye out for the next big trend, coming up with radical innovations and being willing to take risks. A firm is said to be entrepreneurial if it is innovative, proactive and risk-taking. This orientation, in turn, can lead to superior firm performance. For example, consider the 3M Company and Google. These firms are known to be creative and innovative and are perhaps exemplars of entrepreneurial-oriented firms.

Google's two most popular features of thread sorting and unlimited archiving of one's email were developed by an engineer within the firm. Google advises its employees to work 20 per cent of their office time on projects that don't have an immediate impact but may be promising in the future.[19] To be innovative and cater to new and emerging customer demands, 3M sends 9000 technical employees to different countries into customers' workplaces to view their customers' problems first-hand.

To measure EO, Engelen and his co-authors used text-mining methods. As EO is related to a concurrent focus on innovativeness, proactiveness and risk-taking, the authors used words that indicate these three behaviours in a company's letters to shareholders in the annual report. They used a dictionary-based approach to measure EO. For this, the authors used the text analysis software DICTION.[20] See Table 19.1 below for the words that were used to measure EO.[21]

Construct	Measure	Source
Entrepreneurial orientation	Computer-aided text analysis of letter to shareholders ad-lib, adroit, adroitness, adventuresome, adventurous, anticipate, audacious, bet, bold, bold-spirited, brash, brave, bright-idea, chance, chancy, change, clever, cleverness, conceive, concoct, concoction, concoctive, conjure-up, courageous, create, creation, creative, creativity, creator, danger, dangerous, dare, daredevil, daring, dauntless, dicey, discover, discoverer, discovery, dream, dream-up, enterprising, envisage, envision, expect, expert, exploration, exploratory, explore, fearless, forecast, fore-glimpse, foreknow, foresee, foretell, form, formulation, forward-looking, frame, framer, freethinker, gamble, genesis, genius, gifted, gutsy, headlong, hit-upon, imagination, imaginative, imagine, improvise, incautious, ingenious, ingenuity, initiative, initiator, innovate, innovation, inquire, inquiry, inspiration, inspired, intrepid, invent, invented, invention, inventive, inventiveness, inventor, investigate, investigation, look-into, make-up, mastermind, masterstroke, metamorphose, metamorphosis, neoteric, neoterism, neoterize, new, new-wrinkle, novel, novelty, opportunity-seeking, original, originality, originate, origination, originative, originator, patent, plunge, precarious, proactive, probe, prospect, radical, rash, recast, recasting, reckless, research, resourceful, resourcefulness, restyle, restyling, revolutionize, risk, risky, scrutinization, scrutiny, search, see-things, stake, study, survey, temerity, think-up, trademark, uncertain, venture, venturesome, vision, visionary, visualize, wager	DICTION 6.14.5 Corporate websites Investor relations departments

Table 19.1: Words to measure entrepreneurial orientation

Okay, now we have a textual measure for EO. Firms with EO use these words more in their letters to the shareholders.

What might happen to EO firms when they hire a narcissistic CEO? To answer this question, the authors used similar text-mining methods and indicators as Chatterjee and Hambrick for measuring narcissism. The authors first tested for a positive relationship between EO and firm performance. They indeed found one. Google and 3M do well for a reason. They have an entrepreneurial mindset. Let's see what happens when such firms have a narcissistic CEO.

The authors found narcissistic CEOs weaken the positive association between a firm's EO and firm performance. There is reason to believe that such CEOs might put themselves first and care less about the objectives of the firm. However, these CEOs help in some industries. Like Chatterjee and Hambrick, the authors found narcissistic CEOs strengthen the positive association between EO and firm performance in dynamic sectors and markets with few competitors. So, it is best to have Elon Musk at the helm in an industry like electric vehicles, which is remarkably dynamic.

What about firms with few rivals? Why might narcissists do well there? Markets with few competitors tend to pay more attention to the actions of every other player in a market. These markets are closely followed by the media, a situation that motivates narcissists and allows them to practice what they do best. Show who is in power. Indeed, Engelen and his co-authors find that narcissists do better in these markets because of the following reasons. First, markets with few players have lower competitive pressures. Thus, ignoring subordinates that may lead to tension between the CEO and their employees and consequently delay a new product introduction, for example, is less of an issue in a market with few players than in a market with a lot of players. Second, narcissists ignore trial-and-error thinking. This can be a bigger issue in a market with a lot of players. Third, narcissistic CEOs tend to be very controlling. In a market with few firms, they tend to be significantly endowed with many resources. So, such markets will be affected less detrimentally by having a narcissistic CEO at the top.

In essence, a narcissistic CEO positively impacts firm performance, but only in specific contexts.

Till now, we have talked about using the text in press releases and interviews to measure CEO narcissism.

What about other modes of a CEO's communication, which are textual, and can enable one to understand if a CEO is narcissistic?

In an exciting study, Charles Ham from Washington University in St Louis, Nicholas Seybert from the University of Maryland and Sean Wang at the Southern Methodist University used a textual characteristic pertinent to someone's identity and of supreme legal importance to explore narcissistic personalities.[22]

Signatures.

Ham and his colleagues used the size of a CEO's signature in a firm's annual report to determine the narcissism of a CEO. They then used their narcissism measure to see how a narcissistic CEO affects firm investments and performance.

Why use signatures?

We know signatures are used for identity validation. We know that this textual characteristic is a very important item in determining the authenticity of a painting or work of art. For example, French painter Paul Cézanne signed his paintings as 'P. Cezanne'. Cézanne signed in a stylized cursive, which now, in fact, is also a popular computer font. But it is also an indicator of someone's personality and her intention that her work is for posterity. Let's briefly look at the signature styles of some famous painters and what signature enthusiasts think the signatures indicate about their personalities.

Surrealistic Mexican painter Frida Kahlo's signature has a changing pressure, a determined right slant and measured spacing. Graphologists have speculated that the changing pressure signifies someone with a very sensitive yet troubled mind. The determined right slant and the measured spacing show Kahlo's pride in her femininity and indigenous identity.

Frida Kahlo.

Source: teepublic.com

British-based street artist Banksy uses an array of signatures, but they all are consistently large, bold letters that are spaced closely together. These characteristics in his signature indicate someone confident, tenacious and who is an intellectual.

Source: https://www.irishnews.com/magazine/entertainment/2017/12/12/news/
danny-boyle-and-banksy-stage-alternative-nativity--1208657/

Source: https://www.bimago.com/canvas-prints/street-art/
banksy-signature-68016.html

Source: https://www.themarginalian.org/2008/10/10/bansky-pet-shop/

Pablo Picasso's signature has a heavy line pressure and wide letters, with large gaps between the letters. It is surmised that this indicates someone happy, expansive in his persona, and with a great and consistent work ethic.[23]

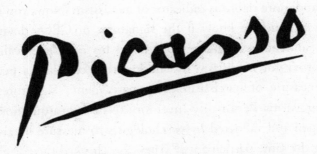

Source: https://www.gallery.ca/sites/default/files/picasso.jpg

Note that in the medieval period, artists did not think of their signatures as something that was meant to show their style and personality, nor was it a legal tool. Artists generally thought of themselves as just craftsmen. Signatures played a more down-to-earth role then. It stood for an indicator, which allowed these craftsmen to be paid for their work. It was during the Renaissance that an artist signing their work of art became more common. The use of the signature as a legal tool and the way we understand it today was primarily due to the Statute of Fraud Acts passed by the English Parliament in 1677.[24] A signature thus now acts not just as an indication of a person's identity but also works as a legal tool.

Indeed, signatures matter for all of us, but it does matter more for some people responsible for thousands, such as a CEO. A CEO's signature has weight, can change the lives of many and is a tool that can indicate their personality.

Past research[25] has demonstrated that signature size can be an implicit measure of ego and dominance, which are strong indicators of narcissism. The beauty and elegance of using the signature as an indicator of narcissism is that the signatory is more than likely to be oblivious that her ego would affect something as simple as their signature.[26] Thus, the measure is implicit and could be said to be a fairer and more rigorous indicator of narcissism. Now, you might think, how do we know if the signatures of CEOs do indeed reflect someone's narcissism? Lam and his colleagues validated their proxy for narcissism by checking the correlation between their measure of narcissism using participants' signatures and the Narcissistic Personality Inventory (NPI-16), a questionnaire developed and validated by psychologists to measure narcissism, among the same participants.[27] They also checked the correlation between their measure and a prior study's narcissism score that had employees' perceptions of the narcissism of their CEOs.[28]

How did the authors use the signature to measure narcissism?

This text-mining method the authors used is what I would define as size-based. This is a rare and creative use of text to create a measure. To measure narcissism using signatures, the authors first drew a rectangle around each CEO's signature, where each side of the rectangle touched the most extreme endpoint of the signature. The area used by the signature was then calculated by multiplying the length and width of the rectangle. As long names can affect the narcissism measure, they controlled for the length of the CEO's name by dividing the square area by the number of letters in the CEO's name. The authors then examined the effects of the signatures of narcissistic CEOs on 741 CEOs from 411 firms over the period 1992–2015 on a firm's investments and performance.

What did they find?

Lam and his co-authors found that narcissistic CEOs overinvest in R&D and acquisitions and that their firms experience lower profitability and operating cash flows. However, despite these adverse outcomes, narcissistic CEOs enjoy higher compensation. Thus, similar to the study by the German team of social scientists, these authors find that narcissistic CEOs don't help firms. However, in some contexts, as we saw in the earlier studies, a narcissistic CEO helps.

In essence, it appears that having a narcissistic CEO can indeed be a double-edged sword. On one hand, a narcissistic CEO can often be detrimental. Narcissistic CEOs pursue too many acquisitions that aren't seen to their end and overinvest in research and development. For acquisitions, one example is Jack Welch's fervid bid to acquire Honeywell Industries, which eventually failed.[29] These CEOs also influence and decrease a firm's entrepreneurial spirit and often lead a firm to suffer lower profits and cash flows.

On the other hand, a narcissistic CEO can be beneficial for firms in dynamic industries and in industries with low competition. Findings that narcissistic CEOs tend to be more active and strengthen the positive association between EO and firm performance in dynamic industries suggest that it may indeed be a manna for a company like Tesla, which competes in one of the most dynamic sectors, to have a leader like Elon Musk as a CEO.

Given Elon Musk's ostentatious actions, he should rate high on the narcissistic scale and even though that has its problems, his narcissistic tendencies also allow Tesla, SpaceX and the Boring Company to scale new heights.

So, what do these studies mean for businesses?

First, some CEOs make decisions based on self-absorption and don't look at objective facts. Firms would be remiss to ignore that proper care and scrutiny must be done when someone is appointed CEO. Chatterjee and Hambrick give the example of Jean-Marie Messier. He was the CEO of Paris-based Compagnie Generale des Eaux, which was a global leader in water, electrical and waste utilities. One day, Messier decided to move to the entertainment and media business, which we now know as Vivendi. So, a utility company diversified and moved into entertainment. This is like Toyota Motors deciding to move into selling mineral water. Generale des Eaux was doing well, but their capabilities did not match up at all with what a media and entertainment business would need. Messier himself had no clue about the media and entertainment business. Vivendi was formed in 1997 and suffered losses of €13.6 billion in 2001 and €23.3 billion in 2002. Messier was described as someone who is 'colourful', 'self-absorbed', and 'egomaniacal'.[30] It would not be a surprise if Messier ranked very high on the narcissism scale. Consider his signature, which he sometimes used in his emails: 'J6M'—short for Jean-Marie Messier Moi-Même, Maître du Monde (Jean-Marie Messier Myself, Master of the World). You get the picture.

Second, if firms are working in a dynamic context with few competitors, hiring someone at the top who is self-absorbed might be a good idea. Narcissists tend to go for the jugular and are bold and risk-takers. Perhaps in settings such as an industry that is highly dynamic and has few rivals, firms need someone who is more of a maximum man than a minimum man.*

* In their book *Power and the Corporate Mind*, Zaleznik and Kets de Vries define two types of executives: the 'Minimum Man', who is plain, a conformist, cares about equality, one who plays for the team and is mostly satisfied with the status quo. These executives

Third, investors have an array of various textual sources by which they can measure narcissism in CEOs or other top management personnel. Narcissism can be measured by what these top management personnel say in their interviews or write in their letters to shareholders or the manner in which they sign. The identification of narcissism in top management personnel may lead investors to be more cautious in their investment strategies.

Finally, we see that narcissistic CEOs get higher pay despite their low performance. The board of directors of firms should be more mindful of such inflation in salaries and decide accordingly.

There is a quote by Dwight Shrute, a textbook narcissist, of the American version of the TV show *The Office*, which I thoroughly enjoy. The quote goes as this, 'I am ready to face any challenge that might be foolish enough to face me.'

It would be foolish to be unaware of how narcissistic CEOs can be a double-edged sword for a company.

---

do things in a cautious manner and gradually. The second type, the 'Maximum Man', is colourful, adventurous and a maverick. Firms led by these executives are entrepreneurial, come up with innovations, take risks, move fast and bravely.

VI

ENEMIES, FRIENDS AND LOVERS

The way we use language differs for someone or something we hate, love, like or simply don't care about. We may use the same word or phrase differently depending on who we talk to and who we are talking about. In business, generally, a firm's rivals are its enemies as they are trying to steal market share from the firm. In online dating, a person's matches are their potential lovers. In social media and online communities, a user's connections are their friends whose posts they like, share or disagree with. And many a time, our posts about ourselves, family, friends, acquaintances, brands, artists, governments and celebrities are read by people we don't know.

In this set of chapters, I will take you through articles that examine directly or indirectly talk about enemies, friends and lovers. We will examine if Honda should be worried if Toyota has a product defect due to what people say online, learn whether vague language has a place in business, and see if one has a better chance of finding friends online and perhaps a romantic partner, depending on the way one wields words.

20

Wayward Brands and Innocent Rivals

Most of us know what happens if a firm has a product failure and has to recall its products. Generally, there are negative consequences for a firm's reputation, sales and even stock prices. Sometimes the consequences can be seriously dire. Sorry to be a downer but consider a product recall where a food processing company must recall its potentially tainted peanut butter. The cause of the recall is a major salmonella outbreak from consuming peanut butter, and the outbreak has killed several people and made hundreds sick.

Recalls like this have tremendous repercussions. Sometimes even bankruptcy.

In the case of the peanut butter, the culprit was the Peanut Corporation of America (PCA), which has now ceased to exist.

PCA was a peanut-processing business founded in 1977. It used to cater to food makers for usage in various snacks, cookies, ice cream and even dog treats through its processing plants in Blakely, Georgia, Suffolk, Virginia and Plainview, Texas. Its core market was 'institutional food', which included jails, nursing homes and schools.[1]

Between late 2008 and early 2009, because of the salmonella contamination and the consequent food poisoning in PCA's peanut products, nine people died and at least 714 people got sick. Half of them were children.[2] The contamination led to the most extensive food recall in American history.[3] Over 3900 different products made by 361 different companies were recalled. All used PCA ingredients.[4] The consequences for PCA were dire.

On 13 February 2009, PCA filed for bankruptcy. Stewart Parnell, the CEO and president of PCA was sentenced to twenty-eight years in prison—the longest punishment ever handed out to a producer in a food-borne illness case.[5]

But what do you think happened to other innocent peanut butter manufacturers? What do you think could happen to a blameless manufacturer whose plant facilities were spick and span and did not have 'dusty beams, leaky roofs, and birds flying through the building'[6] unlike PCA?

Let's consider another famous scandal. The Volkswagen (VW) emissions scandal, sometimes known as Dieselgate or Emissionsgate.[7]

Volkswagen was charged with deploying software that fooled US emissions testing and using its false ecological ratings to qualify for green car subsidies and tax exemptions.[8] According to the Environmental Protection Agency (EPA), VW insisted for a year that the discrepancies were just technical glitches. On 20 September 2015, VW admitted its deception and issued a public apology. VW's global recall of diesel cars allegedly designed to mislead environmental regulators ate up a substantial amount of money from the company's coffers. As of 1 June 2020, the emissions scandal cost VW $33.3 billion through fines, penalties, financial settlements and buyback costs.[9]

Volkswagen got hammered and deserved it. I had a Volkswagen Jetta SportWagen at the time of this recall and

I can tell you I was angry with myself for trusting Volkswagen and overall disappointed with this well-known brand. Though my car ran on petrol/gasoline, I wanted to sell the car but was finding it hard to find any buyer unless I reduced the price really low. Blatant cheating is not easily forgiven. Even a product recall caused by an honest mistake damages a company's finances and consumers' perceptions of the brand.[10]

What do you think happened to other car manufacturers? Firms such as Ford, Tesla and General Motors? These are American brands. Perhaps there were repercussions for these automakers. What about German car manufacturers such as BMW and Daimler? Did they suffer too because of VW's folly? No wonder even Angela Merkel, the then Chancellor of Germany, urged 'complete transparency' and engaged the German Transport Minister, Alexander Dobrindt, to coordinate with Volkswagen and manage the crisis so that it didn't dent the reputation of the German auto manufacturing industry.

One of the most famous product recalls is the Japanese car manufacturer Toyota's unintended acceleration crisis in 2009 and 2010. Beginning in August 2009, the accelerator pedals in some Toyota vehicles suddenly became stuck. Drivers panicked and automobiles spun out of control, resulting in many crashes.

The crisis began in San Diego, California, in August 2009. While driving with his family, a man called 911 to report that the accelerator pedal in his Toyota Lexus was stuck and he could not get his car to stop. His brakes were not working either. The car crashed. Nobody riding in the Lexus survived the wreck. The 911 call became viral, and Toyota had to face the consequences. They had slipped up.

By February 2010, the company had recalled more than 8 million vehicles worldwide with more than 6 million in the US itself.[11] Over the next five years, an estimated ninety people died. Toyota was accused of hiding information, and in 2014, Toyota paid $1.2 billion to avoid prosecution.[12] This penalty and the costs associated with more than 10 million recalls and other punitive damages caused a dent in Toyota's financial performance.[13] Toyota's reputation also took a nosedive. A company that had previously stood for quality, reliability, safety and innovation had become notorious.

But what about other car manufacturers like Honda, Nissan and Chrysler? Did they suffer too because of the wrongdoings of Toyota? Or did they benefit from Toyota's mishaps?

Consider Honda. Toyota's arch-rival and a car manufacturer from the same country as Toyota.

Did consumers punish Honda too because of Toyota's crisis? What do you think happened?

There are three possible scenarios.

Scenario 1: Honda gains. Suppose we follow the general logic of firm competition and market share effects. In this case, new buyers might decide to stop buying Toyota cars and buy Honda cars, or current Toyota car owners might sell or trade in their Toyotas for another car manufacturer, most probably Honda. Honda is regarded as the most ostensible substitute for Toyota. In a *Time* magazine article,[14] when asked who the biggest beneficiary of Toyota's crisis would be, analysts from Deutsche Bank surmised that 'We see Honda as being the best positioned across a broad range of vehicles to gain'.

Scenario 2: Nothing happens to Honda's sales. There is no change in Honda's sales as buyers ignore Toyota's crisis, the world of buying and selling cars sees no upheaval, and Honda's sales remain the same. A Honda spokeswoman mentioned that the company did not change its sales forecast due to Toyota's problems.[15]

Scenario 3: Honda suffers too. There could be a contagion effect where consumers might perceive other Japanese brands as having defects and therefore also being less trustworthy. In a CNN article, the author speculated that 'Toyota's recall problems could hurt more than its own reputation' and 'Honda and Nissan could suffer collateral damage if consumers no longer give Japanese cars the same deference as in the past.'

What do you think happened? What happens to rivals or competitors when there is a product recall for one firm?

In a study that I published with Gerard Tellis at the University of Southern California, we examined this very question: Can a product recall for one firm, the culprit, influence how innocent rivals are perceived online and what are the consequent effects on the innocent rivals' sales and stock price?[16]

As you have seen through the examples, a product recall is never good news for a firm. It is also bad for consumers. Besides the severity of the consequences of product recalls, the other problem is that they are also rampant. In 2019, before the onset of COVID-19, around 39 million vehicles and about 14 million motor vehicle parts were taken off US roads.[17] And this statistic is just for the automobile industry.

Tellis and I advanced the idea that though it might seem like a great occasion for the rivals of the culprit firm, a product recall is not necessarily good news for competitors. We proposed a phenomenon that we named a 'perverse halo effect', whereby negative online comments about a recalled brand increase negative online comments for an innocent competitor. These negative comments, in turn, lead to a decrease in sales and stock market performance for innocent rivals.

But why will an innocent brand that has nothing to do with a product recall get hammered by users on social media?

To theorize why a perverse halo occurs, we relied on a seminal paper by Jack Feldman and John Lynch in the prestigious *Journal of Applied Psychology*. Feldman and Lynch proposed a theory called the accessibility–diagnosticity theory. In the context of a product recall, the theory works like this.[18]

If a consumer thinks brand A is diagnostic of (i.e., informative about) brand B, the consumer will use perceptions of brand A's quality to infer the quality of brand B. However, this presumption only occurs when both brands and their quality perceptions are accessible (i.e., retrievable from memory) simultaneously. In essence, the possibility of a perverse halo between car models of different brands depends on the existence and strength of association between brands in a consumer's memory.

Consumers implicitly have networks wherein information about brands and their attributes (e.g., country of origin, size) resides in their knowledge network as interconnected nodes.[19] Brands are interconnected in the consumer's mind through linkages between such nodes. The accessibility of brand A when brand B is mentioned rises with increasing linkage strength between the two brands. We argued that a perverse halo occurs when two brands are similar. High similarity leads to an increase in both accessibility and diagnosticity. An array of factors can increase the perception of similarity between brands. Brands could be owned by the same owner or have similar attributes, such as size, country of origin and production processes.

So, how did we go about testing our idea?

For the study, we tracked forty-eight car models from four different brands: Toyota, Honda, Nissan and Chrysler. We analysed the daily traffic, topic and sentiment on more than 1000 automotive social media sites following product recall announcements during a sixteen-month period from the beginning of 2009 to mid-April 2010. The online comments spanned postings about the four brands and their forty-eight car models on various social media platforms. We collected such comments from automotive forums and blogs such as Thetruthaboutcars. com and review sites such as Edmunds.com.

Now let's get to the text-mining algorithm we used to generate our outcome variable of interest, negative comments about a car model's safety. We used a natural language processing (NLP) algorithm to generate our outcome variable. The algorithm starts by generating tag data (similar to classifying a document as x or y) on three dimensions at the sentence level: subject, attribute and sentiment. For example, in an online comment with a sentence such as, 'One cannot be safe in a Corolla', the subject is Corolla, the attribute is safety and the sentiment is negative. So, if one is interested in collecting the volume of negative sentiment about Toyota Corolla, the algorithm first screens for references of the car model 'Toyota Corolla' in a sentence. It then filters for the keyword 'safety' and its synonyms in the same sentence and evaluates whether that sentence is negative. It then adds the count of negative sentences about the safety attribute in a poster's comment. We then added all negative comments about the safety attribute for the Corolla car model for the brand Toyota every day to arrive at a daily negative comments score for Corolla.

Let's now get to the results.

We first examined if there was a perverse halo among brands of the same car manufacturer.

Could a Lexus LS recall also damage Toyota Tacoma's online comments and further hurt its sales? A Lexus LS is very different from the Toyota Tacoma. The Lexus LS is a full-size luxury sedan and is the flagship model of Toyota's Lexus division. On the other hand, the Toyota Tacoma is a pickup truck.

We found that a recall for Lexus LS could also hurt Toyota Tacoma. Across a range of analyses, we found that negative comments about a car model from one brand influenced other car models of the same brand. So, a Toyota Corolla recall incited worries about the Tacoma, Prius and RAV4, which are distinctly different classes of Toyota vehicles. In essence, if Toyota has an issue with one car model, people perceive that Toyota's other car models have the same problem, which creates negative comments or chatter about the innocent car models of Toyota.

What about a perverse halo among different brands? First, let's observe what happens to the negative online comments for innocent rival brands when a brand undergoes a product recall.

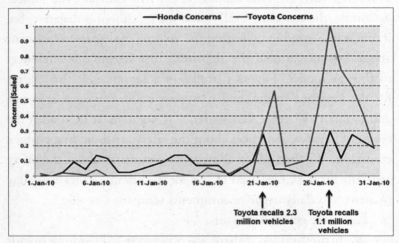

Figure 20.1: Graph of Toyota's major product recalls and negative online comments for Toyota and Honda

Figure 20.1 clearly shows that negative comments about Toyota increased when Toyota issued large product recalls due to its unintended acceleration crisis in January 2010. What we also see is that a Toyota recall not only sparked negative comments about Toyota but also for Honda—a brand whose cars had a clean bill of health at the time.

Interestingly, we observed increased negative comments about Honda when Toyota made extensive recalls. Note that our study not only looked at Toyota's product recalls and its spillovers on other brands but also at recalls of each of the other brands and their subsequent spillovers. Honda's recall on 16 March 2010 increased negative online comments for both Toyota and Nissan. And these negative online comments were more than just talk.

The negative comments spurred by a product recall amplified damage to the bottom line of domestic rivals. To assess the impact on company stock price, when we aggregated the online comments about car models across each brand, we found that such comments sparked by a rival's recall erased $7.3 million, on average, from an innocent firm's market capitalization over six days. The negative online buzz about the culprit brand's innocent rival also negatively affected the innocent brand's sales.

One might think that the effects are symmetric. We found that the perverse halo effect appears to be asymmetric in terms of market dominance. A recall for a top seller like Toyota Corolla has a more significant negative impact on a rival with a smaller market share like Nissan Sentra. In contrast, a Sentra recall left less of a dent in Corolla. Intriguingly, we found that the perverse halo has an inverse effect on car companies identified with different nations of origin. Specifically, a recall of a Toyota car (recognized as a Japanese brand) resulted in a decrease in negative chatter about Chrysler cars (recognized as an American brand). We also found that a Toyota recall can increase Chrysler's sales and its market cap, at least temporarily. This finding suggested that a brand like Chrysler should be cashing in when a competitor from another country has a recall event.

Using text-mining tools, our study of the automotive industry
revealed that product recalls provoked a sharp increase in negative
chatter on social media sites for the culprit brand. We found
this online trash talk amplifies the damage, slashing sales and the
market cap of the recalling company.

But the damage does not end there. Innocent firms—especially
rival firms of the same national origin faced a similar fate when
they got caught in a 'perverse halo' of negativity created by the
recalled firm. In general, bad news travels fast on social media,
and our study demonstrated that a recall event not only increases
negative chatter for innocent rivals but also damages the sales and
stock market performance of rivals.

Let's get back to the initial examples I posed at the beginning
of this chapter. PCA's salmonella scandal and Volkswagen's
diesel emissions scandal. What happened to PCA's rivals and
Volkswagen's competitors?

PCA's peanut butter fiasco had strong and negative
repercussions not just for PCA but for the whole category.
Consumers got scared, stopped trusting and avoided peanut butter
altogether. Sales of brands that were innocent went down by 25 per
cent.[20] The industry suffered. The effects of the recession further
exacerbated the industry's doom and estimated losses primarily
due to the scandal were estimated to be to the order of $1 billion.[21]

What about Volkswagen and its rivals?

During the Volkswagen emissions scandal, I did an analysis
to find out what happened to car manufacturers.[22] I calculated
the stock market returns[*] for nine automobile brands after 20

---

[*] I calculated the abnormal stock market return, which is the difference between the
actual return of a security and the expected return. I used the country's main index
such as the DAX, which is a stock market index consisting of forty major German
companies.

September 2015, the day that VW admitted its deception and issued a public apology. I selected three German brands (Volkswagen, BMW, Daimler), one European (Fiat), two American (Ford and GM), two Japanese (Toyota and Honda) and one Korean (Kia).

All four European brands (VW, BMW, Daimler and Fiat) suffered in the stock market after VW's dark day. Volkswagen's stock market return was -18.95 per cent on 21 September, while BMW, Daimler and Fiat followed suit with -1.8 per cent, -1.8 per cent, and -3.3 per cent, respectively. The returns remained negative till 22 September for all four brands. When I examined the stock market returns for the non-European brands, the negative effect was weaker, with only Kia showing a negative return of -2.4 per cent on 21 September. So, the pattern found in our focal study of Toyota, Honda, Nissan and Chrysler repeated itself.

So, what do these results imply for managers?

First, innocent rivals should be on the lookout for competitors from the same country facing a product recall. As I discussed, one factor that increases associations between two brands is similarity. Rival firms can lie low and avoid comparisons with the recalled firm during a recall event. Many firms pursue a strategy of denial, stating that the firm has nothing to do with the recalled firm and that its scientific processes, facilities and suppliers are different. Such a strategy can sometimes backfire.[23]

Second, firms should deliberate on what consumers think online about their firm and how similar or dissimilar they are perceived in consumers' eyes to other firms in the same industry. This information can enable firms to position themselves differently from their rivals. One important thing that I can keep talking to my MBA students about is brand positioning and differentiation. Firms can create a distinct positioning by correctly understanding customer needs and the competition. This should reduce consumer perceptions of similarity that can emerge from comparative advertising or messages in traditional mediums like television or social media. If there is a recall, a firm perceived to be similar to a recalling firm may need to deviate from its positioning.

Third, for recalling firms, it is imperative that they manage the tide of negative comments that will emerge during such events. Such negative comments spread like wildfire. Generally, firms focused on mass media like television and newspapers to manage such crises. But as our research showed, it is vital that they also handle the crisis on social media. Firms could create a page on their website about the product recall with FAQs that answer commonly asked questions, inform their consumers as soon as possible about the recall on all social media channels and ensure that all information regarding the recall is on one dedicated website.

Finally, rivals' managers from the same country as the recalling firm can use the product recall's online comments to predict what would happen to their own online comments, sales and stock market performance. Online comments tinged with negativity can be a leading indicator of impending doom and can help firms organize and plan some of the aforementioned strategies.

In essence, online chatter does matter, and a perverse halo exists.

Innocent rivals—beware of wayward brands.

21

The Unexpected Upsides of Vagueness

Let's consider some expressions:[1]

- We are exploring many options.
- We should wait till we get all the facts.
- This is a possibility.
- It could go up or it could go down.

All four expressions seem to say something, but, in fact, say nothing. If you are a firm in this current topsy-turvy world of societal, economic, financial and political upheavals, it is inelegant and naïve for a business executive to utter these expressions.

Don't firms have to act on imperfect information all the time? Adding more imperfect information and ambiguity in business communications will just exacerbate the complexity that firms in our modern-day world have to contend with.

What these terms genuinely mean is unclear. According to the Oxford English Dictionary, vagueness is the 'lack of certainty or distinctness'. The notion of vagueness was first introduced in 1902 to describe 'words with blurred edges'.[2] Yes, our understanding does become blurry when we come across vague content.

Indeed, we, as humans, do not appreciate vagueness. We appreciate communicators who can express themselves, clearly articulate their thoughts and feelings, and provide us with a complete picture of any situation or context. As Aesop, in his wonderful quip, states, 'I can't be friends with a man who blows hot and cold with the same breath.' In an age that worships accurate information, vagueness indeed feels like intentional laziness and an indication of a sloppy attitude.[3]

But vagueness still exists and is used.

We see it often in lyrics in songs.

Take, for example, Bryan Adams' hit single 'Summer of '69' from 1984. It apparently is not about the summer of 1969 but more about the other 69. I think we all know what the other 69 means. In a TV interview (*The Early Show* on CBS), Bryan Adams confirmed what he meant.[4] Until I read about this, I always thought the song was about the actual 'Summer of 1969'. Whenever I heard this song, I wished to be young and restless where I would be strumming a guitar in open fields with the sun shining brightly. My best friends would then join in . . . and so on. A song that triggered happy nostalgia. Oops, I misunderstood it. Not my fault though. The title of the song and lyrics were well . . . vague!

Another song with vague lyrics is Rihanna's hit that mixes pop, hip-hop, R&B and rock, 'Umbrella'. I always thought that the song was about love, with the usage of the word 'umbrella' and the lyrics that go with it, indicative of love and caring. I was mistaken.

Apparently, 'umbrella' in the song is supposed to symbolize a condom.

In fact, in creative work, vagueness can be a good thing. Many musicians have quite a lot of difficulty in explaining their songs. Perhaps it is part of the mystique.[5] Musicians know what something means or does not mean in their songs, but maybe they want listeners to create their own narrative and interpretation of what a piece means.

For example, consider rapper M.I.A.'s hit single, 'Paper Planes'. Many must have thought that the song was about drug dealers and the idea of getting high. At least, I did. The song also had some controversy, as some claimed it was pro-gun and pro-terrorism. M.I.A., a Sri Lankan who sought refuge in the UK due to the displacement caused by the Sri Lankan Civil War, has said she wants the song to be open to interpretation. However, she hinted that the song is a political satire on big business and stereotypes about immigrants. In a 2009 interview, when asked about the song, she stated, 'It could be about, you know, gun corporations selling guns and making billions of dollars, or it could be about immigrants coming over and being like, the scary thing that's going to take everyone's jobs . . . I kinda want to leave it ambiguous.'[6]

Consider Bob Dylan, undoubtedly one of the greatest songwriters of all time and the first musician to win the Nobel Prize in Literature. Just ponder on all the speculations and hunches of what his lyrics mean. There have been hundreds of books written about what people 'think' his lyrics mean. If Dylan came out now and expressed what his songs meant, he would perhaps be a spoilsport and dull all the feelings and emotions we associate with his songs. Many musicians endorse the idea of the importance of vagueness in lyrics. American singer-songwriter John Mellencamp says, 'One quality of a good songwriter is to be vague. A vague notion, a vague image, but enough to give the listener the opportunity to make more out of what's being said than is there. That's the great thing about Bob Dylan's songs: We the listeners have made more out of them than he ever intended.'[7]

There are websites devoted to what songs mean. SongMeanings. com, a music website with over half a million members, allows users to discuss and provide their understanding of the underlying meanings of individual songs. The website's objective, which has around 1 million lyrics, is to discuss 'factual song meanings, personal experiences through the song, or even just their dismay for a song'.

Vague words or words with more than one meaning (i.e., polysemous words and homographs) also enable us to make rich connections between contrasting concepts. This nature of ambiguity is even an art form, which we call poetry.[8] Indeed, the Nobel Prize committee awarded Bob Dylan the Nobel Prize in Literature 'for having created new poetic expressions within the great American song tradition'. Moreover, who can doubt my favourite painter Claude Monet's masterpieces that make vagueness a joy to behold and a dream to the senses?

Vagueness is all good in creativity and the arts. But what about the pragmatic world of business which is generally unsentimental and unromantic? Will vagueness work here?

Vagueness and the consequent possible misinterpretation should have no role in business, right?

How about a company being vague to its stakeholders, such as its customers, investors, regulators, policymakers and employees? As you might guess, being mysterious with your investors, for example, is a no-no. Investors crave clear, factual, and objective information. They constantly seek information; the clearer and more precise it is, the better their odds of profiting in the stock market.

What about competitors?

Competition is at the heart of strategy. Competitive strategy is what firms plan to fend off current competitors and new entrants. It is, in essence, a long-term plan to gain a competitive advantage over its rivals in the industry. In business, competitors are your nemesis.

In their sharp little book, *Marketing Warfare*, Al Ries and Jack Trout apply military thinking to marketing problems, confronting and overcoming competitors with different warfare strategies to generate distinct brand positioning and consumer demand.[9]

Will being vague benefit firms when they confront competitors, which on most occasions is like warfare?

What do you think?

Strategy professors Wei Guo at China Europe International Business School, Tieying Yu at Boston College and Javier Gimeno at INSEAD combined forces to provide a different perspective of how vagueness might work in business, and when it could sometimes be helpful.[10] First, they examined if firms used vague language in their corporate communications, especially when confronted by new competitors. Second, they wanted to explore if being vague in a firm's corporate communications could have positive repercussions.

Wei and his colleagues had two primary questions.

- Do firms use vague language in profitable markets and where there is a higher likelihood of potential entrants?
- Will the vague language used by incumbents in a market (i.e., the firms that are already present in a market) be negatively related to potential entrants' probability of market entry and under what conditions will potential rivals react to such vagueness?

Firms have a lot to lose if new entrants move into their markets. Take, for example, firms such as Kodak, Sony, General Electric and DishTV. In the last couple of decades, these incumbents have been disrupted by technologies embraced by newer entrants such as Apple, Samsung, NextEra Energy and Netflix, respectively, in each of their markets. New entrants bring considerable resources and distinct positioning, and, of course, like all other firms, these companies yearn for market share.

Wei and his colleagues argued that when managers of incumbents realize that there is a high possibility of new entrants in their market, a market in which they currently are doing well, they are more likely to use vague language in their communications that would make their strategies and tactics harder to determine. This diminished understanding would then result in fewer firms entering their markets.

Who knew vagueness could be helpful in business?

Now, what is the primary idea here? Entrants or future rivals need clear and valuable information.

Future entrants need this clarity to come up with a competitive strategy. Potential entrants can only respond convincingly and effectively to an incumbent's plans if they are first aware, and importantly, they can interpret the strategy put forward by the incumbent. Vagueness in an incumbent's communication hinders the entrant's understanding of the firm's actions and predicting their reactions.

So, how did Wei and his colleagues go about answering their research questions?

Wei and his colleagues focused on the US domestic airline industry between 1995 and 2001. How did they define a market where the incumbents and the potential entrants waged war, to use Ries and Trout's jargon? They defined a market as a pair of cities where customers demand air travel using either non-stop or one-stop flights. The 'market' here refers to the marketplace or product category where final goods or services are sold, and firms compete. For example, Apple overshadowed Kodak in the camera market. At the same time, Netflix, via its streaming technology, has almost decimated firms like DishTV, which uses traditional cable TV technology in the direct broadcast TV market.

'Incumbents' were defined as airlines with either a market share of at least 5 per cent or a minimum of ten travellers per day in a specific city-pair market. For identifying potential entrants, they only picked airline carriers that 'had flights to or from both of the two endpoints of a route but did not yet operate a route linking the two endpoints'.

Now let's go into the text-mining method Wei and his colleagues used.

What document can help firms understand a competitor's strategies and is publicly available? Remember, it is the prerogative of a firm to disclose information. In most cases, firms would be remiss to state their strategies and tactics to the outside world. One such report that firms have to provide to the public is their annual report. Moreover, according to the US Securities and Exchange Commission (SEC), firms can't provide false information in their annual reports. Along with a narrative about a firm's operations and financial conditions in the preceding year, the annual report also includes plans and forecasts about the future of the firm. Wei and his colleagues thus used the incumbent firm's annual report to determine vagueness.

A firm's annual report has several sections. To capture their measure of vagueness, the authors focused on the following areas generally believed to be most pertinent to competition. These four were 'Business', 'Properties', 'Management Discussion and Analysis (MD&A)' and 'Financials'.

How did the research team go about capturing vagueness?

To compute the vagueness of the text in the four sections of the annual report, the authors used a dictionary-based approach. They used a vagueness dictionary developed by Jack Hiller at Southern Illinois University.[11] The original intention for creating the dictionary was to analyse vagueness in the delivery of university lectures, but since then, it has been used to uncover ambiguity in settings such as questionnaire design, political speeches and strategic management research.[12] The dictionary contains 362 different vague words and expressions on ten dimensions of vagueness.

As elaborated above, vagueness alludes to the use of words and expressions in communication, making interpreting the communication complicated and inexact.

Some examples of vague words are words like 'about', 'around' and 'nearly' before a number to make the number less precise; terms like 'a couple', 'a little', 'a high rate of' to refer to undetermined amounts; terms like 'may', 'could be', 'perhaps', and the use of phrases like 'as a matter of fact', 'in any event', 'as far as' that transfer the onus on the receiver of the information to make sense of the communication.

Wei and his colleagues next computed the vagueness score using the four sections of the annual report for eighteen domestic airlines across 5156 markets that saw 8095 new market entries from 1995 to 2001. To account for document length, they created a vagueness metric that was 'calculated as a count of vague words and expressions normalized by the total number of words in each document'.

Consider this statement from United Airlines[13:]

> Beginning January 1, 2001, the Company will decrease the
> commission it pays to travel agents from ten percent to eight
> percent for ticketless bookings.

This would be less vague compared to the following statement
from Vanguard Airlines:[14]

> The company revised its pricing system to compete more
> effectively against airlines that offered a limited number of seats
> at fares at or below the Company's then existing fares.

So, what did they do and find after calculating the vagueness
metric?

They first ran a regression analysis to find a relationship
between a predictor and a response variable. The statistical
output from a regression enables one to see if the relationship is
statistically valid.

In their first analysis, where vagueness was the outcome
variable, they found that firms resort to using vague language when
the market is attractive and when there are many incumbents. In
the second analysis, they ran a survival model (this is another
form of regression where the outcome variable is an event that
occurs in time, such as getting fired from a company after a
period). In this survival model, the outcome variable is coded as
a 'yes' if a potential entrant enters a market at a point in time and
a 'no' if the potential entrant does not enter a market at a point
in time. They found that when an incumbent firm uses fifty-
nine additional vague words in an annual report (while holding
all other variables in the regression at their mean values), this
reduces the probability of a potential entrant entering the same
market by 11.4 per cent.

Vagueness in providing information by an incumbent firm thus decreases the possibility of a potential entrant into an attractive market. What about contexts when the likelihood of a potential entrant entering an attractive market reduces even further when incumbent firms provide vague information? What could be some of these contexts?

Size is one. The size of an existing firm in an industry can influence how much attention entrants pay to the firm. Big firms have many advantages such as brand awareness and equity, economies of scale, ease of raising capital, and, of course, their experience and learnings in the market.[15] A potential entrant will thus consider a large incumbent a threat and will surely monitor what the large incumbent says. The authors carried out this analysis and found that firm size amplified the effect of vagueness in reducing the likelihood of market entry by a potential entrant. Potential entrants perhaps surmise that gaining market share will be tricky if there are big incumbents and when it is also hard for them to understand their strategies. Consider the telecommunications market. Few firms can compete with players like AT&T and Verizon, who dominate the market. This market requires ownership of the spectrum. To indulge in warfare with these firms would take a fair amount of courage, investments and resources. Plus, if, say, the information provided by AT&T and Verizon appears vague in their annual reports, which these potential entrants pay attention to, this should dwindle the hopes of these entrants seeing a bright future ahead.

Another context that could affect how much attention potential entrants pay to an incumbent is the market's concentration. I am using an economics-related word here and most of you may have heard and know about this term. However, for the uninitiated, market concentration measures the extent to which market shares are concentrated amongst a small number of firms. A high market concentration means that a small number of firms hold a substantial market share in a given market.

How should market concentration affect the likelihood of a potential entrant entering?

First, if the market concentration is high, there are only a few incumbents. This should make it easier for potential entrants in terms of resource use, as there are only a few firms to pay attention to. So, a potential entrant will pay more heed to firms in concentrated markets where few players dominate. However, the information provided by these dominant incumbents is vague and this lack of clarity should reduce their desire to enter such a market. The authors carried out this analysis and indeed found that the influence of vagueness in decreasing the likelihood of market entry increased when there were only a few firms in an attractive market.

Imagine you are the CEO of a firm considering entering the travel search market, a highly concentrated market with two leading players: Expedia and Priceline. Expedia owns Travelocity and Orbitz, and Priceline owns Kayak. If you are the CEO, while you would surely put a lot of effort into unearthing information about the leading players, it is likely that the information you will obtain is vague.[16] And, if Expedia and Priceline are already doing well, your chances of doing well are slimmer, and thus this will reduce the likelihood of entry.

Overall, Wei and his colleagues found that incumbent firms in attractive markets introduce vagueness in their communication to counter invasion by rivals, which works. It works even more when the incumbent is huge, and only a few players are in the market. So, what do these results imply for managers?

First, as Wei and his colleagues state, the Chinese general, military strategist and philosopher Sun Tzu had a saying, 'The supreme art of war is to subdue the enemy without fighting.' The study shows that language can be a strategic tool. Thus, it is important that firms learn to understand how language is used by their rivals and pay careful attention to the different tones and subtle cues used when they read their rival's information. A proper understanding of language can enable firms to understand what is being said and not said. Sometimes, the rival information can be vague, and this could be a voluntary strategy by a firm to cloud their actual strategies. A firm's behaviour in acting and reacting to its rival's competitive warfare is generally driven by its motivation to act and its capabilities.[17] This study, in essence, shows that a firm's behaviour can also be driven by the information that its rivals convey.

Second, companies that increase information asymmetry between two firms by being vague should acknowledge that their rivals might know what they are doing and thus be aware of their sophistry.

Third, the authors used only annual reports to identify vagueness. But given the various ways that firms nowadays communicate, such as via press releases, interviews, conference calls and social media like X, there is ample opportunity for a firm to understand if a rival is being deliberately vague.

So, vagueness has a benefit in business. Using the study above as one case, vagueness provides an upside for the incumbent. It deters market entry.

What about vagueness in our personal lives? Can there be an upside to vagueness here too?

A fascinating paper by Arul Mishra and Himanshu Mishra at the University of Utah and Babu Shiv at Stanford University finds an interesting upside of vagueness for common folk.[18] The authors argue that vague numerical ranges and deadlines are more potent in helping people pursue a goal and sustain it (e.g., lose weight) rather than exact numbers, dates and deadlines.

We tend to see our goals as ranges, and our minds focus on the more easily achievable portions of those ranges, which we perceive as within reach. I remember training for a marathon years ago. A marathon involves running 26.2 miles or 42 kilometres. My goal was to finish a marathon at an 8-minute mile pace (i.e., 3 hours, 29 minutes, 45 seconds to complete a marathon). Training for a marathon involves months of running intelligently and gaining endurance with training runs that increase every week till you taper off three weeks before the race. If it is a 16-week marathon programme, you want the longest run for your first week to be around 6 miles. You run your longest run of 22 miles three weeks before the actual run to train your body to suffer. Yes, it is suffering no matter what they say. I remember finishing my 22-mile training run at 2:59:40, which was slower than my 8-minute mile pace goal. Knowing that I did not achieve my precise goal demotivated me. However, when a friend of mine suggested that I think of my goal of running a marathon as something between around 3 hours and 28 minutes and 3 hours 32 minutes, my training run instead of being a demotivator, in fact, egged me on.

In essence, vagueness has positive repercussions not only for the creatives among us but can also be beneficial for firms and normal folks. It has its upsides.

22

How to Talk to Your Date

Consider this: you are on a date after using one of those apps that help you meet someone online and then after a few online conversations about some physical activity like yoga or running, concerts, travel and eating (have I hit on the general things that prospective couples talk about?) you are one on one with that person over coffee or a drink in the real world.

Now, I am going to give you two choices. One is the person you are on a date with speaks similarly to you. That is, the person has a similar style of talking. Perhaps the person uses similar sentence phrasing, phrases and idioms, and words.

The other choice is a person who speaks in a very different style than you. They use phrases that you have never heard of or are unfamiliar with, words that you don't generally use and perhaps use short and curt sentences compared to you who likes using complete sentences.

Whom would you prefer?

Research in psychology has shown that how a person communicates with another not only reveals their personality but also induces how this person will be in a relationship with another person or others.[1]

Let me introduce you to a theory called CAT.

Developed by Howard Giles, a British-American social psychologist and a Distinguished Research Professor of Communication in the Department of Communication at the University of California in Santa Barbara, CAT stands for Communication Accommodation Theory.[2] The theory concerns the changes in behaviour that people make to adapt their communication with their partner, and the extent to which people perceive their partner as suitably adapting to them.[3] In other words, the theory's core idea is that we adjust our style of speech to one another.

A consequence of this theory is that the more convergence in the way we communicate with another person, via voice, posture, gestures, etc., the more connected we feel with that other person.[4]

Can this kind of convergence and synchronization also work for text?

Indeed, research shows that in text-based conversations, when there is a dialogue between two people and when both use function words such as pronouns, conjunctions, etc., the two people seem to establish common ground.[5]

However, can this convergence work in online settings and group settings? Is there a possibility whereby participants of an online platform adapt to the linguistic style of a community or product interest group, which then positively influences the online platform's growth and performance? Or is such linguistic matching, in fact, bad for an online community and firm performance?

Let's get down to business. Why should firms like Amazon, Apple or Yelp first care about linguistic similarity or dissimilarity among their users and communities?

Well, more than 65 million firms use online brand communities to connect with customers.

It has been shown that these communities increase a firm's reputation and performance.[6] More and more firms are exploring ways to build an online community that allows their customers to learn, share and collaborate. This helps firms to build loyalty and retention. You may have heard the term 'customer lifetime value' or CLV. It is the net present value of all future streams of profits that a customer generates over the life of his or her business with a firm. The formula for CLV of a firm's customer goes something like this:[7]

$$CLV = m\left(\frac{r}{1+i-r}\right) - AC$$

I don't want to scare you, but this is a formula that is more simplistic than the original equation that uses a mathematical function called a Taylor series expansion. The term m here denotes margin or profit, r is the retention rate, i is the discount rate to take care of the time value of money (money today is more valuable than money tomorrow) and AC is the firm's acquisition costs for acquiring the customer. This formula enables firms to calculate how much value each customer is worth over their lifetime and can be calculated at different time intervals, such as monthly or annually.

If you examine the most important term enabling firms to make the most out of their customers, it is r, the retention rate.

Retention rate is the percentage of customers a business retains over a given period.

Moreover, it appears twice in the formula. If it is high, it helps the CLV as the numerator increases and the denominator decreases. We subtract the retention rate in the denominator. In essence, the retention rate is crucial for firms to derive higher value from their customers. High retention rates mean you can cross-sell other products to your existing customers (who else has bought club T-shirts, club scarves and overpriced beer from their favourite sports clubs!). You can sell products that are of higher value (at least among my friends—they started with a Johnnie Walker Red whisky, which costs around $22.99 to $24.99 for 750 ml and now, after landing a cushy job, drink Johnnie Walker Platinum, which costs about $100 for 750 ml. Yes, they rose up the ranks in drinking whisky and made Diageo's managers, Johnnie Walker's owner, happy). You have more data over time about your customers that can enable you to create products that satisfy their needs, your customers generate positive word of mouth about your product and you don't need to spend too much money acquiring new customers. Higher retention rates drive up each customer's CLV, which drives up the customer equity (the sum total of the CLVs of all your customers), which increases a firm's earnings and market value. Having a high retention rate is essential for firms to prosper and grow. Also, CLV connects marketing with finance as higher customer value leads to higher profits and cash flow, which in turn increases the firm's value (for publicly listed firms in the stock market, it would be the firm's market capitalization). See Figure 22.1 for the framework.

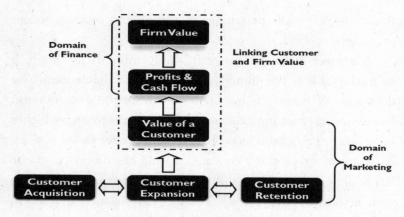

Figure 22.1: Customer value and firm value linkage

As the world moves towards more subscription-based business models, you can see why retention rate is an important ingredient that firms focus on. In the past, newspapers, magazines and telecommunications companies focused on subscription-based businesses, but now we see firms across a range of industries whose survival, profitability and growth are inherently tied to doing well in their subscription-based business. We see examples of such businesses in online entertainment (Netflix), online learning (Lynda, Coursera), food preparation (Blue Apron), health and beauty products (Ipsy, Dollar Shave Club) and a multitude of companies using software-as-a-service (SaaS) in the B2B space.[8]

What is the primary element that drives customer loyalty or retention?

You guessed it.

It is customer satisfaction. The relationship between customer satisfaction and customer loyalty is convex, which means that there are increasing returns to customer loyalty if customers are satisfied. See Figure 22.2 below for a delineation of this relationship.

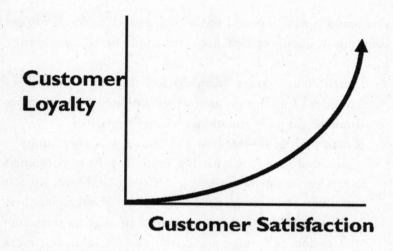

Figure 22.2: Relationship between customer satisfaction and customer loyalty

Thus, if customers are happy and satisfied and are deeply loyal, which means higher retention, it increases the CLV.

Which brands do you think have the highest customer loyalty?

If you are in a marketing class or a presentation on customer loyalty, the professor or the presenter will invariably refer to Apple or Harley-Davidson as exemplars of customer loyalty. These brands have built long-term relationships with their customers. Loyalists of these brands don't just think of themselves as customers but as members of a tribe. Yes, a tribe, a fellowship, a community. Firms that can create a harmonious and engaged community will be able to increase each customer's loyalty, CLV, consequently increasing firm performance and market value.

What are the ingredients of such communities? In a seminal paper that has been cited about 8200 times (which is a lot! I would be happy if one of my papers gets 500 citations) on Google Scholar, Albert M. Muniz, Jr. of DePaul University and Thomas O'Guinn of the University of Wisconsin put forward the idea of a brand community and the critical characteristics of a brand community. They proposed three markers of a brand community:[9]

- Shared consciousness: members feel they know each other (consider a Jeep Bronco user, who mentions, 'Who else drives Broncos? Guys like me and guys who like engines.'
- Rituals and traditions: how the meaning of community is reproduced (consider a Kit-Kat candy bar. Most consumers have a particular way of eating a Kit-Kat, and loyal Kit-Kat consumers feel a strong need to be correct about eating these candy bars. The brand created a ritual through its marketing strategy and used simple and intrinsic behaviour in customers to create a special ritual).
- Sense of moral responsibility: sense of duty to community (consider Apple Mac users who help each other in forum sites).

We see examples of such communities for brands such as Jeep, Lego, Airbnb, Sephora and Lomo cameras, among many others. And all these firms are doing well and prospering. Thanks to their communities.

Thus, firms care about brand communities and strategize on how to build, engage and sustain these communities. Suppose members have a shared consciousness, rituals and traditions, and a sense of moral responsibility. In that case, such brands have reached a level of brand resonance[10] whereby customers will be deeply tied with the brand over a long time—in turn, increasing a firm's profits and firm value.

One crucial element in an online community is how members talk to one another. If the conversations between community members break down, it can strongly affect the firm's prospects.

Is adapting to the linguistic style of a community or product interest group in an online setting helpful in increasing sales for a firm? Or is it better for members to use their own distinct style in conversing with other members online?

Stephan Ludwig, a professor of marketing at Monash University in Australia examined this very question, with a group of colleagues.[11]

Let's begin with a theory that Ludwig and his co-authors used. There is a notion of so-called language games whereby members of an online group adopt and adhere to a group's collective communication style to show their affiliation.[12]

For example, consider Amazon.com. On Amazon, many users typically write and read reviews for particular types of products or product interest groups. Examples of product interest groups can be a group focused on science fiction books or one focused on political books. In these groups, users share a common interest and they interact with each other repeatedly. Ludwig and his colleagues proposed that if someone writes a review that increases her perceived representativeness to the group in a linguistic sense, the review can subsequently increase conversion rates or sales. Research in psycholinguistics has demonstrated that synchronization in a conversational style, irrespective of the content being written, increases affinity, trustworthiness and shared experiences among the participants in a conversation.[13]

Here is an example from the study. Consider the following descriptions of book experiences for a science fiction book called *The Reckoning* on Amazon.com:

- Reviewer A: 'One of my favourite series.'
- Reviewer B: '[. . .] The best in the world!! Loved it!'
- Reviewer C: 'A very fine finish to a thrilling trilogy.'

All three reviews talk about the same book and the same thing, but each has a different style. These reviewers differ in the manner they express themselves in terms of the usage of pronouns, use of conjunctions and other function words (I will explain what function words mean later in this chapter).

Let's speculate on what each of these reviews says about the reviewer's personality.

- Reviewer A is positive towards the book, but in a muted way. Perhaps she is an introvert.
- Reviewer B seems to have just won the lottery and is effervescent in her opinion of the book. This person seems to be an extrovert.
- Reviewer C reminds me of my English teacher in high school. Tight and too formal for high school students to be fond of.

As you can observe, all of them talk about the book in a positive light, but the way the reviewers have written their positive opinions about the book in effect communicates their personalities.

The authors state the product interest group for science fiction books on Amazon uses more of the linguistic style as reviewer A. Thus reviewer A's review will be more persuasive and further affect the decision-making of readers on Amazon.

How does this happen?

Prior research finds that the level of linguistic synchrony between two conversationalists also has implications on the behaviour of the conversationalists. People who communicate in the same style tend to find common ground. If two people speak in the same style, it also denotes high psychological synchrony. In a sense, a high match in the language style between conversationalists leads to an increase in understanding and perceptions of a shared social identity. It increases rapport and agreement between two people. Don't you see this among your closest friends who speak in the same style as you? At least at my end, I can guarantee that a stranger will think my friends and I are talking in a different language if she accompanies us for dinner.

Moreover, closer linguistic synchrony decreases perceptions of social distance in communication. Note that this bonding does not just happen between two people. Indeed, this bonding also happens in group settings, as members use the same style to show their affiliation with a group.[14] As text is one of the only means one can communicate their language style in online reviews, such reviews lead group members to feel the reviewer is like them. Research shows that people who get messages from others who are like them trust these messages and tend to comply with the content of the message.[15]

So how did Ludwig and his colleagues go about testing their prediction? And what text-mining techniques did the authors use?

They first gathered online reviews from Amazon.com using the JavaScript programming language to access and parse the various HTML and XML describing books available for sale on Amazon.com. The authors also collected the conversion rates or sales of books, which was a lucky break, as this kind of data is now unavailable. During that time, Amazon made users' conversion behaviour, i.e., whether they bought a book or not, publicly available.[16] This data availability allowed Ludwig and his colleagues to link the online reviews for books with actual sales. It is impossible to do this kind of analysis now, as Amazon does not share such data any more.

Their final sample consisted of 18,681 online reviews for 591 books from different sub-genres, from 5 April to 5 May 2010.

The authors then categorized the books into different sub-genres to analyse the data by product groups.

Now, how did they measure linguistic style similarity?

Ludwig and his co-authors created a measure called Linguistic Style Matching (LSM), which is the amount of synchronization between each review for a book and the common linguistic style of each book sub-genre or product interest group. The authors measured the common linguistic style for each sub-genre or product interest group by taking the average of the usage intensity for every function word (the number of function words divided by the total words) in the English language.

Now why function words? Okay, before that, what are function words?

In general, affective content words, which convey emotions such as love, happiness, hate, sadness, etc., express the emotional intent of a text.

As shown by the example of the three reviewers above, all three liked the book, but each had a different writing style. Affect such as liking or loving is an 'internal feeling state'[17] and is not a linguistic property. Ludwig and his colleagues applied prior research in linguistics, which shows that function words are powerful indicators of linguistic style.[18]

The authors first clarified the difference between linguistic content and style.

If we focus on words, 'content words are generally nouns, regular verbs, and many adjectives and adverbs. They convey the content of a communication'. However, one cannot communicate content without style words.[19] Yla Tausczik from the University of Maryland and James Pennebaker, professor of psychology at the University of Texas in Austin and, if I may say so, one of the gurus of computational linguistics, state, 'Intertwined through these content words are style words, often referred to as function words. Style or function words are made up of pronouns, prepositions, articles, conjunctions, auxiliary verbs and a few other esoteric categories.'[20]

Previously known as 'junk words', several researchers have worked on the importance of function words and how they affect the outcome of a conversation and various other behaviours.[21] Initially neglected in the past by psychologists, function words are fundamental and crucial in how we deal with our personal and professional lives. We use function words all the time without knowing it.

Let's get into why function words matter. If we take nouns such as 'house', 'car', 'school', and verbs such as 'run', 'eat' and 'sing', these words are content-heavy. We know what people are talking about when someone uses these words. However, there is much more to communication than just content. We, as human beings, are quite attentive to the way someone conveys a message. Just as the way we pay attention to how someone walks or stands, we also pay attention to the linguistic style of a communicator. We pay attention to how the communicator puts the words together in a message.[22] These words don't have anything to do with the content but as Cindy Chung and James Pennebaker in their article on the psychological uses of function words so elegantly write, they 'serve as the cement that holds the content words together'.[23]

Two trivia questions now:

A. How many function words do you think there are in the English language?

   a. 100?
   b. 1000?
   c. 500?

B. How many of these words affect our daily vocabulary
    percentage-wise—that is, what is roughly the percentage
    usage of these words in our everyday lives?
    a. 33 per cent
    b. 66 per cent
    c. 55 per cent

In fact, there are only about 500 function words in the English
language and believe it or not, we use this moderately small
number of words roughly 55 per cent of the time in our daily
conversations.[24] Function words are generally very short, spoken
and read quickly. We tend to gloss over them, yet they matter
without us knowing their importance. The next time you are
trying to learn a new language, pay more attention to function
words. It seems if you are trying to learn a new language, function
words are the hardest to master.[25] If I go back to the example of
the three reviewers, one can ascertain their linguistic style using
the function words each use.

In the end, you might think that function words are trivial,
but they have a deep connection with our brains. Compared
to other mammals, humans have a much bigger cerebral cortex
frontal lobe.[26] Many social skills, such as understanding someone's
emotions and desires, and the ability to connect with others,
depend on the frontal lobe. Language has a strong connection
to this frontal lobe. Many of the uses of language are stored in
the frontal and temporal lobes. The left temporal lobe, known
as Wernicke's area, is essential for using advanced words such

as nouns, adjectives and verbs. The left frontal lobe, known as Broca's area, is important for utilizing function words.

Let's do a counterfactual. If someone has a damaged Wernicke's and a functional Broca's area, they would be regular in the way a good speaker is, one who speaks pleasantly and maintains eye contact. But they will only tend to use function words. On the other hand, someone with a damaged Broca's area but a functioning Wernicke's area would speak passively, hesitatingly, and use speech without any function words. As you can see, function words are strongly linked to how we connect with others.

Because of its deep linkage with how we use language, using 'junk words' can have significant repercussions. For example, they can be indicative of our personalities. Using self-references, for instance, is linked to someone with a Type A personality.[27] Higher testosterone levels are associated with using fewer non-I pronouns.[28] Using more first-person pronouns like 'I' or 'me' is associated with depression.[29] In fact, poets who died by suicide tended to use more first-person singular pronouns than poets who did not.[30]

Repeated usage of references to the self may indicate social isolation and self-absorption. These 'junk words' can also have effects on physical health. There is a positive correlation between using non-I pronouns and good physical health as people tend to focus less on the self and start sharing their lives with friends and family.[31] We also tend to use more third-person plural pronouns and fewer first-person pronouns as we age.[32] Overall, these function words reflect our state of mind and impact our social behaviours.

Ludwig and his colleagues thus used these words to arrive at linguistic similarity.

The authors calculated a different LSM score for each function word to determine how a review is similar to a product interest group or sub-genre. They used the formula below to calculate the difference in usage intensity of a particular function word such as 'his' between a review i and the average usage intensity of that same word such as 'his' in the sub-genre or product interest group of review:

$$LSM_{\text{"his" review}_i} = 1 - \left| \frac{\left(\frac{\sum \text{"his"}_i}{\sum N_i - \mu \text{"his"}_j} \right)}{\mu N_j} \right|$$

Here, LSM 'his'$_i$ refers to the similarity of the usage intensity for the word 'his' between a review and the subgenre's general style, $\sum$ 'his'$_i$ signifies the number of times the word 'his' appears in review i, $\sum N_i$ is the total number of words in review i, μ'his'$_j$ refers to the average number of times the word 'his' appears in all reviews for the same subgenre $_j$, and μN_j is the average words that appear in reviews in subgenre j.

Finally, as I mentioned above, the authors focused on function words, calculating the LSM score of a review by taking the average LSM score across all function words. For example, if a particular review used a word such as 'despite' four times in a review with 100 words, the score would be .04. If the average intensity for all reviews for the same subgenre or product interest group is .02, the LSM value for the word 'despite' will be .98. The authors apply this formula across all function words and average the LSM scores per review to get a final composite LSM score, which varies from 0 to 1. A higher score indicates more stylistic similarity between a review and the style of the subgenre.

Now, what next?

Of course, the analysis to examine the relationship between LSM and sales of the books.

For their analysis, the authors ran a regression model to examine the effect of linguistic style similarity on sales. Their model used weekly data, and because they were focused on rigorously ensuring that the result could be as causal as possible, they took the difference for each of the consequential variables each week to arrive at their findings.

What did the analysis uncover? The authors found that as the degree of LSM in reviews increased, so did the conversion rates for the book. The authors also wanted to see the impact of the content of the words. Thus, they used LIWC to measure positive and negative emotions in a review. See Table 22.1 below for the categories and example words that the authors used in their research.

The authors found that for reviews with positive changes in affective content, i.e., reviews for a book, which became more positive week to week, higher levels of LSM significantly enhanced conversion rates for the book. In another interesting finding, the authors saw that the effect of positive content on conversion rates or sales is asymmetrical.

Greater increases in positive content in linguistically similar reviews have a more negligible effect on increasing conversion rates. That is, there are non-linear effects for positive content. However, they did not see such tapering-off happen for changes in negative content in reviews that are linguistically similar. This indicates that an adverse change in the negative content of similar reviews is more detrimental than an increase of the same size in positive content in similar reviews. This finding aligns with a lot of research in behavioural economics related to prospect theory and loss aversion, which states that losses loom larger than gains.[33]

Word Categories Used to Calculate LSM and Affective Content

Category	Examples
Affective Content	
Positive affective content	*Love, nice, sweet*
Negative affective content	*Ugly, dumb, hate*
LSM	
Personal pronouns	*I, his, their*
Impersonal pronouns	*it, that, anything*
Articles	*a, an, the*
Conjunctions	*and, but, because*
Prepositions	*in, under, about*
Auxiliary verbs	*shall, be, was*
High-frequency adverbs	*very, rather, just*
Negations	*no, not, never*
Quantifiers	*much, few, lots*

Table 22.1 Example words for linguistic style similarity matching

So, we see that linguistic style similarity in reviews positively affects sales on sites like Amazon, which have product groups. What about communities?

Stephan Ludwig assembled another team to show that linguistic style matching also benefits user communities and not just online e-commerce platforms like Amazon.[34] Analysing about 74,000 members across 37 communities, Ludwig and his co-authors found that when a member's linguistic style matches with the community's overarching linguistic style, it demonstrates their identification with the community and, in turn, influences the member's participation in the community. When members use a linguistic style continuously, they participate more in terms of their quality and quantity. On the other hand, when a member changes her linguistic style often, they only participate in quantity, but quality suffers. The authors also found that if there is greater synchronicity in a community's linguistic style, that, in turn, increases the participation of all community members.

Overall, these studies show that beyond the content, linguistic style matters. And we tend to like, listen and change our behaviour towards people with similar language styles.

What do these results imply for managers, and what can they do with them?

First, besides focusing on sentiment (positive vs negative), online platforms also need to pay heed to the linguistic style within the communities in their media. Not only does content matter, but the style matters too. For example, monitoring the linguistic style using function words can enable firms to grasp why a community or product group is doing worse than expected.

Second, managers of online sites with reviews and forums can encourage users to write in a style consistent with the writing style of the community or group. Such encouragement can build strong communities on their platforms, leading to more satisfaction and loyalty. As I have discussed, retention rates deeply influence a customer's lifetime value. For example, online platforms can provide examples that match the linguistic style of a community when a user first intends to comment or review.

If a group or community prospers, a firm's performance will flourish. Generally, conversion rates average about 2 per cent–3 per cent across online retail sites.[35] We all know how big a company like Amazon is. Even a subtle increase in these conversion rates can translate into millions of dollars on websites like Amazon.

Third, another idea could be that comments that are linguistically similar to the overall linguistic style of the community can appear first. This will allow a user to understand the style and then write or engage with the community in a similar style. However, the current tide of consumer privacy and consumer

welfare is an important phenomenon, and online platforms
would be remiss to neglect it. Thus, platforms can also allow
users themselves to sort comments and reviews that match their
linguistic style.

Fourth, as Ludwig and his colleagues show that linguistic style
matches increase sales, online platforms can use their in-house
analytics and show reviews that are linguistically aligned with the
community and positively affect them. Note, consumers tend
to discount positive reviews, so perhaps providing linguistically
aligned reviews with diverse opinions may be a better strategy.

Now, let's return to my question at the beginning of this
narrative. Remember the dating question I put forward at the
beginning of this chapter? Who would you choose?

Of course, the one who is like you in their linguistic style.

Research shows that for potential romantic couples on a
first date, synchronizing their use of function words predicts the
subsequent beginning of a relationship and permanence.[36]

We often hear the phrase 'opposites attract'. However, in
language, we tend to seek someone who matches our style. We
seek someone who matches us in how we think and communicate.
And you will never know unless you pay heed. Those function
words or 'junk words' affect us more profoundly than we think.

Epilogue

There is this wonderful quote by British linguist David Crystal: 'Language has no independent existence apart from the people who use it. It is not an end in itself; it is a means to an end of understanding who you are and what society is like.'[1]

In this book, I have provided a glimpse of how intelligently and creatively mining language from consumers, firms and artists can generate a slew of insights for businesses. Knowing how language is used not only by others but also by us enables us to understand how we think and act. Text mining is a wonderful tool to grasp this understanding—be it firms trying to understand their customers, shareholders and competitors or us trying to discern what we say and what others say.

As I write this, large language models (LLMs) like Generative Pre-trained Transformer (GPT) and Bidirectional Encoder Representations from Transformers (BERT) have arrived and now the discourse is how such LLMs will affect the way we work. These models have tremendous ramifications for us as humans and, of course, for businesses too. The artificial intelligence (AI) chatbot ChatGPT has made AI more human-like and now mimics and communicates with us. Among many other tasks, these LLMs can write poetry, essays, stories and code, and generate art and music. Though, currently, there are many issues with these models, such as biases and hallucinations, which will hopefully be resolved as these models get better, the use of these models just goes to show the tremendous potential of mining language.

My field of quantitative marketing has taken enormous steps in utilizing text mining to unearth powerful and actionable insights that can help firms. Research can now figure out what kind of stories and trajectories of stories succeed, what kind of movie scripts are likely to succeed and what kind of content in social media posts will drive consumer engagement, to name a few.

I finished my PhD in 2013 but sometimes feel like doing a PhD again. Never have there been so many opportunities to study interesting social science problems using tools from natural language processing. The wonderful thing about all these scientific developments is that one can even learn these techniques from online courses sitting at home. There is a gamut of text mining, natural language processing and machine learning courses offered by online education providers such as Coursera, Udemy and LinkedIn Learning, among others. Thus, the potential to learn and utilize these tools for business insights is beyond promising. I would advise readers to try to learn these tools if they are deeply interested in text mining.

More so, firms now need to buckle up and ensure that they collect, analyse and monitor online content such as reviews, messages, tweets, blogs, etc. If firms can also collect offline content via consumer diaries or focus groups, the amalgamation of online and offline content can only help firms to get better. There is no drawback to such endeavours. If a firm's goal is to appease its customers and shareholders, it is paramount that they collect such information.

Language has power and can move and change us. If one ever doubts the power of language, consider these four words— 'A diamond is forever'. This slogan by De Beers was named the ad slogan of the twentieth century by *Advertising Age*.[2] You may ask why.

In 1939, when De Beers enlisted the ad agency N.W. Ayer to change the way the American public perceived diamonds, the annual sales for De Beers were $23 million. By 1979, mainly because of the power of those four words, De Beers' sales were more than $2.1 billion.[3] So, in forty years, the revenue increased by about ninety-one times. Those four words, 'A diamond is forever', signify a metaphor.[4] A diamond is as old as the earth itself, over three billion years, and is unbreakable and enduring. In a sense, a diamond literally is *forever*. Those four words worked like a mantra and made normal people apart from the rich aspire to buy a diamond ring for their engagements. The four-word mantra captured the idea of eternal romance and protection, which comes with owning a diamond. It made people change their behaviour.

What worked in the twentieth century will in all likelihood work in the twenty-first too. Words and language have an effect on people. Understanding how language affects *us* using text mining should now be the mantra of all businesses.

Acknowledgements

There are many who have been helpful and inspired me in writing this book.

I want to thank Holly Edgar for helping in developing and structuring the manuscript in its initial stages. A massive thank you to Brittany Chung Campbell for her vital work in proofreading and helping me find a home for the book. Thanks to Ritvik Rai for his earnest research assistance. This book would not have been possible without the intuition, experience, and guidance of my editor Venkatesh Karthik at Penguin. Thank you for that. Thanks to Ralph Rebello for seeing the book through to its final stages.

I want to thank all my teachers at Holy Cross School in Dimapur, Assam Rifles Public School in Shillong, Hindu College in Delhi, the Operations Research department at the University of Delhi, and the University of Southern California in Los Angeles for helping me discover and enjoy learning.

I want to thank all my ex-colleagues at the Foster School of Business at the University of Washington in Seattle who nurtured me during my initial years as an assistant professor. A big thank

Acknowledgements

you to my current colleagues at INSEAD for your continual support and encouragement.

Thanks to all researchers whose work I have cited in the book. Your research is an inspiration to me, and I have tried my best to convey your findings in the simplest and most effective manner.

To my students whom I have taught in various universities, such as INSEAD, University of Washington in Seattle, Wharton School of Business, and University of Southern California. My students are what keeps me going and I am grateful to have this tremendous opportunity to perhaps motivate my students to scale all the heights they aspire for.

To my co-authors. Thank you for bearing with me and your friendship. None of my papers would have seen the light of your day without your ideas and insights. And of course, the late nights to tackle reviewer 2 :)

I want to thank my sister and her family for always being there.

My journey as an academic has been deeply shaped by my adviser, Gerard Tellis at the University of Southern California. I continually strive to think, critique and write like him.

My friends are an integral part of who I am. Thank you Pongkhi, Amlan, Gautam, Swati, Baijanta, Kanaki, Dmitriy, Neil, Peter, Julien and Aparna.

Finally, I want to thank my parents, who were professors and librarians and have passed on. I am sure they are surprised and smiling from above. Never would have they once thought that this very naughty and always kinetic young boy would sit down to write a book. A book I hope finds a home in at least one library.

Research Methods and Helpful References

I have discussed various methods and technical concepts across the chapters. Here is a summary description of these chapter-wise, which could be useful if you want to quickly find the chapter related to a specific method or concept. I also provide what I believe are relevant and helpful references if you want to learn more about the method or concept. These references will in turn lead you to seminal books or articles on the topic.

I. TWISTS AND TURNS

1. Improv on Social Media

Synthetic Control Method: The Synthetic Control Method (SCM) is a statistical approach used to evaluate the treatment effect in comparative case studies. An SCM estimates the effect of a treatment (or intervention) of interest by comparing the evolution of an outcome variable for a unit affected by the treatment to the evolution of the same outcome variable for a synthetic control group.

Abadie, A., A. Diamond, and J. Hainmueller. 2010. Synthetic control methods for comparative case studies: Estimating the effect of California's tobacco control program. *Journal of the American Statistical Association*, 105(490): 493–505.

Event Study Method: An event study conducted on a specific firm examines any changes in its stock price and how it relates to a given event.

Sorescu, A., N.L. Warren, and L. Ertekin. 2017. Event study methodology in the marketing literature: an overview. *Journal of the Academy of Marketing Science*, 45: 186–207.

2. Should Metallica Be More Justin Bieber?

Regression: The regression model is a statistical model that finds a relationship between an outcome (or label) and one or more predictors (or features).

Gallo, A. (2015). A refresher on regression analysis. *Harvard Business Review*, 4.

3. Spoiler Alert: The Tale of a Nordic Thriller

Supervised and Unsupervised Machine Learning: Supervised and unsupervised are two types of machine-learning models. In supervised learning, a model is given labelled data that it learns from and then predicts the label. In unsupervised learning, a model finds patterns in data that has no pre-specified labels.

Devin, S. (2018). Supervised vs. Unsupervised Learning, Understanding the differences between the two main types of machine learning methods. *Towards Data Science.* https://towardsdatascience.com/supervised-vs-unsupervised-learning-14f68e32ea8d.

Binary Logistic Regression Model: A binary logistic regression model is a type of regression model that estimates the likelihood of an outcome occurring versus the outcome not occurring based on one or more predictors. For example, the outcome can be 'win the lottery' or 'did not win the lottery' based on certain predictors such as age, star sign, gender, etc. An analyst tries to find which predictors are most potent in predicting an outcome.

Penman, Paul (2022). Binary Logistic Regression—An introduction. *Data Science Institute.* https://www.datascienceinstitute.net/blog/binary-logistic-regression-an-introduction.

II. FIRMSPEAK

5. The Concrete Benefits of Being Concrete in Language

Natural Language Processing (NLP): NLP helps machines such as computers 'read' text by mimicking the capability of humans to understand a natural language, such as English or Chinese. Text mining employs a range of methodologies to process text and speech, and one of the most common and important ones is NLP.

Machine Learning: NLP is the field related to how machines such as computers understand language, but for the machine to understand language, machine learning is the means. Machine learning involves developing algorithms that teach machines to automatically learn and become better from experience. Artificial Intelligence (AI) is the overall term utilized used for machines, which can resemble human intelligence. Both NLP and machine learning are a part of AI.

Yse, Diego Lopez (2019). Your Guide to Natural Language Processing (NLP). *Towards Data Science.* https://towardsdatascience.com/your-guide-to-natural-language-processing-nlp-48ea2511f6e1.

6. When 'You' Can Make the Difference

Dictionary-Based Approach: The dictionary-based approach uses a dictionary of words to identify if a piece of content uses words that belong to a construct or dimension. The most widely used measurement for the dictionary-based approach is the frequency of the words that belong to a construct or dimension in a textual corpus.

Humphreys, A., and R.J.H. Wang. 2018. Automated text analysis for consumer research. *Journal of Consumer Research*, 44(6): 1274–1306.

Human Coding: Human coding or manual coding in text mining is the process of labelling (e.g., positive or negative sentiment) or rating (1-low to 5-high) textual data using human assessors.

White, M.D., and E.E. Marsh. 2006. Content analysis: A flexible methodology. *Library Trends*, 55(1): 22–45.

7. On the Internet, Everybody Knows You're a Dog

Behavioural Targeting: Behavioural targeting uses people's behavioural data, such as what people are or are not doing in an app, on a website, or with ad campaigns, to trigger personalized marketing, determining the advertisements that resonate most with them.

McGinley, Corinne (2023). Behavioral Marketing: What Is It & How Is It Beneficial? [+ Examples]. Hubspot. https://blog.hubspot.com/marketing/what-is-behavioral-marketing.

Abnormal Stock Market Returns: Abnormal stock market returns are calculated by subtracting the expected normal stock returns of a firm that would have been observed if an analysed event had not taken place from the actual stock market returns because of the analysed event.

Sorescu, A., N.L. Warren, and L. Ertekin. 2017. Event study methodology in the marketing literature: an overview. *Journal of the Academy of Marketing Science*, 45: 186–207.

Propensity Score Matching: Propensity score matching is a technique used when a group of entities receives a treatment and the other group does not. This method creates a counterfactual of the control group, ensuring the predictors have the same distribution for the treated and counterfactual groups. After the matching, the treatment and control group's outcomes are compared.

Heinrich, C., A. Maffioli, and G. Vazquez. 2010. A primer for applying propensity-score matching. Technical Note No. IDB-TN-161, *Inter-American Development Bank*, 2010.

III. CONSUMERSPEAK

11. Words That Gonna Make you Sweat (Virtually)

Decision Tree: A decision tree is a supervised machine-learning approach that is used for both classifying labels and for regression tasks. Each tree starts with a root node, which has outgoing branches that feed into internal nodes. In each node, based on a test for a feature or predictor, the data is divided into two or more nodes so that the subsequent nodes have data that are homogenous in the feature or predictor utilized for the test. Each branch is the outcome of the test. The terminal node contains the class label.

Paplinger, Thomas (2017). What is a Decision Tree? *Towards Data Science.* https://towardsdatascience.com/what-is-a-decision-tree-22975f00f3e1.

13. #Boycott[Insertyourfirmname]: Shunning Shitstorms on Social Media

Random Forest Model: A random forest model is a machine-learning model that divides a dataset into decision trees and takes the majority voting across the decision trees for the final classification. The idea is that although a single tree may provide an inaccurate prediction, taking the collective decision will likely lead to a more correct prediction.

Gradient Boosting: Gradient boosting takes a dataset and creates a decision tree one at a time. It takes wrongly classified samples from a prior decision tree and corrects errors from the previous one in the next decision tree. In essence, each subsequent tree improves upon the earlier ones and learns from the previous tree's mistakes. The final classification is based on weighting each decision tree's performance in the classification. In essence, it aggregates weak models to create an overall strong model.

Glen, Stephanie (2019). Decision Tree vs Random Forest vs Gradient Boosting Machines: Explained Simply. *Data Science Central.* https://www.datasciencecentral.com/decision-tree-vs-random-forest-vs-boosted-trees-explained/.

IV. MONEY AND MARKETS

16. Is All That Twitters Gold?

Granger Causality: Correlation is not causation. One can find that there is a high positive correlation between ice-cream sales and drownings. But this does not mean that enjoying an ice cream will lead to death. The variable, which is leading to this strong correlation, is the summer season. Causation is when a variable or an event causes another variable or event to occur. Establishing causation is hard and can only be determined from an appropriately designed test. Granger causality or temporal causality uses the assumption that if a variable X causes Y then changes in X will systematically happen before any changes happen in Y. Thus, in a statistical sense, lagged values of X will show a statistically significant correlation with Y.

Padav, Pallavi. Granger Causality in Time Series—Explained using Chicken and Egg problem. *Analytics Vidhya*. 2021. https://www.analyticsvidhya. com/blog/2021/08/granger-causality-in-time-series-explained-using-chicken-and-egg-problem/.

V. BOSSES

17. A Crash Course on Charisma from Barack Obama and Mahatma Gandhi

Cluster Analysis: Cluster analysis is a method that groups similar observations into a number of clusters or segments.

Kaufman, L., and P.J. Rousseeuw. 2009. Finding groups in data: an introduction to cluster analysis. John Wiley & Sons.

Notes

Introduction

1. *The Lyrics: 1956 to the Present* by Paul McCartney, https://www.insider.com/paul-mccartney-yesterday-original-title-scrambled-eggs-the-beatles-2021-10.
2. Barry Miles, *Paul McCartney: Many Years From Now* (New York: Henry Holt & Company, 1997), ISBN 0-8050-5249-6.
3. https://www.thebeatles.com/yesterday.
4. https://web.archive.org/web/20060910071729/http://www.guinnessworldrecords.com/content_pages/record.asp?recordid=50867.
5. Sibi Jeyya, 'Highest Number of Languages Spoken in This City?', 5 September 2021, https://www.indiaherald.com/Politics/Read/994407975/Highest-Number-of-Languages-is-Spoken-in-this-City.
6. Sruthy Susan Ullas and Petlee Peter, 'At 107, Maximum Languages Spoken in Bengaluru', the *Times of India,* 4 September 2021, https://timesofindia.indiatimes.com/city/bengaluru/at-107-max-languages-spoken-in-bengaluru/articleshow/85914744.cms.
7. Steven Pinker, *The Language Instinct: How the Mind Creates Language,* (Penguin UK, 2003).
8. 'Four Fundamental Shifts in Media & Advertising During 2020', 23 September 2020, https://doubleverify.com/four-fundamental-shifts-in-media-and-advertising-during-2020/.

9.   Ying Lin, '10 Internet Statistics Every Marketer Should Know in 2023', 3 October 2022, https://www.oberlo.com/blog/internet-statistics.

10. Facebook Revenue and Usage Statistics, Mansoor Iqbal, 18 July 2023, https://www.businessofapps.com/data/facebook-statistics/.

11. Daniel Ruby, '44+ TikTok Statistics—Users, Financials and Trends', 21 June 2023, https://www.demandsage.com/tiktok-user-statistics/.

12. Twitter Users, Stats, Data and Trends, 11 May 2023, https://datareportal.com/essential-twitter-stats.

13. Branko Krstic, '25+ Astounding Amazon Statistics for 2023', 20 May 2023, https://webtribunal.net/blog/amazon-stats/#gref

Chapter 1: Improv on Social Media

1.   'Ratings—164.1 Million Watch All-or-Part of CBS's Super Bowl XLVII Coverage', *TheFutonCritic.com*, accessed 19 July 2022, http://www.thefutoncritic.com/ratings/2013/02/04/1641-million-watch-all-or-part-of-cbss-super-bowl-xlvii-coverage-648314/20130204cbs06/.

2.   'FIFA World Cup Final Breaks Records for TV Broadcasters', ACT, accessed 19 July 2022, https://www.acte.be/publication/fifa-world-cup-final-breaks-records-for-tv-broadcasters/.

3.   Marc Berman, 'Super Bowl 2023: 113 Million Viewers Ranks as the Third Most-Watched Telecast Historically', *Forbes*, 13 February 2023, https://www.forbes.com/sites/marcberman1/2023/02/13/super-bowl-2023-113-million-viewers-ranks-as-the-third-most-watched-telecast-historically/?sh=6cd1986d45d4

4.   https://www.si.com/fannation/soccer/futbol/news/how-fifa-world-cup-final-beat-super-bowl-lvi-in-tv-ratings#.

5.   'Super Bowl Blackout Caused by "Failure of Device Protecting Power Supply"', the *Guardian*, Guardian News and Media, 8 February 2013, https://www.theguardian.com/sport/2013/feb/08/super-bowl-blackout-power-device.

6.   The Eredivisie is the highest level of professional football in the Netherlands.

7.   Nick Miller, 'World Cup Stunning Moments: Luis Suárez Bites Giorgio Chiellini in 2014', the *Guardian*, Guardian News and Media, 27 March 2018, https://www.theguardian.com/football/blog/2018/

mar/27/world-cup-stunning-moments-luis-suarez-bites-giorgio-chiellini-in-2014.

8. https://www.theguardian.com/music/2014/jun/26/springsteen-suarez-biting-has-no-place-in-sports.

9. M. Wedel and P.K. Kannan, 'Marketing Analytics for Data-Rich Environments', *Journal of Marketing* 80(6) (2016): 97–121; Edward B. Keller and Brad Fay, *The Face-to-Face Book: Why Real Relationships Rule in a Digital Marketplace* (New York: Free Press, 2012).

10. Tim Wu, *The Attention Merchants: The Epic Scramble to Get inside Our Heads* (New York, Vintage Books, a division of Penguin Random House LLC, 2017).

11. Catherine E. Tucker, 'Social Networks, Personalized Advertising, and Privacy Controls', *Journal of Marketing Research* 51, no. 5 (January 2013): 546–62, https://doi.org/10.1509/jmr.10.0355.

12. Abhishek Borah et al., 'Improvised Marketing Interventions in Social Media', *Journal of Marketing* 84, no. 2 (2020): 69–91, https://doi.org/10.1177/0022242919899383.

13. Haewoon Kwak et al., 'What Is Twitter, a Social Network or a News Media?', *Proceedings of the 19th International Conference on World Wide Web*—WWW '10 (2010), https://doi.org/10.1145/1772690.1772751.

14. 'Keller Center Report Research—Baylor University', accessed 19 July 2022, https://www.baylor.edu/business/kellercenter/doc.php/375705.pdf.

15. @Oreo. 'Power out? No problem.' Twitter, 3 February 2013, 8.48PM, https://twitter.com/Oreo/status/298246571718483968?s=20&t=5SbQqXd1oj5hKtzb8wNaNQ.

16. Angela Watercutter, 'How Oreo Won the Marketing Super Bowl with a Timely Blackout Ad on Twitter', *Wired*, 4 February 2013, https://www.wired.com/2013/02/oreo-twitter-super-bowl/.

17. Chen Lin, Sriram Venkataraman, and Sandy D. Jap, 'Media Multiplexing Behavior: Implications for Targeting and Media Planning', *Marketing Science* 32, no. 2 (2013): 310–24, https://doi.org/10.1287/mksc.1120.0759.

18. Angela Watercutter, 'How Oreo Won the Marketing Super Bowl with a Timely Blackout Ad on Twitter', *Wired*.

19. Loulla-Mae Eleftheriou-Smith, 'Snickers Tells Suarez It's "More Satisfying than Italian"', *Campaign UK*, 3 February 2015, https://www.

campaignlive.co.uk/article/snickers-tells-suarez-its-more-satisfying-italian/1300560.

20. 'Mars Chocolate North America Snickers—Suarez Tweet', The Shorty Awards, accessed 19 July 2022, https://shortyawards.com/7th/soccer-tweet.

21. James Vincent, 'Elon Musk Explains Why Tesla's Cybertruck Windows Smashed during Presentation', the Verge, 25 November 2019, https://www.theverge.com/2019/11/25/20981489/tesla-cybertruck-glass-window-fail-elon-musk-explanation.

22. Charles S. Brant, 'On Joking Relationships', American Anthropologist 50, no. 1 (1948): 160–62, https://doi.org/10.1525/aa.1948.50.1.02a00270.

23. A. Borah, S. Banerjee, Y.T. Lin, A. Jain, and A.B. Eisingerich, 'Improvised Marketing Interventions in Social Media', Journal of Marketing, 84(2) (2020): 69–91.

24. Caleb Warren and A. Peter McGraw, 'Differentiating What Is Humorous from What Is Not', Journal of Personality and Social Psychology 110, no. 3 (2016): 407–30, https://doi.org/10.1037/pspi0000041.

25. Salvatore Attardo and Lucy Pickering, 'Timing in the Performance of Jokes', Humor—International Journal of Humor Research 24, no. 2 (2011): https://doi.org/10.1515/humr.2011.015.; Lambert Deckers and John Devine, 'Humor by Violating an Existing Expectancy', The Journal of Psychology 108, no. 1 (1981): 107–10, https://doi.org/10.1080/00223980.1981.9915251.; Martin Eisend, 'A Meta-Analysis of Humor in Advertising', Journal of the Academy of Marketing Science 37, no. 2 (2008): 191–203, https://doi.org/10.1007/s11747-008-0096-y; Sigmund Freud, 'Humour', International Journal of Psychoanalysis, 9 (1) (1928): 1–6.

26. Sigmund Freud, 'Humour', International Journal of Psychoanalysis, 9 (1), (1928): 1–6.

27. Charles S. Brant, 'On Joking Relationships', American Anthropologist, 50 (1) (1948): 160–62.

28. Robert S. Wyer and James E. Collins, 'A Theory of Humor Elicitation', Psychological Review 99, no. 4 (1992): 663–88, https://doi.org/10.1037/0033-295x.99.4.663; Nancy A. Yovetich, J. Alexander

Dale, and Mary A. Hudak, 'Benefits of Humor in Reduction of Threat-Induced Anxiety', *Psychological Reports* 66, no. 1 (1990): 51–58, https://doi.org/10.2466/pr0.1990.66.1.51.

29. Linda D. Henman, 'Humor as a Coping Mechanism: Lessons from PoWs', *Humor—International Journal of Humor Research* 14, no. 1 (May 2001), https://doi.org/10.1515/humr.14.1.83; Stanislav Treger, Susan Sprecher, and Ralph Erber, 'Laughing and Liking: Exploring the Interpersonal Effects of Humor Use in Initial Social Interactions', *European Journal of Social Psychology*, 2013, https://doi.org/10.1002/ejsp.1962.

30. BBC, 'Penguin Chicks Rescued by Unlikely Hero | Spy in the Snow—BBC', YouTube (YouTube, 26 December 2018), https://www.youtube.com/watch?v=Z7PlUGbsXlQ.

31. Ibid.

32. Colleen McClain et al., 'The Internet and the Pandemic', Pew Research Center: Internet, Science & Tech, 28 April 2022, https://www.pewresearch.org/internet/2021/09/01/the-internet-and-the-pandemic/.

33. 'Covid-19 Barometer: Consumer Attitudes, Media Habits and Expectations', Kantar, Understand People. Inspire Growth, accessed 19 July 2022, https://www.kantar.com/Inspiration/Coronavirus/COVID-19-Barometer-Consumer-attitudes-media-habits-and-expectations.

Chapter 2: Should Metallica Be More Justin Bieber?

1. Chris Gorski, 'Why It's so Hard for a One-Hit Wonder to Have a Lasting Music Career', *Science News*, 9 May 2022, https://www.sciencenews.org/article/music-one-hit-wonder-pop-songs-lasting-career.

2. Cass Sunstein, 'Opinion | Why Is Success so Hard to Predict?', the *Washington Post*, 23 October 2021, https://www.washingtonpost.com/news/volokh-conspiracy/wp/2016/06/01/why-is-success-so-hard-to-predict/.

3. Joel McIver, 'A History of Thrash Metal', *MusicRadar*, 29 April 2010, https://www.musicradar.com/news/guitars/a-history-of-thrash-metal-249162.

4. Keith Kahn-Harris, *Extreme Metal: Music and Culture on the Edge* (Oxford: Berg, 2007).

5. 'Metallica', Recording Academy, accessed 24 July 2022, https://www.grammy.com/artists/metallica/10686.

6. Clive Stafford Smith, 'How US Interrogators Use Music as a Tool of Torture', the *Guardian*, 18 June 2008, https://www.theguardian.com/world/2008/jun/19/usa.guantanamo.

7. 'R/Metallica—the Most Common Words in Metallica Lyrics (Excluding "and," "the," etc. I Left in "Yeah" Because . . . well, Come on Lol)', reddit, accessed 24 July 2022, https://www.reddit.com/r/Metallica/comments/nn4211/the_most_common_words_in_metallica_lyrics/.

8. Lauryn Schaffner, 'Here's the Most Commonly Used Word in Slipknot's Lyrics', *Loudwire*, 19 June 2019, https://loudwire.com/most-commonly-used-word-slipknot-lyrics/.

9. Deena Weinstein, 'Just So Stories: How Heavy Metal Got Its Name—a Cautionary Tale', *Rock Music Studies* 1, no. 1 (December 2013): 36–51, https://doi.org/10.1080/19401159.2013.846655.

10. J. Arnett, 'Three Profiles of Heavy Metal Fans: A Taste for Sensation and a Subculture of Alienation', *Qualitative Sociology*, 16(4) (1993): 423–43.

11. Lauren Dana, '21 Justin Bieber Love Songs to Play at Your Wedding', Brides (Brides, 23 April 2021), https://www.brides.com/justin-bieber-love-songs-5180192.

12. Keith Caulfield, 'Justin Bieber Tops Billboard 200 with "My World 2.0"', *Billboard*, 7 August 2013, https://www.billboard.com/music/music-news/justin-bieber-tops-billboard-200-with-my-world-20-1209176/.

13. Lars Brandle, 'Justin Bieber Beats One Direction to the Top Down Under', *Billboard*, 23 November 2015, https://www.billboard.com/pro/justin-bieber-direction-aria-charts/#!.

14. Billboard Staff, 'Hispanic Heritage Month: The 50 Best Latin Songs of All Time', Billboard, 8 October 2021, https://www.billboard.com/music/latin/best-latin-songs-of-all-time-6760654/.

15. http://www.rollingstone.com/reviews/album/32714131/review/32735160/my_world_20.

16. Ben Rayner, 'Bieber Bonanza "Just Thrown Together"', thestar.com (*Toronto Star*, 22 December 2011), https://www.thestar.com/

entertainment/2011/12/21/bieber_bonanza_just_thrown_together. html.

17. https://www.nbcwashington.com/news/national-international/ justin_bieber_complains_over_twitter_trending_topics_ takedown/1888078/.

18. Jonah Berger and Grant Packard, 'Are Atypical Things More Popular?', *Psychological Science* 29, no. 7 (2018): 1178–84, https://doi. org/10.1177/0956797618759465.

19. Marvin Zuckerman, *Sensation Seeking: Beyond the Optimum Level of Arousal* (Hillsdale, NJ: Erlbaum, 1979).

20. Belle Beth Cooper, 'Why Getting New Things Makes Us Feel so Good: Novelty and the Brain', Buffer Resources, 24 June 2020, https:// buffer.com/resources/novelty-and-the-brain-how-to-learn-more-and- improve-your-memory/.

21. Nico Bunzeck and Emrah Düzel, 'Absolute Coding of Stimulus Novelty in the Human Substantia Nigra/VTA', *Neuron* 51, no. 3 (2006): 369–79, https://doi.org/10.1016/j.neuron.2006.06.021.

22. www.billboard.com/biz.

23. David M. Blei, 'Probabilistic Topic Models', *Communications of the ACM* 55, no. 4 (2012): 77–84, https://doi.org/10.1145/ 2133806.2133826.

24. 'Car Insurance Experts Reveal Which Country Music Stars Love Their Trucks the Most', accessed 24 July 2022, https://www.money.co.uk/ guides/truck-yeah.

25. Stef Schrader, 'Your Ears Are Right: Country Music Is Singing Way More about Trucks Now', The Drive, 23 January 2021, https://www. thedrive.com/news/38777/your-ears-are-right-country-music-is- singing-way-more-about-trucks-now.

26. Simon Frith, 'Why Do Songs Have Words?', *The Sociological Review* 34, no. 1_suppl (1986): 77–106, https://doi.org/10.1111/j.1467- 954x.1986.tb03315.x.

27. '"Hey Ya" by Outkast Was the First Song on iTunes to Reach One Million Downloads | DailyRapFacts', dailyrapfacts.com, 21 October 2019, retrieved 22 March 2021.

28. '500 Best Songs of All Time: 50-1', *Rolling Stone*, retrieved 15 September 2021.

29. Jeff Giles, 'Extreme's Nuno Bettencourt Celebrates 25th Anniversary of "More than Words" Going to No. 1', Ultimate Classic Rock, 9 June 2016, https://ultimateclassicrock.com/extreme-more-than-words-no-1/.

30. 'Official Singles Chart Top 100', Official Charts Company, retrieved 28 April 2020.

31. William Raft Kunst-Wilson and R.B. Zajonc, 'Affective Discrimination of Stimuli That Cannot Be Recognized', Science 207, no. 4430 (1980): 557–58, https://doi.org/10.1126/science.7352271.

32. Rob Copsey, 'Remixes That Gave Songs a Big Chart Boost', Official Charts, 22 April 2020, https://www.officialcharts.com/chart-news/remixes-that-gave-songs-a-big-chart-boost__14351/.

33. https://blabbermouth.net/news/metallica-shapes-setlist-around-what-fans-are-listening-to-on-spotify-says-daniel-ek.

Chapter 3: Spoiler Alert: The Tale of a Nordic Thriller

1. 'Spoiler Definition & Meaning', Merriam-Webster (Merriam-Webster), accessed 22 July 2022, https://www.merriam-webster.com/dictionary/spoiler.

2. 'SpoilerTV', SpoilerTV, accessed July 22, 2022, https://www.spoilertv.com/. 'Similarweb.com Website Traffic, Ranking, Analytics [June 2022]', Semrush, accessed 22 July 2022, https://www.semrush.com/website/similarweb.com/overview/.

3. Amanda Kooser, 'Avengers: Endgame Spoilers? Just Don't, Russo Brothers Say', CNET (CNET, 16 April 2019), https://www.cnet.com/culture/entertainment/avengers-endgame-spoilers-just-dont-russo-brothers-say/.

4. Jun Hyun Ryoo, Xin (Shane) Wang, and Shijie Lu, 'Do Spoilers Really Spoil? Using Topic Modeling to Measure the Effect of Spoiler Reviews on Box Office Revenue', Journal of Marketing 85, no. 2 (2020): 70–88, https://doi.org/10.1177/0022242920937703.

5. 'Press Room', IMDb (IMDb.com), accessed 22 July 2022, https://www.imdb.com/pressroom/stats/.

6. David M. Blei and John D. Lafferty, 'A Correlated Topic Model of Science', The Annals of Applied Statistics 1, no. 1 (January 2007), https://doi.org/10.1214/07-aoas114.

7. D.M. Blei, A.Y. Ng, and M.I. Jordan, 'Latent Dirichlet Allocation', *Journal of Machine Learning Research*, 3 (Jan.), (2003): 993–1022.

8. Y. Liu, (2006), 'Word of Mouth for Movies: Its Dynamics and Impact on Box Office Revenue', *Journal of Marketing*, 70 (3), 74–89.

9. Joseph W. Alba and Elanor F. Williams, 'Pleasure Principles: A Review of Research on Hedonic Consumption', *Journal of Consumer Psychology* 23, no. 1 (2013): 2–18, https://doi.org/10.1016/j.jcps.2012.07.003.

10. Tanya (Ya) Tang, Eric (Er) Fang, and Feng Wang, 'Is Neutral Really Neutral? The Effects of Neutral User-Generated Content on Product Sales', *Journal of Marketing* 78, no. 4 (2014): 41–58, https://doi.org/10.1509/jm.13.0301.

11. Kyle Bagwell, 'Chapter 28 the Economic Analysis of Advertising', ed. R. Porter and M. Armstrong, *Handbook of Industrial Organization*, (2007): 1701–1844, https://doi.org/10.1016/s1573-448x(06)03028-7.

12. Morris B. Holbrook, 'Popular Appeal versus Expert Judgments of Motion Pictures', *Journal of Consumer Research* 26, no. 2 (1999): 144–55, https://doi.org/10.1086/209556.

13. Sangkil Moon, Paul K. Bergey, and Dawn Iacobucci, 'Dynamic Effects among Movie Ratings, Movie Revenues, and Viewer Satisfaction', *Journal of Marketing*, 74 (1) (2010): 108–21.

Chapter 4: Mistaking the Value of Mistakes in Online Reviews

1. T. Reich, and S.J. Maglio, 'Featuring Mistakes: The Persuasive Impact of Purchase Mistakes in Online Reviews', *Journal of Marketing*, 84(1) (2020): 52–65.

2. https://www.qualtrics.com/blog/online-review-stats/.

3. Maynard Mack, *Alexander Pope: A Life* (Yale University Press, 1985, ISBN 0-300-03391-5).

4. S. Nieuwenhuis, K.R. Ridderinkhof, J. Blom, G.P. Band, A. Kok, 'Error-Related Brain Potentials Are Differentially Related to Awareness of Response Errors: Evidence from an Antisaccade Task', *Psychophysiology*. 38 (5), (September 2001): 752–60. doi:10.1111/1469-8986.3850752. PMID 11577898.

5. K. Overbye, R. Bøen, R.J. Huster, and C.K. Tamnes, '*Learning from Mistakes: How Does the Brain Handle Errors?*. *Everything You and Your Teachers Need to Know about the Learning Brain*, 20, (2020*)*.

6. J.F. Cavanagh, and M.J. Frank, '*Frontal Theta as a Mechanism for Cognitive Control*', *Trends Cogn. Sci.* 18 (2014): 414–21. doi: 10.1016/j.tics.2014.04.012.

7. K. Overbye, K.B. Walhovd, T. Paus, A.M. Fjell, R.J. Huster, and C.K. Tamnes, 'Error Processing in the Adolescent Brain: Age-Related Differences in Electrophysiology, Behavioral Adaptation, and Brain Morphology', *Dev. Cogn. Neurosci.*, 38:100665 (2019). doi: 10.1016/j.dcn.2019.100665.

8. J.B. Hirsh, and M. Inzlicht, 'Error-Related Negativity Predicts Academic Performance', *Psychophysiology* 47 (2010): 192–6, doi: 10.1111/j.1469-8986.2009.00877.x.

9. https://www.amazon.com/Fablehaven-Brandon-Mull/dp/1590385810.

10. Ashlee Humphreys and Rebecca Jen-Hui Wang, 'Automated Text Analysis for Consumer Research', *Journal of Consumer Research* 44, no. 6 (2017): 1274–1306, https://doi.org/10.1093/jcr/ucx104.

11. 'YouTuber Jenna Marbles Quits over Blackface', BBC News, 26 June 2020.

12. https://www.cnn.com/2020/06/26/entertainment/jenna-marbles-quits-youtube-intl-hnk-scli/index.html.

13. https://thehill.com/blogs/pundits-blog/finance/332777-the-art-of-the-corporate-apology-truth-reflection-and-growth/.

14. Jon Springer, 'Skittles Says Sorry for Ditching Lime Flavor in the First Place', *AdAge*, 23 March 2022, https://adage.com/article/marketing-news-strategy/skittles-says-sorry-ditching-lime-flavor-it-recently-brought-back/2407796.

15. L. ten Brinke, and G.S. Adams, 'Saving Face? When Emotion Displays during Public Apologies Mitigate Damage to Organizational Performance', *Organizational Behavior and Human Decision Processes*, 130, (2015). 1–12.

Chapter 5: The Concrete Benefits of Being Concrete in Language

1. Gary Lupyan and Bodo Winter, 'Language Is More Abstract than You Think, or, Why Aren't Languages More Iconic?', *Philosophical*

Transactions of the Royal Society B: Biological Sciences 373, no. 1752 (2018): 20170137, https://doi.org/10.1098/rstb.2017.0137.

2. Ibid.

3. Marc Brysbaert, Amy Beth Warriner, and Victor Kuperman, 'Concreteness Ratings for 40 Thousand Generally Known English Word Lemmas', *Behavior Research Methods* 46, no. 3 (2013): 904–11, https://doi.org/10.3758/s13428-013-0403-5.

4. Ibid.

5. Ashley Marcin, 'Piaget Stages of Development: What Are They and How Are They Used?', Healthline (Healthline Media, 29 March 2018), https://www.healthline.com/health/piaget-stages-of-development.

6. 'Concrete and Specific Language – Idaho State University', accessed 19 July 2022, https://www.isu.edu/media/libraries/student-success/tutoring/handouts-writing/editing-and-mechanics/Concrete-and-Specific-Language.pdf.

7. PwC, 'PwC Future of Customer Experience', 2018, https://www.pwc.com/us/en/advisory-services/publications/consumer-intelligence-series/pwc-consumer-intelligence-series-customer-experience.pdf#page=8.

8. Grant Packard and Jonah Berger, 'How Concrete Language Shapes Customer Satisfaction', *Journal of Consumer Research 47,* no. 5 (2020): 787–806, https://doi.org/10.1093/jcr/ucaa038.

9. A. Parasuraman, Leonard L. Berry, and Valarie A. Zeithaml (1988), 'SERVQUAL: A Multiple-Item Scale for Measuring Consumer Perceptions of Service Quality', *Journal of Retailing*, 64 (1), 12–40.

10. 'What Is Text Mining, Text Analytics and Natural Language Processing?', Linguamatics, accessed 19 July 2022, https://www.linguamatics.com/what-text-mining-text-analytics-and-natural-language-processing.

11. Lucia Specia, 'Inferring Psycholinguistic Properties of Words', Proceedings of the 2016 Conference of the North American Chapter of the Association for Computational Linguistics: Human Language Technologies, 2016, https://doi.org/10.18653/v1/n16-1050.

12. Max Coltheart, 'The MRC Psycholinguistic Database', *The Quarterly Journal of Experimental Psychology*, Section A 33, no. 4 (1981): 497–505, https://doi.org/10.1080/14640748108400805.

13. All about Linguistics, accessed July 19, 2022, https://all-about-linguistics.group.shef.ac.uk/branches-of-linguistics/morphology/what-is-morphology/.

14. 'Psycholinguistics', Oxford Bibliographies, accessed 19 July 2022, https://www.oxfordbibliographies.com/view/document/obo-9780199828340/obo-9780199828340-0153.xml.

15. Max Coltheart, 'The MRC Psycholinguistic Database', *The Quarterly Journal of Experimental Psychology*.

16. 'Apa PsycNet', American Psychological Association, accessed 19 July 2022, http://psycnet.apa.org/index.cfm?fa=search.displayRecord&uid=2005-11504-006.

17. Grant Packard and Jonah Berger, 'How Concrete Language Shapes Customer Satisfaction', *Journal of Consumer Research 47*.

18. One standard deviation more from the average of the concreteness score. Standard deviation is a measure of the degree of variation around a value.

19. Frank V. Cespedes, and Christopher Wallace, 'Executives and Salespeople Are Misaligned – and the Effects Are Costly', *Harvard Business Review*, 21 September 2017, https://hbr.org/2017/01/executives-and-salespeople-are-misaligned-and-the-effects-are-costly; Blake Morgan, 'Customer Service Is a $350 Billion Industry, and It's a Mess', *Forbes*, 25 September 2017, https://www.forbes.com/sites/blakemorgan/2017/09/25/customer-service-is-a-350b-industry-and-its-a-mess/.

Chapter 6: When 'You' Can Make the Difference

1. Billboard Hot 100 Singles chart listing for the week of 28 November 1992. *Billboard*, 28 November 1992, retrieved 24 September 2010.

2. Wendy Geller, 'It Was 40 Years Ago: Dolly Parton Bids Adieu to Porter Wagoner, Writes "I Will Always Love You"', Yahoo!, 21 February 2014, https://www.yahoo.com/entertainment/blogs/our-country/40-years-ago-this-week--dolly-parton-bids-adieu-to-porter-wagoner--writes--i-will-always-love-you-175857744.html.

3. Jon Pareles, 'Review/Pop; Bryan Adams, More Mr. Nice Guy', the *New York Times*, 8 March 1994, https://www.nytimes.com/1994/03/08/arts/review-pop-bryan-adams-more-mr-nice-guy.html.

4. 'European Airplay Top 50' (PDF). *Music & Media*, 3 August 1991, retrieved 31 July 2019.
5. Lowenna Waters, '10 of the Best Mariah Carey Songs', the *Telegraph*, Telegraph Media Group, 10 October 2017, https://www.telegraph.co.uk/music/what-to-listen-to/best-mariah-carey-songs/.
6. Gary Trust, 'Mariah Carey's "All I Want for Christmas Is You" Continues at No. 1 on Billboard Hot 100', *Billboard*, 4 January 2022, https://www.billboard.com/music/chart-beat/mariah-carey-all-i-want-for-christmas-is-you-eighth-week-number-one-hot-100-eighth-week-1235015250/.
7. Gary Trust, 'Mariah Carey & "Charlie Brown Christmas" Top Billboard's Greatest of All Time Holiday Charts', *Billboard*, November 18, 2021, https://www.billboard.com/music/chart-beat/mariah-carey-charlie-brown-greatest-of-all-time-holiday-charts-1234999010/.
8. Plácido Domingo, Frances Moore, Global Music Report, 24 April 2018: Annual State of the Industry (PDF). *International Federation of the Phonographic Industry*, archived from the original (PDF) on 24 April 2018, retrieved 28 August 2018.
9. 'Adele: Someone Like You', *Bitesize*, retrieved 19 May 2020.
10. Gary Trust, 'Is Adele's "Someone like You" the First No. 1 Piano-and-Vocal-Only Ballad?', *Billboard*, 14 January 2013, https://www.billboard.com/pro/is-adeles-someone-like-you-the-first-no-1-piano-and-vocal-only/.
11. 'Someone like You (Adele Song)', Wikipedia (Wikimedia Foundation, 28 June 2022, https://en.wikipedia.org/wiki/Someone_like_You_(Adele_song).
12. Gary Trust, 'Ariana Grande's "7 Rings" Spends Third Week atop Billboard Hot 100, Marshmello Makes Fortnite-Fueled Flight to No. 2', *Billboard*, 12 February 2019, https://www.billboard.com/pro/ariana-grande-7-rings-hot-100-number-one-third-week/.
13. Tim Ingham, 'Over 60,000 Tracks Are Now Uploaded to Spotify Every Day. That's Nearly One per Second', *Music Business Worldwide*, 1 March 2021, https://www.musicbusinessworldwide.com/over-60000-tracks-are-now-uploaded-to-spotify-daily-thats-nearly-one-per-second/.

14. You can listen to the song here: https://www.youtube.com/watch?v=BZ9S6XOs2X0.

15. Grant Packard and Jonah Berger, 'Thinking of You: How Second-Person Pronouns Shape Cultural Success', *Psychological Science 31*, no. 4 (2020): 397–407, https://doi.org/10.1177/0956797620902380.

16. John Lyons, *Semantics*, vol. II, Cambridge University Press, 1977.

17. Tad T. Brunyé et al., 'When You and I Share Perspectives', *Psychological Science 20*, no. 1 (2009): 27–32, https://doi.org/10.1111/j.1467-9280.2008.02249.x.

18. 'Digital Song Sales', *Billboard*, 24 March 2022, http://www.billboard.com/charts/digital-song-sales.

19. J.W. Pennebaker et al., 'The Development and Psychometric Properties of LIWC2015', 2015, https://doi.org/10.15781/T29G6Z.

20. M. Davies, 'Word Frequency Data', Word frequency: based on one billion word COCA corpus, accessed 24 July 2022, http://www.wordfrequency.info/.

21. Ariana Orvell, Ethan Kross, and Susan A. Gelman, 'How "You" Makes Meaning', *Science 355*, no. 6331 (2017): 1299–1302, https://doi.org/10.1126/science.aaj2014.

22. Rachel A. Simmons, Peter C. Gordon, and Dianne L. Chambless, 'Pronouns in Marital Interaction', *Psychological Science 16*, no. 12 (2005): 932–36, https://doi.org/10.1111/j.1467-9280.2005.01639.x.

Chapter 7: On the Internet, Everybody Knows You're a Dog

1. Charles Duhigg, 'How Companies Learn Your Secrets', the *New York Times*, 16 February 2012, https://www.nytimes.com/2012/02/19/magazine/shopping-habits.html.

2. 'How Target Figured Out A Teen Girl Was Pregnant Before Her Father Did', Kashmir Hill, *Forbes*, 16 February 2012, https://www.forbes.com/sites/kashmirhill/2012/02/16/how-target-figured-out-a-teen-girl-was-pregnant-before-her-father-did/?sh=38c88cc86668.

3. https://www.cbc.ca/news/business/woman-targeted-by-baby-product-marketers-after-miscarriage-1.4989945.

4. Glenn Fleishman, 'Cartoon Captures Spirit of the Internet', the *New York Times*, 14 December 2000, https://www.nytimes.com/

2000/12/14/technology/cartoon-captures-spirit-of-the-internet. html.

5. Kate Cox, 'Gambling Services Use Big Data to Target Recovering Gamblers, Low-Income Families', Consumerist, 31 August 2017, https://consumerist.com/2017/08/31/gambling-services-use-big-data-to-target-recovering-gamblers-low-income-families/.

6. Peter Vidani, 'The New Yorker – A cartoon by Kaamran Hafeez, from this week's . . .' tumblr.com, the *New Yorker*, 23 February 2015, archived from the original on 20 September 2016, retrieved 29 July 2016.

7. Robert W. Palmatier and Kelly D. Martin, *The Intelligent Marketer's Guide to Data Privacy: The Impact of Big Data on Customer Trust* (Cham, Switzerland: Palgrave Macmillan, 2019).

8. Robert J Shapiro, 'What Your Data Is Really Worth to Facebook', *Washington Monthly*, 9 January 2022, https://washingtonmonthly. com/magazine/july-august-2019/what-your-data-is-really-worth-to-facebook/.

9. 'The Trust Center', Cisco, 30 June 2022, https://www.cisco.com/c/en/us/about/trust-center.html.

10. K.D. Martin, A. Borah, and R.W. Palmatier, Data Privacy: Effects on Customer and Firm Performance, *Journal of Marketing*, 81(1), (2017): 36–58.

11. Nicholas Confessore and Gabriel J.X., 'The Follower Factory', the *New York Times*, 27 January 2018, https://www.nytimes.com/interactive/2018/01/27/technology/social-media-bots.html.

12. Maggie Astor, 'Your Roomba May Be Mapping Your Home, Collecting Data That Could Be Shared', the *New York Times*, 25 July 2017, https://www.nytimes.com/2017/07/25/technology/roomba-irobot-data-privacy.html.

13. 'Data Breach', Definition, accessed 23 July 2022, https://www. trendmicro.com/vinfo/us/security/definition/data-breach.

14. RBS (2020), '2020 Year End Data Breach QuickView Report', accessed at https://pages.riskbasedsecurity.com/en/en/2020-yearend-data-breach-quickview-report.

15. Michael Hill and Dan Swinhoe, 'The 15 Biggest Data Breaches of the 21st Century', *CSO Online*, 16 July 2021, https://www.csoonline.com/article/2130877/the-biggest-data-breaches-of-the-21st-century.html.

16. Ramkumar Janakiraman, Joon Ho Lim, and Rishika Rishika, 'The Effect of a Data Breach Announcement on Customer Behavior: Evidence from a Multichannel Retailer', *Journal of Marketing 82*, no. 2 (2018): 85–105, https://doi.org/10.1509/jm.16.0124; Huseyin Cavusoglu, Birendra Mishra, and Srinivasan Raghunathan, 'The Effect of Internet Security Breach Announcements on Market Value: Capital Market Reactions for Breached Firms and Internet Security Developers', *International Journal of Electronic Commerce 9*, no. 1 (2004): 70–104, https://doi.org/10.1080/10864415.2004.11044320.

17. Eugene F. Fama, 'Market Efficiency, Long-Term Returns, and Behavioral Finance', *SSRN Electronic Journal*, 1997, https://doi.org/10.2139/ssrn.15108; William F. Sharpe, 'Capital Asset Prices: A Theory of Market Equilibrium under Conditions of Risk', *The Journal of Finance 19*, no. 3 (1964): 425, https://doi.org/10.2307/2977928.

18. R.I. Dunbar, 'Gossip in Evolutionary Perspective', *Review of General Psychology 8*, no. 2 (2004): 100–10, https://doi.org/10.1037/1089-2680.8.2.100; Eric K. Foster, 'Research on Gossip: Taxonomy, Methods, and Future Directions', *Review of General Psychology 8*, no. 2 (2004): 78–99, https://doi.org/10.1037/1089-2680.8.2.78.

19. Ibid.

20. Bianca Beersma and Gerben A. Van Kleef, 'Why People Gossip: An Empirical Analysis of Social Motives, Antecedents, and Consequences', *Journal of Applied Social Psychology 42*, no. 11 (2012): 2640–70, https://doi.org/10.1111/j.1559-1816.2012.00956.x.

21. Roy F. Baumeister, Liqing Zhang, and Kathleen D. Vohs, 'Gossip as Cultural Learning', *Review of General Psychology 8*, no. 2 (2004): 111–21, https://doi.org/10.1037/1089-2680.8.2.111.

22. Nicholas Emler, 'Gossip, Reputation and Social Adaption', in *Good Gossip*, R.F. Goodman and A. Ben-Ze'ev, eds. Lawrence: University of Kansas Press, 119–40.

23. Colleen Mills, 'Experiencing Gossip: The Foundations for a Theory of Embedded Organizational Gossip', Group; *Organization Management 35*, no. 2 (November 2010): 213–40, https://doi.org/10.1177/1059601109360392; Eliot R. Smith, 'Evil Acts and Malicious Gossip', *Personality and Social Psychology Review 18*, no. 4 (December 2014): 311–25, https://doi.org/10.1177/1088868314530515.

24. Jonnathan Coleman, 'Here's How Long It Would Take to Read All the New Privacy Updates', *Medium*, 25 May 2018, https://jonnathancoleman.medium.com/heres-how-long-it-would-take-to-read-all-the-privacy-updates-you-ve-been-getting-cd4f215cff6d.

25. Olivia Adams, 'What Is a Privacy Policy & How to Write It: The Definitive Guide', WebsitePolicies, 23 June 2022, https://www.websitepolicies.com/blog/what-is-privacy-policy.

26. K.D. Martin, A. Borah, and R.W. Palmatier, Data Privacy: Effects on Customer and Firm Performance, *Journal of Marketing*.

27. K.D. Martin, A. Borah, and R.W. Palmatier, 'A Strong Privacy Policy Can Save Your Company Millions', *Harvard Business Review*, 2018.

28. Robert W. Palmatier and Kelly D. Martin, *The Intelligent Marketer's Guide to Data Privacy: The Impact of Big Data on Customer Trust* (Cham, Switzerland: Palgrave Macmillan, 2019).

29. George R. Milne, Andrew J. Rohm, and Shalini Bahl, 'Consumers' Protection of Online Privacy and Identity', *Journal of Consumer Affairs* 38, no. 2 (2004): 217–32, https://doi.org/10.1111/j.1745-6606.2004.tb00865.x.

30. George R. Milne, Mary J. Culnan, and Henry Greene, 'A Longitudinal Assessment of Online Privacy Notice Readability', *Journal of Public Policy and Marketing 25*, no. 2 (2006): 238–49, https://doi.org/10.1509/jppm.25.2.238.

31. Smith, Dinev, and Xu, 'Information Privacy Research: An Interdisciplinary Review', *MIS Quarterly 35,* no. 4 (2011): 989, https://doi.org/10.2307/41409970.

32. Kate O'Flaherty, 'iPhone Users' Favorite IOS 14.5 Feature Is a Rip-Roaring Success', *Forbes*, 30 June 2021, https://www.forbes.com/sites/kateoflahertyuk/2021/05/14/iphone-users-favorite-ios-145-feature-is-a-rip-roaring-success/?sh=3f9e327e6e76.

Chapter 8: When 'I' Is More than 'we'

1. PricewaterhouseCoopers, 'Consumer Intelligence Series', PwC, accessed 24 July 2022, https://www.pwc.com/us/en/services/consulting/library/consumer-intelligence-series.html.l—the figure is 49 per cent.

2. https://www.forbes.com/sites/danielnewman/2015/10/13/customer-experience-is-the-future-of-marketing/?sh=ddc3804193d5.

3. Nasir Naveed et al., 'Bad News Travel Fast', Proceedings of the 3rd International Web Science Conference on - WebSci '11, 2011, https://doi.org/10.1145/2527031.2527052.

4. 'PWC: Audit and Assurance, Consulting and Tax Services', accessed 24 July 2022, https://www.pwc.com/us/en/zz-test/assets/pwc-consumer-intelligence-series-customer-experience.pdf.

5. G. Packard, S.G. Moore, and B. McFerran, '(I'm) Happy to Help (You): The Impact of Personal Pronoun Use in Customer–Firm Interactions', *Journal of Marketing Research*, 55(4), (2018): 541–55.

6. C. Nathan DeWall et al., 'Narcissism and Implicit Attention Seeking: Evidence from Linguistic Analyses of Social Networking and Online Presentation', *Personality and Individual Differences 51*, no. 1 (2011): 57–62, https://doi.org/10.1016/j.paid.2011.03.011.

7. Yla R. Tausczik and James W. Pennebaker, 'The Psychological Meaning of Words: LIWC and Computerized Text Analysis Methods', *Journal of Language and Social Psychology 29*, no. 1 (August 2009): 24–54, https://doi.org/10.1177/0261927x09351676.

8. G.A. Fine, and P. Manning, Erving Goffman, *The Blackwell Companion to Major Contemporary Social Theorists*, (2003): 34–62.

9. Jeanne Fahnestock, *Rhetorical Style: The Uses of Language in Persuasion* (Oxford: Oxford University Press, 2011); Peter C. Gordon, Barbara J. Grosz, and Laura A. Gilliom, 'Pronouns, Names, and the Centering of Attention in Discourse', *Cognitive Science 17*, no. 3 (1993): 311–47, https://doi.org/10.1207/s15516709cog1703_1.

10. Elizabeth Dori Tunstall, 'How Maya Angelou Made Me Feel', The Conversation, 22 July 2022, https://theconversation.com/how-maya-angelou-made-me-feel-27328.

11. Larry Scherwitz, Kent Berton, and Howard Leventhal, 'Type A Behavior, Self-Involvement, and Cardiovascular Response', *Psychosomatic Medicine 40*, no. 8 (1978): 593–609, https://doi.org/10.1097/00006842-197812000-00002.

12. Katie Wales, *Personal Pronouns in Present-Day English* (Cambridge: Cambridge Univ. Press, 2006).

13. Cindy Chung, and James W. Pennebaker, 'The Psychological Functions of Function Words', *Social Communication*. K. Fiedler, ed. Chicago, IL: Psychology Press (2007).

14. Ananthanarayanan Parasuraman, Leonard L. Berry, and Valarie A. Zeithaml, 'SERVQUAL: A Multiple-Item Scale for Measuring Consumer Perceptions of Service Quality', *Journal of Retailing*, 64 (1), (1988): 12–40.

15. Regression analysis examines the association between an outcome variable and predictors. If the outcome variable is sales, a manager will try to see if a predictor such as advertising has a positive, negative, or no association with the number of sales.

16. William Ickes et al., 'Naturalistic Social Cognition: Empathic Accuracy in Mixed-Sex Dyads.', *Journal of Personality and Social Psychology 59*, no. 4 (1990): 730–42, https://doi.org/10.1037/0022-3514.59.4.730.

17. Rachel A. Simmons, Peter C. Gordon, and Dianne L. Chambless, 'Pronouns in Marital Interaction', *Psychological Science 16*, no. 12 (2005): 932–36, https://doi.org/10.1111/j.1467-9280.2005.01639.x.

Chapter 9: Do Not Read This Book in Print: Save the Trees

1. R.E. Denton Jr, 'The Rhetorical Functions of Slogans: Classifications and Characteristics', *Communication Quarterly*, 28(2), (1980): 10–18.

2. https://www.etymonline.com/word/slogan

3. George E. Shankel, *American Mottoes and Slogans* (New York: H.W. Wilson Co., 1941), 5.

4. Timothy R.V. Foster, 'The Art and Science of the Advertising Slogan', adslogans.co.uk.

5. K.L. Keller, 'Conceptualizing, Measuring, and Managing Customer-Based Brand Equity', *The Journal of Marketing*, 57(1), (1993): 1–22.

6. https://recyclecoach.com/resources/7-revealing-plastic-waste-statistics-2021/.

7. https://www.epa.gov/facts-and-figures-about-materials-waste-and-recycling/plastics-material-specific-data.

8. https://www.indystar.com/story/news/2018/07/29/plastic-waste-pollution-people-cant-resits/818703002/

9. James P. Dillard, and Lijiang Shen, 'On the Nature of Reactance and Its Role in Persuasive Health Communication', *Communication Monographs*, 72 (2), (2005): 144–68.

10. Joseph, Grandpre, Eusebio M. Alvaro, Michael Burgoon, Claude H. Miller, and John R. Hall, 'Adolescent Reactance and Anti-Smoking Campaigns: A Theoretical Approach', *Health Communication*, 15 (3), (2003): 349–66; Brian L. Quick and Michael T. Stephenson (2007), 'Further Evidence That Psychological Reactance Can Be Modelled as a Combination of Anger and Negative Cognitions', *Communication Research*, 34 (3), 255–76; Brian L. Quick, and Jennifer R. Considine, 'Examining the Use of Forceful Language When Designing Exercise Persuasive Messages for Adults: A Test of Conceptualizing Reactance Arousal as a Two-Step Process', *Health Communication,* 23 (September), (2008): 483–91.
11. Gaylen D. Paulson, and Michael E. Roloff, 'The Effect of Request Form and Content on Constructing Obstacles to Compliance', *Communication Research,* 24 (3), (1997): 261–90.
12. A. Kronrod, A. Grinstein, and L. Wathieu, 'Go Green! Should Environmental Messages Be So Assertive?', *Journal of Marketing*, 76(1), (2012): 95–102.
13. Anne R. Clark, 'The Impact of Cost of Compliance, Deservingness of Aid, and Directness of Request on Reactions to the Request', *Southern Communication Journal*, 58 (3), (1993): 215–26.
14. Ying Zhang, Jing Xu, Zixi Jiang, and Szu-Chi Huang, 'Been There, Done That: The Impact of Effort Investment on Goal Value and Consumer Motivation', *Journal of Consumer Research*, 38 (1), (2011): 78–93.
15. J. Henrich, S.J. Heine, and A. Norenzayan, 'Most People Are not WEIRD', *Nature*, 466(7302), (2010): 29.
16. https://www.creativereview.co.uk/make-love-not-war-slogan/.
17. https://www.un.org/development/desa/en/news/population/world-population-prospects-2019.html.

Chapter 10: The Force of Four-Letter Words in Online Reviews

1. Katy Steinmetz, 'Why We Swear: Profanity Is Powerful', *Time*, 15 December 2016, https://time.com/4602680/profanity-research-why-we-swear/.
2. Timothy Jay, 'The Utility and Ubiquity of Taboo Words', *Perspectives on Psychological Science 4*, no. 2 (2009): 153–161, https://doi.org/10.1111/j.1745-6924.2009.01115.x.

3. 'Watch Your Mouth!', NBCNews.com, NBCUniversal News Group, 29 March 2006, https://www.nbcnews.com/id/wbna12063093.

4. David Anderson, 'The Average American Utters 80 to 90 Curse Words Every Day. Here's Why It's Good for You.', *Business Insider*, 16 May 2021, https://www.businessinsider.com/swearing-good-for-workouts-work-life-health-2018-12.

5. Rob Chirico, 'When Lyrics Were Clean, Almost', *Slate*, 27 June 2016, https://slate.com/human-interest/2016/06/a-history-of-swearing-in-music.html.

6. 'Ban the F-Bomb: Is There Too Much Bad Language in Pop Music?', the *Guardian*, 18 November 2016, https://www.theguardian.com/music/2016/nov/18/is-there-too-much-swearing-in-pop-emeli-sande-chvrches-beyonce.

7. Musixmatch, 'Profanity in Lyrics: Most Used Swear Words and Their Usage by Popular Genres', Medium, Musixmatch Blog, 1 June 2016, https://blog.musixmatch.com/profanity-in-lyrics-most-used-swear-words-and-their-usage-by-popular-genres-d8a12c776713.

8. Wenbo Wang et al., 'Cursing in English on Twitter', Proceedings of the 17th ACM Conference on Computer Supported Cooperative Work and Social Computing, 2014, https://doi.org/10.1145/2531602.2531734.

9. Katy Steinmetz, 'Why We Swear: Profanity Is Powerful', *Time*.

10. Steven Pinker, *The Stuff of Thought: Language as a Window into Human Nature* (London: Penguin Books, 2008).

11. '"Fuck" Is One of the Most Beautiful Words: Osho News', Osho News | Osho News brings articles and news items for people on the path, Osho lovers, sannyasins and meditators, 11 August 2019, https://www.oshonews.com/2012/01/18/fuck/.

12. David Edmonds, 'Why Do People Swear?', BBC News, 27 February 2017, https://www.bbc.com/news/magazine-39082467.

13. David Anderson, 'The Average American Utters 80 to 90 Curse Words Every Day. Here's Why It's Good for You.', *Business Insider*.

14. 'Traffic Congestion Ranking: Tomtom Traffic Index', Traffic congestion ranking | TomTom Traffic Index, accessed 22 July 2022, https://www.tomtom.com/en_gb/traffic-index/ranking/.

15. Mudambi and Schuff, 'Research Note: What Makes a Helpful Online Review? A Study of Customer Reviews on Amazon.com', *MIS Quarterly 34*, no. 1 (2010): 185, https://doi.org/10.2307/20721420.

16. Sarah G. Moore, 'Attitude Predictability and Helpfulness in Online Reviews: The Role of Explained Actions and Reactions', *Journal of Consumer Research 42*, no. 1 (January 2015): 30–44, https://doi.org/10.1093/jcr/ucv003.

17. Jared M. Spool, 'The Magic behind Amazon's 2.7 Billion Dollar Question', UX Articles by UIE, 8 March 2016, https://articles.uie.com/magicbehindamazon/.

18. Stephan Ludwig et al., 'More than Words: The Influence of Affective Content and Linguistic Style Matches in Online Reviews on Conversion Rates', *Journal of Marketing 77*, no. 1 (2013): 87–103, https://doi.org/10.1509/jm.11.0560.

19. Pratibha A. Dabholkar, 'Factors Influencing Consumer Choice of a "Rating Web Site": An Experimental Investigation of an Online Interactive Decision Aid', *Journal of Marketing Theory and Practice 14*, no. 4 (2006): 259–73, https://doi.org/10.2753/mtp1069-6679140401.

20. Katherine C. Lafreniere, Sarah G. Moore, and Robert J. Fisher, 'The Power of Profanity: The Meaning and Impact of Swear Words in Word of Mouth', *Journal of Marketing Research*, 2022, p. 002224372210786, https://doi.org/10.1177/00222437221078606.

21. Yelp 2017.

22. J.W. Pennebaker, R. Boyd, K. Jordan, and K. Blackburn, 'The Development and Psychometric Properties of LIWC2015. University of Texas at Austin, (2015), https://doi.org/10.15781/T29G6Z.

23. Yla R. Tausczik and James W. Pennebaker, 'The Psychological Meaning of Words: LIWC and Computerized Text Analysis Methods', *Journal of Language and Social Psychology 29*, no. 1 (August 2009): 24–54, https://doi.org/10.1177/0261927x09351676.

24. A stem is the form of a word before inflectional affixes are added to it.

Chapter 11: Words That Are Gonna Make You Sweat (Virtually)

1. Sean P. Egen, '10 Quotes about Finance & Credit: Credit One Bank', Credit Education and Personal Finance Articles | Credit One Bank, accessed July 24, 2022, https://www.creditonebank.com/articles/10-famous-quotes-about-finances-credit.

2. myFICO.com.

3. J. Merritt Melancon, 'How Social Media Posts Could Affect Credit Scores', UGA Today, 17 May 2022, https://news.uga.edu/how-social-media-posts-could-affect-credit-scores/.

4. Evelyn M. Rusli, 'Bad Credit? Start Tweeting', the *Wall Street Journal*, 2 April 2013, https://www.wsj.com/articles/SB100014241278873248 83604578396852612756398.

5. 'Fact Sheet: Cash-Flow Data in Credit Underwriting', accessed 24 July 2022, http://www.idealenterprises.in/fact-sheet-cash-flow-data-in-credit-underwriting-10/.

6. https://patft.uspto.gov/netacgi/nph-Parser?Sect1=PTO1 &Sect2=HITOFF&p=1&u=/netahtml/PTO/srchnum. html&r=1&f=G&l=50&d=PALL&s1=8302164.PN.

7. Nizan Geslevich Packin, 'Social Credit: Much More than Your Traditional Financial Credit Score Data', *Forbes*, 13 December 2019, https://www.forbes.com/sites/nizangpackin/2019/12/13/social-credit-much-more-than-your-traditional-financial-credit-score-data/?sh=72644e825a82.

8. J. Merritt Melancon, 'How Social Media Posts Could Affect Credit Scores', UGA Today.

9. 'Press Releases', FDIC, accessed 24 July 2022, https://www.fdic.gov/news/press-releases/2019/pr19117.html.

10. 'Consumer Financial Protection Bureau', Consumer Financial Protection Bureau, accessed 24 July 2022, https://www.consumerfinance.gov/.

11. O. Netzer, A. Lemaire, and M. Herzenstein, 'When Words Sweat: Identifying Signals for Loan Default in the Text of Loan Applications', *Journal of Marketing Research*, 56(6), (2019): 960–80.

12. 'Personal Loans Made Easy: Prosper, Online Loans are Easy with Prosper—Apply Today for Low Rates!', accessed 24 July 2022, https://www.prosper.com/about.

13. 'About Experian', Experian, accessed 24 July 2022, https://www.experian.com/corporate/about-experian.

14. Jeffrey T. Hancock et al., 'On Lying and Being Lied to: A Linguistic Analysis of Deception in Computer-Mediated Communication', *Discourse Processes* 45, no. 1 (2007): 1–23, https://doi.org/

10.1080/01638530701739181; Myle Ott, Claire Cardie, and Jeff Hancock, 'Estimating the Prevalence of Deception in Online Review Communities', Proceedings of the 21st International Conference on World Wide Web, 2012, https://doi.org/10.1145/2187836.2187864.

15. Ellen K. Nyhus and Paul Webley, 'The Role of Personality in Household Saving and Borrowing Behaviour', *European Journal of Personality 15*, no. 1_suppl (2001), https://doi.org/10.1002/per.422.

16. Daniel M. Oppenheimer, 'Consequences of Erudite Vernacular Utilized Irrespective of Necessity: Problems with Using Long Words Needlessly', *Applied Cognitive Psychology 20*, no. 2 (2006): 139–156, https://doi.org/10.1002/acp.1178.

17. G. Harry McLaughlin, 'SMOG Grading—A New Readability Formula', *Journal of Reading*, 12 (8), (1969): 639–46.

18. Sarah K. Harkness, 'Discrimination in Lending Markets', *Social Psychology Quarterly 79*, no. 1 (September 2016): 81–93, https://doi.org/10.1177/0190272515623459.

19. Variance in machine learning refers to changes in the model's predictions when a researcher uses different portions of the training data. It shows how spread out are the predictions. Bias refers to how inaccurate are the predictions.

20. Dokyun Lee, Kartik Hosanagar, and Harikesh S. Nair, 'Advertising Content and Consumer Engagement on Social Media: Evidence from Facebook', *Management Science 64*, no. 11 (2018): 5105–31, https://doi.org/10.1287/mnsc.2017.2902.

21. M. Pasupathi, 'Telling and the Remembered Self: Linguistic Differences in Memories for Previously Disclosed and Previously Undisclosed Events', *Memory 15*, no. 3 (2007): 258–270, https://doi.org/10.1080/09658210701256456.

22. Gary D. Bond and Adrienne Y. Lee, 'Language of Lies in Prison: Linguistic Classification of Prisoners' Truthful and Deceptive Natural Language', *Applied Cognitive Psychology 19*, no. 3 (2005): 313–29, https://doi.org/10.1002/acp.1087.

23. Tal Yarkoni, 'Personality in 100,000 Words: A Large-Scale Analysis of Personality and Word Use among Bloggers', *Journal of Research in Personality 44*, no. 3 (2010): 363–73, https://doi.org/10.1016/j.jrp.2010.04.001.

24. H. Andrew Schwartz et al., 'Personality, Gender, and Age in the Language of Social Media: The Open-Vocabulary Approach', *PLoS ONE 8*, no. 9 (2013), https://doi.org/10.1371/journal.pone.0073791.

25. Brent Weiss and Robert S. Feldman, 'Looking Good and Lying to Do It: Deception as an Impression Management Strategy in Job Interviews', *Journal of Applied Social Psychology 36*, no. 4 (December 2006): 1070–86, https://doi.org/10.1111/j.0021-9029.2006.00055.x.

26. Ellen K. Nyhus and Paul Webley, 'The Role of Personality in Household Saving and Borrowing Behaviour', *European Journal of Personality 15*.

27. James W. Pennebaker, 'The Secret Life of Pronouns', *New Scientist 211*, no. 2828 (2011): 42–45, https://doi.org/10.1016/s0262-4079(11)62167-2.

28. 'Gao-22-104380, Mortgage Lending: Use of Alternative Data Is Limited but . . .', accessed 24 July 2022, https://www.gao.gov/assets/gao-22-104380.pdf.

Chapter 12: How to Become Sherlock Holmes Online

1. R. Mohawesh, S. Xu, S.N. Tran, R. Ollington, M. Springer, Y. Jararweh, and S. Maqsood, 'Fake Reviews Detection: A Survey', IEEE Access, 9, (2021): 65771–802.

2. 'Love Everything You Buy', Fakespot, accessed 24 July 2022, https://www.fakespot.com/press#:~:text=About%2042%25%20of%20720%20million,millions%20of%20virus%2Davoiding%20shoppers.

3. Greg Sterling, 'Study Finds 61 Percent of Electronics Reviews on Amazon Are "Fake"', MarTech, 13 May 2021, https://martech.org/study-finds-61-percent-of-electronics-reviews-on-amazon-are-fake/.

4. Teodora Dobrilova, 'What Percentage of Amazon Reviews Are Fake', Review42, 18 January 2022, https://review42.com/resources/what-percentage-of-amazon-reviews-are-fake/.

5. A. Mukherjee, V. Venkataraman, B. Liu, and N. Glance, 'Fake Review Detection: Classification and Analysis of Real and Pseudo Reviews', UIC-CS-03-2013, Technical Report, 2013.

6. Bella M. DePaulo et al., 'Cues to Deception', *Psychological Bulletin 129*, no. 1 (2003): 74–118, https://doi.org/10.1037/0033-2909.129.1.74; M. Zuckerman, and R.E. Driver, 'Telling Lies: Verbal and Nonverbal

Correlates of Deception', *Multichannel integrations of nonverbal behaviour*, (1985): 129–47.

7. Amit Katwala, 'The Race to Create a Perfect Lie Detector – and the Dangers of Succeeding', the *Guardian*, 5 September 2019, https://www.theguardian.com/technology/2019/sep/05/the-race-to-create-a-perfect-lie-detector-and-the-dangers-of-succeeding.

8. Bella M. DePaulo and Deborah A. Kashy, 'Everyday Lies in Close and Casual Relationships.', *Journal of Personality and Social Psychology 74*, no. 1 (1998): 63–79, https://doi.org/10.1037/0022-3514.74.1.63.

9. Paul V. Trovillo, 'A History of Lie Detection', *Journal of Criminal Law and Criminology* (1931–1951) 29, no. 6 (1939): 848, https://doi.org/10.2307/1136489.

10. Bella M. DePaulo et al., 'Cues to Deception', *Psychological Bulletin 129*.

11. Bella M. DePaulo, 'Spotting Lies: Can Humans Learn to Do Better?', *Current Directions in Psychological Science 3*, no. 3 (1994): 83–86, https://doi.org/10.1111/1467-8721.ep10770433.

12. '10 Surprising Facts about Divorce around the World', Worthy, July 2, 2019, https://www.worthy.com/blog/divorce/entertainment/divorce-around-the-world/.

13. Charles F. Bond et al., 'Lie Detection across Cultures', *Journal of Nonverbal Behavior* 14, no. 3 (1990): 189–204, https://doi.org/10.1007/bf00996226.

14. Laura Zimmerman, 'Deception Detection', Monitor on Psychology, American Psychological Association, March 2016, https://www.apa.org/monitor/2016/03/deception.

15. Charles F. Bond and Bella M. DePaulo, 'Accuracy of Deception Judgments', *Personality and Social Psychology Review* 10, no. 3 (2006): 214–34, https://doi.org/10.1207/s15327957pspr1003_2.

16. E.T. Anderson, and D.I. Simester, 'Reviews without a Purchase: Low Ratings, Loyal Customers, and Deception', *Journal of Marketing Research*, 51(3), (2014): 249–69.

17. Lina Zhou et al., 'Automating Linguistics-Based Cues for Detecting Deception in Text-Based Asynchronous Computer-Mediated Communications', *Group Decision and Negotiation 13*, no. 1 (2004): 81–106, https://doi.org/10.1023/b:grup.0000011944.62889.6f.

18. Judee K. Burgoon et al., 'Detecting Deception through Linguistic Analysis', *Intelligence and Security Informatics*, 2003, 91–101, https://doi.org/10.1007/3-540-44853-5_7.

19. Myle Ott, Yejin Choi, Claire Cardie, and Jeffrey T. Hancock, 'Finding Deceptive Opinion Spam by Any Stretch of the Imagination', in *Proceedings of the 49th Annual Meeting of the Association for Computational Linguistics*. Portland, OR: Association for Computational Linguistics, (2011): 309–319.

20. S. Moon, M.Y. Kim, and D. Iacobucci, 'Content Analysis of Fake Consumer Reviews by Survey-Based Text Categorization', *International Journal of Research in Marketing*, 38(2), (2021): 343–64.

21. Dina Mayzlin, Yaniv Dover, and Judith Chevalier, 'Promotional Reviews: An Empirical Investigation of Online Review Manipulation', *American Economic Review 104*, no. 8 (January 2014): 2421–55, https://doi.org/10.1257/aer.104.8.2421.

22. Xinxin Li and Lorin M. Hitt, 'Self-Selection and Information Role of Online Product Reviews', *Information Systems Research 19*, no. 4 (2008): 456–74, https://doi.org/10.1287/isre.1070.0154.

Chapter 13: #Boycott[Insertyourfirmname]: Shunning Shitstorms on Social Media

1. C.E. Cresci, '#Deleteuber: How Social Media Turned on Uber', the *Guardian*, 30 January 2017, https://www.theguardian.com/technology/2017/jan/30/deleteuber-how-social-media-turned-on-uber.

2. Paige Leskin, 'Uber Says the #DeleteUber Movement Led to "Hundreds of Thousands" of People Quitting the App', *Business Insider*, 11 April 2019, https://www.businessinsider.com/uber-deleteuber-protest-hundreds-of-thousands-quit-app-2019-4.

3. Allison Benedikt, Dan Kois, and Jennifer Lai, 'How Slate Tracked down a Year of Anger and Outrage', *Slate*, 3 August 2015, http://www.slate.com/articles/life/culturebox/2014/12/the_year_of_outrage_2014_behind_the_scenes_of_everything_you_were_angry.html.

4. J. Pfeffer, T. Zorbach, and K. M. Carley, 'Understanding Online Firestorms: Negative Word-of-Mouth Dynamics in Social Media

Networks', *Journal of Marketing Communications 20*, no. 1–2 (October 2013): 117–28, https://doi.org/10.1080/13527266.2013.797778.

5. Tweetbinder sentiment report on @McDonaldsCorp or 'McDonald's' or McDonalds (https://dash.tweetbinder.com/report/f4ad2a80) showed that negative retweets generated 3.1 per cent more impact than positive retweets. https://www.refinery29.com/en-us/2017/11/182412/mcdonalds-twitter-black-friday-jokes.

6. https://www.businessinsider.com/burger-king-women-belong-in-kitchen-tweet-international-womens-day-2021-3.

7. YouTube (YouTube, 2009), https://www.youtube.com/watch?v=5YGc4zOqozo.

8. A. Borah, S. Banerjee, Y. Lin, and A. Eisingerich, 'Why So Tactless? Untactful Social Media Messages, Its Consequences and Mitigation Strategies', Working Paper, 2023.

9. Iris Murdoch, The Sovereignty of Good (London: Ark, 1985).

10. Ibid.

11. Christian Homburg, Laura Ehm, and Martin Artz, 'Measuring and Managing Consumer Sentiment in an Online Community Environment', *Journal of Marketing Research 52*, no. 5 (2015): 629–41, https://doi.org/10.1509/jmr.11.0448; David A. Schweidel and Wendy W. Moe, 'Listening in on Social Media: A Joint Model of Sentiment and Venue Format Choice', *Journal of Marketing Research 51*, no. 4 (2014): 387–402, https://doi.org/10.1509/jmr.12.0424.

12. Andrea Everard and Dennis F. Galletta, 'How Presentation Flaws Affect Perceived Site Quality, Trust, and Intention to Purchase from an Online Store', *Journal of Management Information Systems 22*, no. 3 (2005): 56–95, https://doi.org/10.2753/mis0742-1222220303; Evert Gummesson, 'Extending the Service-Dominant Logic: From Customer Centricity to Balanced Centricity', *Journal of the Academy of Marketing Science 36*, no. 1 (2007): 15–17, https://doi.org/10.1007/s11747-007-0065-x.

13. Manuel Castells and Gustavo Cardoso, (eds), 'The Networked Society: From Knowledge to Policy', Washington, DC: Center for Transatlantic Relations, 2006; Paul H. Nitze School of Advanced International Studies, Johns Hopkins University. Washington, DC: Brookings Institution Press; Manuel Castells, 'The Rise of the Network Society' (Cambridge, Massachusetts: Blackwell Publishers 1996).

14. Neil M. Alperstein, 'Celebrity and Mediated Social Connections: Fans, Friends, and Followers in the Digital Age' (Springer Nature, 2019).

15. Joshua D. Angrist and Pischke Jörn-Steffen, 'Mostly Harmless Econometrics: An Empiricist's Companion (Princeton: Princeton University Press, 2009).

16. N. Hansen, A.K. Kupfer, and T. Hennig-Thurau, 'Brand Crises in the Digital Age: The Short-and Long-Term Effects of Social Media Firestorms on Consumers and Brands', *International Journal of Research in Marketing*, 35(4), (2018): 557–74.

17. Richard E. Petty and John T. Cacioppo, 'The Elaboration Likelihood Model of Persuasion', *Advances in Experimental Social Psychology*, (1986): 123–205, https://doi.org/10.1016/s0065-2601(08)60214-2.

18. D. Herhausen, S. Ludwig, D. Grewal, J. Wulf, and M. Schoegel, 'Detecting, Preventing, and Mitigating Online Firestorms in Brand Communities,' *Journal of Marketing*, 83(3), (2019): 1–21.

19. Sigal G. Barsade, 'The Ripple Effect: Emotional Contagion and Its Influence on Group Behavior', *Administrative Science Quarterly 47*, no. 4 (2002): 644–75, https://doi.org/10.2307/3094912.

20. Molly E. Ireland and James W. Pennebaker, 'Language Style Matching in Writing: Synchrony in Essays, Correspondence, and Poetry.', *Journal of Personality and Social Psychology 99*, no. 3 (2010): 549–71, https://doi.org/10.1037/a0020386.

21. 'The Stanford Natural Language Processing Group', accessed 23 July 2022, https://nlp.stanford.edu:8080/parser/.

Chapter 14: When Bytes Matter More than Words

1. https://owlcation.com/humanities/12-Words-Youve-Probably-Never-Heard-Of.

2. Gunning Fog Index, accessed 23 July 2022, http://gunning-fog-index.com/fog.cgi.

3. F. Li, 'Annual Report Readability, Current Earnings, and Earnings Persistence,' *Journal of Accounting and Economics*, 45(2–3), (2008): 221–47.

4. Julien Le Maux and Nadia Smaili, 'Annual Report Readability And Corporate Bankruptcy', *Journal of Applied Business Research (JABR) 37*, no. 3 (2021).

5. Kin Lo, Felipe Ramos, and Rafael Rogo, 'Earnings Management and Annual Report Readability', *Journal of Accounting and Economics 63*, no. 1 (2017): 1–25, https://doi.org/10.1016/j.jacceco.2016.09.002.

6. Gary C. Biddle, Gilles Hilary, and Rodrigo S. Verdi, 'How Does Financial Reporting Quality Relate to Investment Efficiency?', *Journal of Accounting and Economics 48*, no. 2–3 (2009): 112–31, https://doi.org/10.1016/j.jacceco.2009.09.001.

7. Brian P. Miller, 'The Effects of Reporting Complexity on Small and Large Investor Trading', *The Accounting Review 85*, no. 6 (January 2010): 2107–43, https://doi.org/10.2308/accr.00000001.

8. The Premerger Notification Office Staff and DPIP and CTO Staff, 'Businessperson's Guide to Federal Warranty Law', Federal Trade Commission, 7 August 2020, https://www.ftc.gov/business-guidance/resources/businesspersons-guide-federal-warranty-law.

9. Michael J. Wisdom, 'An Empirical Study of the Magnuson-Moss Warranty Act', *Stanford Law Review 31*, no. 6 (1979): 1117, https://doi.org/10.2307/1228455.; F. Kelly Shuptrine and Ellen M. Moore, 'Even after the Magnuson-Moss Act of 1975, Warranties Are Not Easy to Understand', *Journal of Consumer Affairs 14*, no. 2 (1980): 394–404, https://doi.org/10.1111/j.1745-6606.1980.tb00677.x.

10. Tim Loughran and Bill McDonald, 'Measuring Readability in Financial Disclosures', *The Journal of Finance 69*, no. 4 (2014): 1643–71, https://doi.org/10.1111/jofi.12162.

11. Will Kenton, 'What You Should Know About 10-KS', Investopedia, 8 July 2022, https://www.investopedia.com/terms/1/10-k.asp.

12. Tim Loughran and Bill McDonald, 'Measuring Readability in Financial Disclosures', *The Journal of Finance 69*.

13. Kin Lo, Felipe Ramos, and Rafael Rogo, 'Earnings Management and Annual Report Readability', *Journal of Accounting and Economics 63*, no. 1 (2017): 1–25, https://doi.org/10.1016/j.jacceco.2016.09.002.

14. 'The One Number You Need to Grow', *Harvard Business Review*, 16 July 2015, https://hbr.org/2003/12/the-one-number-you-need-to-grow.

15. Joshua Evan Blumenstock, 'Fighting Poverty with Data', *Science 353*, no. 6301 (2016): 753–54, https://doi.org/10.1126/science.aah5217.

16. Joshua Blumenstock, Gabriel Cadamuro, and Robert On, 'Predicting Poverty and Wealth from Mobile Phone Metadata', *Science 350*, no. 6264 (2015): 1073–76, https://doi.org/10.1126/science.aac4420.

17. Rex Yuxing Du, Ye Hu, and Sina Damangir, 'Leveraging Trends in Online Searches for Product Features in Market Response Modeling', *Journal of Marketing 79*, no. 1 (2015): 29–43, https://doi.org/10.1509/jm.12.0459.

18. Zhi Da, Joseph Engelberg, and Pengjie Gao, 'In Search of Attention', *The Journal of Finance 66*, no. 5 (2011): 1461–99, https://doi.org/10.1111/j.1540-6261.2011.01679.x.

Chapter 15: Can Noise Be Information? A 'Sound Story' about Financial Markets

1. Michele Debczak, 'Why Is White Noise "White"?', Mental Floss 1 March 2016, https://www.mentalfloss.com/article/76069/why-white-noise-white.

2. Glenn Elert, 'The Nature of Sound', *The Physics Hypertextbook* (hypertextbook), accessed 23 July 2022, https://physics.info/sound/.

3. Unknown, 'The Propagation of Sound', accessed 23 July 2022, https://pages.jh.edu/virtlab/ray/acoustic.htm.

4. Meghan Neal, 'The Many Colors of Sound', the *Atlantic* 16 February 2016, https://www.theatlantic.com/science/archive/2016/02/white-noise-sound-colors/462972/.

5. 'Sound of Sleep', Sound of Sleep, 10 March 2017, https://www.soundofsleep.com/white-pink-brown-noise-whats-difference/.

6. Nelly A. Papalambros et al., 'Acoustic Enhancement of Sleep Slow Oscillations and Concomitant Memory Improvement in Older Adults', *Frontiers in Human Neuroscience 11*, August 2017, https://doi.org/10.3389/fnhum.2017.00109.

7. https://www.tiktok.com/tag/brownnoise?lang=en.

8. Carolyn Steber, 'TikTok Is Obsessed with Using Brown Noise for Productivity Right Now', Bustle 30 June 2022, https://www.bustle.com/wellness/white-pink-brown-noise-difference-experts.

9. 'Architectural', IAC Acoustics, 28 June 2022, https://www.iacacoustics.com/blog-full/comparative-examples-of-noise-levels.html.

10. Simon Haykin, *The Neural Networks: A Comprehensive Foundation* (Macmillan College Publishing Company, 2007).

11. Brain and Health: The Basics of Brainwaves,http://www.brainandhealth.com/brain-waves.

12. Esther Ramdinmawii and Vinay Kumar Mittal, 'Effect of Different Music Genre: Attention vs. Meditation', 2017 Seventh International Conference on Affective Computing and Intelligent Interaction Workshops and Demos (ACIIW), 2017, https://doi.org/10.1109/aciiw.2017.8272603.

13. Nick Perham, 'Heavy Metal's Bad Rep Is Unfair – It Can Actually Have Numerous Health Benefits for Fans', The Conversation, 3 September 2020, https://theconversation.com/heavy-metals-bad-rep-is-unfair-it-can-actually-have-numerous-health-benefits-for-fans-118476.

14. Hannah Sparks, 'These Cheesy '80s Pop Songs Are the Best for Beating Stress: Study Says', *New York Post* 15 February 2021, https://nypost.com/2021/02/15/why-80s-pop-is-the-best-music-genre-for-reducing-stress/.

15. Philiptrapp, 'Report: Black Metal, Death Metal Good for Focus + Productivity', Loudwire, 13 June 2019, https://loudwire.com/black-death-metal-good-focus-productivity-report/.

16. J.D. Coval, and T. Shumway, 'Is Sound Just Noise?', *The Journal of Finance*, 56(5), (2001): 1887–1910.

17. Will Kenton, 'What Is the Pit?', Investopedia, 8 February 2022, https://www.investopedia.com/terms/p/pit.asp#:~:text=Electronic%20Trading-,What%20Is%20the%20Pit%3F,shouting%20and%20through%20hand%20signals.

18. 'Open Outcry', Wikipedia, 18 May 2022, https://en.wikipedia.org/wiki/Open_outcry.

19. Elise Payzan-LeNestour et al., 'Impact of Ambient Sound on Risk Perception in Humans: Neuroeconomic Investigations', *Scientific Reports 11*, no. 1 (August 2021), https://doi.org/10.1038/s41598-021-84359-7.

20. This plot is the average of the sound level over a typical day for each second across the forty-six days of the sample period.

21. John Coates, *The Hour between Dog and Wolf: How Risk Taking Transforms US, Body and Mind* (New York: Penguin Press, 2013).

22. Elise Payzan-LeNestour et al., 'Impact of Ambient Sound on Risk Perception in Humans: Neuroeconomic Investigations', *Scientific Reports 11*, no. 1 (August 2021), https://doi.org/10.1038/s41598-021-84359-7.

23. R.M. Sapolsky, 'McEwen-Induced Modulation of Endocrine History: A Partial Review,' *Stress 2*, (1997): 1–12.

24. C. Philip Beaman, 'Auditory Distraction from Low-Intensity Noise: A Review of the Consequences for Learning and Workplace Environments', *Applied Cognitive Psychology 19*, no. 8 (2005): 1041–64, https://doi.org/10.1002/acp.1134.

25. Scott D. Gronlund et al., 'Role of Memory in Air Traffic Control.', *Journal of Experimental Psychology: Applied 4*, no. 3 (1998): 263–80, https://doi.org/10.1037/1076-898x.4.3.263.

Chapter 16: Is All That Twitters Gold?

1. Karina Luz Bocanegra Salcedosays, and Brian Deansays: 'How Many People Use Twitter in 2022? [New Twitter Stats]', Backlinko, 5 January 2022, https://backlinko.com/twitter-users.

2. 'The Number of Tweets per Day in 2020 – David Sayce', accessed 23 July 2022, https://www.dsayce.com/social-media/tweets-day/.

3. https://www.businessofapps.com/data/twitter-statistics/.

4. Becky Oskin, '#Earthquake! Tweets Beat Official Quake Alerts', *LiveScience* 6 May 2014, https://www.livescience.com/45385-earthquake-alerts-from-twitter.html.

5. Guardian 2013.

6. Mark Jurkowitz and Jeffrey Gottfried, 'Twitter Is the Go-to Social Media Site for U.S. Journalists, but Not for the Public', Pew Research Center, 27 June 2022, https://www.pewresearch.org/fact-tank/2022/06/27/twitter-is-the-go-to-social-media-site-for-u-s-journalists-but-not-for-the-public/.

7. Thomas H. Davenport and John C. Beck, *The Attention Economy: Understanding the New Currency of Business* (Boston: Harvard Business School, 2005).

8. J. Bollen, H. Mao, and X. Zeng, 'Twitter Mood Predicts the Stock Market', *Journal of Computational Science*, 2(1), (2011): 1–8.

9. Q4 Web Systems, 'Public Companies and Their Use of Twitter for Investor Relations: An Analysis of Corporate Reporting Using Social Media', 2009, available at: http://www.q4blog.com/about/research-reports/.; Elizabeth Blankespoor, Gregory S. Miller, and Hal D. White, 'The Role of Dissemination in Market Liquidity: Evidence from Firms' Use of Twitter™', *The Accounting Review 89*, no. 1 (January 2013): 79–112, https://doi.org/10.2308/accr-50576.

10. Mark L. Mitchell and J. Harold Mulherin, 'The Impact of Public Information on the Stock Market', *The Journal of Finance 49*, no. 3 (1994): 923–50, https://doi.org/10.1111/j.1540-6261.1994.tb00083.x.; Paul C. Tetlock, 'Giving Content to Investor Sentiment: The Role of Media in the Stock Market', *The Journal of Finance 62*, no. 3 (August 2007): 1139–68, https://doi.org/10.1111/j.1540-6261.2007.01232.x.

11. Gerard J. Tellis and Joseph Johnson, 'The Value of Quality', *Marketing Science 26*, no. 6 (2007): 758–73, https://doi.org/10.1287/mksc.1070.0286.

12. Seshadri Tirunillai and Gerard J. Tellis, 'Does Chatter Really Matter? Dynamics of User-Generated Content and Stock Performance', *Marketing Science 31*, no. 2 (2012): 198–215, https://doi.org/10.1287/mksc.1110.0682.

13. Paul M. Healy and Krishna G. Palepu, 'Information Asymmetry, Corporate Disclosure, and the Capital Markets: A Review of the Empirical Disclosure Literature', *Journal of Accounting and Economics 31*, no. 1–3 (2001): 405–40, https://doi.org/10.1016/s0165-4101(01)00018-0.

14. David Sayce, 'The Number of Tweets per Day in 2020', David Sayce, Paper Gecko Ltd., 16 December 2020, https://www.dsayce.com/social-media/tweets-day/.

15. James Surowiecki, 'The Wisdom of Crowds: Why Many Are Smarter than the Few and How Collective Wisdom Shapes Business, Economies, Societies, and Nations', n.d.

16. Eugene F. Fama, 'The Behavior of Stock-Market Prices', *The Journal of Business 38*, no. 1 (1965): 34, https://doi.org/10.1086/294743.

17. Sitaram Asur and Bernardo A. Huberman, 'Predicting the Future with Social Media', 2010 IEEE/WIC/ACM International Conference on Web Intelligence and Intelligent Agent Technology, 2010, https://doi.

org/10.1109/wi-iat.2010.63.; Hal R. Varian and Hyunyoung Choi, 'Predicting the Present with Google Trends', *SSRN Electronic Journal*, 2009, https://doi.org/10.2139/ssrn.1659302.

18. Robert P. Schumaker, A. Tomasz Jarmoszko, and Chester S. Labedz, 'Predicting Wins and Spread in the Premier League Using a Sentiment Analysis of Twitter', *Decision Support Systems 88* (2016): 76–84, https://doi.org/10.1016/j.dss.2016.05.010.

19. 'Twitter Character Counter: Check Your Tweet Length and More!', accessed 23 July 2022, https://charactercounter.com/twitter.

20. Theresa Wilson et al., 'Opinionfinder', Proceedings of HLT/ EMNLP on Interactive Demonstrations, 2005, https://doi.org/10.3115/1225733.1225751.

21. D. McNair, M. Lorr, and L. Doppleman, POMS Manual for the Profile of Mood States, San Diego, CA: *Educational and Industrial Testing Service,* 1971.

22. C.W. Granger, 'Investigating causal relations by econometric models and cross-spectral methods', *Econometrica: Journal of the Econometric Society*, (1969): 424–38.

23. Derek Thompson, 'The World's First Twitter-Based Hedge Fund Is Finally Open for Business', *The Atlantic*, 18 May 2011, https://www.theatlantic.com/business/archive/2011/05/the-worlds-first-twitter-based-hedge-fund-is-finally-open-for-business/239097/.

24. M. Van Dieijen, A. Borah, G.J. Tellis, and P.H. Franses, 'Big Data Analysis of Volatility Spillovers of Brands across Social Media and Stock Markets', *Industrial Marketing Management*, 88, (2020): 465–84.

25. Kit Smith, '60 Incredible and Interesting Twitter Stats and Statistics', Brandwatch, 2 January 2020, http://www.brandwatch.com/blog/twitter-stats-and-statistics/.

26. Ewelina Lacka et al., 'Measuring the Real-Time Stock Market Impact of Firm-Generated Content', *Journal of Marketing* (2021): 002224292110428, https://doi.org/10.1177/00222429211042848.

27. Brendan Brown, Trump Twitter Archive, accessed 23 July 2022, https://www.thetrumparchive.com/.

28. Peder Gjerstad et al., 'Do President Trump's Tweets Affect Financial Markets?', *Decision Support Systems 147* (2021): 113577, https://doi.org/10.1016/j.dss.2021.113577.

Chapter 17: A Crash Course on Charisma from Barack Obama and Mahatma Gandhi

1. R. J. House, and B. Shamir, 'Toward the Integration of Transformational, Charismatic, and Visionary Theories of Leadership', in M. Chemers, and R. Ayman (eds.), *Leadership: Perspectives and Research Directions* (New York: Academic Press, 1993), 81–107.

2. Annette L. Ranft et al., 'Marketing the Image of Management', *Organizational Dynamics 35*, no. 3 (2006): 279–90, https://doi.org/10.1016/j.orgdyn.2006.05.003.

3. 'The Dark Side of Charisma', *Harvard Business Review*, 7 August 2014, https://hbr.org/2012/11/the-dark-side-of-charisma.

4. Paul Joosse, 'Becoming a God: Max Weber and the Social Construction of Charisma', *Journal of Classical Sociology*, 14 (2014): 266–83. 10.1177/1468795X14536652.

5. 'Charisma (Disambiguation)', Wikipedia, 23 October 2021, https://en.wikipedia.org/wiki/Charisma_(disambiguation).

6. 'The Nature of Obama's Charismatic Leadership', *Harvard Business Review*, 23 July 2014, https://hbr.org/2009/01/the-nature-of-obamas-charismat.

7. John E. Baur et al., 'More than One Way to Articulate a Vision: A Configurations Approach to Leader Charismatic Rhetoric and Influence', *The Leadership Quarterly 27*, no. 1 (2016): 156–71, https://doi.org/10.1016/j.leaqua.2015.08.002.

8. YouTube (YouTube, 2012), https://www.youtube.com/watch?v=sR-qL7QdVZQ.

9. L. R. Pondy, 'Leadership Is a Language Game', in Morgan W. McCall and Michael M. Lombardo, in *Leadership: Where Else Can We Go?* (Durham, NC: Duke University Press, 1978).

10. Raed Awamleh and William L. Gardner, 'Perceptions of Leader Charisma and Effectiveness', *The Leadership Quarterly 10*, no. 3 (1999): 345–73, https://doi.org/10.1016/s1048-9843(99)00022-3.; Sherry J. Holladay and W. Timothy Coombs, 'Communicating Visions', *Management Communication Quarterly 6*, no. 4 (1993): 405–427, https://doi.org/10.1177/0893318993006004003.

11. Boas Shamir, Michael B. Arthur, and Robert J. House, 'The Rhetoric of Charismatic Leadership: A Theoretical Extension, a Case Study,

and Implications for Research', *The Leadership Quarterly* 5, no. 1 (1994): 25–42, https://doi.org/10.1016/1048-9843(94)90004-3.; John E. Baur et al., 'More than One Way to Articulate a Vision: A Configurations Approach to Leader Charismatic Rhetoric and Influence', *The Leadership Quarterly* 27, no. 1 (2016): 156–171, https://doi.org/10.1016/j.leaqua.2015.08.002.

12. R.G. Lord, R.J. Foti, and C.L. de Vader, 'A test of leadership categorization theory: Internal structure, information processing, and leadership perceptions', *Organizational Behavior and Human Performance*, 34, (1984): 343–378. http://dx.doi.org/10.1016/0030-5073(84)90043-6.

13. Boas Shamir, Michael B. Arthur, and Robert J. House, 'The Rhetoric of Charismatic Leadership: A Theoretical Extension, a Case Study, and Implications for Research', *The Leadership Quarterly* 5, no. 1 (1994): 25–42, https://doi.org/10.1016/1048-9843(94)90004-3.; Michelle C. Bligh, Jeffrey C. Kohles, and James R. Meindl, 'Charisma under Crisis: Presidential Leadership, Rhetoric, and Media Responses before and after the September 11th Terrorist Attacks', *The Leadership Quarterly* 15, no. 2 (2004): 211–39, https://doi.org/10.1016/j.leaqua.2004.02.005.

14. Boas Shamir, Michael B. Arthur, and Robert J. House, 'The Rhetoric of Charismatic Leadership: A Theoretical Extension, a Case Study, and Implications for Research', *The Leadership Quarterly* 5; Boas Shamir, Robert J. House, and Michael B. Arthur, 'The Motivational Effects of Charismatic Leadership: A Self-Concept Based Theory', *Organization Science 4*, no. 4 (1993): 577–94, https://doi.org/10.1287/orsc.4.4.577.

15. J.E. Baur, B.P. Ellen III, M.R. Buckley, G.R. Ferris, T.H. Allison, A.F. McKenny, and J.C. Short, 'More than One Way to Articulate a Vision: A Configurations Approach to Leader Charismatic Rhetoric and Influence', *The Leadership Quarterly*, 27(1), (2016): 156–71.

16. R.P. Hart, 'Redeveloping DICTION: Theoretical Considerations', *Progress in Communication Sciences*, (2001): 43–60.

17. Michelle C. Bligh, Jeffrey C. Kohles, and James R. Meindl, 'Charisma under Crisis: Presidential Leadership, Rhetoric, and Media Responses before and after the September 11th Terrorist Attacks', *The Leadership Quarterly* 15; K.M. Davis, 'The Presidential Crisis Rhetoric of September 11th, 2001 and Hurricane Katrina: Examples

of Charismatic Leadership or Not?', (Doctoral dissertation, Clemson University), 2007.

18. https://www.nytimes.com/elections/2008/president/debates/transcripts/second-presidential-debate.html.

19. Michelle C. Bligh and Jeffrey C. Kohles, 'The Enduring Allure of Charisma: How Barack Obama Won the Historic 2008 Presidential Election', *The Leadership Quarterly 20*, no. 3 (2009): 483–92, https://doi.org/10.1016/j.leaqua.2009.03.013.

20. https://hi.hofstede-insights.com/national-culture.

21. https://www.goodreads.com/author/quotes/5810891.Mahatma_Gandhi.

22. M. Weber, 'Legitimate Authority and Bureaucracy: The Theory of Social and Economic Organisation', (1947): 328–40.

23. Michelle C. Bligh and J.L. Robinson, 'Was Gandhi 'Charismatic'? Exploring the Rhetorical Leadership of Mahatma Gandhi', *The Leadership Quarterly*, 21(5), (2010): 844–55.

24. M.K. Gandhi, *The Story of My Experiments with Truth*, (Beacon Press, Boston, 1957).

25. https://www.hofstede-insights.com/country-comparison/india,the-usa/.

Chapter 18: Letter-Writing Skills for Leaders

1. https://www.businessinsider.com/ex-tesla-employees-reveal-what-its-like-work-elon-musk-2019-9#he-has-very-high-standards-6.

2. Ibid.

3. Rajesh Chandy, 'Cancel Your Meetings—You Need Time to Think', *Wired*, 14 February 2012, https://www.wired.co.uk/article/rajesh-chandy

4. https://en.wikipedia.org/wiki/Wang_Laboratories.

5. AnnaLee Saxenian, 'Inside-out: Regional Networks and Industrial Adaptation in Silicon Valley and Route 128', *The Sociology of Economic Life* (2018): 357–74, https://doi.org/10.4324/9780429494338-20.; Glenn Rifkin and George Harrar, *The Ultimate Entrepreneur: The Story of Ken Olsen and Digital Equipment Corporation*, (Chicago: Contemporary Books, 1988).

6. Glenn Rifkin, 'Ken Olsen, Who Built DEC Into a Power, Dies at 84', 7 Feb 2011, the *New York Times*, https://www.nytimes.com/2011/02/08/technology/business-computing/08olsen.html.

7. 'Epistolography Definition & Meaning', Merriam-Webster, accessed 22 July 2022, https://www.merriam-webster.com/dictionary/epistolography.

8. Hoakley, 'A Message on an Apple, and Two Abandoned Lovers', The Eclectic Light Company, 5 March 2017, https://eclecticlight.co/2017/03/05/a-message-on-an-apple-and-two-abandoned-lovers/.

9. G.F. Kohut and A.H. Segars, 'The President's Letter to Stockholders: An Examination of Corporate Communication Strategy', *Journal of Business Communication 29*, no. 1 (January 1992): 7–21, https://doi.org/10.1177/002194369202900101.

10. G. Jacobson, 'How Valuable Is the Annual Report?', *Management Review*, 77(10), (1988): 51.

11. Baruch Lev and Feng Gu, *The End of Accounting and the Path Forward for Investors and Managers*, (Hoboken: John Wiley & Sons, 2016).

12. Huili Wang, and Lixin Li. 'Lexical Features in Corporate Annual Reports: a Corpus-based Study' (2012).

13. C. Marlene Fiol, 'A Semiotic Analysis of Corporate Language: Organizational Boundaries and Joint Venturing', *Administrative Science Quarterly 34*, no. 2 (1989): 277, https://doi.org/10.2307/2989899.

14. Edward H. Bowman, 'Content Analysis of Annual Reports for Corporate Strategy and Risk', *Interfaces 14*, no. 1 (1984): 61–71, https://doi.org/10.1287/inte.14.1.61.

15. C. Marlene Fiol, 'Corporate Communications: Comparing Executives' Private and Public Statements', *Academy of Management Journal 38*, no. 2 (1995): 522–36, https://doi.org/10.5465/256691.

16. Pascal Balata and Gaétan Breton, 'Narratives vs Numbers in the Annual Report: Are They Giving the Same Message to the Investors?', *Review of Accounting and Finance 4*, no. 2 (January 2005): 5–14, https://doi.org/10.1108/eb043421.

17. Lorenzo Patelli and Matteo Pedrini, 'Is the Optimism in CEO's Letters to Shareholders Sincere? Impression Management versus Communicative Action during the Economic Crisis', *Journal of Business Ethics 124*, no. 1 (September 2013): 19–34, https://doi.org/10.1007/s10551-013-1855-3.

18. Manjit S. Yadav, Jaideep C. Prabhu, and Rajesh K. Chandy, 'Managing the Future: CEO Attention and Innovation Outcomes', *Journal of Marketing 71*, no. 4 (2007): 84–101, https://doi.org/10.1509/jmkg.71.4.84.

19. David A. Nadler, and Jeffrey D. Heilpern, 'The CEO in the Context of Discontinuous Change', in *Navigating Change: How CEOs, Top Teams, and Boards Steer Transformation*, D.C. Hambrick, D.A. Nadler, and M.L. Tushman, eds. (Boston: Harvard Business School Press, 1998), 3–27.

20. James W. Pennebaker, Matthias R. Mehl, and Kate G. Niederhoffer, 'Psychological Aspects of Natural Language Use: Our Words, Our Selves', *Annual Review of Psychology 54*, no. 1 (2003): 547–77, https://doi.org/10.1146/annurev.psych.54.101601.145041.

21. Daniel Thomas, 'Tesla Surpasses $1 Trillion Valuation after Hertz Order', BBC News, 25 October 2021, https://www.bbc.com/news/business-59045100.

22. Mark Matousek, 'Former Tesla Employees Reveal What It's like to Work with Elon Musk', *Business Insider*, 1 October 2019, https://www.businessinsider.com/ex-tesla-employees-reveal-what-its-like-work-elon-musk-2019-9.

Chapter 19: Me, Myself and I: Can Narcissism be a Good Thing?

1. https://hbr.org/2017/01/are-you-solving-the-right-problems.

2. Rachel Ranosa, 'Fun Friday: Top Ten Most Hated Employee Traits', *HRD America*, 26 September 2019, https://www.hcamag.com/us/news/general/fun-friday-top-ten-most-hated-employee-traits/178999.

3. 'Narcissus', *Encyclopædia Britannica*, accessed 22 July 2022, https://www.britannica.com/topic/Narcissus-Greek-mythology.

4. 'The History of the Psychoanalytic Movement', in J. Strachey (ed.), *The Standard Edition of the Complete Psychological Works of Sigmund Freud*, 14: 7–6, 1957.

5. Robert Raskin and Howard Terry, 'A Principal-Components Analysis of the Narcissistic Personality Inventory and Further Evidence of Its Construct Validity', *Journal of Personality and Social Psychology 54*, no. 5 (1988): 890–902, https://doi.org/10.1037/0022-3514.54.5.890.

6. Robert A. Emmons, 'Narcissism: Theory and Measurement', *Journal of Personality and Social Psychology 52*, no. 1 (1987): 11–17, https://doi.org/10.1037/0022-3514.52.1.11.

7. Arijit Chatterjee and Donald C. Hambrick, 'It's All about Me: Narcissistic Chief Executive Officers and Their Effects on Company Strategy and Performance', *Administrative Science Quarterly 52*, no. 3 (2007): 351–86, https://doi.org/10.2189/asqu.52.3.351.

8. Robert A. Emmons, 'Factor Analysis and Construct Validity of the Narcissistic Personality Inventory', *Journal of Personality Assessment 48*, no. 3 (1984): 291–300, https://doi.org/10.1207/s15327752jpa4803_11.

9. Dazed, 'Anonymous Calls out "Narcissistic Rich Dude" Elon Musk', Dazed, 6 June 2021, https://www.dazeddigital.com/science-tech/article/53080/1/anonymous-calls-out-narcissistic-rich-dude-elon-musk-cryptocurrency-bitcoin.

10. 'Tesla (TSLA) – Market Capitalization', CompaniesMarketCap.com – Companies Ranked by Market Capitalization, accessed 22 July 2022, https://companiesmarketcap.com/tesla/marketcap/.

11. Arijit Chatterjee and Donald C. Hambrick, 'It's All about Me: Narcissistic Chief Executive Officers and Their Effects on Company Strategy and Performance', *Administrative Science Quarterly 52*.

12. MarketsandMarkets™, 'Blockchain Market Worth $39.7 Billion by 2025 – Exclusive Report by MarketsandMarkets™', 5 May 2020, https://www.prnewswire.com/news-releases/blockchain-market-worth-39-7-billion-by-2025--exclusive-report-by-marketsandmarkets-301052885.html.

13. R.A. Emmons, 'Narcissism: Theory and Measurement', *Journal of Personality and Social Psychology*, 52(1), (1987): 11.

14. Christopher Y. Olivola et al., 'Republicans Prefer Republican-Looking Leaders', *Social Psychological and Personality Science 3*, no. 5 (April 2012): 605–13, https://doi.org/10.1177/1948550611432770.

15. Justin M. Carré, Cheryl M. McCormick, and Catherine J. Mondloch, 'Facial Structure Is a Reliable Cue of Aggressive Behavior', *Psychological Science 20*, no. 10 (2009): 1194–98, https://doi.org/10.1111/j.1467-9280.2009.02423.x.

16. Timothy Aeppel and Alwyn Scott, '"Neutron Jack" Welch, Who Led GE's Rapid Expansion, Dies at 84', Reuters, 2 March 2020, https://

www.reuters.com/article/us-people-jackwelch/neutron-jack-welch-who-led-ges-rapid-expansion-dies-at-84-idUSKBN20P20T.

17. Paul R. La Monica, 'Tesla's Stock Slide Raises Doubts about Elon Musk's Twitter Purchase', CNN, 11 May 2022, https://www.cnn.com/2022/05/11/investing/tesla-stock-elon-musk-twitter/index.html.

18. Andreas Engelen, Christoph Neumann, and Susanne Schmidt, 'Should Entrepreneurially Oriented Firms Have Narcissistic CEOS?', *Journal of Management 42*, no. 3 (May 2013): 698–721, https://doi.org/10.1177/0149206313495413.

19. Bill Murphy Jr., 'Google Says It Still Swears by the 20 Percent Rule to Find Big Ideas, and You Should Totally Copy It', Inc.com, 1 November 2020, https://www.inc.com/bill-murphy-jr/google-says-it-still-uses-20-percent-rule-you-should-totally-copy-it.html.

20. R.P. Hart, 'DICTION 5.0: The Text Analysis Program', Thousand Oaks, CA: Sage-Scolari, 2000.

21. J.C. Short, J.C. Broberg, C.C. Cogliser, and K.H. Brigham, 'Construct Validation Using Computer-Aided Text Analysis (Cata): An Illustration Using Entrepreneurial Orientation', *Organizational Research Methods*, 13(2), 320–47.

22. C. Ham, N. Seybert, and S. Wang, 'Narcissism is a bad sign: CEO signature size, investment, and performance', *Review of Accounting Studies*, 23, (2018): 234–64.

23. '12 Famous Artists' Signatures and What They Can Tell You', The Study, 15 December 2021, https://www.1stdibs.com/blogs/the-study/artist-signatures/.

24. 'The Signature: A Brief History', The Grizzly Labs, accessed 22 July 2022, https://blog.thegrizzlylabs.com/2020/11/history-of-signatures.html.

25. Richard L. Zweigenhaft, 'The Empirical Study of Signature Size', *Social Behavior and Personality: an International Journal 5*, no. 1 (January 1977): 177–85, https://doi.org/10.2224/sbp.1977.5.1.177; Dale O. Jorgenson, 'Signature Size and Dominance: A Brief Note', *The Journal of Psychology 97*, no. 2 (1977): 269–70, https://doi.org/10.1080/00223980.1977.9923972.

26. Laurie A. Rudman, Matthew C. Dohn, and Kimberly Fairchild, 'Implicit Self-Esteem Compensation: Automatic Threat Defense',

Journal of Personality and Social Psychology 93, no. 5 (2007): 798–813, https://doi.org/10.1037/0022-3514.93.5.798.

27. Robert Raskin and Howard Terry, 'A Principal-Components Analysis of the Narcissistic Personality Inventory and Further Evidence of Its Construct Validity', *Journal of Personality and Social Psychology 54*, no. 5 (1988): 890–902, https://doi.org/10.1037/0022-3514.54.5.890.

28. Charles A. O'Reilly et al., 'Narcissistic CEOS and Executive Compensation', *The Leadership Quarterly 25*, no. 2 (2014): 218–31, https://doi.org/10.1016/j.leaqua.2013.08.002.

29. Michael Elliott, 'The Anatomy of the GE-Honeywell Disaster', *Time*, 8 July 2001, http://content.time.com/time/business/article/0,8599,166732,00.html.

30. K.N. Cukier, 'Frenchie Goes to Hollywood: Vivendi's Jean-Marie Messier Has Put Together a Combination of Content and Distribution. Can He Make It Work—and Make Mr. Murdoch Work with Him?', Red Herring, 13 November (2000): 128–32.; Daren Fonda, 'The French Rejection', *Time*, 29 April 2002, https://content.time.com/time/subscriber/article/0,33009,1002315,00.html.

Chapter 20: Wayward Brands and Innocent Rivals

1. 'Peanut Salmonella Trial Shows Food Safety Relies on Honor System', accessed 20 July 2022, https://newsadvance.com/news/local/peanut-salmonella-trial-shows-food-safety-relies-on-honor-system/article_67596124-2004-11e4-bef5-0017a43b2370.html.

2. Bill Marler, 'Yes, Stewart Parnell and PCA, You Killed People with Salmonella Peanut Butter', Marler Blog, 2 July 2015, https://www.marlerblog.com/legal-cases/yes-stewart-parnell-and-pca-you-killed-people-with-salmonella-peanut-butter/.

3. 'Food Recall' (PDF), www.fns.usda.gov. 2014, retrieved 14 July 2019.

4. Peanut Butter and other Peanut Containing Products Recall List (Current Update), Food and Drug Administration

5. 'Former Peanut Company Officials Sentenced to Prison for Their Roles in Salmonella-Tainted Peanut Product Outbreak', The United States Department of Justice, 1 October 2015, https://www.justice.

gov/opa/pr/former-peanut-company-officials-sentenced-prison-their-roles-salmonella-tainted-peanut.

6. Lyndsey Layton; Nick Miroff, 'The Rise and Fall of a Peanut Empire', the *Washington Post*, retrieved 11 April 2009.

7. 'Volkswagen Emissions Scandal', Wikipedia, 26 June 2022, https://en.wikipedia.org/wiki/Volkswagen_emissions_scandal.

8. Abhishek Borah, 'Dieselgate and the "Perverse Halo" of Volkswagen', Foster Blog, 30 September 2015, https://blog.foster.uw.edu/dieselgate-and-the-perverse-halo-of-volkswagen/.

9. Christie Smythe and Patricia Hurtado, 'Volkswagen Probed by States Over Pollution Cheating', Bloomberg.com, 22 September 2015.

10. Niraj Dawar and Madan M. Pillutla, 'Impact of Product-Harm Crises on Brand Equity: The Moderating Role of Consumer Expectations', *Journal of Marketing Research 37*, no. 2 (2000): 215–26, https://doi.org/10.1509/jmkr.37.2.215.18729.

11. Eric S. Page, 'Toyota Offers Condolences to Family Killed in Crash', NBC 7 San Diego, 23 February 2010, https://www.nbcsandiego.com/news/local/toyota-offers-condolences-to-family-killed-in-crash/1865838/.

12. Meagan Parrish, 'The 2009 Toyota Accelerator Scandal That Wasn't What It Seemed', Manufacturing.net, 17 June 2022, https://www.manufacturing.net/automotive/blog/13110434/the-2009-toyota-accelerator-scandal-that-wasnt-what-it-seemed.

13. Greene Broillet and Wheeler, 'Toyota Sudden Acceleration Defect Case: $1.1 Billion Settlement', Greene Broillet & Wheeler, LLP, 14 December 2017, https://www.gbw.law/blog/2017/december/toyota-sudden-acceleration-defect-case-1-1-billi/.

14. Alex Taylor III, 'Who Benefits from Toyota's Recall Problem?', *Time*, 2 February 2010, http://content.time.com/time/business/article/0,8599,1958379,00.html.

15. Staff Writer, 'Honda's Sales Eclipse Toyota's', the *Columbus Dispatch*, 20 February 2010, https://www.dispatch.com/story/business/2010/02/20/honda-s-sales-eclipse-toyota/23547240007/.

16. A. Borah, and G.J. Tellis, 'Halo (Spillover) Effects in Social Media: Do Product Recalls of One Brand Hurt or Help Rival Brands?', *Journal of Marketing Research*, 53(2), (2016): 143–160.

17. Mathilde Carlier, 'Automotive Vehicle and Equipment Recalls - U.S.', Statista, 20 April 2022, https://www.statista.com/statistics/541703/united-states-vehicle-recalls/.

18. J.M. Feldman, and J.G. Lynch, 'Self-Generated Validity and Other Effects of Measurement on Belief, Attitude, Intention, and Behavior', *Journal of Applied Psychology*, 73(3), (1988): 421.

19. Allan M. Collins and Elizabeth F. Loftus, 'A Spreading-Activation Theory of Semantic Processing', *Psychological Review 82*, no. 6 (1975): 407–28, https://doi.org/10.1037/0033-295x.82.6.407.; R. Janakiraman, C. Sismeiro, and S. Dutta, 'Perception Spillovers across Competing Brands: A Disaggregate Model of How and When', *Journal of Marketing Research,* 46(4), (2009): 467–81.

20. Andrew Martin and Liz Robbins, 'Fallout Widens as Buyers Shun Peanut Butter', the *New York Times*, 6 February 2009, https://www.nytimes.com/2009/02/07/business/07peanut.html.

21. Christopher Doering, 'Peanut Recall Having Big Impact on Small Firms', Reuters, 11 March 2009, https://www.reuters.com/article/domesticNews/idUSTRE52A4AT20090311.

22. https://blog.foster.uw.edu/dieselgate-and-the-perverse-halo-of-volkswagen/.

23. George Siomkos and Paul Shrivastava, 'Responding to Product Liability Crises', *Long Range Planning 26*, no. 5 (1993): 72–79, https://doi.org/10.1016/0024-6301(93)90079-u.

Chapter 21: The Unexpected Upsides of Vagueness

1. Bryce Sanders, 'How to Be Masterful at Being Vague (When It's Necessary)', Bizjournals.com, 2 March 2016, https://www.bizjournals.com/bizjournals/how-to/growth-strategies/2016/03/how-to-be-masterful-at-being-vague.html.

2. C.S. Peirce, 'Vagueness', in M. Baldwin (ed.), *Dictionary of Philosophy and Psychology II,* (London, England: Macmillan, 1902).

3. Jonah Lehrer, 'In Praise of Vagueness', *Wired* 21 July 2011, https://www.wired.com/2011/07/in-praise-of-vagueness/.

4. 'Bryan Adams: Hit Was about Sex, Not 1969', CBS News, 8 September 2008, https://www.cbsnews.com/news/bryan-adams-hit-was-about-sex-not-1969/.

5.   Paul Cantor, 'How Being Vague Gives You Extraordinary Creative Powers', Medium, 1 November 2017, https://paulcantor.medium.com/how-being-vague-gives-you-extraordinary-creative-powers-ebb0b6f6a098.

6.   Shanee Edwards, and Jennifer Edelston, 'The Hidden Meanings behind Your Favorite Pop Songs', SheKnows, 7 October 2021, https://www.sheknows.com/entertainment/slideshow/3555/the-hidden-meaning-behind-pop-songs-including-hit-me-baby-one-more-time/27/.

7.   https://www.brainyquote.com/quotes/john_mellencamp_776380.

8.   'The Surprising Benefits of Ambiguous Language', BBC Future, accessed 22 July 2022, https://www.bbc.com/future/article/20140313-the-benefits-of-talking-vague.

9.   'Marketing Warfare by Al Ries', Goodreads, 13 December 2005, https://www.goodreads.com/book/show/2595.Marketing_Warfare.

10. Wei Guo, Tieying Yu, and Javier Gimeno, 'Language and Competition: Communication Vagueness, Interpretation Difficulties, and Market Entry', *Academy of Management Journal 60*, no. 6 (2017): 2073–98, https://doi.org/10.5465/amj.2014.1150.

11. J.H. Hiller, 'Communication Vagueness Dictionary (WordStat version 7) [Computer software], Montreal, Quebec, Canada: Provalis Research, 2014; Jack H. Hiller, Donald R. Marcotte, and Timothy Martin, 'Opinionation, Vagueness, and Specificity-Distinctions: Essay Traits Measured by Computer', *American Educational Research Journal 6*, no. 2 (1969): 271–86, https://doi.org/10.3102/00028312006002271.

12. John M. Ford et al., 'Automated Content Analysis of Multiple-Choice Test Item Banks', *Social Science Computer Review 18*, no. 3 (2000): 258–71, https://doi.org/10.1177/089443930001800303.; R.L. Hogenraad and R.R. Garagozov, 'Textual Fingerprints of Risk of War', *Literary and Linguistic Computing 29*, no. 1 (2013): 41–55, https://doi.org/10.1093/llc/fqt015.; Antoaneta P. Petkova, Violina P. Rindova, and Anil K. Gupta, 'No News Is Bad News: Sensegiving Activities, Media Attention, and Venture Capital Funding of New Technology Organizations', *Organization Science 24*, no. 3 (2013): 865–88, https://doi.org/10.1287/orsc.1120.0759.

13. United Air Lines, Inc. 2001, Form 10-K 2001, retrieved 20 April 2013 from https://www.sec.gov/Archives/edgar/

data/101001/000010100101500005/0000101001-01-500005-index. htm.

14. Vanguard Airlines, Inc. 1999, Form 10-K 1999, retrieved 20 April 2013 from https://www.sec.gov/Archives/edgar/ data/1000578/0001000578-99-000005-index.html.

15. M.J. Chen, and D.C. Hambrick, 'Speed, Stealth, and Selective Attack How Small Firms Differ from Large Firms in Competitive Behavior', *Academy of Management Journal*, 38, (1995): 453–82: References – Scientific Research Publishing, accessed 22 July 2022, https://www. scirp.org/(S(351jmbntvnsjt1aadkposzje))/reference/ReferencesPapers. aspx?ReferenceID=1322803.

16. 'Monopoly by the Numbers', Open Markets Institute, accessed 22 July 2022, https://www.openmarketsinstitute.org/learn/monopoly-by-the-numbers.

17. Ming-Jer Chen and Danny Miller, 'Competitive Attack, Retaliation and Performance: An Expectancy-Valence Framework', *Strategic Management Journal 15*, no. 2 (1994): 85–102, https://doi. org/10.1002/smj.4250150202.

18. Himanshu Mishra, Arul Mishra, and Baba Shiv, 'In Praise of Vagueness', *Psychological Science 22*, no. 6 (2011): 733–38, https://doi. org/10.1177/0956797611407208.

Chapter 22: How to Talk to Your Date

1. James W. Pennebaker, 'Your Use of Pronouns Reveals Your Personality', *Harvard Business Review*, 1 August 2014, https://hbr.org/2011/12/ your-use-of-pronouns-reveals-your-personality.

2. H. Giles, 'Communication Accommodation Theory' in L.A. Baxter and D.O. Braithewaite (eds.), *Engaging Theories in Interpersonal Communication: Multiple Perspectives* (Sage Publications, Inc., 2008): 161–73.

3. Howard Giles and Philip Smith, *Accommodation Theory: Optimal Levels of Convergence* (Baltimore: University Park Press, 1979).

4. Martin J. Pickering and Simon Garrod, 'Toward a Mechanistic Psychology of Dialogue', *Behavioral and Brain Sciences 27*, no. 02 (2004), https://doi.org/10.1017/s0140525x04000056.

5. Molly E. Ireland and James W. Pennebaker, 'Language Style Matching in Writing: Synchrony in Essays, Correspondence, and Poetry', *Journal of Personality and Social Psychology 99*, no. 3 (2010): 549–71, https://doi.org/10.1037/a0020386.

6. Andrew M. Baker, Naveen Donthu, and V. Kumar, 'Investigating How Word-of-Mouth Conversations about Brands Influence Purchase and Retransmission Intentions', *Journal of Marketing Research 53*, no. 2 (2016): 225–39, https://doi.org/10.1509/jmr.14.0099.

7. Peter S. Fader and Bruce G.S. Hardie, 'Probability Models for Customer-Base Analysis', *Journal of Interactive Marketing 23*, no. 1 (2009): 61–69, https://doi.org/10.1016/j.intmar.2008.11.003.

8. Daniel M. McCarthy, Peter S. Fader, and Bruce G.S. Hardie, 'Valuing Subscription-Based Businesses Using Publicly Disclosed Customer Data', *Journal of Marketing 81*, no. 1 (2017): 17–35, https://doi.org/10.1509/jm.15.0519.

9. Albert M. Muniz and Thomas C. O'Guinn, 'Brand Community', *Journal of Consumer Research 27*, no. 4 (2001): 412–32, https://doi.org/10.1086/319618.

10. Kevin Lane Keller, 'Building Customer-Based Brand Equity: A Blueprint for Creating Strong Brands' (2001).

11. S. Ludwig, K. De Ruyter, M. Friedman, E.C. Brüggen, M. Wetzels, and G. Pfann, 'More than Words: The Influence of Affective Content and Linguistic Style Matches in Online Reviews on Conversion Rates', *Journal of Marketing*, 77(1), (2013): 87–103.

12. Anne-Laure Fayard and Gerardine DeSanctis, 'Enacting Language Games: The Development of a Sense of 'We-Ness' in Online Forums', *Information Systems Journal 20*, no. 4 (2009): 383–416, https://doi.org/10.1111/j.1365-2575.2009.00335.x.

13. Molly E. Ireland and James W. Pennebaker, 'Language Style Matching in Writing: Synchrony in Essays, Correspondence, and Poetry', *Journal of Personality and Social Psychology 99*.

14. Anne-Laure Fayard and Gerardine DeSanctis, 'Enacting Language Games: The Development of a Sense of 'We-Ness' in Online Forums', *Information Systems Journal 20*.

15. Marci Kramish Campbell et al., 'Varying the Message Source in Computer-Tailored Nutrition Education', *Patient Education and*

Counseling 36, no. 2 (1999): 157–69, https://doi.org/10.1016/s0738-3991(98)00132-3.

16. Mike Bray and L.J. Martin, *Internet Rich: Your Blueprint to Book Sales* (Wolfpack Publishing, 2011).

17. Joel B. Cohen, Michel Tuan Pham, and Eduardo B. Andrade, 'The Nature and Role of Affect in Consumer Behavior', *Handbook of Consumer Psychology*, n.d., https://doi.org/10.4324/9780203809570.ch11.

18. Martin J. Pickering and Simon Garrod, 'Toward a Mechanistic Psychology of Dialogue', *Behavioral and Brain Sciences 27*, no. 02 (2004), https://doi.org/10.1017/s0140525x04000056.

19. Yla R. Tausczik and James W. Pennebaker, 'The Psychological Meaning of Words: LIWC and Computerized Text Analysis Methods', *Journal of Language and Social Psychology 29*, no. 1 (August 2009): 24–54, https://doi.org/10.1177/0261927x09351676.

20. Ibid.

21. David A. Huffaker, Roderick Swaab, and Daniel Diermeier, 'The Language of Coalition Formation in Online Multiparty Negotiations', *Journal of Language and Social Psychology 30*, no. 1 (2010): 66–81, https://doi.org/10.1177/0261927x10387102.; C. Chung, and J. Pennebaker, 'The Psychological Functions of Function Words', in K. Fiedler (ed.), *Social Communication* (Psychology Press, 2007), 343–359.

22. Gordon Willard Allport, *Pattern and Growth in Personality* (New York: Holt, Rinehart and Winston, 1961).

23. C. Chung, and J. Pennebaker, 'The Psychological Functions of Function Words', in K. Fiedler (ed.), *Social Communication* (Psychology Press, 2007).

24. Helen Bird, Sue Franklin, and David Howard, '"Little Words"—Not Really: Function and Content Words in Normal and Aphasic Speech', *Journal of Neurolinguistics 15*, no. 3-5 (2002): 209–37, https://doi.org/10.1016/s0911-6044(01)00031-8.

25. Christine Weber-Fox and Helen J. Neville, 'Sensitive Periods Differentiate Processing of Open- and Closed-Class Words', *Journal of Speech, Language, and Hearing Research 44*, no. 6 (2001): 1338–53, https://doi.org/10.1044/1092-4388(2001/104).

26. Antonio Damasio, *Descartes' Error: Emotion, Reason and the Human Brain* (London: Vintage Digital, 1995).

27. Larry Scherwitz, Kent Berton, and Howard Leventhal, 'Type A Behavior, Self-Involvement, and Cardiovascular Response', *Psychosomatic Medicine 40*, no. 8 (1978): 593–609, https://doi.org/10.1097/00006842-197812000-00002.
28. James W. Pennebaker et al., 'Testosterone as a Social Inhibitor: Two Case Studies of the Effect of Testosterone Treatment on Language', *Journal of Abnormal Psychology 113*, no. 1 (2004): 172–75, https://doi.org/10.1037/0021-843x.113.1.172.
29. Walter Weintraub, *Verbal Behavior in Everyday Life* (New York: Springer Pub. Co., 1989).
30. Shannon Wiltsey Stirman and James W. Pennebaker, 'Word Use in the Poetry of Suicidal and Nonsuicidal Poets', *Psychosomatic Medicine 63*, no. 4 (2001): 517–22, https://doi.org/10.1097/00006842-200107000-00001.
31. R. Sherlock Campbell and James W. Pennebaker, 'The Secret Life of Pronouns', *Psychological Science 14*, no. 1 (2003): 60–65, https://doi.org/10.1111/1467-9280.01419.
32. James W. Pennebaker and Lori D. Stone, 'Words of Wisdom: Language Use over the Life Span', *Journal of Personality and Social Psychology 85*, no. 2 (2003): 291–301, https://doi.org/10.1037/0022-3514.85.2.291.
33. Daniel Kahneman, *Thinking, Fast and Slow* (New York, NY: Farrar, Straus and Giroux, 2013).
34. Stephan Ludwig et al., 'Take Their Word for It: the Symbolic Role of Linguistic Style Matches in User Communities', *MIS Quarterly 38*, no. 4 (April 2014): 1201–17, https://doi.org/10.25300/misq/2014/38.4.12.
35. Econsultancy and RedEye (2011), 'Conversion Rate Optimization Report'.
36. Molly E. Ireland and James W. Pennebaker, 'Language Style Matching in Writing: Synchrony in Essays, Correspondence, and Poetry', *Journal of Personality and Social Psychology 99*, no. 3 (2010): 549–71, https://doi.org/10.1037/a0020386.

Epilogue

1. Joy Lo Dico, 'Watch What You're Saying!: Linguist David Crystal on Twitter, Texting and Our Native Tongue', 14 March 2010, the *Independent*.

2. https://www.aaaa.org/timeline-event/diamond-forever-unforgettable-de-beers-tagline-thats-still-shining/?cn-reloaded=1.
3. https://crisscut.stevenstone.co.uk/jewellery/the-most-brilliant-advertising-campaign-of-all-time/.
4. https://www.forevermark.com/en/now-forever/a-diamond-is-forever/the-power-of-a-diamond-is-forever/.

Sources for Figures and Tables

Figure 1.1: Borah, A., Banerjee, S., Lin, Y.T., Jain, A., and Eisingerich, A.B., (2020), 'Improvised Marketing Interventions in Social Media', *Journal of Marketing*, *84*(2), 69–91.

Figures 1.2a, 1.2b, 1.2c, 1.2d: Borah, A., Banerjee, S., Lin, Y.T., Jain, A., and Eisingerich, A.B., (2020), 'Improvised Marketing Interventions in Social Media', *Journal of Marketing*, *84*(2), 69–91.

Figure 4.1: Reich, T., and Maglio, S.J., (2020), 'Featuring Mistakes: The Persuasive Impact of Purchase Mistakes in Online Reviews', *Journal of Marketing*, *84*(1), 52–65.

Table 5.1: Packard, G., and Berger, J., (2021), 'How Concrete Language Shapes Customer Satisfaction', *Journal of Consumer Research*, *47*(5), 787–806.

Figure 7.1: Martin, K.D., Borah, A., and Palmatier, R.W., (2018), 'A Strong Privacy Policy Can Save Your Company Millions', *Harvard Business Review*.

Figure 8.1: Author-created.

Figure 9.1: Kronrod, A., Grinstein, A., and Wathieu, L., (2012), Go Green! Should Environmental Messages Be So Assertive?', *Journal of Marketing*, *76*(1), 95–102.

Table 13. 1: Hansen, N., Kupfer, A.K., and Hennig-Thurau, T., (2018), 'Brand Crises in the Digital Age: The Short-and Long-Term Effects of Social Media Firestorms on Consumers and Brands', *International Journal of Research in Marketing*, 35(4), 557–74.

Image _ When Bytes Matter More (Formula image): https://en.wikipedia.org/wiki/Gunning_fog_index.

Figure 14.1: https://trends.google.com/trends/.

Figure 15.1: Coval, J.D., and Shumway, T., (2001), 'Is Sound Just Noise?', *The Journal of Finance*, 56(5), 1887–910.

Figure 16.1: Gjerstad, P., Meyn, P.F., Molnár, P., and Næss, T.D., (2021), 'Do President Trump's Tweets Affect Financial Markets?', *Decision Support Systems*, 147, 113577.

Figure 16.2: Gjerstad, P., Meyn, P.F., Molnár, P., & Næss, T.D., (2021), 'Do President Trump's Tweets Affect Financial Markets?', *Decision Support Systems*, 147, 113577.

Figure 17.1: Baur, J.E., Ellen III, B.P., Buckley, M.R., Ferris, G.R., Allison, T.H., McKenny, A.F., and Short, J.C., (2016), 'More than One Way to Articulate a Vision: A Configurations Approach to Leader Charismatic Rhetoric and Influence', *The Leadership Quarterly*, 27(1), 156–71.

Figure 17.2: Author-created.

Table 18.1: Yadav, M.S., Prabhu, J.C., and Chandy, R.K., (2007), 'Managing the Future: CEO Attention and Innovation Outcomes', *Journal of Marketing*, 71(4), 84–101.

Table 19.1: Engelen, A., Neumann, C., and Schwens, C., (2015)., '"Of Course I Can": The Effect of CEO Overconfidence on Entrepreneurially Oriented Firms', *Entrepreneurship Theory and Practice*, 39(5), 1137–60.

Me, Myself – Sig 1: https://society6.com/product/frida-kahlos-signature_print.

Me, Myself _ Signature 2: https://www.irishnews.com/magazine/entertainment/2017/12/12/news/danny-boyle-and-banksy-stage-alternative-nativity--1208657/.

Me, Myself _ Signature 3: https://www.bimago.com/canvas-prints/street-art/banksy-signature-68016.html.

Me, Myself _ Signature 4: https://www.themarginalian.org/2008/10/10/bansky-pet-shop/.

Me, Myself _ Signature 5: https://www.gallery.ca/sites/default/files/picasso.jpg.

Figure 20.1: Author-created.

How to Talk To Your Date – Figure 1: Author-created

How to Talk To Your Date – Figure 2: Author-created

How to Talk To Your Date – Fig. 3: Author-created

How to Talk to Your Date – Formula: Ludwig, S., De Ruyter, K., Friedman, M., Brüggen, E.C., Wetzels, M., and Pfann, G., (2013), 'More than Words: The Influence of Affective Content and Linguistic Style Matches in Online Reviews on Conversion Rates', *Journal of Marketing*, *77*(1), 87–103.

Table 22.1: Ludwig, S., De Ruyter, K., Friedman, M., Brüggen, E.C., Wetzels, M., and Pfann, G., (2013), 'More than Words: The Influence of Affective Content and Linguistic Style Matches in Online Reviews on Conversion Rates', *Journal of Marketing*, *77*(1), 87–103.

Scan QR code to access the
Penguin Random House India website